IntergalacticMatch.com

ISBN 978-1954095-09-0 (Paperback)
IntergalacticMatch.com

Yorkshire Publishing
1425 E 41st Pl
Tulsa, OK 74105
www.YorkshirePublishing.com
918.394.2665

Printed in the USA

IntergalacticMatch.com

{The Love Ops/Special Forces of Romantic Love}

–

How I Met My Cosmic True Love, and You Can, Too

Michael Ellegion & Celeste

TULSA

CONTENTS

Lady Celeste (Illustrated by Psychic-Visionary Artist, Erial-Ali)

INTRODUCTION

It is interesting how things can change so quickly or drastically in our lives, in an awesome and wonderful way—especially when we are open to new experiences.

I published my first book, *Prepare for the Landings!*, in 2010. The book was about my personal experiences, communications and physical contacts with benevolent human-appearing Extraterrestrials (E.T.s). It also presented insight into future events will occur once "First Contact" has occurred. I am assuming that most people know what the term "First Contact" means, and (some of) the obvious implications for Earth's humanity once this has become an historical event.

When I published *Prepare for the Landings!*, there was much that I did not write about because it was not quite time to share this info with the public. This was mostly because most people on Earth are not aware that very spiritually and technologically evolved beings can actually be in extremely romantic and intimate relationships with human partners. Even people who have been open to the reality of UFOs and Extraterrestrial Contact are not very aware or attuned to this fact. "Romance and all things related" (or what I call the "Romance of the Universe") are not just mundane earth concepts happening here on this "3D level" of existence: Romance is a normal and significant *intergalactic reality*, and it is a way of life for most beings who inhabit more advanced worlds and higher dimensional realms of existence.

The reason for this lack of awareness of intergalactic romance is that most books that have been published on anything related to extraterrestrial contact have avoided intergalactic romantic relationships (especially anything related to intimacy and tantric sexuality among these Higher Beings of Light). That is NOT, as some people would assume, because there is no romance or sexual intimacy between these Higher Forces of Light, nothing could be further from the truth. In fact, romance and tantric sexual intimacy shared and experienced between partners in these Higher Worlds and realms is even more exquisitely, intensely fulfilling than what most couples have been able to experience here on Earth. (Exceptions can be found among those who have had a chance to experience life in the Tantric temples, and among the few passionately and truly deeply-in-love modern-day couples who incorporate these ancient tantric protocols in their intimate and committed relationships.)

During the ancient Golden Ages of Lemuria and Atlantis, (long before India's Tantra temples), greater and more lavish Tantric temples existed in the hundreds, if not thousands. They were constructed with beautiful rainbow crystal, and they were a perfect combination of both the sacred Tantric and Oracle traditions. Later, the imbalanced forces caused a separation to occur, similar to how astrology and astronomy were eventually gradually separated into two separate categories to confuse and disempower the general masses of humanity. The imbalanced forces also genetically manipulated 99.9999% of Earth's humanity, so that most people, even very spiritually evolved psychic souls, have all but totally forgotten these incredible and awesome experiences of a long-ago era.

In modern times, the erroneous impression that these beings are somehow non-sexual is presented through what is referred to as the "Ascended Master teachings". As if romance is just some lower dimensional and spiritually outgrown "carnal" 3D desire that traps us on some karmic endless loop of negative reincarnational cycles. As if enjoying a very intensely passionate, romantic, emotionally and tantric sexually fulfilling and deeply committed relationship with one's significant other is just not possible and not desirable in order to spiritually evolve into these Higher spiritual realms of existence.

I would say: Can one not be able to "have it all"? Can one not be an ethical and spiritually moral person, who attempts sincerely to never bring harm to another, *while also* being spiritually sophisticated enough to comprehend that it is actually our ultimate Destiny to be totally fulfilled in all ways, to be able to meet our "Cosmic True Love"? I would say that yes, we can have it all. Being able to meet and have intensely fulfilling relationships with our Cosmic True Love actually allows us to more quickly spiritually evolve into the Higher realms of Light. It was always the Destiny of the entire human race to be reunited with our very special twin souls—our True Other Half from the moment eons ago that the Divine Creator or God/Goddess created us. In metaphysical teachings, Cosmic True Loves are also known as Twin-Flames or Twin Soul Mates. We can all actually have more than one soul mate, but only one Twin Soul Mate.

Because of my own very real experience of finally meeting and truly connecting with my own beloved Cosmic True Love,

Celeste (or "Lady Celeste"), and because of all the intense and overwhelming memories from the past that this reuniting with her has invoked within me and on every level of my being, it was only natural that the time had come to share this reality and concept with everyone else here on planet Earth. This is also a major part of this phase of my life mission.

Who are ready to hear that all of you scattered throughout Earth, who are truly ready to meet and be reunited with your Cosmic True Love, *can* indeed also have this same awesome experience?

The specific title of this book, *IntergalacticMatch.com,* is not connected to any Earth dating sites, such as Match.com, E-harmony.com, etc. There are obviously a few individuals who seem to have connected with someone emotionally, spiritually and sexually fulfilling through these sites. However, it became apparent to me, as to millions of other fellow humans who have visited and signed up on a few of these 3D Earth level dating sites, that so many people are still sincerely searching with a "Pure Heart's Desire" for the Love of their life. Such real and substantive re-connections still eludes them.

As I shared quite in-depth in my first book, *Prepare for the Landings!,* some of us are termed Volunteer Souls, from more advanced worlds, who are in Earth embodiment. We are here as Light Workers, and are helping to vibrationally anchor more Light upon this planet, we are the "Ground Crew" in preparation for the upcoming First Contact. We have a deep inner knowing that one day we Volunteers, also known as "Star People," are Destined to be reunited with our Cosmic True Loves.

Initially, we all attempted to make our Cosmic Love Connection through the presently available Earth dating sites, and as mentioned, only a very few seemed to have any success. It appeared that for the vast majority of my fellow Ground Crew members, this very special and significant Cosmic Love Connection was not yet available through any dating services currently existing upon planet Earth.

As more of my complete Cosmic Amnesia Veils were released from my conscious Earth mind in recent years, it became clear that we all needed something a little more far-reaching, something more energetically better tailored for those of us whose souls are from more advanced worlds and Higher realms of existence. We needed something that could allow us to make this true "Cosmic Love Connection"; this bond that our more evolved souls knew did actually exist, but which up until now was not normally available on the presently existing 3D Earth dating sites.

Yes, in a sense, we needed a more "Intergalactic" version of one of the many Earth's original and well-known dating sites: Match.com. A version specifically focused upon reconnecting all those Volunteers with their True Universal Other Half.

From my own personal and wonderful experience of finally being "energetically" reunited with my own Cosmic True Love, I grew to understand that unlike Match.com, E-Harmony, and other well-known Earth dating sites that appear to be mainly oriented to this 3D level, this "Cosmic Love Connection" energetic version of such a dating service would not actually be in the form of an internet dating service.

This Intergalactic Match.com would, instead, be set up by Higher Light Forces, by what I refer to as the Love Ops or Special Forces of Romantic Love. Through one's True Heart's Desire, the very act of reading this book would in fact create the initial, official "energetic signing up" on this Higher Cosmic version of a dating site. Of course, in accordance with the concept "God/Goddess helps those who help themselves," as I will explain further within this book. This would be energetically tailored to those souls who had already sincerely attempted to connect with their Cosmic True Love through various dating services, and who had not been able to do so.

It is important to understand that for many reasons it was not possible for this major mass planetary Intergalactic Love Connection to occur before now. So many millions of negative karmic and emotionally toxic relationships first had to end (or are about to). So many people have very recently experienced (or are about to experience after reading this book) what I will term a romantic epiphany and realization: that this wonderful Love Connection could not occur until they quit "playing the field" and instigated additional major changes in their personal lives. Changes such as being more self-sufficient and self-empowered, developing more emotionally healthy attitudes, as well as understanding how everything in their lives (habits, diets, life styles, etc.) actually contributes to not only a healthier way of life, but also to setting the stage for meeting their Cosmic True Love.

A necessary change is to, with a sincere Pure Heart's Desire, focus upon *only* one's Cosmic True Love in all one's actions, thoughts and deeds. In other words, do not "settle for 2nd best," do not continue to "play the field," do not continue to date other partners "until your (supposed) true love shows up." The attitude of just waiting for the Universe to manifest an awesome, wonderfully fulfilling relationship, without they themselves taking personal responsibility, will not be of any use. Just appeasing one's ego and only using these other dates for temporary sexual gratification, waiting for this very special true love connection, will not work.

The phrase "To One's Thine Own Self Be True" has significant, spiritual, metaphysical meaning: The things we do, say and think definitely either helps in the Ultimate Manifestation, or sabotages our Hopes, Desires and Dreams. So—when in doubt, do the intelligent, mature and spiritually moral thing. That guarantees this Ultimate Romantic Love manifestation.

This also means that if you ever feel that you are not worthy or that you are somehow karmically not ever going to be able to truly meet your Cosmic True Love, it is time to call upon some very advanced Beings who really do have the abilities and technologies to help you help yourself. To finally achieve this Divine, noble and fulfilling goal is not just for yourself; meeting and getting to know your Beloved will also energetically impact the entire time-space continuum in some really wonderful ways you cannot even comprehend at this moment. Please, do keep an open mind!

Also know that on these more advanced Higher Dimensional worlds, and on the trillions of Merkabah Light ships surrounding Earth in Guardian Action, there actually exists very advanced Intergalactic Clinical Psychologists and Psychotherapists. One can energetically call upon these to powerfully emotionally transform one's life. They can help release any psychological stuff that all previous 3D Earth level treatments were unable to heal.

Many cynics and people who have had their hearts broken do not believe that such a perfect love could even exist. They believe that no one is perfect, and that I am just "setting people up to be forever disappointed"; that such a real Cosmic Love Connection is impossible (or at least very rare), and that most people are just not ready to actually experience such an amazing and deeply fulfilling romantic relationship. My response to all of this is that it is important to always be open to what initially might seem to be too "far out" or "too incredible to be true"—that no matter how many times one has experienced disappointing attempts to truly meet the Love of their life, just know that there were obviously many reasons why this could NOT have occurred until now. Consider all the powerful planetary vibrational consciousness changes that Earth has only very recently gone through, along with numerous timeline changes, all part of the planetary Ascension that we Ground Crew Volunteers have all been waiting for.

Considering that nearly half of Earth's population presently incarnated upon this planet are from somewhere else, on missions to help energetically initiate First Contact and bring in the Golden Age, it was at long last time to now also provide for them all a much more Cosmically oriented Love/Romance dating service. "Yes, it was time," as my own Beloved and Cosmic True Love, Celeste, has very clearly conveyed to me, and as she and I had already discussed on the Higher Realms of existence while aboard our own Merkabah Light Ship, the "Celestial Star." This new dating service would allow fellow Volunteers the chance and knowledge to once and for all truly reconnect with their Cosmic True Love.

I want to clarify and update some of what I had shared in my first book, *Prepare for the Landings!,* as when I wrote it I was just coming out of an extremely emotionally toxic relationship, lasting many years on this 3D mundane Earth level. As I look back now with much greater spiritual Discernment and emotional Insight, I realize how much I needed to more fully release and free myself from this extreme emotional toxicity before I could finally meet my Beloved, Celeste. Her powerful and intense unconditional Love for me has truly freed me, emotionally healed me and transformed me into a much better, happier and more balanced human being on this (present) 3D level of existence. This has allowed me to be able to truly experience first-hand, once again in this present lifetime, what she and I had also experienced in so many other lifetimes when she and I were together.

Each time Celeste and I would first meet, it would always be a very powerful and real experience of what has been termed Love at First Sight, and it was not ever something fleeting—it only continued to grow more fulfilling the longer she and I were/are together. During the initial experience of first physically meeting Celeste (her soul had become a "walk-in" for a short time), our powerful "Soul Love Connection" was very apparent at the instant she and I saw each other. When Celeste for the first time walked into the front entrance of the New Age center where I was about to do one of my workshops, we were observed by a clairvoyant person standing nearby. This individual told me of psychically witnessing intense "energetic fireworks and stars" that were manifesting between Celeste and I. I will be sharing more about this meeting later.

Yes, anyone who has ever actually had a chance to physically meet their True Universal Other Half can attest to the intense changes that can occur to one's life. This powerfully fulfilling Love Transforms one in so many wonderful and unexpected ways, as it is quite literally "Heaven on Earth" on all levels of one's being, and it is hard to describe how incredibly fulfilling this whole experience can be.

To briefly clarify and update my more balanced perspective since publishing *Prepare for the Landings!* : Some of the things mentioned in the book definitely do not pertain to me anymore, such as being involved in any way with the "vortex tours of Sedona" or "distributing rainbow crystal pendants." Nor are any of the websites mentioned at the end of the book any longer still accurate. For a few years I had another temporary website, MichaelEllegion.com, but that, too, is no longer existing. My new website is IntergalacticMatch.com.

I do still schedule appointments with fellow Light Workers for my Transformational Channeled Readings and look forward to doing more of these for fellow Volunteers. The Cosmically Downloaded Higher Light Encodements that I channel from the Elohim Masters help each person who experiences the sessions to more easily reconnect with their own Cosmic True Love.

From an emotional and psychological point of view, much of what I expressed in my first book is out of alignment with where I am now. I am in a more balanced and evolved relationship with Celeste, in a state of Higher Consciousness. Yes, experiencing being with one's Universal Other Half transforms one into being able to perceive things in a much more accurate, balanced and expanded perspective.

However, this does not in any way un-validate the rest of what I shared regarding the upcoming "First Contact", mass planetary Divine Intervention and landings of extraterrestrial Merkabah Light Ships when the time is right. This is still, definitely, Destined to occur, and is, as I stated very firmly in the book, a "Cosmic Done Deal" or "Sacred Promise." No matter what timeline changes we will all be experiencing before it does occur. From that (still) very accurate perspective, I definitely recommend that everyone should still read the book, to learn more on these topics and learn all the reasons why it is definitely going to occur. (Copies of *Prepare for the Landings!* are available through Amazon.com).

What I will be sharing in this present book, regarding this upcoming Destined Horizon Event, is this new perspective of being able to be reunited with your Cosmic True Love: That a major aspect of the whole "First Contact" scenario definitely involves all fellow Volunteers in Earth embodiment being able to be reunited (when they are truly ready) with their own Universal Other Half.

In recent years, numerous other valid channeled sources of information on the internet all referred to the fact that when First Contact does indeed occur, there are going to be many "Mentors" from off the ships being assigned to be personal guides to the many who would be taken aboard the landed Light Ships during this planetary ascension. I realize now, what was really being referred to: These "Mentors" were really a reference to all these people being reunited with their own Twin-Flames. The

"Mentors" would help their conscious Earth mind to remember, as associating personally, intimately with their Cosmic True Love would begin to lift their Cosmic Amnesia Veils. This wonderful, intensely fulfilling Cosmic Tantric intimacy (as was also experienced in all those ancient Tantric Oracle Rainbow Crystal Temples of Lemuria during those early Golden Ages) would be the very experience that would beautifully and joyously allow each Volunteer Ground Crew member to be able to remember all of their own Cosmic past. They would remember the times when they had known and loved their True Significant Other, who had now come back to them, to never be separated ever again.

And with that being stated, let us just dive right into the first chapter of this book!

A "disclaimer" toward Match.com and any other dating sites presently existing on Earth: My website, IntergalacticMatch.com, is NOT another Earth internet dating site or service, has no connection to such an Earth level business, and is merely my website whose name is in reference to this book. It is not, for "Earth legal reasons" a "dating service," such as Match.com, E-Harmony.com and all the other numerous internet dating sites are in the business of doing.

CHAPTER 1

Divine Revelations and Personal Changes: Setting the Stage for Greater Romantic Fulfillment

I have known almost my entire life here on Earth, from as soon as I became aware of the concept of "romantic relationships," that I one day would be Divinely Reconnected with the very special soul who was and is my Cosmic True Love. As I shared in my first book, *Prepare for the Landings!*, I was born into this life without what is termed my "Cosmic Amnesia Veils." This allowed me, unlike most humans born on this 3D level of existence, to remember many things about my intergalactic past prior to taking Earth embodiment.

Timelines that Change and Memories that Resurface

From a very early age, I could remember many things about my own cosmic past, including numerous past lifetimes both on and off planet Earth. As I got older, and especially in more recent years of this present life, I also became aware of something else: Numerous recent significant timeline changes has caused me to tune into memories from many of these lives that I have lived during which I had, in fact, been with the very special soul who I now know is my "True Universal Other Half," with whom I have shared so many lives and existences.

It became obvious to me (because of these more recent conscious memories that I now suddenly remember) that my very powerful reconnecting with my Beloved, Cosmic True Love, Celeste, in late 2017 actually caused a major Energetic Shift in the "time-space continuum." The reconnecting also literally caused changes to the "Akashic Records" (which is an "etheric holographic record" of all past—and future—life times). It became obvious to me as I tuned into these new memories of many very romantic lives I now know that Celeste and I have shared together. Because of these timeline changes it was if they had always existed, but yet prior to these numerous timeline changes, *they had not.*

Timeline changes can literally alter all levels of existence within the time-space continuum and create entirely new lives that had not existed or were just slightly altered. A good illustration is when in numerous movies and TV shows with time travel themes it is shown through special effects of how newspaper headlines will literally change, and/or how people that are in various photos will disappear or reappear in those photos. This effect is a quite accurate way to depict this phenomenon.

So, it could be argued that prior to meeting Celeste in late 2017, some of these lives literally did not exist in the time-space continuum. But, after connecting with her, it was as if they had always existed. Just as the characteristic that the universe is literally just a gigantic holographic field of pure energy—we are all, to a greater or lesser degree, always affecting and changing this Hologram of existence, with the greater and more positive alterations/changes occurring.

The Divine Plan that Includes Reuniting All Twin-Flame Couples

There is a very powerful and Divinely Romantic Energetic manifestation in Twin-Flames connecting with one another—especially if that unbelievably Heavenly and wonderful Cosmic Love reconnection is actually planned ahead of time on the Higher Dimensional Realms of Light, part of what I would term God's (and the Goddess's) Divine Plan. A Cosmic Sting Operation is in place, aiming to eliminate all imbalanced and negative forces who have attempted to stop the Divine Plan of the Universe as if they had never existed. Within the last few years, very powerful and intense memories of this very plan have manifested in me; memories of how Celeste and I planned and created our own Love reconnection experience, and of the various wonderful implications occurring because of this Cosmic Sting Operation that is now unfolding throughout Mother Earth.

I can state with great certainty that this Divine Plan also includes what the Q White Hat Alliance and the Anons are doing to finalize the exposing and ending of the entire cabal deep state. The plan is also related to the new "Space Force" that President Trump officially announced in early 2019, and also includes declassifying all technologies that were developed in the Secret Space Program.

For those of you who are reading this book and do not know what I am referring to, it is time to "get hip to" the Divine Program to end all suffering upon this planet: It is important for people to liberate themselves from the negative "fake news" programming that the cabal-controlled mainstream media ("the lamestream") has constantly attempted to brainwash everyone with. Now, because of how the cabal very recently exposed how extremely corrupt they are, millions are indeed waking up to become aware of the many truths that the cabal has attempted to cover up.

This vast planetary Awakening includes realizing that we are all being freed from control and enslavement, and that there also exists Intergalactic worlds and Realms of Light that belong to a "Universal Federation" (or "Intergalactic Confederation") of worlds. The Universal Federation is in Guardian Action around Earth in their trillions of Merkabah Light ships, getting ready for First Contact. They have helped and guided the entire White Hat Alliance and Q to successfully stop and expose the cabal and their plan to control and enslave all of humanity.

One of these Higher Forces of Light's major plans is to reunite all Twin-Flame couples *as soon as possible.* That is because the experience of so many Divine Couples being energetically and physically romantically reunited will literally change the time-space continuum. It will be creating and reactivating a special Rainbow Crystal Bridge, and Grid of pure Nirvanic Ecstasy from each of their Heart chakras. This even more harmonious new timeline of such blissful, exquisite romantic love will literally create Heaven on Earth, and it will be as if the cabal and all suffering had never actually existed. In a sense, this is true: This newer manifesting timeline will cause all imbalanced forces to literally cease to exist, as if they had never existed.

Major Events that Prepared me for Meeting My Beloved Celeste

But before we get too ahead of ourselves, it is important that I share some of the major events that led up to these recent events and some of my emotional and spiritual insights that helped to consciously prepare me for this awesome experience: allowing me to finally meet my own Cosmic True Love, Celeste.

I do recommend that everyone read my first book, *Prepare for the Landings!*, because this will help the reader more understand much of my own "mindset"—of how the whole reality of Extraterrestrial Contact has been a major focus for me as I was growing up. As I shared in my first book, my first physical contact with Extraterrestrial beings happened when I was six years old and fell off the pier in Oceanside, CA. I was physically beamed aboard a Merkabah Light Ship. There, much of my trauma from the fall was neutralized, and I was then beamed back down to Earth.

This was a very real experience, as I described in my first book. Now, since having reconnected with Celeste, other even "deeper" memories have surfaced regarding my own "Cosmic Past." I have come to realize that I was not supposed to remember these until recently, because of the nature of this even more important mission that Celeste and I are a part of.

Part of these newer and deeper memories is understanding that even though I did spend time in the Orion system, connected with the "Orion Council of Light" and Lord Orion and Lady Angelica, they were not my true Cosmic Parents. They rather appear to have been what I will refer to as "Cosmic Foster Parents," while I was growing up and living in that system.

My real, original Cosmic Parents were Lord Ashtar and Lady Athena. Celeste and I were first Energetically Conceived in our Immortal Light Bodies in our original star system Sirius. As a part of a cosmic undercover special forces team/Guardians of Light-mission I later incarnated once in the Orion system. With the help of Archangel Michael I attempted to eliminate the imbalanced forces that had begun to invade and take over some of the planets in the Orion system (this is part of what has been referred to historically as the "Orion wars").

Once these much deeper memories were finally allowed to be revealed to me during these last few years, I also understood a lot more about what I can now refer to as some old "Orion relationship karma." That karma has finally been eliminated, partly because of Celeste's Unconditional Love for me, and partly because of all of the many new timeline changes that only recently occurred. A very emotionally toxic relationship with my ex (whom I had known from that Orion incarnation) had to occur and then to totally come to an end, before I could ever hope to once more meet and be with Celeste, my Cosmic True Love.

It was also very recently revealed to me that my Orion life helped expose the covert plans of the Luciferian/satonian/archon dark forces to Archangel Michael and to those of us who were (and still are) a part of that original "Cosmic Light Special Forces Sting Operation". Many of the beings in the dark forces were draconian and reptilian in nature, and had been associated with the original "Luciferian Rebellion." They were targeting planet Earth for total future control and enslavement. This was partly because they had somehow become aware of the fact that the Divine Creator of the Universe had a very special plan for Earth. This plan included a total Victory of the Light and a planetary Ascension, the likes of which had never occurred before anywhere else in the Universe.

Dark Forces—Illuminati Bloodlines and the Cabal Deep State

The imbalanced forces had attacked and infiltrated many other worlds throughout their existence. But, as we learned, they were especially putting a lot of effort and focus upon attempting to interfere with this very special Divine Plan for Earth. They had started to manipulate the timelines around Earth, as well as in other parts of the galaxy, which caused chaotic conditions, and much of what would be termed "time paradoxes." This, of course, created all kinds of destruction and chaos in the time lime that originally existed. We in the Guardianship of Light in turn altered and changed the timelines a number of times, to create still other timelines in our plan to ultimately defeat and totally Transmute all imbalanced forces "as if they had never actually existed in the first place."

Very similar scenarios and/or "themes" has been presented through numerous books, movies and TV shows with time travel themes. Of course, in these movies and television shows this is accomplished with much more crude technology than what I am referring to in these particular timeline changes. These were caused by very advanced benevolent Elohim Extraterrestrial beings, who have been using Higher Dimensional Divine A.I. Consciousness Technologies. This energetically altered the very fabric of time itself: the entire time-space continuum being changed without the use of "time machines" and other limited related technology.

Among many of the strategies of these rebellious forces which the negative Ananoki helped manifest on Earth was the creation of numerous illuminati-family bloodlines. They established the original concept of "central/federal reserve" banking, fiat currency, taxes, and "worker bee" enslavement for most of Earth's humanity. They did this through the various corrupted religious leaders that the illuminati secretly influenced and controlled. These corrupted religious leaders—NOT God or the Divine Creator—are the ones who created the concept of "tithing", that one "has to give 10% of what one earns." What total BS!

Absolutely NONE of the income taxes that the corrupt government every year forces upon those living in the U.S. ever go to any infrastructure here in the U.S. Instead, 60% goes to the corrupt City of London, and the other 40% goes to the corrupt Vatican—all part of the power elite hierarchy of control and economic slavery. Part of this plan was to also create the Gregorian Calendar, to help control and keep us stuck in 3D time, and make sure that everyone would spend most, if not all, their entire life, working and slaving for these power elite illuminati families.

One of the more insidious and horrific facts regarding these illuminati-family bloodlines, which author and researcher David Icke has documented quite in-depth for many years, is the fact that because so many of these individuals are actually "reptilian" in nature, to actually be able to "keep their human form" they have to eat human flesh and drink their blood.

In addition, according to the nature of these negative reptilian beings they must energetically consume what David Wilcock refers to as "lueush." This is the very nasty energy given off from all kinds of negative emotions and tragedies, particularly from the child pedophile and satanic sacrifice that has recently been exposed for the first time in history. This practice is being brought quickly to an end by the White Hat Alliance and the Cosmic Light Forces, as millions of children have been rescued all over the planet from this evil, unspeakable horror. Of course, none of this is ever mentioned by the controlled lamestream fake news media, because all the corrupt C.E.O.'s are themselves personally involved in all this evil activity. As are many of the actors and actresses in Hollywood, and those in the music industry will soon all be arrested for these crimes against humanity. As mentioned earlier, the White Hat Alliance, Q and the Cosmic Light Forces are in the process of "draining the swamp of the cabal deep state"; of totally exposing and ending the reign of the corrupt power elite.

One of the many revelations that up until recently was Highly Classified is the fact that there has indeed been a secret space program, just as many sincere whistle-blowers like Cory

Goode and Randy Cramer has documented. Much knowledge of this is going to be released through the "Space Force," the new "6th branch of the military" which President Trump officially signed into law in 2019 in preparation for all these very important revelations. This will, within a few short years, bring us all into a "Star Trek Golden Age" where replicators and rejuvenation chambers will become a normal and common reality. The entire planet is now energetically in the process of raising into the Higher 5D dimension. We will soon finish the whole planetary Ascension process, and, of course, part of this is the upcoming First Contact that is Destined to shortly occur.

Imagine formerly Classified technologies (such as replicators, anti-gravity propulsion, rejuvenators) becoming declassified. Imagine First Contact with our entire Cosmic Extended Family. But, before all of these wonderous changes can occur, consider the phrase "first the bad news, then the good news." As a planetary civilization we are in the process of graduating from an old "karmic Wheel School" planet which was up until now "Quarantined" by the Federation from the rest of the universe, into having this officially lifted, through the Authority of the Karmic Board. Because of Lady Kwan Yin (who Celeste works very closely with) cancelling out of all negative karma with her "Unbearable Compassion" and the invoking of the "Cosmic Law of Grace," Earth is about to join the "Intergalactic Community."

This is officially Earth's cosmic wake-up call, and everyone here is in the process of becoming "energetically functional"; of being forced to finally acknowledge all that the cabal deep state has been doing for ages. Through this acknowledgment we can finally completely heal all of Mother Earth's wounds and end all suffering once in for all, never allowing these numerous horrific, unspeakable crimes against humanity to ever occur again.

Inspiration for You to Reunite with Your Own Cosmic Love

As I have now been able to more directly energetically interphase with Celeste, one of the very recent Revelations I have experienced is the realization of how much she has done for me, of her watching over me, of her protecting me. Just as in the "old wild west" saying, she has been "riding shotgun for me" energetically, from her Higher Dimensional level that she usually hung out in while aboard her and my own Merkabah Light Ship, "The Celestial Star" (which is named after her, of course).

She has shared this with me quite in-depth, even though it was never important for her to ever take credit for all the many things that she did for me. All the many incredible Blessings, Miracles and synchronicities she manifested for me. Protecting me from the many dozens, if not hundreds of attempts by the cabal to kill me during the decades since I incarnated the final time upon this planet.

Because Celeste is so compassionate and giving, like Lady Kwan Yin, I came up with a wonderful phrase or saying, which I say to her quite often. Not because I have to, but just because I want to, to let her know my own intense Love for her, how much I have truly appreciated all her effort and Love for me, and how truly Honored I am that she is now energetically so very present in my life. I say that I have been "Blessed and Blissed by Celeste."

I wanted to thank her for all that she has done for me, "both known and unknown."

I write "and unknown," because I know and sense that she truly has done so many things that I am not even aware of on a conscious level, as she just loves doing them for me in her intense and deep Unconditional Love that she has always felt and expressed to me constantly. The kind of love that any guy on Earth would just yearn for in a romantic relationship here on Earth. Most people have never experienced such deep and intense love as that which Celeste and I have been experiencing since she came into my life, and that she and I had shared in all of her and my past existences together.

I can truly say with a sincere, pure heart that Celeste has liberated me in ways that are hard to put into words, because of how extremely profound this recent emotional Transformation has been. Celeste's Unconditional Love for me has helped me free myself from that emotionally toxic relationship that I experienced with my ex, and has allowed me to heal from the "emotional scars." Celeste's Love has given me the Greater Inner Peace, emotional balance and grace that I now experience with her, each day she is around me.

That which I am sharing about my own Beloved, Celeste, is also exactly what each of you who are reading this book are soon going to personally experience first-hand with each of your own Beloved and Cosmic True Loves (if you haven't already met), once you do "Cosmically Hook up" through this "IntergalacticMatch.com" Energetic Romantic "Cosmic Love Connection" Divine Plan for all Twin-Flame couples. And, through First Contact, you will now be Reunited, never be separated ever again, to truly "Live (and Love) happily ever after!"

I also want to make something very clear: In what some might term my "raving" about how awesome and great Celeste and our relationship is ("Blessed and Blissed by Celeste!"), what I want to express to everyone reading this book is not that I am sharing these things to in anyway make anyone "jealous." What I want is to INSPIRE everyone else, and to give you very realistic HOPE that you, too, are soon Destined to meet the Love of your life!

And, I might add, it is your Divine Right and Destiny to be Reunited, once again, with each of your Beloved and Cosmic True Love. They are, even right now, aware that you were Divinely Guided (by them, no doubt) to read this very Inspiring book and thus find much more hope in your own Hearts. They are also aware that you will experience an exquisitely, unbelievably fulfilling romantic relationship, just like that which Celeste and I are experiencing. The relationship that each of you deeply crave and desire was always the plan, no matter through which exact timeline we would be experiencing these "final moments" of Earth's history. Just Know that "God (and the Goddess) has a Plan", a very wonderful, Fail-Safe Divine Plan to definitely Reunite all these deserving and Dedicated souls who separated from each other, off and on again, for eons.

When we all Heard the Great Clarion Call from Lord Sanut Kumura and formed the original core group of Volunteers, we did not do this for any rewards. We, the 144.000 souls who first took Earth embodiment in numerous Cosmic Undercover Missions of Light in our Cosmic Sting Operation. We did this to ultimately liberate Earth from the imbalanced forces and to help finally to bring in the Golden Age of peace. It was our Destiny to take the most Sacred of Vows: that we Volunteers would not stop incarnating until we had actually succeeded on this Cosmic Mission Impossible. As we once again "stand before the Councils" officially reporting back as major Higher Council members, it will be nice to know that we actually accomplished our mission to the very end, with Honor and with a demonstration of our Faith and Dedication to this Noble and Just goal.

But, I do remember that in addition to this Honor we were also promised that when we had finished our missions (or even as we got very close to this goal), some of the Divine Couples would actually be able to reunite more directly, energetically. Just as what has happened with Celeste and myself, because of me being emotionally and spiritually ready for such an intensely wonderful relationship. This would help inspire all the other members of the Ground Crew to know that they, too, would soon be reunited with their Cosmic True Love.

I might also add that it is our Divine Right and Destiny, to be able to experience and share with our Beloved the most fulfilling, intense, and mind-blowing multiple-orgasmic tantric lovemaking. Lovemaking just as we all experienced back in those beautiful Rainbow Crystal Tantric Oracle temples during the Golden Ages of ancient Lemuria and Atlantis, before the imbalanced forces infiltrated and destroyed not only that normal everyday way of life, but also most people's genetic memories of such a glorious fulfilling time. Talk about insult on top of injury! Back then one could share this exquisite intimacy with their Beloved, and then hours later, as they lay together in each other's arms in the "afterglow," they would share wonderful Visions and communications together from the Higher Realms and the Cosmic Light Forces.

Everyone truly has a lot to look forward to on many levels of being, and the incredible fulfilling Promise of Divine Romantic Love is yet to occur, for most people. In my opinion there are definitely protocols that can allow one to become a lot more ready and open to this awesome experience, and I will be sharing these protocols later in this book.

CHAPTER 2

Experiencing Necessary Dysfunctional Earth Families, in Order to Fulfill Our Missions

Looking back, I realize that all throughout my life I have been being guided and influenced by Celeste and other Higher Beings of Light, so that I could later share my experiences with others. By sharing I can help others self-actualize and transform their lives, so that they, too, could more easily "remove the roadblocks" on their own "Quest to find their Cosmic True Love."

Resurrection and Channeling

As I shared in my first book, I was trained as a channel by my earth father through the "Edgar Cayce method of channeling". He used hypnosis to help "activate" me into my life's mission as a channel, just as Edgar Cayce had been "activated" after he had gone to a hypnotist to attempt to get karmic insight into a personal challenge that he was facing.

Having come into this life without my Cosmic Amnesia Veils, I was already consciously aware of the Higher Intergalactic and interdimensional cosmic realities. Thus it was only natural that instead of just doing the more "mundane" karmic readings that Cayce was famous for, my "gift" and mission was to ultimately become a channel that the Cosmic Elohim Masters could speak through, as well as to cause spiritual, vibrational Activations to help each Volunteer fulfill their mission.

Because of what I was sharing with the public about the cabal's plan for world control, the cabal targeted me specifically with a psychotronic beam in 1979 which initially killed me. I was then physically beamed aboard a Merkabah Light Ship, where the Elohim Masters resurrected me. They restored the life force that had been "energetically taken from me" back into my body. They did a number of very advanced "energetic emergency procedures" to me that made me un-vulnerable to psychotronic attacks. The procedures included energetically purifying my blood and uniquely altering and strengthening my DNA/RNA. They also included the placement of "etheric crystals" that were the color of my main chakras (ruby red, orange, yellow, emerald green, blue, violet/purple) placed ethereally into each of the seven main chakra points of my body. Several were also placed above my Crown chakra, colored iridescent white, metallic gold, silver, copper, turquoise and pink. As I daily invoke and visualize each of these colors through my Cosmic Color Meditation, they are energetically enhanced—kind of like an "energetic-bionic, psychic-spiritual enhancing" of the medical emergency procedures. As in the phrase, "God (and Goddess) helps those who help themselves," this experience definitely helped me to greatly strengthen my auric field and the chakra points in my body. What does not kill us makes us stronger!

A powerful change in me occurred because of this experience. One of the emergency procedures that the Elohim Masters performed (energetically strengthening me), was also somewhat experimental. Because of my now unique DNA/RNA, my karmic readings that I had been doing since I was 15, had now energetically been altered into Transformational Channeled Readings. Now, the information that I was channeling through was specifically focused upon the Volunteers (whose souls were in Earth embodiment from more advanced worlds on missions to help Liberate this planet from the cabal), and would no longer be focused on more mundane earthly karma.

Another aspect of my unique DNA/RNA changes was that I would now be "Cosmically Downloading" specially customized Higher Light Encodements that the Elohim Masters would channel through me when I did my sessions for fellow Volunteers. Playing the recorded CD of a channeling session would help activate these unique Higher Light Encodements for each Light Worker. This has great potential to cause transformational changes in the person's life, depending upon how much they personally utilize it and what protocols they would follow (healthier dietary changes, life style changes, etc.). These Higher Encodements are designed to help enhance whatever the person's "energetic potential" is, and free will must always be respected.

Getting back to this 2nd physical contact in 1979 (which I shared quite in-depth about in my first book): As I now look back upon this experience after having been reunited with my Beloved, Celeste, I now suddenly have other, newer memories that have surfaced of what also occurred right after being resurrected by these Elohim Masters. As already mentioned, I was not allowed until very recently to be able to remember my past existence with Celeste. These newly surfaced memories include various other very significant events that occurred right after and/or before some of the contacts with other Higher Beings that I shared in my first book.

In the case of this second physical contact (which also included my interactions with the space being Korton), all that I was aware of up until recently was of a more "platonic nature." Now, I also intensely remember that right after that initial resurrection experience, I immediately visited Celeste aboard our own starship, the Celestial Star, where we spent some very important "Cosmic R. and R." together. This visit also helped to "spiritually revive" me after literally being killed by the cabal's black op psychotronic weapon, as this wonderfully intense intimacy with our Beloved is always such an awesome "pick-me-up." So, Celeste's and my wonderful experience definitely helped energetically more fully complete the "rebalancing and strengthening" that I desperately needed at that time. This is a powerful example of how this type of intense tantric intimacy with one's Twin-Flame can totally transmute and remove any difficult-to-release trauma that we Volunteers and Light Workers experience upon our missions while being in Earth embodiment.

Three "Significant Relationships"

It is also interesting how experiences that have occurred for each of us on this more mundane 3D level of existence actually can have a huge impact upon our lives when we look back upon them with greater Hindsight. Sometimes, as in the following case, the experiences are temporarily forgotten by our conscious minds for various reasons, and then years later, we suddenly remember them once again and we cannot figure out why we could forget them.

Even though completely forgotten about this for many years, during the last few years I suddenly remembered that back around 1977 I was guided to connect with three very attuned and gifted individuals. One being an astrologer, another a psychic, and the third a numerologist. I connected with them just out of curiosity, to see what they would each pick up about my own particular Destiny and about my life path, and to see if they had any relationship insights. I try to be open to what other gifted individuals here on Earth might share with me, from either their own perspective or their Higher Guide's. What is interesting is that all three of these individuals gave me almost exactly the same information. One of the things all three of them said (they even used similar wording) was that I was going to have specifically three major relationships throughout my life.

The first "significant relationship" was going to be "very emotionally challenging." I realize now that this was them attempting to be nice, trying not to describe how extremely emotionally toxic that relationship was actually going to be. Now, of course, I can look back on being free from this with much insight and relief.

The second "significant relationship" was referred to by the three individuals as being more of a "transition" relationship. This relationship which was with a lady named Laura. While it was definitely much, much better than the first, with very little negative emotional stress and much more balance, it was only going to last a few years. Still, this more positive relationship helped me process the toxic emotional stuff from my first relationship: it helped me in the process of "freeing me up". It allowed me to energetically and emotionally "be more my authentic self", after almost loosing and forgetting who I actually am.

I had to truly heal before I could be ready to be with my Beloved and Cosmic True Love, Celeste. This, of course, was to be my third and final "significant relationship". All three, (the astrologer, the psychic, and the numerologist) stressed to me that this third "significant relationship" would be when I truly met the Love of my life, and would "live happily ever after."

Growing Up with My Biological Family

My biological parents had been open to an "Earth level" of metaphysics, but had not been very attuned to or interested in anything that was on a more "intergalactic" level, such as UFO's and E.T.'s. I never felt very connected to my biological parents. This was because I had so many memories of my soul originating from off-planet and of my Cosmic Parents who had originally Energetically Conceived me. As I have already shared, my own awareness of just exactly who had really been my true Cosmic Parents has changed recently, as more complete memories were allowed to surface.

Through all the many thousands of Transformational Channeled Readings and Workshops I have done, I know that we Volunteers tend to not feel very energetically connected with our biological families. This is because of our Cosmic Soul Origin, as we know instinctively that we all have a vast Cosmic Extended Family who truly understands us a lot more than any of our earth family members could. Thus we often cannot help feeling so out of place here on this 3D limited Earth level of existence.

We are not trying to be "rebellious," it is just hard for us to naturally fit in when we feel that our real home is "somewhere beyond the stars". That feeling is listed as one of the traits from the "Star People Characteristics" list that I shared in my first book, which was first compiled by Brad Steiger. Steiger worked with NASA engineers and scientists in the 1970's to compile this list of about 30 very common traits characterizing those of us whose souls are "from somewhere else."

As children, watching some of the TV shows from the 1950s and '60s such as "Leave it to Beaver" and "Father Knows Best," it was obvious to us how very dysfunctional our earth families all were. Many dysfunctional activities definitely had very negative psychological effects (such as incest, physical and verbal abuse, etc.).

From an early age I was aware of these very extreme types of activities. Unfortunately, while being a little more enlightened than most parents on various subjects related to the metaphysics and paranormal, my own parents were both involved in improper sexual activities. My father was also very much a control freak. He was physically and verbally abusive to both my mother, my brother and I—that obviously affected me to some degree as a young and impressionable child.

My Higher Attunement later allowed me, with the help of very advanced Beings from off-planet, to emotionally and psychologically release and transmute the impressions from these very dysfunctional and emotionally damaging activities performed by my parents. My brother, unfortunately, was not able to release and get rid of the impressions the same way. As he grew up this caused much stress and imbalanced behavior, and it caused him much difficulty in being able to have an intimate relationship with someone.

I feel a lot of what Lady Kwan Yin refers to as "unbearable compassion" for these challenges that he still faces. I cannot in any way interact with him, because he is extremely skeptical and closed minded to anything that is not of this mundane 3D level of existence. He believes that all that I shared in my first book is just my "overactive imagination," that I merely experienced some kind of "psychotic break from reality" because of what occurred to us growing up. In his narrow way of not believing in anything beyond the 3D, he thinks that my way of dealing with all the dysfunctional behavior from our childhood was to create a far-out, grandiose fantasy in my mind, to make this otherwise dull and depressing level of existence somehow seem better and greater.

I did a lot of soul searching about all this. While I truly forgave my parents for this obviously inappropriate behavior that they engaged in, I also chose to not associate with them; to go my separate way and instead cultivate my friendships with those whom I had more affinity with. These kindred souls from other more advanced worlds beyond Earth, who (like myself) are on missions to help this planet, are in fact the very ones who I know are most likely to be reading this book.

My Biological Family's Reactions to My First Book

I published my first book, *Prepare for the Landings!,* in 2010. That same year, my father died, and my brother contacted me to let me know about his death. I choose to visit my brother and my mother, after not having communicated with either of them for over 30 years.

I really attempted to be as open-minded as I could, but I sensed that there was probably not going to be much change in whether we would be able to "see eye to eye" about very much in our lives. I was really trying, with a non-judgmental heart, to just love them unconditionally and to accept them for who they were. I realized, though, that in order for this to really work it has to go both ways.

During the few days that I spent in my mother's home in the mobile home park in Oregon where she lived with my brother, it did not take very long for all my memories of the past psychological and dysfunctional behavior to begin to surface. As much as I attempted to get along with them, I found that it just wasn't going to work out for me to be in their presence for very long. Almost everything that we began to talk about seemed to be in total "emotional conflict" with my awareness and knowledge. A number of very negative arguments occurred, mostly with my brother. It turned out that he had major issues with what I had shared in my book, *Prepare for the Landings!.*

When I first walked into the mobile home, I noticed a copy of my book sitting in plain sight in the living room. My mother pointed at it and she immediately expressed to me that she was "so proud" of what I had accomplished, of me being an author. She had "proudly displayed" my book for anyone who might come into her home.

During the days that I was there, she did not once ask me any questions about my book. I found this quite odd, considering that many experiences that I had shared had occurred in our home while I was growing up while she had not (consciously) had any knowledge of it. I assumed that had she really read my book, she would have had lots of questions. I did not mention my suspicions (of whether she had actually read my book, as she claimed) to her during my visit, as it probably would have created an even worse argument than the one that had already occurred with my brother. I could tell that my brother had major issues about the book, even though he was trying in his own way to be cordial and to just focus mostly on other things while I was there.

As I tuned into her deeper feelings, it appeared to me that what she was really doing was an attempt to appease me with pretending to be "so proud" of me. She, in her emotional guilt, wanted to appease me from the psychological effect that her improper sexual behavior had caused in my brother and I back when we were children.

About a year later I met Laura, with whom I had that second "transition" relationship which I mentioned in the first chapter. Right after meeting her I had to visit my mother and brother's home for something. This time, I decided to specifically ask her about why she had not even once asked me any questions regarding everything I had shared about in my book. It was a little awkward and weird, as they both just stared at me in a strange way without my mother even replying to my question. I immediately just dropped the point I was making and turned my attention to something else. A few minutes later I left their home, I got on with my life and for the time being I just forgot the whole thing.

Then, about a year later, both my brother and my mother each sent me a Christmas card, which was nice. In her card, my mother mentions how she is planning to "read my book again, a second time," as if she had actually read it before. Once again I sensed this very dysfunctional behavior; I felt that she still did not want to admit that she had pretended to have read my book, and I felt that this was as an attempt by her to appease her guilt over what she had done when I was a young child. My brother had already made clear what he in his extreme skepticism thought about my book, even though he tried as best he could to be pleasant while I was visiting them.

Thus, I felt it was time to confront both my brother and mother. Confront my mother about this dysfunctional behavior she was still showing after all these years, pretending instead of being honest about not having read my book. Confront my brother by sharing information that would make it much more difficult for his skeptical mind to just intellectually explain everything away that I had shared in my book.

When I was in the process of writing this book, Celeste suggested that I find the letter that I had written to my mother and brother. She suggested that I share much of it in this book, because so much of what I expressed in the letter would be something other people could really relate to regarding their own very dysfunctional earth family members.

I include the parts of the letter especially to those of you who are reading this book and are looking forward to being reunited with your Cosmic True Loves, to show how important it is to truly deal with as much abuse and trauma as you can. I want you to know that even though so many fellow Volunteers have attempted traditional Earth psychotherapy without success, there are still more advanced and more successful solutions out there that you can try. These solutions can be experienced and utilized through very advanced Elohim Masters: Cosmic Psychotherapists and Intergalactic Clinical Psychologists (such as Voltra) are indeed available 24/7 for all kinds of wonderful and powerful methods, protocols and treatments that are literally out of this world!

I want to make something very clear here: By sharing what I am sharing, I am not in any way "giving medical advice" to anyone. All I am doing is sharing my own and hundreds of other people's personal experiences. Sharing our own very unique (but yet somewhat similar) experiences of having advanced beings of Light Divinely Intervene and help us. The beings of Light are willing to do the same with each of you. This will happen through your own Free Will and Inner Discernment, NOT because of me in any way giving so-called "medical advice."

All I am suggesting is that anyone with a pure heart's desire to be set free of any emotional or psychological trauma and abuse can choose to *also* experience "something else," something that can provide guidance to help you help yourself. Through this you can be freed from stuff that may have bothered you for most of your life, stuff you desire to be free from before being reunited with each of your Beloveds.

The Letter to my Mother and Brother

Thus, here is most of my letter to my mother and brother, quoted verbatim:

> Dear Mother & Peter,
>
> After reading your card and Peter's letter, I felt I wanted to respond to what you both said.
>
> Mother, you stated that you are "rereading" my book again. What I found strange, when you told me that you had read my book before, the first time, supposedly, but considering that so much that I share in my book occurred to me, which you, Paul and Peter obviously had no knowledge of at the time that it occurred. And yet, you had no "questions" or "comments" for me about how so many things happened to me as I share in my book, without you, Peter and Paul being aware of it.
>
> I would have thought, that these experiences would have been very "shocking" to have found out after so many years, of what

actually had occurred while I was growing up in Vista, CA. I mean I had assumed that with most families, if one of their family members had published a book which described so many "out-of-this-world" type of experiences—And they had no [conscious] knowledge that such had, indeed, occurred, that this "revelation" would be very hard to believe, and most families would in many cases have a very hard time believing that such had occurred.

So, I'm supposed to assume, Mother, that you were actually not "shocked" or "incredulous" that I had actually had such experiences and knowledge as I have shared in my book, and that you truly feel that what I Am describing actually occurred? I am only questioning you because as stated, most families would normally have a difficult time accepting and believing what I shared, when the other family members obviously had no [conscious] knowledge that such experiences had actually occurred.

Peter, I understand how you might think that all of the things that I have shared in my book, is just merely some kind of "psychological response-psychotic break from reality" to all of the abuse that Paul dished out to you and I. That in order to be able to psychologically survive, I somehow, in an "over-active imagination" just conjured up these experiences in an attempt to "escape" the horrible abuse that you and I experienced.

Yes, Peter, I do know and remember those very negative things that you have referred to, and for awhile, I did specifically focus upon all of the very horrible abuse that Paul dished out to you and I, because I wanted to ultimately be able to Clear the horrible emotional, psychological and physical abuse that I received. So yes, Peter, I "started" a number of years ago, to clear, release and transmute all of the negative abuse that I do acknowledge did take place.

But, obviously, the difference between you and I, at this stage in our life, because of our differences on many levels, just like everyone else in this planet are all very unique and different, with various different "strengths" & "weaknesses." Some people who experience very "little" psychological abuse, have trouble ever being able to fully clear it, and also forgive those who abused them. Others, who have gone thru many times worse the degree of psychological & physical abuse, for an even greater amount of time, are able to overcome it in a much shorter amount of time [as well as being able to totally forgive their abusers].

Just like the example of someone who experiences a physical injury in a car accident which for some may be "life threatening," while for others it is something they are able to overcome and come back to full vibrant health very quickly. Yes, someone else experiences such major physical injuries, that the doctors do not expect the person to survive for more than a few minutes, as their body is practically ripped apart in pieces. But not only does this other person survive their injuries, despite the extreme nature of their wounds, they totally heal with absolutely not scaring and live to a "ripe old age."

Of course, I Am giving an example of how in every situation in life, how one person responds to and recovers from very stressful and challenging situations, which includes extreme psychological and physical abuse, is always much different to each person. Some people recover very fast, while another takes much longer to do so. And there are so many reasons why this is so, from personality differences, differences in their mental & natural psychological outlook on life, and "last but not least" their [spiritual] Consciousness & Awareness level and philosophy in life, etc.

So for me, which I know you just think or assume, Peter, that because of what you, in your own specific way, have gone through and are still experiencing, that somehow because I do not mention [and focus upon this still, now] as you do, that I am somehow "not facing reality" or that I supposedly never "dealt" with all of the negative things that occurred to me and you while I lived in our house in Vista.

But besides you and I having different psychological qualities of how we each "deal with" and "process" experiences, I also had some very powerful help from the very Beings who have been Intervening all my life.

One of these beings named Voltra, who is a "Cosmic Psychotherapist-psychologist" helped me, with their very advanced "Elohim Consciousness Technology" & techniques to be able in a very short period of time, of what would have normally taken years and decades on earth. Of "release work" to be able to clear, all of this intense negative trauma, in a very short period of time, so that I could, in-deed, live a more "normal" life, "psychologically & emotionally."

I know, Peter, that you have trouble believing me when I share this with you, or any of the other many things that I have shared in my book. But I know what I know, and as stated, after this earlier, very intense and powerful work on myself, that Voltra and other beings helped me with to fully release all the trauma. Unlike you, I now choose not to focus upon the many negative experiences while growing up.

And while I will acknowledge that yes, that one statement in my book may be "technically" inaccurate, of having grown up in a so-called "normal" childhood because of all the abuse from Paul. This aspect of my life, all these negative human abusive experiences that you and I went through, was not what I was focusing on in my book. It is a book that is focused exclusively upon the Extraterrestrial aspect & subject, not my abusive, dysfunctional and psychologically imbalanced parents.

I am sorry, Peter, that you are still so psychologically and emotionally damaged, after all these years, and yes, perhaps, it may be that as you stated, you will be dealing with these affects for the rest of your earth life. And I truly do have much compassion for you and these problems you obviously still face.

But, and this is the big "BUT", just because you are still "dealing with" these psychological conditions after all these years, do not assume that I, too, [still] have the same or even some of this same psychological damage that you are still experiencing. I know, you think that

I Am just in total denial and are refusing to "deal with" these earlier negative experiences. And, also, that I somehow just "psychotically created" this ["other-worldly"] reality-fantasy in my imagination to be able to deal with such horrific abuse.

Well, this point right here, I would like to share with you, Peter, and Mother, of the fact that four different people, who I met in the last 20 years, individually and separately, confirmed to me, of their personal knowledge regarding my experience of falling off the Oceanside Pier in the summer of '59. And of my experience of being aboard the spaceship that had beamed me up into it while I was falling off the pier. Actually, two of these people, who are now much older, shared with me of them remembering how they saw me, when I was a very young child, of falling off the pier back then.

One of these two, a man, who I do not specifically remember back in '59, came running up to me during one of my many public lectures, when right after I had shared about this first UFO & ET encounter. This man was very emotional and stated that he was the one who had jumped off the pier to rescue me from the ocean after I had fallen in. Of course, he had not known about the fact that as I shared at the lecture and in my book, that in the process of falling, I had been physically beamed up into the UFO/spaceship. And then after being on board the craft, they then beamed me back down to the very instant they had beamed me up ("time-space warp"). But I had mentioned that while I could not specifically remember who it was that had jumped off the pier, I did have the strong impression at the time that I knew that someone other than my parents, had actually jumped off the pier. It was at this moment during that public lecture, that this man had jumped up very emotionally and excitedly exclaimed that he was the person who, that indeed, jumped off the pier after me.

There was no reason for someone who for most of my life was a stranger to me, to have just made this up, of his participation, in rescuing me out of the ocean. I and everyone else who were attending my event that evening, could tell how spontaneous and genuine he was in his sudden response to what I was sharing at the time. It obviously was a very emotional moment for him, because of what he had done, years before, of being the one to rescue a fellow human being, especially a very young child [me] who had fallen off the pier into the ocean.

I know, Peter, that you are probably having a difficult time accepting this, that why would Paul not have jumped over the side of the pier to have rescued me, rather than someone else, a stranger at the time?

Well, this point right here, is one of the many things that thousands of UFO cases that I have studied & researched through the years, have in common. Of how so often only one member of a biological earth family, will have any [conscious] memory of what happened. Part of this reason is because of the affects on their minds and "mundane earth level consciousness." Of the very intense "higher dimensional frequencies" and "other-worldly" influences that causes the other people to not be able to even remember what had happened. Because, it would be too overwhelming and too much to deal with on a conscious level as compared to their "mundane" earthly lives. But for those of us, whose souls are not from earth, but a Volunteer in Earth embodiment, and who also was not born with the "cosmic amnesia veils" (as with myself) this experience was not too surprising, considering what my mission was for being in Earth embodiment.

The second person who also remembers me falling off the Oceanside pier, when she was also very young, and who was also 6 years of age at the time, shared a very interesting story with me, after I had connected with her about ten years ago. She stated that she grew up in a military family, in Canada, that her father was in Canadian military intelligence. And in the summer of '59, her father had traveled with her to the U.S. to go specifically to the Camp Pendleton military base, which was not far from Oceanside, and for the first and only time in her life, her father decided to briefly go visit the Oceanside pier. As she and her father were walking along the pier, she specifically remembers seeing a very young child that she somehow knew was about her same age, suddenly climb up on the railing of the pier and then fall off the pier. Of all the commotion and that she also remembers some man nearby who quickly climbed over the railing to jump down into the ocean and that he did rescue the child [me] from the ocean.

The other two individuals, one a man and the other a woman, both experienced my personal 90 min. Transformational Channeled Readings, in the last ten years. One of them, the man, who I never met, because he experienced his session with me over the phone, rather than in person (actually in more recent years, a large number of my sessions

I do over the phone, and Skype [if someone is in another country] besides doing them in person). The other person, the woman, I did meet, when I did the 90 min. Reading for her. Both these people, individually & separately, who lived in different areas of the U.S., told me the exact same story, that they remember very vividly, as very young children, of being physically beamed aboard a spaceship in '59, during the summer, and that they specifically remember being on the same ship that I was taken into. That they remember seeing me suddenly standing amongst the beautiful human appearing beings who were dressed just as I remember them, in metallic blue and silver jumpsuits. While I, myself, do not specifically remember any other fellow earth human children being aboard the ship with me, this was understandable, since they were not in the same room or chamber that I was in. They both told me that they were standing in the corridor that was just outside the room and that my back was toward them, so I would not have seen them unless I had turned around and looked the other way from where I was facing during most of my own interaction with these Elohim ET's. Both the man and woman's experience was basically the same, of just seeing me standing there in the nearby chamber, with the glowing white walls. They then remembered me also suddenly disappearing later (which was when the ET's had beamed/teleported me back down to earth, to that same moment they had first beamed me into the ship to help take away most of the trauma of having fallen off the pier in the first place).

Now I know that those who tend to be skeptical and cynical about the reality of UFO's & ET contact, and/or that I had actually had such experiences. myself, would attempt to explain away these four individual's testimonies, that they may have just been attempting to somehow use my public presentation to also get some kind of "notoriety" or "fame" for themselves, or that they each had something to "gain" by connecting with me. But these types of cynical and/or skeptical (and totally untrue) opinions by others, have no basis of Truth. As a matter of fact, I only briefly interacted and communicated with them that one time, for a few hours, to do Readings for them, and/or to speak to them in person or over the phone. That was it. Besides, I have had a very busy life, with having met and connected with thousands of people through the years, who experienced Reading sessions with me, and who I met at the many, literally hundreds of public lectures and Workshops [and media interviews] that I have done throughout the years and decades since the late '70's.

Even though I did not need this type of "collaborative conformational personal testimonies" from four other people, to verify that I had, indeed, experienced what I did in '59. It was still wonderful to have Connected with them and to hear what they each knew first hand from their awareness of the incident. And also so that for those who would tend to be skeptically not believe that it had actually happened (or that it was merely the "overactive imagination" of a young child who had later "psychotically created an entire other-worldly fantasy life to help deal with all the horrible and traumatic abuse in my life"). I realized that this was to still get individual witness confirmation from four different/separate individuals who also knew first hand of the Truth of what I have shared in my book and all those numerous public events I have done. So that someone like you, Peter, would have a much greater difficulty in explaining away my experiences.

There is also quite a few very fascinating (and "confirming" aspects) to what is often shared thru me by the various Higher Beings who have channeled through me. That has, many dozens, in fact many hundreds of times, been reported by so many of the people (fellow "Light Workers"/"Star People") who have experienced one of my personal 90 min. Transformational Channeled Readings with me.

One of these aspects, which has been mentioned or brought up by Ashtar (one of the main beings who usually channels thru me). Ashtar has often referred to the "Excelerator Chair" on board a Lightship called the Jupiter One, that Voltra (the "Cosmic Psychotherapist-Psychologist" that I referred to earlier) is in charge of. Ashtar would just briefly mention each time, in all of these various different Readings for the person who was experiencing the session. To [sincerely] ask right before going to sleep at night, to be taken etherically aboard the Jupiter One (while their physical body was sleeping). And to sit in the "Excelerator Chair," in the Jupiter One, (to have all their psychological stress, trauma and abuse, released and transmuted, that they had experienced while also growing up on earth with abusive & extremely dysfunctional earth parents and relatives). Over a few month's time, all of the intense trauma and stress they had experienced would all be released & transmuted.

In each of these cases, Ashtar had not described what the "Excelerator Chair" actually looked like, just that it would definitely help them to now be able to release all their trauma that was still bothering them and making their life a very "hellish" and unhappy experience. So many of these had gone to various earth psychiatrists & psychotherapists for many years and had not really been able to release and let go of all of these horrible after-affects of how they had been treated when much younger.

Later, after their Channeled Reading with me, these same individuals, who would often ask (and with a sincere open heart & "unbiased skeptical mind & intellect") for some kind of "confirmation" that not only verified that the "Excelerator Chair on board the Jupiter One" really did exist. But, that by doing so (of sincerely asking) to be taken aboard to experience this "Cosmic Psychotherapy Technique," and that such an experience would really help themselves to be healed.

What is fascinating, is that dozens, or more accurately, hundreds of different people, who did not know each other (even though their "Higher Self" on board the various [billions of] Light Ships hovering over the Earth on Higher Dimensions, did know each other because of all being Volunteers in Earth embodiment). All, later, got back with me to share the fact that they each had a very brief, but powerful glimpse/psychic vision or dream of having seen themselves sitting in a very comfortable, crystalline, futuristic looking chair. With very intense, iridescent, beautiful multi-rainbow colored lights and rays shooting through and around them in the Light filled chamber where the chair was.

But much more than that, what was really wonderful was what they also shared with me later. That after having personally, individually, Connected with Voltra and his fellow "Cosmic Psychotherapist-Psychologists", and of utilizing this very advanced Higher Elohim ET Healing Technology. They all started to quickly release all of their own psychological & emotional trauma and "dysfunctional" earth habits that they had been experiencing for so many years.

Understand, that the Higher Beings never give "advice" nor "medical advice" to anyone who experiences sessions with me (unlike astral or spirit entities from the spirit world/astral plane that usually channel thru most earth mediums & psychics). Higher

Light Beings, such as the Higher Dimensional Elohim ET's and Ascended Earth Masters who work with them, merely give very excellent Suggestions, and it is up to the person, through their own free will, whether they want to do what has been suggested. But those that do, and so often it has always been those individuals who have attempted through more "traditional" earth medical doctors, psychiatrists and psychotherapists. Who, after many years of so-called "traditional medical therapy", and not really being able to overcome these types of challenges, have been guided by Higher Light Forces to connect with me. And in so doing, are offered an opportunity, through this more "alternative out-of-this-world" option, to truly experience a very wonderful and uplifting, as well as Empowering experience, of finally being healed.

One of the activities and practices that I have "religiously" been doing for the last several years, and which I do every other day, is yoga. This is not only a great exercise for "body, mind and spirit", but also helps those who have been abused and traumatized in earlier years, which includes all kinds of "Post Traumatic Stress." It's been scientifically studied and shown to be very rejuvenating for one's immune system, as well as building strength in the body, and allows one to slow down the "aging process" in the body, etc. I feel very blessed to be able to do this, and of the many benefits from this practice.

Well, even though I know that this letter has been much longer than I had planned to write, I felt it was necessary to finally "get a few things off my chest" regarding some of both of your comments that I felt needed to be more clarified. Regarding my earlier experiences that you both knew nothing of until you read it in my book, and the eye-witness reports of those who also had first-hand knowledge of what I had indeed experienced in my early childhood.

It really doesn't matter to me whether you still do not believe me, or not, Peter, of the fact I really have had UFO & ET contact and continued authentic communications with these beings all my life, both while I was living at our home in Vista and after I left, or whether I have REALLY "dealt with" all that abuse that Paul dished out to you and I. What matters is that I do love you and mother, both. But, understand, because we have so much "not in common", I do not feel either that because of these extreme differences in my and your "outlook in life", beliefs and interests, etc., that there is very little that we can [usually] even talk about.

I cannot pretend that I have a desire to usually interact with others who I cannot even speak or communicate with, and where our conversations would just be "mundane, small talk" and not being able to speak of so many other really important things and subjects as I can with the many thousands of fellow Light Workers who I have met and interacted with through the years who are attuned to these things that I Am "into". I find it very hard to just relate to a very extremely [and yes, very "superficial"] narrow view of reality that you, Peter, are always focused on, and also the other many strong differences in our "philosophical" and so-called "political" views, etc.

Because of the fact that Higher Beings, operate in a Universal "Service to Collective" (as verses "service to self"), that the entire Intergalactic Community is in cooperation to every other planet and galaxy, as verses the way that earth has been stuck in a competitive, "dog eat dog", everyone-for-themselves" attitude.

But this all is about to drastically change once "First Contact" & full public ET Disclosure officially occurs. So, until then, we'll just have to "agree to disagree" with so many things in our lives. Again, this is okay, but honestly, I just do not have much incentive, because of these many differences in how we see life, or to communicate very much with you because I know that we do not "see eye to eye" in most areas, and if I Am not enjoying the interaction, then I do not feel that I Am required to have to interact or communicate at all. Again, I Am being honest, rather than in some kind of "dysfunctional" way that so many biological earth families pretend to, of "having anything in common" and that they feel somehow because they are connected merely by their "biological blood" connection, that they are somehow "required" to always communicate.

But for me, this is not enough of a reason to always stay in contact; that there must be much more of a true [spiritual] connection, which causes true "rapport & affinity" and quality of the relationship, in a true functional way, of being the true basis of why one should want to interact and associate with someone else. Yes, in my opinion, it is extremely "dysfunctional" and perhaps even "dishonest" for the other person, and to themselves, to just pretend that they have a lot "in common" when they really don't. So, please forgive me, if I do not want to very often interact and communicate with you, when there is not much we can speak about that we would be able to agree with, Peter.

And, mother, the same applies to you, in that I feel that with you stating that you had [really?] "read" my book before, and now you state that you were going to "read it again." And yet, the point I made earlier, of the "incongruity" of you claiming you had actually read it, and yet, strangely, you had absolutely no "comments" and "questions" to me ever, since we reconnected in late 2010, after so many years. About so many things that I shared that you obviously had no knowledge of, and yet you never brought this up, of how I could have experienced all those things. You see the point I Am making.

This is, at the very least, a type of more "dysfunctional" behavior, of not questioning, of addressing, at least in the minds of some people, what is so obvious, quite a different version of what I experienced, than what you, yourself, remembers, but yet you never questioned me regarding these "revelations." In fact, even though I know you are not trying to do this, but a psychologist might even state that you have been in some kind of "dysfunctional" way, of not being "honest" with me or yourself, to acknowledge the "conflict" between your past awareness of what happened [on a more "mundane" level] and my narrative of what [also] was going on [at least on other levels of reality]—and not even question such an extreme difference in what I reported.

At least, I feel that Peter is actually being more "straight forward" in his skepticism regarding my experiences. Unless, of course, (which you have not explained how you have "reconciled" the differences of your and my narrative of our past early years together), you were actually being very intuitive and psychically tuning in to the authenticity of what I had actually experienced, and that is why you "accept in stride" all that I have shared in my book?

Please be really honest [and "functional"] with me. Am I right in questioning this point of psychological "contradiction" as I have made in this letter, or were you truly being very psychic and intuitively sensed the authenticity of what I have shared about my early ET encounters? And, first of all, please be honest with yourself, as much as I hope that you are honest with me. I really felt that this point needed to be cleared up, once and for all. Thanks. Love to you both,

Michael

After the Letter

Just as I assumed, since having written this letter to both my mother and my brother, I never heard from them. I understand that they both in their own way did not want, not even a little bit, to acknowledge any of what I shared with them: that would mean having to change their entire "paradigm of reality," and such a change is often too challenging. I truly have much compassion for both of them, I have long since forgiven my mother for her and my father's dysfunctional and abusive behavior that I experienced while growing up.

I do not consider myself in any way a "victim." I felt that I was evolved and strong enough to overcome, process and transmute all of the 3D dysfunctional and abusive treatment that I went through while growing up. This was because I was one of the few souls ever allowed to be born without my "Cosmic Amnesia Veils" and because of my connection with Voltra (and other intergalactic psychotherapists) with their very advanced Elohim Consciousness Technologies.

Already prior to taking Earth embodiment this final lifetime, I knew this: Despite the very abusive and inappropriate behavior that my Earth biological parents were often guilty of, I also saw that the more positive conditions and qualities they would provide for me would be important to my mission. Not too many Earth parents were aware of metaphysical things back when I was born. My parents were "enlightened" enough to have known the dangers of vaccinations and the truth regarding Flouride, as well as other things that have been publicly forced upon the masses of ignorant humanity for many years. In addition, my father's knowledge and abilities in the area of hypnosis allowed me to be "Activated" here on this 3D level, so that I could then expand this initial experience into my Transformational Channeled Readings.

The Last 3D Embodiment

My final Earth embodiment is the fulfillment of a sacred vow from many millions of years ago (I discussed this in my first book). That was when we Volunteers heard the "Great Clarion Call" all over the universe and the original core group of the 144,000 souls first volunteered to incarnate upon Earth. We would be on Earth until we finally Liberated this planet and brought the "endless wheel of karma" to a close, to allow Earth to finally experience the Victory of the Light and a planetary Ascension.

In recent years it has become clear that this would be the final embodiment of us fulfilling this original sacred vow. Almost half of the world's current population have souls that incarnated upon Earth from "somewhere else" who have joined this vast Intergalactic Mission of Light; us Volunteers, as well as more recent souls from the Higher Realms.

But the point is: As I knew that this was the last 3D embodiment, I was willing on a Higher level to endure some final dysfunctional and imbalanced behavior by my biological Earth parents if through that I could fulfill my mission. I had enough effort and determination of my own and I had awesome Love and Higher protection on another level, initially unbeknownst to my conscious earth mind. I had the help of Celeste, my own

Twin-Flame, just as every other Volunteer presently incarnated upon Earth will also be receiving similar help and protection.

I knew that in these new and recent timeline changes eventually I was Destined to write and publish this book with Celeste. This would help the rest of the Ground Crew to remember that they, too, are Destined (as was Promised) to be Reunited with their own Cosmic True Love before or during First Contact, possibly as early as within the next several years.

CHAPTER 3

Meeting My Twin-Flame

In 2017, right after my relationship with Laura had been completed, I was guided to travel to Florida to be hosted and sponsored for workshops and readings with various fellow Light Workers. I would be in town to do workshops and to schedule in my 90-minute Transformational Channeled Readings at a New Age center, as well as for networking with other Light Workers and other New Age centers who might also be interested in sponsoring me for further events.

Being Guided by Celeste

I deliberately use the word "guided," as I have recently realized (now that my Beloved, Celeste, energetically and etherically has been around me "24/7") that Celeste has been Guiding me in all of the major moves and changes that have occurred throughout this final lifetime on planet Earth.

Even though various other Higher Beings have also helped to guide me as well, I now know it was mainly Celeste. Her main purpose was to personally watch over me, to protect me from all kinds of attempts from the cabal and the imbalanced forces to endanger and interfere with my mission. She has helped me connect and network me with the many thousands of fellow Light Workers I have met, spoken to over the phone/skype, and interacted with at all my numerous public events. Of course, I always did what I could and needed to do as the "boots of the ground", which in years past included contacting and setting up interviews with various media, both mainstream and more alternative.

I remember that a number of times in the 1980's and '90s, right before I contacted various newspapers and radio and TV interview shows in different major cities around the U.S., Hawaii, Canada and Great Britain to attempt to set up an interview with one of their reporters, there suddenly occurred one or more major UFO sightings in those same areas. This, of course, immensely helped me by causing a sudden new openness and interest in the subject of "UFOs and Extraterrestrial Contact." Celeste has shared with me that these UFOs were often her and my Higher Self's ship, the "Celestial Star." She had manifested it to get the attention of the local media. Her "intergalactic public relations photo op program" was obviously very successful, if I may say so myself!

I did a lot of media interviews back in the '80s and '90s, in addition to having my own radio and internet show named the "Cosmic Connection". This came to a close in 2012: I was strongly guided not only by my own Higher Self, but also by Celeste, to finally take a much deserved major break from all of the media work. I would begin to focus more upon my long overdue and much needed emotional rest and healing, which I had been ignoring for many years.

In 2012 I had just started my relationship with Laura, which made this "emotional break" extra important. She lived in Washington until 2016, when I helped her move to Virginia. Once our relationship had been completed, I Knew Within that it was only a matter of time until I would be reconnecting with my Cosmic True Love/Twin-Flame—when the time WAS truly right.

Publicly Announcing That I Was Seeking My Twin-Flame

I was guided at one point to be a guest on a New Age radio and Internet show, during which I specifically made the "public announcement" that I was searching for my Twin-Flame.

For a few years prior to this I had signed up on a few different dating sites. Even though quite a few women showed an interest in me, but none were the one specific soul that I was attempting to find and connect with. I was always as considerate and courteous as I could when I would inform them that I knew I had not yet found "the One" that I was looking for. I thanked them for their interest, and eventually I decided to end my membership to each of these dating sites. I now realize with Hindsight that Celeste had informed me that it would definitely not be through any Earth internet dating site that I would connect with and meet my Beloved, rather it was more likely that we would meet at some upcoming public event or workshop that I would be conducting.

The only reason that I went on that New Age radio show was that I have always attempted to live according to the phrase

"God helps those who helps themselves." I felt that I needed to exhaust all possibilities—even if this included going public with the message that I was Looking and Searching for my Twin-Flame. "Who knows," I thought—"maybe someone who hears this radio interview indirectly knows someone who might turn out to be my Beloved. Or, perhaps even my Twin-Flame herself will listen to the interview." I did not know if anything at all would actually come out of publicly sharing this.

When one is trying with a True Heart's Desire to manifest something or someone that is very important to them, one of the techniques (or "protocols") that one can use is to not only truly Know from Within this ultimate goal, but also to truly exhaust every conceivable option. I knew that based upon the "Law of Divine Manifestation," in doing this I definitely had nothing to lose and all to gain. If nothing more, my effort behind what I did would add to the collective manifestation fulfillment of my innermost desires and my Destiny of finally meeting my Beloved. I did what I could to help the Universe Manifest my Beloved into my life.

I did not feel in any way "desperate" to meet her; I was in fact willing to wait as many years as it might take for this awesome and sublime event to eventually occur. I just Knew from the very depths of my being that it was Destined to occur: something that is guaranteed as long as we are patient, determined and courageous enough to not only believe and Know, but also to do as much as we can to Help the Universe manifest our Desire. (It was not just some "fantasy" conjured up by our overactive imagination to make our otherwise dull and unfulfilling life have some greater meaning and purpose.) It was Destined to occur for me, just as I Know that it is also soon to occur to every other fellow Ground Crew Member—it is a "Cosmic Done Deal", a "Sacred Promise".

Late August/early September 2017 I had just scheduled a weekend workshop for early November at a New Age Center in Florida, when I suddenly received a phone call from Ann, another very clear Channel. She is an elderly lady living in Texas, who has experienced one of my 90-minute Transformational Channeled Readings. Ann had received a specific message from Higher Cosmic Light Forces, regarding me meeting my Twin-Flame. They wanted to inform me through Ann that I was definitely going to meet my Twin-Flame at that upcoming workshop, and they wanted me to prepare for this. Ann emphasized several times how beautiful (inside and out) my Beloved was, and that the moment I met her was going to be very intense and mind-blowing for me.

So—one can imagine how challenging it was for me to be patient until my event in November, but I did my best. Finally, the two months had passed.

Our Meeting (the First Day of the Workshop)

The first day's workshop was titled "Who's Who in the Cosmic Directory," it was a three-hour Power Point Presentation on members of the Spiritual Hierarchy and how they have helped this planet throughout its history. It included copies of more than thirty oil painting portraits of various Ascended Masters and Higher Dimensional Space Beings.

The next day's workshop was titled "The Dynamics of Cosmic Telepathy." This was a three-hour Channeling Class, teaching how one can channel and communicate with the Higher Light Forces. The title was intended as an homage to a book with the same title, published back in the '80s by the famous channel Tuella. Tuella also published the book *Project: World Evacuation By the Ashtar Command,* which I quoted a lot from in my first book, *Prepare for the Landings!.*

I arrived about an hour before the start of my workshop, to make sure that everything was in place and to prepare for my presentation. I had the chairs and tables positioned where they needed to be, sign-in tables set up, and my projector and lap top computer plugged in and ready. Following that I just attempted to relax the best I could, as I felt that the expectation of what was about to occur had risen within me to a fever pitch. It was as if I could already energetically sense my Beloved's presence, as if she was approaching from somewhere out there.

Various attendees began to arrive at the front entrance to the center. As they came up to the sign-in table and signed in, Barbara[1] and I greeted each person. Barbara was the lady in charge of the center. I had positioned myself standing a few feet behind the sign-in table to make it very easy for me to see my Twin-Flame at the very instant she would walk through the front door. Even though I had been assured that it would occur

---

[1] Right after Celeste guided me to write this book, I decided to use some fictional names in this book. Because of the unintended emotional "fallout and aftermath" that happened within a few moments of actually physically meeting my Twin-Flame (which I will explain more about soon), I decided that it would be better if I did not use the actual Earth level name of my Twin-Flame and the few others who were involved in this whole event.

that very day, I was starting to wonder whether she was actually going to arrive.

And then suddenly there SHE was, walking through the front door. I sensed that the very energy of the room suddenly shifted. It seemed as if it happened an instant *before* she had actually physically entered, and it seemed too that the room became slightly brighter.

What I felt and experienced at that moment, the moment of first seeing HER, my Beloved, is so incredibly challenging to adequately put into words. As she was walking up toward me and the sign-in table I sensed not only her physical beauty, but also her inner beauty. I realized that my mouth had dropped open, as I could only just stare at her for a few moments. As her eyes and mine met, it was as if the room momentarily disappeared around us. I sensed intense electrical, magnetic attraction and chemistry shooting back and forth between her and I, in that first awesome moment of being in her Divine Goddess Presence.

Then she must have realized that there were more people waiting in line behind her, because she suddenly bent down quickly to sign her name on the sign-in pad that was laying on the table. I knew she did not want to inconvenience them by her just standing there staring at me.

I really was overwhelmed, to put it mildly, by what I was feeling. For a few moments I could only just stand there, attempting to recover my composure. Then I moved toward her, as I saw her standing in the hallway by herself. She appeared to be merely checking out the bulletin board in the hallway, but I sensed she was really waiting for me to come over to speak to her. So, I walked up to her, trying to decide just exactly what I was first going to say to this Divine gorgeous goddess who I had been waiting for my entire life to finally meet.

Out of friendly curiosity as she had never seen her come to her center before, Barbara had asked my Twin-Flame during her sign-in if she was local or from out of town. I heard her briefly mention that she had recently moved to Florida from another state.

As I walked up to her, I was still feeling an energetic overload from the intense feelings and chemistry that I could not deny and ignore, and I knew that she was definitely experiencing similar feelings. But, I was definitely NOT prepared for what she was about to say in response to my first question, "I couldn't help but overhear that you said you just recently moved to Florida. So, are you here with family?" I sensed her hesitate slightly as she responded, "I'm here with my partner." Her statement nearly floored me, it felt like I had been kicked in the solar plexus. All I could do the next moment was to stand there, stunned at what she had just said.

I had just assumed that when I finally got to meet my Twin-Flame she would not be presently in a relationship. I had assumed that there would be nothing to stop her and I from being together right away. I knew that she too would definitely want this once she and I actually met. I had definitely just experienced what has traditionally been termed "Love at First Sight": Two souls physically meeting, whose attraction, energetic connection and Love is so intensely strong. It literally is not only "Instant soul recognition": the moment we met, the energy in the room had powerfully changed because of this intense and overwhelming attraction.

Carol, Barbara's assistant, had been standing a few feet away from me during the moment that I met Cindy, my Twin-Flame. Carol was also very clairvoyant, and she later told me how she had seen energetic fireworks and stars shooting out between both of us the moment that Cindy had walked up to the sign-in table. It had been very obvious to her how powerful this instant Love Connection was. Carol had sensed the "Destiny potential" for Cindy and me at that powerful moment of our meeting in this lifetime.

But—now I suddenly had another emotion that seemed to be in conflict with my first awesome and wonderful feelings of intense love and attraction for my Beloved. I had somehow just assumed that the Universe would have worked it all out: I expected a type of modern-day fairy tale, where she and I would meet with nothing that could or would ever get in the way of our Love and our happiness. I believe this usually *is* the case when it is Destiny that two Twin-Flames actually meet. Thus I expected this for us too, as I felt that I had no negative karma that would stop me and her from being able to be together.

Now, though, I was facing an emotional and moral dilemma: I consider myself a moral person, I value other people's personal feelings and sovereignty, and I don't approve of interfering with another's relationship nor of ever causing any emotional pain. I had no desire to break up her relationship with someone else, but this was conflicting inside me with my intense feelings for her. Feelings that I knew that she, too, must be feeling for me as well, complicated by her own feelings for her present partner. I did not want to cause her partner any emotional pain because of how she and I felt for each other.

Then I realized that no matter what would later occur, I had to fulfill my own present responsibilities. I had to start my workshop right away in the other room, as it was now a few minutes past the time when the workshop was supposed to start. I did not want anyone to be waiting for me to start, despite this sudden overwhelming emotional love challenge that was now also a part of my awareness.

As I walked into the room to begin my presentation, there SHE sat. Cindy, just staring at me with her wonderful, deep intense eyes. I could feel all the love that she was feeling for me, and my intense feelings for her. This was definitely very distracting for me while attempting to concentrate on what I needed to share for the next three hours. Especially so every time I looked in her direction and saw how intensely she was looking at me.

Somehow, I got through the first 90 minutes of my power point presentation, "Who's Who In the Cosmic Directory", and I had everyone take a short break to stretch and go to the restroom if they needed. Cindy immediately came over to stand near me. She began to tell me how much she was enjoying my presentation, and how glad and excited she was to be able to attend.

I was having extreme difficulty being in close proximity to her without being able to express all my feelings for her, and it was hard to restrain the natural desire to be affectionate and physical with her. I was feeling somewhat dizzy in a wonderful "blissed out" way, and I was struggling to keep it together to finish the second half of my workshop without letting my feelings and physical attraction for Cindy get the best of me. I knew and sensed that she must be feeling these same or similar intense feelings and sensations, and wondered what she was going to do or say in acknowledgment of these feelings.

I was attempting to take it slow, not allowing this intense desire to be with her make me say or do anything that might be considered "too much, too fast" by her. I was afraid to scare her off and mess up this incredible experience and opportunity of getting to know her. I did not want to force myself upon her in any way, and only wanted to respect her space as much as I could. All kinds of intense feelings and desires for her were just coursing intensely through my body. She seemed, almost subconsciously, to move even closer to me—as if she too were feeling all these same intense, wonderful feelings and sensations of physical and spiritual attraction and chemistry. To me this was a total bliss out, so I knew she was obviously feeling similar sensations. I finally apologized to her that even though I truly wanted to talk with her a lot longer, I had better quickly take a restroom break before I continued with the second half of my presentation.

I got through the next 90 minutes, and finished my presentation. After a short question-and-answer period at the end, I officially ended the workshop for the day. I had found out that Cindy was staying in town with her partner. She came over to me once again, and looking at me intensely she said, "I would like to invite you to come stay with me and my partner, if you are interested. I would really enjoy personally learning much more about the Cosmic Color Meditation that you do. I could also sponsor and host you for a while in the town, at my home. Just think about it, and if you are interested, let me know." She again told me how much she really enjoyed being there at my first day's workshop, and mentioned that she would be back the day after for the Channeling workshop. I could sense that she actually wanted to say a lot of other things, but that she was forcing herself to be totally platonic with me. As she was in town with her partner, she must have also been in some kind of inner conflict of her own with the struggle of not giving into all these new feelings that must have been overwhelming her to some degree.

Her suddenly inviting me to actually come visit with her and her partner caused me to feel even more of an emotional dilemma. What was I to do with all these intense feelings of attraction and desire for her, while not wanting to break up her present relationship.

The Dream and Its Message

This inner emotional conflict seemed to intensify early that evening as I went back to Barbara's house, where I had been staying. In fact, that very night I had a very vivid dream of a past life where I was living on an island somewhere in the Malaysia area. It was very obvious in this very vivid dream that Cindy and I were in an intensely fulfilling romantic relationship. In my current life and in all of the other many very romantic lifetimes that she and I have been together, I have always been able to easily and passionately express my True feelings of Love for her. However, for some reason my heart had been very closed in that Malaysian lifetime because of some other earlier relationship. My heart had been broken quite severely, and of course the imbalanced forces were behind that horrible experience. I had closed my heart totally down; it was so closed and hurt that when I had met her in that lifetime, I had great difficulty being able to tell her all my feelings for her.

To make a long story short, I did not express to her all of the Love that I Truly felt for her—*at least not in that particular timeline.* Because marriages were often arranged by the couple's parents in that timeline in the dream, Cindy ended up marrying someone else and I ended up alone and later died of a broken heart. The one thing that seemed to be a "message" to me, the reason that I had that dream, was that no matter WHAT the so-called circumstances happen to be in this present life, I really must—despite the consequences—tell her about my sincere, True, Pure Heart's Desire and feelings for her.

My "ego conscious self" and my Higher Self kept arguing and struggling with this dilemma, what I truly felt set against not wanting to hurt her present partner. When Carol heard about my dream, her immediate response was that this was definitely a Sign or confirmation that I should tell Cindy my True feelings. To Carol it was obvious that I was a very moral and ethical person and that it was not my intent or motive to try to hurt her partner. But, she felt very strongly that the dream did confirm that I needed to tell Cindy, to get it off my chest and just let things happen naturally without making it more complicated than it already was. It was then, right after me telling her about the dream, that she told me about clairvoyantly seeing all those energetic fireworks and stars shooting out between Cindy and

I when she first entered the center. It was obvious to her how intensely connected Cindy and I were.

Seeing Her Again, and Seeing Her Leave (the Second Day of the Workshop)

The next day, Sunday afternoon, I returned back to the center a half hour before I was to start my Channeling Class. I helped set up the chairs in a large round circle, as I always do for this particular event as it allows everyone attending to more easily be able to see and share with everyone whatever they are experiencing during the workshop.

About 15 minutes before my Channeling workshop was scheduled to begin, Cindy arrived and immediately came over to where I was sitting. She quickly sat down beside me, with a warm and wonderful smile on her face. She told me, again, how much she had enjoyed my workshop and Power Point presentation from the day before, how much she had learned, and that she was really looking forward to the day's event.

Then she suddenly seemed to act a little disappointed, she got up and said that she did not want to be inconsiderate of others who might also want to speak with me. She said she would go find another seat for herself for my workshop. I could very clearly sense that she was a very considerate and kind type of person who was only getting up because she felt that she was somehow being selfish if she continued to stay in that chair, and that this was why she had reluctantly decided to move to another chair.

I wanted to have said to her that it was okay if she wanted to stay.

However, because of me feeling awkward with all of these intense feelings coursing through me, I decided that for the present I would just focus on beginning my 2nd workshop day and on what I needed to share with everyone regarding Channeling. During the second half of the workshop I would allow everyone present to also experience being able to channel for the first time if they wanted to.

Even though I had conducted literally hundreds of Channeling workshops though since the early '80s, for me this was definitely the most intense one I had ever conducted. I could intensely feel Cindy's physical presence, even from across the room from where she was sitting, and felt very distracted by all my feelings and emotions concerning her. This made it much more challenging for me to be as emotionally detached as I needed to be to avoid interfering with what everyone else was there to experience and learn.

I attempted to stay focused on things in an impersonal way, rather than give into these wonderful and conflicting feelings that I was struggling with. Finally, the Channeling workshop came to a close, after everyone at the very end had shared what they each had experienced during the class.

I was particularly interested, of course, to hear what Cindy had experienced. She shared briefly that she had definitely felt the energetic presence of a number of Higher Light Beings who had etherically made their presence known to her in the room while the class was going on. She was definitely interested in personally exploring more with me about the whole Channeling experience, and learning more (both individually and privately with me) about how to more effectively and powerfully do the Cosmic Color Meditation that I had done at the very beginning of the session of the class. During that meditation everyone who wanted to had been given some time to tune in and channel.

The Cosmic Color Meditation had lasted about 30 minutes. It helped to balance, align and strengthen everyone's chakras and auric fields, so that they would all be more open and attuned to channel and receive any Higher Messages and/or Visions from the Higher Light Forces that were present. After the meditation we all spent the next hour being open to whatever experience of Channeling and communications with Higher Light Forces was to occur for each person attending the class.

I wanted so much to be able to talk to Cindy right after the class was over. Unfortunately, because some of the other participants wanting to speak with me, I did not have very much time before Cindy had to leave. She would go back with her partner, who had driven up shortly after the workshop was over.

But Cindy came up to me, and again she invited me to come stay with her and her partner when my schedule would allow. She specifically wanted me to personally teach her more about Channeling and the Cosmic Color Meditation, and she was interested in hosting and sponsoring me for other events in the area where she lived. I could tell how much she was wanting this, and I could also sense her own intense feelings for me. She quickly came up to me and affectionately hugged me for a few moments, thanked me again, then turned and walked out the front door of the Center.

She was going back to her home which was about three hours away, on the East coast of Florida. I just stood there in sort of a daze as I watched her walk out of the front entrance.

CHAPTER 4

Getting to Know my Twin-Flame

It was very difficult to pretend to be calm on my outer level, while on my inside I had my intense feelings for her and my moral challenge: I knew that Cindy was my Beloved/True Love/Twin-Flame, despite that I had just met the day before. But, because she already was in another relationship, I was struggling to know what to do. I did not want to cause emotional pain to her present partner by causing their relationship to break up because of these intense feelings between Cindy and I. Complicating things further were her own feelings toward her partner.

I packed up the few items that I had brought with me and prepared to go with Barbara and Carol back to Barbara's home where I was staying. It was a little after 6 P.M. and I planned to make one of my healthy gourmet pasta dinners for the evening. I was going to share it with Barbara and Carol, if they wanted to try some of it. They did, and they raved about how delicious it was. However, as I sat down to enjoy what was normally very tasty for me (what I jokingly often refer to as an "oral orgasm"), I was astonished to realize that I wasn't really hungry. In fact, I really wasn't that interested in eating at all, because of all these intense feelings for Cindy that were totally enveloping me.

Projects on Time Travel

A few days prior to my two workshops that weekend, I had shared some info with Barbara and Carol about time travel. The info was very factual, I knew it from having interviewed many whistle-blowers. One of them were Andrew Basiago, who had been personally involved in Highly Classified projects regarding actual time travel technology (such as "Project Pegasus", the "Montauk Project", etc.).

Many years before, I had met and interviewed Al Beileck. He had been one of the original survivors of what has been referred to as "The Philadelphia Experiment"/"Project Invisibility"/"Project Rainbow," where the Navy had literally teleported the Navy ship the U.S. Eldridge through a "time-space warp"/"wormhole" and back again. This highly Classified, Top Secret experiment was of course officially debunked by the cabal deep state, but according to Al Beileck it was very factual. He explained that the movie that was produced about it in Hollywood was at least 70% true, and did quite accurately depict what occurred when Al and his brother jumped over the side of the U.S.S. Eldridge when it got caught in the time-space warp in 1943: they suddenly found themselves in 1983, in Montauk, New York state. All the incredible things did actually occur, despite the attempt to ridicule and suppress the facts of this historical event.

I interviewed Andrew Basiago a few times on my radio show, "Cosmic Connection," that I used to host up until ten years ago. Andrew shared many fascinating facts regarding his personal experience of traveling as a child through time in "Project

Pegasus" (part of D.A.R.P.A.), and I am convinced that these facts are very real.

Andrew also told me about a photograph that he claims was taken of him in 1863. At nine years of age he had been sent from 1972 back to 1863 to listen to President Lincoln's Gettysburg Address in real time. You can probably find this photo on the internet, using this search phrase: "photo of Andrew Basiago, in 1863 at President Lincoln's Gettysburg Address." You will see one of the most fascinating real-life time travel photos ever taken, it gives evidence of time travel. The historical photo is taken by a well-known Union photographer of that time. And, as Andrew himself mentioned: A facial recognition test upon the image of the young child that is shown in this very photo, has shown a definitive match with his much older facial features that he has now as an adult. So, yes, check it out!

What is extra fascinating about this particular photographic evidence of actual time travel, is what I learned years earlier by interviewing other whistle-blowers who had been involved in intelligence espionage work for the government. They told me that the cabal (deep state) had ordered various intelligence agents throughout the years to go to various photo archives and remove any photos from the Civil War period that had contained possible photographic evidence depicting time travelers who had just "happened to be" in some of the photos taken at that time. The cabal wanted them to remove any photos that might be a "problem" for them, but in my communications with various Higher Light Beings, such as Ashtar and others of the Federation of Light, I learned that not all of these photos were confiscated by these cabal agents. The Higher Forces purposely made sure that the agents would not be able to get all of the photos. In fact, the Higher Forces told me that in the future I would personally meet one or more individuals who were personally involved in time travel, and who also happened to be fellow Volunteer in Earth embodiment. I was told that these Volunteers would show me one or more photos that very accurately documented one or more actual time travel experiences.

Message Via "Déjà Vu"

Andrew had also shared the fact that many of the time travel-themed movies and TV shows that have been produced through the years actually often depicted "truth presented in fictional form," and that much of the technology that was shown in such movies as "Timeline" and "Déjà vu" was based upon actual technology that had been developed in these Highly Classified time travel projects. Barbara was fascinated about this, and wanted to see the movie, "Déjà vu," which she had not seen before. I had seen this particular movie a couple times already, but thought it would be fun to watch it again with Barbara and Carol.

For those who have not seen "Déjà vu," I will give a short synopsis of the script. This time while I was watching it, something extraordinary occurred; something seemed to be giving me some kind of cryptic-energetic message about whether I should actually tell Cindy my feelings for her or not.

In "Déjà vu," the actor Denzell Washington plays an ATF agent. He investigates an apparent terrorist attack upon a ferry that was hosting a party with hundreds of Navy personnel on board, which was blown up leaving almost everyone killed. During the investigation he discovers that very advanced optical scanning technology is being used, which allows the officials the ability to see events that are supposedly recorded three days before. He soon discovers that this technology is actually not scanning recordings, but is instead scanning and observing *live* what is actually happening three days before. The other investigators were claiming to him that what they are all seeing is just recordings being played back.

Denzel picks up a small laser pointer on the desk and shoots the small laser beam bouncing off the mirror beside the young lady who is being scanned at that moment. The laser beam bouncing off the mirror proved that they are actually watching her live, and that these are not merely recorded images from three days before. This is significant, as the body of the young beautiful lady, who is very much alive at that moment, was found washed up ashore around the time of the ferry explosion. The investigators had figured out that she had not died in the ferry explosion, but that a psychotic killer had actually killed her prior to blowing up the ferry. The killer had also cut off three of her fingers. It is very obvious that Denzel is attracted to the lady and that he wished there was a way for him to somehow save her life before she would be killed three days ago and a way for him to stop the horrific destruction of the ferry.

To make a long story short, Denzel devises a way to use the scanning technology to travel back in time to save the lady from being killed. Denzel gets slightly wounded by the killer. In the next scene, the lady and Denzel are sitting in her bathroom while she is dressing his wound. She is trying to understand how he was able to intervene and rescue her right before she would have been killed and her body thrown into the river.

Denzel then says to her this dramatic statement, "*What if you had to tell someone the most important thing in the world, but you knew they would never believe you, what would you do?*"

The lady looks at him, and then responds, "*I would try to understand, for you never know what someone might go through.*"

As I was watching and listening to the movie, even though I had seen it a couple times before, for some reason this question to the lady and her response to him seemed to energetically jump out at me. It was as if someone was attempting to tell me something that I needed to realize regarding the moral conflict that I was feeling concerning Cindy. As if this specific question from the movie had been projected to me like some kind of mantra, telling me to go ahead and tell Cindy all that I was feeling about her—despite that a "fall out" was likely to occur afterwards.

At the end of the movie, Denzel is shown walking up to the pier where the lady's dead body had originally been laying; this time (in this new timeline) she is alive with a towel wrapped around her. Denzel helps her get into his car to take her down town to his office to fill out forms pertaining to what had just occurred.

In the final scene, as she gets into his car, she turns to him and very dramatically repeats what he had said to her before, "*What if you had to tell someone the most important thing in the world, but you knew they would never believe you, what would you do?"*

And this time, Denzel turns to look at her with a very quizzical and strange look on his face, as if her question somehow seems vaguely familiar, as if he had "heard" this same question once before, or as if he, himself, had actually said the same thing to her (hence the title of the movie, "Déjà Vu"). He responds to her, almost automatically, *"I would try to understand."*

Hearing this question and the response again as it was repeated by the actors in the movie, its indirect energetic cryptic message had a very strong effect upon me. Again, I sensed that someone was definitely attempting to get my attention regarding my inner struggle concerning Cindy.

In life here on planet Earth on this 3D level, it often appears to be true that despite our best intent, things sometimes seem to get all complicated—leaving us without any apparent solution to all that is happening. Yet, despite that, I had always felt that if we would just try hard enough—with the Highest Intent, with a sincere, True Pure Heart's Desire—we can somehow find a way to make everything a "win-win." Even if it initially seems difficult or impossible to solve whatever the challenge happens to be.

I feel that somehow, someway (although we do not at the time understand), with enough positive Intent and focus, and asking God/Divine Intelligence and Higher Light Forces to help us help ourselves, literal Miracles can and do occur. No matter what the so-called situation actually is, as long as we will believe and Know Within that Miracles can occur for ourselves and all of humanity. At that moment I could not believe that God would just dangle my Beloved in front of me and not let me get to know her and be with her, without causing hurt to someone else (like her partner). I felt there must be some solution that would still allow me to get to know her without causing anyone else any emotional pain.

Transformational Channeled Reading for Cindy

When I saw Cindy walk out of the center that Sunday, I wondered if I would ever be able to see her again and get to actually know her in this lifetime. A couple of days later, I found out that Cindy had signed up for one of my personal 90-minute Transformational Channeled Readings for her on the following Thursday, 2:00 P.M., at the Center.

Even after those two energetic confirmations, I was still conflicted during the next few days about whether I should actually do her Reading or whether I should just temporarily cancel it and attempt to explain to her why I had done so. Despite having done thousands of Readings for various fellow Light Workers/ Volunteers in Earth embodiment, never had I dealt with this type of situation; a Reading involving someone I felt so powerfully Connected to, someone who had her own intense feelings for me. I was concerned that something about her and I would come up during her Reading and that this might freak her out. Maybe she was not ready to hear it all at once but would need to slowly open up to all the romantic feelings and revelations pertaining to her and my past lives together, her and my present life romantic relationship, and her and my possible mission together in the near future.

Finally, Thursday afternoon came. I had arrived early to set up my digital recorder and a couple of chairs in one of the several backrooms of the center, which Barbara had allowed me to use to do my sessions.

For the first time, after doing many thousands of personal Transformational Channeled Readings, I was feeling a little nervous. This was a very unique situation, to put it mildly, and really did not know what to expect. Normally I prided myself at always being able to be emotionally detached from whatever was channeled through me. This was the first session I had ever done in which I was concerned about how my feelings were going to affect what the Higher Light Being, Ashtar, would be sharing through me.

Cindy arrived a few minutes early for her session. As she walked in through the front door I could tell how excited and joyous she was feeling about being able to experience a session with me. I led her to the back room where the two chairs were positioned in front of a large table. On the table was my recorder, ready to be turned on to record the session as soon as I was ready to begin it.

I sat down in one of the two chairs, and Cindy in the other one. Even though the two chairs were already positioned a couple feet apart from one another, Cindy moved hers slightly closer to mine, which caused her and my legs to be touching. Whether this was more of a subconscious desire of hers to be as physically close to me as she could, I do not know. I was feeling very Blissed out and a little dizzy from the wonderful chemistry, feelings of attraction, and Love that I knew she also had to be experiencing. This was wonderfully distracting, and made it somewhat difficult for me to concentrate on energetically aligning and preparing myself for her session.

I forced myself to concentrate upon what I needed to do, to enable Ashtar to begin Channeling through me. As I prepared to close my eyes, Cindy was sitting right across from me with a wonderful, warm smile beaming a lot of love at me. Her feelings that she was feeling for me were obvious now that she was sitting so very close to me.

Even up to that moment, despite those apparent energetic confirmations, I had still been struggling to decide whether to do her Reading or not. But in the next instant, I allowed myself to "surrender" into the very familiar altered state of awareness that allows my conscious mind to move aside and allow the Higher Beings of Light to speak through me.

As always when beginning my sessions, I did my short, summarized version of the Cosmic Color Meditation, which lasted a few minutes. Then within a few moments, as my conscious self moved out of the way, Lord Ashtar's presence was powerfully felt in the room. He began suddenly and dramatically to speak strongly and rapidly, which has always been his style of speaking through me. This lasted for about two thirds of the 90-minute session. Ashtar then ended his part of the session, and one of the Goddesses, Lady Commanders (or Ascended Lady Masters), spoke through me. Then at the very end, during the last 15 to 20 minutes, there was time for a questions and answers-session.

As always when I do one of these 90-minute Transformational Channeled Readings for a fellow Volunteer, it is not until I start to come back to "full waking consciousness" that am I usually able to remember much of what was shared during the session.

Coming back to full consciousness, I remembered that both Ashtar and the Lady Master had purposely kept what they shared with Cindy regarding her and my specific past life connections very impersonal and platonic. They did, though, at least a few times mention that Cindy and I did in fact know each other and that we had crossed each other's path quite a few times throughout our past existence.

At one point toward the end of the session, when Cindy asked the Lady Master a more specific question of exactly how she and I had known each other, the Lady Master said something about allowing me to share with her some things that I personally needed to. This was another confirmation that I needed to share my true feelings with her. Ashtar and the Lady Master were allowing me to break the ice with Cindy in my own way and however I felt I should do it.

Opening my eyes, I saw Cindy looking at me with her beautiful, bright eyes. She obviously was not only very enthralled with what she had already experienced and heard during the session, but now also curious about what I was about to share with her.

I sat for a few moments, feeling awkward while considering how I was going to present to her that which I needed to get off my chest. All the intense feelings were flowing so powerfully through me, especially since Cindy's legs were touching mine. Her close physical presence was overwhelming me with such an intense desire to be physical with her, to suddenly and passionately embrace her and start kissing her. I could not help these natural feelings that were even more intense now than before, but with great effort I restrained myself—I did not in any way want to overwhelm her or take advantage of her. I did not know if she was ready to give into these same or similar feelings and sensations that I was so powerfully experiencing.

I stuttered, still feeling awkward and unsure of what I was going to say first. But then, all of a sudden, a calmness and relief fell over me, finally letting me share with her that which was so important to me. The calmness allowed my heart the opportunity to sincerely express itself to her, while attempting to be as respectful as possible. Being a "gentleman" and she a "lady," I shared with her how I was attempting to respect her space. I did not want to cross the line in any way with her, and I apologized for potentially causing her to feel awkward in any way because of what I was sharing. But I also told her that I did not apologize for what I was feeling, for what I had felt the instant I saw her, nor for all the intense feelings and the Inner Knowing of who she was to me. My feelings just flowed out of me as I shared my True, Pure Heart's Desire for her: that I knew for sure she was my Beloved and Twin-Flame.

For the first few moments, I could tell that she was feeling a little awkward. Then she seemed to open up, as she could tell how sincere I was, and she allowed some of her own feelings to come out. I sensed that she was still holding back from sharing all that she would have liked to. In the back of her mind she was also thinking of her present partner, whom she did not want to betray, hurt or be unfaithful to. In addition, no matter how I attempted to present it to her, me sharing my feelings was still going to be somewhat "so much, so fast." There was a lot to take in and process, contemplating all of the implications.

At one point I suddenly felt so overwhelmed with Love for her that I started to cry. I could not stop these intense deep feelings from coming up and being expressed. Cindy, in her own obvious feelings for me, jumped up and reached over to hug me. The hug lasted for at least a minute. I struggled not to begin passionately kissing her—as I so strongly wanted to, but I felt that I needed to give her more time before I could do so. As I attempted to regain my composure, I spent some more time just sharing my feelings with her. Again I apologized for potentially overwhelming her through my sharing, and explained that I had just had to tell her.

She then began to share a little of her present situation: She did definitely feel some intense feelings of Love for me, but she did not want to hurt her present partner. She felt her partner Tony was a soul mate to her, though she also did know he was not her Twin-Flame. She shared that she had met him earlier in the year. He lived in Florida and had traveled up to Illinois to the city she was living in. They had met and fallen in love, and he had brought her back with him to Florida. But, as she also pointed out, if she had not met him and had not come down with him, she would not have been able to now meet me.

Then she shared something that was going to make this whole thing much more challenging than it already was: When she and Tony met, he had just broken up with another lady who had cheated on him and broken his heart. Cindy had felt much compassion for him, besides her own feelings for him, and this had also been a factor in getting involved with him; her compassionate nature. She did not want to break his heart a second time, from getting involved with me.

At this point, hearing about Tony's situation, I began to feel more awkward than I already did about accepting her invitation of going to stay with her, considering how extremely emotionally challenging this whole thing would be for me and her. I too had much compassion for what Tony had already gone through, and I did not want to create a second broken heart situation. Despite that it could result in me fulfilling my own intense desire and powerful magnetic attraction for Cindy, who obviously also felt this same intense attraction for me.

As she and I continued to share what we were feeling, I suddenly realized that over three hours had passed from the time Cindy had first arrived for her session. I felt that I had better bring our little "sojourn" to a reluctant end, as much as I wanted to still sit and visit with her. I slowly stood up and reluctantly told Cindy that I felt that as much as I wanted to visit with her a lot more, I knew that I must bring it to close. I had to say goodbye for now. Suddenly, all the intense emotions of sadness from having to let her go overwhelmed me, and I started to cry.

Cindy jumped up and immediately began to hug me again. It was extremely difficult to just keep the hug platonic, and I struggled to not give into all those intense feelings and desires to be intimate with her. Somehow, I resisted the urge to do so, and I sensed that she, too, was attempting to just keep this second spontaneous hug merely affectionate. But I lingered in the wonderful and dizzy feelings that were coursing through my entire body from being so very physically close to her.

After about another minute of being lost in her awesome and wonderful energy, I forced myself to let go of her and turned toward the hallway to walk back up to the front of the center where Barbara's and Carol's offices were. Cindy immediately, very affectionately, went up to each of them. She quickly hugged them and thanked them for having the chance of being able to come to their center, of them sponsoring me for my workshops, and of having just experienced such a great session with me.

As Cindy started to turn to go toward the front door, I said goodbye to her one more time. She suddenly ran back over to me and hugged me for the third time, this time even more intensely than the first two hugs I had enjoyed and shared with her earlier. All I could do, once more, was just stand there, and to savor and soak in her wonderful energy and presence that my Essence so craved and desired beyond anything I had ever experienced with anyone else on this planet in this present lifetime.

Then, once more, Cindy turned and walked out the front door, on her way back to her home on the east coast of Florida. I just continued to stand there for a few minutes, attempting to try to figure out if I would really ever see her again, if I would ever be able to actually be with her considering the emotional challenge of her, my Beloved, being in another relationship. I was thinking of her and my very intense Love for each other and whether some miracle could occur that would still allow her and I to be together, despite how impossible this whole thing seemed here on this 3D level of reality and in that particular timeline.

Processing Our Meeting

Now that my two workshops and the Reading appointments that I had scheduled were over, I was next invited to be hosted by another person who had attended my two workshops. After my move I spent the next several days attempting to process all that had occurred, the unique circumstances behind this whole experience: finally meeting Cindy, only to discover the seemingly very difficult (if not impossible) challenge that appeared to be blocking me getting to know my Beloved. I pondered the future and what my options were.

I continued going over and over in my heart, mind and soul the intense feelings of Love that Cindy and I felt for each other. I kept asking Divine Creation and the Higher Light Forces if she and I were supposedly Destined to be together, then why would Cindy also happen to be in another relationship? Especially with someone who had already experienced a broken heart? To me, this seemed utterly contradictory, I just could not understand this apparent "blockage" or "wall" to my True, Pure Heart's Desire being fulfilled. I had expected it to so easily occur once I had met my True Love. Cindy was the One, as I knew inside was true—but how could this other unexpected challenge also exist? I just could not figure it out, and kept praying and meditating for some Insight or answer—yes, even a miracle.

Then, one morning, after having slept on it, and sincerely asking God/Goddess, the Higher Light Forces, and my own I AM Presence/Higher Self what to do about this dilemma. All of a sudden I had a strong inner knowing that I needed to write an email to Cindy and be much more in-depth. I needed to share much more of my true feelings with her, and not to hold anything back. I must speak from my heart of all of my intense feelings of Love for her, and of what a challenge this was, not being able to be with her. I also told her of my compassion for her own dilemma, and of not wanting to hurt her partner either, and of how this was eating me up inside. I also told her that just as she had expressed so strongly about wanting me to come stay with her, I so strongly wanted to teach her all I could about doing the Cosmic Color Meditation and about learning to Channel.

By the time I finished composing my email to her it was quite long, even though I tried to keep it as short as possible. I guess it was like this book; there is just so much I had share, and could not make it any shorter. I sent the email to her about a week after she had returned back home from having experienced her session with me, and I waited with bated breath for her response.

But as the days and weeks began to go by, not having heard back from her, I began to fear the worst. Despite attempting to follow clearly what my Higher Self and the Higher Light Forces were guiding me to do, I wondered if for the first time in my life I had somehow misunderstood what the Higher Guidance had clearly directed me to do. I began to question not only my own inner guidance, but what my purpose in life now really was, and if I would really ever hear from her again. I began to feel that I had after all somehow screwed it all up with "too much, too soon," that my intense feelings for her had caused me to somehow misread what my Higher Self and the Higher Forces had actually been attempting to tell me. I was really in a horrible funk.

I continued to refuse to totally give up Hope, even though my faith was growing weaker with each day that passed. One day as I checked the inbox of my email account as I did each day in my daily ritual, suddenly like a miraculous bolt out of the blue, my mouth dropped open. My eyes stared, incredulously, at the email that had appeared—from Cindy.

I began to read Cindy's email, first with bated breath, not knowing what her response was going to be to me. As I continued to read her email I began to cry, to sob—tears of joy streaming down my cheeks in great relief from what she was sharing with me.

Here, word for word, except for me changing her real name to "Cindy", is what my Beloved shared with me in her email:

> Hello Michael,
>
> I apologize for taking some time to get back with you. I don't frequently check my emails so I didn't open the email until Monday. You probably have been waiting anxiously to hear back from me.
>
> I have had you on my mind. I was very glad to see I had an email from you. Wow, it has been a lot to process. I'm just so very shocked that I am indeed your Twin Flame. I am truly in complete "awe." It is very exciting and heart-warming to know that my Other Half is in Earth Embodiment. Nothing can measure the joy and ecstasy that I am feeling in discovering that you, out of all souls, are my Divine Counterpart.
>
> In your email you said "I know beyond any shadow of a doubt that you are indeed my Twin Flame/Twin Soulmate." I'm just very curious how you know for certain. I have been meditating upon it and feel a sense that I pos-

sibly could be, but I just have a lot of remembering to do. Once I read your email, I knew that it must be so! WOW!!!

When I first pulled up your website and read about you and your story, I just felt this intense drive to do everything in my power to make it to your event. Having the opportunity to attend Sat. & Sun., I felt extremely honored to have met someone like you, to hear of all the incredible things that you have done/do and just simply being in your presence, I knew right away that you were the purest source of divine walking Light that I have ever met.

After Saturday's event I really wanted to speak with you. I waited around for a while, until you were talking with the last person of the event. Then for some reason my ego told me to go ahead and leave. I was quite nervous in trying to find my words to say to you. I felt so much, but could not find words that even came close to expressing myself and the gratitude I have towards you. So, I sadly walked out of the door not wanting to at all. Then I just sat in my car going back and forth about if I should go back in and speak with you. My emotions really built up about it and I began sobbing for the next 20 minutes. I finally built the courage up to do it, then I thought, OMG I have been sitting here for 20 mins. If I go back in there now I will just look like a weirdo. After telling myself that I would be okay, and that I could talk to you the next day, I drove to my hotel. Then Sunday came around. I looked forward all day to being at the Center and getting the chance to speak to you. Then we had our little chat when I came and sat beside you. Which I much enjoyed. I wanted to continue sitting beside you through the whole workshop, but when I went to the restroom and came back I felt I should leave the seat next to you open in case anyone else wanted to chat with you before the session started. Then I just never made my move to sit beside you, and wished I had. My thought then was that it may be my last chance to ever see you or be in your presence in person. Now it all makes sense why I got so emotionally worked up after the workshops.

After Sunday, I was unsure if I would ever get the chance to connect with you again. I remember you stating that you only give readings to Star People. I have always felt that I could possibly be a Star Person/Volunteer in Earth Embodiment, but was unsure.

Getting your call on Tuesday was an enormous, Lovely surprise. I was so thrilled to hear your voice. Also, so thrilled to get the chance to connect with you again, and the news that I am a true Volunteer! Oh, my, I was filled with such radiant joy after receiving your call. I danced around like a fool for hours.

Reconnecting with you at the center, receiving my very powerful reading and reconnecting roots with our Divine Light Family was truly the most amazing blessing. It has had such an impact on my being and consciousness. I definitely felt a difference in my brainwaves after leaving the center and days after. My brain felt like it was connected to cosmic jumper cables, getting an immense power download. As you stated in your email, that our reconnecting would "alter my consciousness." I have been noticing a shift in many ways.

After revealing to me your deepest feelings of Sacred Love, I could, too, feel just a glimpse of what you were feeling in some long ago familiar way. I could truly feel how intense and how real your sincerity was.

One thing I want you to know about myself and my journey in this life, is that I still have much to grow and much lifting of the Veil to do. I am just beginning to really take flight with my wings along my spiritual journey. Every day, I am getting a little more in-tuned and awakened. Learning to have balance, shutting out all the distractions that are being thrown at humanity, especially the youth. My conscious self has a lot of catching up to do.

I'm still developing my Inner senses and getting in touch with my abilities. So, some of the experiences you tell me about that we have shared together in numerous lifetimes, I don't really remember, although I feel some sense of familiarity. Also, the intense feelings and emotions you described, that you felt since the moment we met, I don't exactly feel them so strong. Meeting you at first was just like meeting another lovely fellow Light Worker. This could be for a number of reasons, maybe because you have more of a direct access to your conscious memory bank or because you are vibrating at a more heightened level of awareness or because you have been searching for your Twin Flame for so long.

All my time as [Cindy] I have not really given much thought about Twin Flames and/or if my Twin Flame is in Earth Embodiment. I know little on the significance of the subject. So, you can only imagine my surprise and fascination of what you revealed to me. I am completely blown away beyond any measure.

The news is all such a heavy surprise. You have to understand that this changes my whole reality. This makes everything that

I had planned and expected to do with my life different. I have always felt after meeting [Tony] and falling for him that I was to spend my life with him. We have a deep connection and love for one another. From the first time I came to Florida with him there has been this growing feeling inside of me that says "this is the guy you are going to marry." I was certain that he was my soulmate (I know that there is many, and Twin Flames over ride soul-mates). I have also known that he is not my Twin Flame. But there has always been this sense that he and I were destined to meet and spend this epic life together. This is why I am so utterly confused. I don't understand why I would do this or plan for this to ever happen. I don't understand why my higher self would allow for something like this to take place with such devastating heartbreak. I am just so stunned. I just need some time to go through things. I don't know if I was exactly ready to find out all the info. that was in your email. I guess on some level, everything happens for a reason.

Ever since I read your email I don't know how to feel or react. At first when I opened your email, I read until you wrote, that I Am indeed your One True Divine Twin-Flame. I was so flabbergasted and astonished, that I just had to sit down and take in the significance that I read. With my head spinning for 22 hours, I found the fortitude to read the rest of the email the next day. As I was reading, I was jumping with immense joy and celebration to have found my Sacred Divine counterpart, but sobbing with sorrow and heartbreak that I have this lovely life, [Tony]. I just don't understand at all and I'm extremely confused on what I am supposed to do.

I can't even fathom how you feel through all this. Waiting all this time to reconnect with your True Divine Love, just waiting for her to take embodiment, as the higher portion of myself was finishing other projects before I came down. With you going through this Extraordinary Legendary journey. The lifetime of ALL lifetimes. Like The Ultimate Cosmic Hero, anchoring Light at the most forceful and daring level. With SO much honor and incredible courage. Michael, you have truly taken on the most astonishing heroic role of all times (I have been sitting here for a while, trying to think of words to truly describe how "incredible" you are. I am not great with words. I have come to the conclusion that there is no Earthly language or reference to describe your divine magnificence). So, I can only express that in my love for you.

I have so much that I want to discuss with you. Please forgive me for not instantly knowing that it was you. The amnesia veil is extremely thick and kind of makes you forget everything. I want to apologize for taking so long to reply back to you. I'm dealing with a lot of emotions that have been coming up, as I'm sure you are.

It took me some time to collect myself together to write this email. I'm sure whatever projects I was finishing on the higher realms were very important, or else I would have reincarnated earlier. I have been listening to my reading as often as I can. I believe I Listened to it every day for a week when I got back home and I'm still trying to listen to it often as I can. I would really love to chat sometime on the phone. I feel like I will be ready to talk soon. I know this has probably been really hard for you. I want you to know that I am here for you at all times. We have a lot to catch up on. I'm so happy that we have reconnected, My dear. I wanted to give you my cell number. The number you have was a temporary number I was using until I got my other phone back that I lost at a music festival. My number is ———————. It's truly such a magnificent honor to have found you.

With much Eternal Love & Light,

[Cindy]

CHAPTER 5

Ancient Nirvanic Ecstasy Insights, and My Sacred Romantic Tantric Adventure and Quest

Almost from the moment of meeting Cindy, I began to slowly experience a few "psychic flashbacks." As my own Cosmic Amnesia Veils began to lift a little more, I began to remember the many past lives we had together. Intuitively I sensed that some of what I was tapping into was of such a nature that it was actually a major energetic threat to the imbalanced forces that had controlled this planet for many ages. I suddenly knew that up until now, only a few dozen souls on the entire planet had had the ability to remember and tune into the particular events covered in the memories that were now beginning to emerge back into my conscious mind.

Now that I have been able to consciously remember, we all merge more and more energetically into the new timeline that is in the process of replacing the older one. The process is sped up as you too, fellow Light Workers/Volunteers in Earth embodiment who read this book, will begin to remember. Like the "Hundredth Monkey Effect," more and more individuals will begin to remember as well.

The imbalanced forces had so severely manipulated all of humanity throughout its existence on Earth, ever since the early Golden Ages of Lemuria and Atlantis, that it resulted in making almost everyone genetically forget what an incredibly wonderful Nirvanic Paradise once existed here for thousands of years.

Because of numerous destructive agendas by the imbalanced forces that sadly brought these ancient Golden Ages to an end, almost all memories of these glorious former Paradise existences were wiped from humanity's consciousness as if they never existed. The imbalanced forces had manipulated the DNA/RNA severely, in an attempt to make sure that no one would ever be able to remember just how wonderfully fulfilling this earlier Paradise on Earth actually was.

Millions of Twin-Flame couples had been reunited in the very beginning of the creation of Lemuria and Atlantis as well as throughout its existence. One half of the couples were incarnated upon the Earth, and their Other Half and Divine Compliment would come down from the Higher Cosmic Dimensional worlds to be physically reunited with them in this Paradise on Earth. In my opinion, this is where the biblical phrase, "The Sons of God looked upon the Daughters of man, and found them fair," actually originated from.

I read the entire Old and New Testaments when I was a young child, and immediately felt that while these religious teachings were very limited and had been manipulated and reinterpreted many times throughout the ages, I also felt there was still much Truth in the Bible, if deciphered and interpreted accurately.

In my opinion, the Bible is actually an "Extraterrestrial and UFO case book," considering how many times there is references to things that occurred during the Biblical ages, which if they occurred in more modern times, easily would have been descriptions of both UFOs (Merkabah Light Ships) and the Extraterrestrial Elohim Beings aboard them. This is, in fact, why Reverend Barry Downing wrote his famous book, *The Bible and Flying Saucers.* He is a well-known minister in the U.K., and received his Doctoral Thesis on this same topic, which he says is clearly indicated throughout the Bible.

I found information on the Council of Nicaea, where in the early 4th century, the religious and political elite manipulated and suppressed most things about our past. They wanted to make sure that the ignorant masses would believe their particular, very narrow and extremely incomplete, version of history—while they left out most of what actually occurred.

More modern-day analogies with examples of how the power elite or cabal deep state have manipulated events and history include the suppressed and manipulated true facts of what actually occurred when President Kennedy was assassinated in Dallas, Texas, in 1963 (through the "Warren Commission"), how Project Blue Book and the Condon Report manipulated the reality of E.T.'s and UFO's, and more recently how the "9-11 Commission" manipulated the true facts of "9-11".

Again and again, all these and many more events which were definitely planned by the cabal deep state behind the scenes. Then, insult on top of injury, they manipulated it afterwards to go along with their agenda for world control, in what has been termed both the "Conspiracy of Silence" and the "Conspiracy to Rule the World."

To me, not only did these cabal "editors and rewriters" of the forgotten true history of Earth suppress the Sacred Goddess Tradition of the ancient past, they replaced it with their corrupt Patriarchal tradition. The original and sacred Divine Feminine Goddess tradition, which was originally united with the Divine Masculine tradition, and which created true Balance of Sacred Energies upon Mother Earth, was destroyed and suppressed by this imbalanced organized political and religious power elite.

Yes, the "priests of orthodox religion", who worked with the "priests of power and politics", the "priests of financial control" (of the fiat currency and the federal reserve central banking system), the "priests of the pharmaceutical cabal," the corrupt agencies of the AMA (referred to by many as the "American Murder Association"), the FDA ("Federal Death Agency"), the CDC ("Center for Disease Creation"), and the WHO ("World Hell Organization"). And let us not forget the totally corrupt, cabal-controlled "fake news" mainstream ("lamestream") media, which works in this modern age to manipulate our minds, consciousness and history. All these corrupt agencies have always wanted total control of how we live and what we think, say, and do.

A Short Introduction to the Tantric Oracle Traditions

It was obvious to me, as I began to remember this ancient past of those early glorious Golden Ages, that just as in how these controllers of knowledge caused a separation of astrology and astronomy which before were one, so too were the Tantric and Oracle traditions once merged together in those very ancient and advanced civilizations of Lemuria and (initially in early) Atlantis.

Linking back to that phrase, "the Sons of God looked upon the Daughters of man, and found them fair": It was obvious that these sexually repressed and narrow-minded patriarchal priests of the Council of Nicaea could not handle the more realistic version which originally basically described just how physically beautiful, gorgeous and sexy, the Divine Feminine Earth Goddesses of these early Tantric Oracle Rainbow Crystal Temples actually were. The priests had to describe them as just "fair."

The Goddesses' Divine Other Halves, these handsome gods from the Higher Realms of the Universal Federation/ Intergalactic Confederation, were visiting their Beloveds in temples—there they Reunited with their Cosmic True Loves. There in these beautiful Rainbow Crystal Tantric Oracle Temples they experienced the most awesome, orgasmic tantric lovemaking, which could last for hours and days on end. They experienced the most exquisite, sensuous, erotic multiple-orgasmic lovemaking, beyond what most people have ever been able to experience or even imagine today.

Part of what helped create such an intensely fulfilling experience for these Divine Couples was that all the early Rainbow Crystal Temples were constructed, or rather "manifested," precisely over specific vortex spots all throughout Lemuria, which energetically amplified the intensity of their intimacy. The couples consumed special herbs and seasonings in their delicious and healthy meals (giving them "Oral orgasms in their mouths"!), which also enhanced their orgasmic tantric lovemaking.

They very "religiously" practiced various meditations and Light ceremonies. The Divine Couples also personally shared a very specific "Cosmic Color Meditation," which powerfully Aligned, Balanced and Strengthened all seven main Chakras in their physical body as well as the several Chakras above their Crown Chakra in the etheric.

Each couple sat together naked in a certain intimate position, known as the "Lotus/Shiva-Shakti" position. This is where the man (representing the Divine Masculine) first sits down, withs his legs crossed in front of him. His partner, representing the Divine Goddess, sits on his lap with her arms and legs around him, hugging and kissing him. This allows both to simultaneously share and experience the "kundalini energetic flow" and exquisite emotional connection and intimacy that is usually so missing in most modern-day relationships.

In the Tantric Tradition, the man's penis is referred to as his Lightning Rod, while the woman's vagina is referred to as her Sacred Yoni, and a "Lotus Flower of Divine Ecstasy and Wisdom is Energetically Activated."

During their Divine lovemaking and after, in their "Afterglow" as they lay Blissed out in each other's arms, they experienced wonderful Visions and Communications with God/Goddess/Divine Creation and Higher Light Forces. These were often visions of past lives, insights about their present life, and predictions of possible future events. This was how the original Sacred Oracle Tradition, which was "part and partial" of the Sacred Tantric Tradition, was first activated upon the planet.

The Separation and Censuring of the Tantric and Oracle Traditions

Much later, by the time that the "Oracle of Delphi" existed, these traditions had degenerated into a corrupted and limited tradition, with its false belief about the Oracle supposedly being a virgin (without being able or allowed to experience the ecstasy of tantric, multiple-orgasmic lovemaking).

This denial/repression/suppression of such a healthy, natural, normal and wonderfully fulfilling part of life, would somehow supposedly allow the women "special powers and abilities" that others who were happily engaging in orgasmic sex and romantic love, would not be able to have. (Are you kidding me?!)

The male priests of various orthodox religions who believed that by denying/repressing/suppressing their sexual desires, they would be "worthy enough to get to Heaven." And even worse, flogging themselves and inflicting horrible pain and agony upon themselves was supposedly required in order to be worthy to Jesus and other saints and avatars.

In fact, is it any accident that so many of the priests of the Catholic religion, because of attempting to deny/repress/suppress this natural desire of the body, end up as child pedophiles and are involved in satanic human sacrifice, as has been well documented quite in-depth by many researchers? Of course, this has also been documented concerning many corrupted individuals of the power elite, including the Royal family and the other illuminati blood line families, much of Hollywood and the music industry, most "career" politicians (of all political parties), most C.E.O.'s of major corporations and media, and so many other people in powerful positions. All of the above are very involved in these corrupt, evil and horrific activities.

However, this is all in the process of being totally exposed, and will finally be over because of both the Higher Light Forces and the Q White Hat Alliance. They are part of a vast planetary Cosmic Sting Operation to finally expose the entire cabal deep state and end this evil activity once and for all.

Getting back to the initiates in the ancient Rainbow Crystal Tantric Oracle Temples: Each day they also practiced various Yogic positions, or Asanas (which are still known today), to enhance their ability to enjoy more orgasmic tantric lovemaking.

I now remember many lifetimes just like this, where Cindy was my Sacred Tantric Life Partner, where she and I did experience this same legendary and intensely fulfilling tantric intimacy. In many of these early lifetimes we experienced this for hundreds of years at a time.

We understand that when one experiences and shares this type of intensely fulfilling tantric, nirvanic sexual ecstasy together as a Twin-Flame couple here on Earth, it powerfully energetically creates the exact opposite of what David Wilcock refers to as "loush." (Loush is the negative energy by-product of all kinds of negative and nasty things, that which the imbalanced forces and cabal deep state have created through the years to keep this planet stuck in the old timeline of the "endless wheel of karma." Yes—trapped in the Matrix/Ground Hog Day of illusion, fear, pain, and suffering (remember that f.e.a.r. stands for "False Evidence Appearing Real"). Only once we release/transmute our fear, and "Red Pill" ourselves, we become energetically and truly Liberated and Free.)

This exquisite Divine Nirvanic Ecstasy, which can only be created and experienced as intensely through the Love and electrical-magnetic attraction between Tantric Twin-Flame couples, powerfully transmutes all of the "loush," and the imbalanced forces totally lose their control over the planet. More and more couples are, in fact, beginning to practice and share this very tradition with their romantic partners. The tradition allows greater and more fulfilling emotional harmony and intimacy, and helps heal so much of one's trauma from the past.

The Moral Conflict and the Help from Voltra

I read Cindy's wonderful email a couple times, to allow her own feelings for me to more fully sink in. Then I waited just a few days before I called her on her cell number that she had shared with me.

I could tell how very excited and happy Cindy was to have a chance to talk to me over the phone now that we had "broken the ice between us" and could now share more of our True feelings for each other. It did not take long before we were having several very romantic and intimate conversations over the phone, which caused me to feel so Blissed out afterwards. She, of course, just could not wait for me to come visit with her ASAP and be her personal teacher in experiencing the Cosmic Color Meditation as it used to be done in Ancient Lemuria's Golden Age. She did not "bat an eye" as I told her just exactly how I wanted to do this with her in the "Lotus/Shiva-Shakti" position.

But, in the back of my mind I was still experiencing the moral conflict and feeling awkward about this whole thing, wondering what would happen if I actually did accept her very excited invitation to stay at her home. I felt compassion for what her present partner could feel, and I was still in a type of emotional quandary about what to do. Here was my Twin-Flame/Beloved, who I had just met and fallen instantly in Love with, with her own intense feelings for me. This powerful electrical-magnetic attraction between us was impossible to deny or ignore. But, Cindy's own soul mate partner, Tony, had already had his heart broken once before, and I did not want to put him through a repetition of that. My concern about him totally conflicted with the intense feelings of Love for my Beloved.

I just could not understand (just as Cindy, herself, wondered in her own email to me) why Divine Creation and the Higher Light Forces had set up this whole thing—allowing me to finally meet my True Love only to discover these seemingly conflicting set of circumstances.

I had heard about these so-called "triangle love relationships" which others had gone through in the past. I had vowed strongly that never would I allow or create such a situation in my own life when the time came for me to meet my Divine Other Half. I did not want to be responsible for causing another human being any emotional pain, which had so often happened when these types of relationship challenges and breakups occurred.

This was why I was so confused that Divine Creation and the Higher Light Forces would allow this to occur. It was, frankly, causing much stress. I kept meditating and praying about what I should do about this seemingly impossible challenge I was facing. I also knew that in life it is usually the things we do *not* do (but which we really deep down want to do, with a True, Pure heart's Desire), that we will regret—NOT the things we *do*, that we usually end up regretting.

All of a sudden, while caught in the midst of this moral dilemma and Truly wanting to do the right thing for all concerned, I strongly felt the presence of Voltra. He was the Intergalactic Clinical Psychologist/Cosmic Psychotherapist whom I had communicated with many times throughout my years of being in Earth embodiment.

He knew how to cut to the chase, how to make so many complex and difficult decisions so remarkably simple—he was always making everything a "win-win" for everyone involved, and helping one get much better perspective about whatever they were facing while being here on a Mission in Earth embodiment. He always had such compassion, deep understanding and insight about all issues that Earth's humanity, collectively and individually, constantly have had to face.

I had never known Voltra to ever give poor advice (or rather "suggestions") to those who very sincerely would ask him what to do with such challenging emotional, psychological issues as the Earth human race is presently facing. Voltra very effectively cut through all of these situations that one is facing, and come up with the "best, ultimate or more perfect" solution to any given emotional and/or psychological challenge.

During my many thousands of personal 90-minute Transformational Channeled Readings, Ashtar has often suggested for the person experiencing the session to sincerely ask to be Energetically Connected to Voltra. They would then be invited to be etherically taken aboard Voltra's Merkabah Light Ship, the Jupiter One, to sit in the Accelerator Chair. Within a certain amount of time after having done so, back here on this 3D earth level numerous people would get back with me to share how their emotional and psychological challenges would become much less, if not entirely, healed and resolved.

(Disclaimer: I want to make something very clear here, I am NOT in any way "prescribing" or "giving medical advice" to anyone. I am merely sharing what so many people, entirely on their own, have voluntarily shared with me about what their own unique experience was after deciding to accept this invitation from Voltra to etherically go aboard the Jupiter One. Afterwards they experienced remarkable transmutation and healing from the very problems that had not been solved in all the many years of them having seen various Earth level psychiatrists, clinical psychologists and psychotherapists. Again, I am NOT giving any medical advice to anyone through these sessions, but merely sharing certain very positive suggestions: that in their own free will, and with the understanding that they are using their own free will, they can have the opportunity to also experience something interesting, unique and empowering with this more advanced extraterrestrial Elohim Merkabah Consciousness Technology which is aboard the Jupiter One and all the other Light Ships.

Various Energetic options are available for fellow Volunteers to help them overcome various difficult emotional and psychological challenges. The person True Pure Heart's Desire can help one to more easily overcome, or at least influence in a positive way, what had been more challenging before. Also, unlike how so many of these so-called "mental health experts" of Earth who want to prescribe all kinds of pharmaceutical drugs to their patients, the Higher Beings never prescribe drugs. Instead, they only utilize very advanced energetic "Cosmic Holistic" consciousness technologies. These have no known negative side-effects compared to how these Earth pharmaceutical drugs of Big Pharma so often affect one.)

This was Voltra's sudden and dramatic statement to me:

> Screw awkwardness! Just go and enjoy. Do not attempt to over-analyze this whole thing. Remember, as you already know: when one is coming from a True pure heart's desire to do the right and moral thing (as you are), even though it may appear to be totally, morally or ethically conflicting to your conscious 3D earth mind, Divine Source/Creation is always able to easily manifest the Miracles and Miraculous Infinite Solutions that one on the Earth level is normally not able to perceive or understand right at this moment.
>
> I know your Intent and Motive is not to hurt another fellow human being, but your heart and soul also cannot deny the Love that you feel for your Beloved. So just go and have a good and fulfilling time, and have Faith that all is well and WILL work out for all concerned even if right now or even initially for

> a short time later, it may or might APPEAR to still be a moral conflict. In the end all WILL work out Just Know this.
>
> Also, know that whatever does happen (or this would not be allowed to occur), Cindy's present partner's (Tony's) Higher Self is definitely okay and in total agreement with this whole thing. That is also why you should not worry or be so concerned about how his conscious 3D earth self may or may not feel about what will occur. Cindy also knows or senses this as well, on a deep Inner level.

Immediately, right after Voltra's sudden and insightful message to me, as I tuned in to what he had just shared with me, I knew within, from my own I AM Presence/Higher Self, that it was true. This allowed me to let go of my emotional inner conflict and awkwardness that had been conflicting and interfering with all the intense and wonderful feelings of passionate Love, desire and physical attraction/chemistry that I felt for Cindy, and that I knew she felt for me.

I called Cindy once more, as I shared with her what Voltra had just shared with me, and I felt that this also very much helped her to understand everything from this Higher and more balanced perspective. This perspective was beyond the conscious ego self, beyond how one often allows one's own earth level self-doubts and emotional limitations to block awesome experiences like that which Cindy and I were about to personally experience together.

This can initially be intense and challenging for most humans living here on Earth who have not had direct contact and communications with Higher Beings, as I have had all my life—Beings who have literally saved my life many hundreds of times from the cabal deep state attempting to kill me, to silence me, and to keep me from sharing all that I have throughout the years and decades, which has been such a threat to them.

Now, I was about to embark upon a "sacred romantic tantric adventure and quest" that powerfully, energetically drew me to fulfill whatever Destiny was about to occur once I arrived in Cindy's area and home.

CHAPTER 6

More Insights from the Ancient Temples that Enhanced One's Life and One's Ability to Experience Greater Ecstasy and Joy on All Levels)

Since I had no car of my own, I took a Greyhound bus from the Sarasota area over to the town that Cindy lived in. Cindy was waiting for me, as I could tell from of the large conversion van that was parked near the greyhound bus terminal.

She had told me about the van that belonged to Tony, and about how we could use it to go out to various vortexes and energy spots that were located all over her area. She specifically wanted to experience doing the Cosmic Color Meditation with me at these particular locations. We wanted to not only "activate" these vortexes and energy spots in a way that had not been done before, but also looked forward to being able to experience them as a tantric Twin-Flame couple, just as we had experienced in the Rainbow Crystal Tantric Oracle Temples of ancient Lemuria. While we were not going to be able to actually be inside one of these beautiful temples, we were nevertheless going to be inside the conversion van which would be parked right on or over the energy vortexes of the area. The van had very dark tinted windows, so we would have total privacy and plenty of time to be able to do our Cosmic Rainbow-Tantric-Chakra Meditation and Activation without anyone bothering us.

Cindy was so excited and joyous to see me again. She gave me a long and affectionate hug, which I, of course, very much enjoyed. Despite the powerful feelings of physical attraction and chemistry that was obviously being felt by both of us, we kind of sensed that for right now we must be as impersonal as we could, until a more appropriate moment the following day when we would actually be sharing the Cosmic Color/Chakra aligning, balancing and strengthening Meditation that we had planned.

Cindy had shared with me that Tony had just become very tied up with taking care of a very challenging situation with his business that he was involved in with two business partners. It appeared that the other two individuals had been financially cheating him out of his own equal share in the company, and he suddenly had to spend a lot of extra time (many hours every day), attempting to get to the bottom of what had been occurring. As a result, he was totally immersed in this situation for the next week or so.

This allowed Cindy and I to have as much time together as we wanted for me to teach her as much as I could about the Cosmic Color Chakra Meditation and share my knowledge about the ancient Rainbow Crystal Tantric Oracle Temples; the very ancient and sacred tradition that had allowed the Divine Couples of this long ago era to be so empowered and fulfilled on a very personal level, and which had all been totally forgotten by most everyone upon Earth, only remembered by a few dozen of us.

Cindy also passionately wanted me to help her remember, if I could, and to help her awaken and be activated as a Channel/ Oracle. She sensed very strongly that she had been together with me many times as my Divine Sacred Tantric Oracle life partner. We had shared so very much back then, and had experienced together the most exquisite, mind-blowing tantric multiple-orgasmic lovemaking.

Cindy and Tony lived in a duplex-type house, with two parts divided by the garage. Each part of the home contained a bedroom, bathroom, kitchen, living room, etc.; each part had the exact same rooms and total square feet. Normally Tony had rented out the second portion of the house to someone else, but it was temporarily unoccupied. I was going to stay as a guest in that second side of the duplex, on the other side of the garage from where Cindy and Tony lived.

After Cindy had driven me in the van back to her home, we both got out of the van, and walked into the house, where Tony was busy talking on the phone. Within a few minutes, he finished his conversation with whoever he had been talking to. He immediately turned around, as Cindy quickly introduced me to him, and he smiled very friendly and shook my hand. I begrudgingly had to admit that I really liked him, that he had a very friendly and likable personality. I could see why Cindy would have easily fallen in love with him and that he was also one of her soul mates.

I suddenly felt a little guilty at what Cindy and I were going to be doing for the next week or more. Even though I understood that on another level, his Higher Self had chosen to allow his present earth soul mate partner to experience whatever was going to be experienced between her and I, I still felt somewhat bad that his conscious self would no doubt be jealous, if not angry, to find out that she was about to experience intimacy together with me.

I really felt compassion for him, especially because of his previous relationship where the girl he was with had cheated on him and he had experienced a broken heart. I tried to put myself in his shoes, thinking about what I would have felt like if the roles were reversed; that I was with Cindy, and along came this other individual who happened to be her Twin-Flame, and they had a "fling" (which could end most relationships).

A Mission to Re-manifest the Nirvanic Ecstasy Grid

I felt much compassion for him and did not want to cause him to have to experience this again, even if his Higher Self and Cindy's and my Higher Self had all agreed to do this because of the greater energetic good that was supposed to come out of this: This particular sacred ancient tradition of the past was about to energetically reactivate the ancient Nirvanic Ecstasy Grid, which was going to cause a major shift in the time-space continuum. I was assured by Divine Source and the Higher Light Forces that what Cindy and I would be energetically reactivating was part of the whole Cosmic Sting Operation to help end the control of the imbalanced forces.

Both her and my own unique DNA/RNA, united through our Twin-Flame connection of intimately sharing the Cosmic Color Chakra Meditation on/over the energy vortexes, actually allowed her and I simultaneously to remember, what she and I personally experienced during this ancient and glorious Golden Age of Lemuria (a cosmic energetically enhanced Déjà Vu).

Grounding into the Harmonic Grid through the Energy Vortexes and Energy spots in her area and experiencing this powerful, transformational shift in the time-space continuum through our energetic reenactment as a Tantric Divine Twin-Flame couple, would create a kind of "time loop of Nirvanic Ecstasy". That loop would powerfully transmute massive amounts of the negative loush energy from existence, once and for all—in a way that had not been done before in this modern age. This would officially and energetically reactivate and begin to re-manifest the Nirvanic Ecstasy Grid back into existence.

I also began to sense how angry the present-day imbalanced forces actually were. Not only had I suddenly started to be able to remember exactly what Cindy and I had energetically experienced and activated before, along with all the intense orgasmic tantric lovemaking that we experienced together in those ancient life times in the temple; now that we both were back together as a Sacred Tantric Couple, we would do an even greater job of transmuting the loush. This would powerfully help end the imbalanced forces, and quickly help eliminate them as if they had never existed in the first place.

Because of the very recent timeline changes that allowed the new timeline to manifest, now was also the wisdom of all the other new Romantic life times since when she and I had been together as a Twin-Flame couple encoded into her and my own DNA/RNA. This, in turn, allowed her and I to create these new lifetimes together, to be manifested in the time-space continuum and the Akashic Records as if they had always existed. This is now helping end the reign of those very forces that had suppressed humanity's joy and ecstasy.

Only this intimate, passionate tantric energetic reenactment of what we did in the ancient past was capable of creating the intensity that was needed to transmute all of the suffering the imbalanced forces had caused humanity to experience. The suffering had lasted for eons of time, since that early Golden Age of Lemuria when the imbalanced forces had energetically hijacked this reality and genetically erased its memory from almost all of humanity.

With what Cindy and I were about to do, and because it was our True, Pure Heart's desire to free up humanity both collectively and individually, it would now be too late for the imbalanced forces to stop us once we began what we had planned. I sensed in the back of my mind not only how angry they were, but that they were planning some kind of horrible energetic punishment and torture for me for daring to do this.

But I did not care about threats of possible negative consequences from the imbalanced forces. I had been fearlessly battling them all my life, and was never intimidated by their threats and attempts upon me. This would be no different.

I had a mission to fulfill, and yes, it would be most intensely enjoyable and fulfilling while it was occurring, for both Cindy and I. But I specifically asked Divine Creation and the Higher Light Forces that I did not want Cindy or her partner Tony to have to suffer in any way because of what might come down after a certain phase of this upcoming mission was over, and things went back to (so-called) normal in their own lives.

Manipulation of Earth's True Ancient History

Anatomically, modern man is supposed to only have maximum 4,000 nerve endings in his penis/"Lightning Rod", and women are supposed to only have maximum 8,000 (double the amount of men) nerve endings in her vagina/"Yoni." It is my perception, based partly upon my conscious memory of life back in these ancient Rainbow Crystal Tantric Oracle Temples, that both men and women actually used to have many more nerve endings, which allowed for them to each feel and experience much more extreme levels of sexual multiple-orgasmic ecstasy and pleasure than is even possible today.

The imbalanced forces did all kinds of genetic manipulation to lessen this original greater number of nerve endings, to slowly lower the population's ability to feel so much more orgasmic ecstasy. As in the phrase, "if you don't use it, you lose it," this gradually caused one to lose their original and very strong energetic connection to the Nirvanic Ecstasy Grid. This was done both covertly and overtly over many ages.

As the fanatical, narrow-minded religious beliefs and teachings that stressed denial/repression/suppression and celibacy of one's natural sexual desires and functionings was forced upon the masses, along with guilt and sin (one would burn in hell for all eternity—"fear porn" programming), humanity gradually began to lose their natural pleasure abilities. If one was enjoying themselves too much, well then, they would be "punished by a Wrathful and Revengeful God" for their "lustful" behavior.

So many religious people have even stated how they are a "God Fearing people," as if this very quality of actually fearing someone or something is something positive or to be proud of, or even to aspire to. But I say with clear insight: anything one "has to fear" cannot possibly be a really, true positive force or being. Yes, to totally Love and to Respect is one thing, but to FEAR?! (Remember what the word f.e.a.r. stands for: "False Evidence Appearing Real"!)

So many religious individuals will state, and even believe, that in order to be a truly moral or ethical person, one needs religion. I say: First of all, there is a major difference in my mind and consciousness between being "Spiritual" and being religious. In my opinion, religion is (diabolical) "man-made dogma", or rather "man's interpretation of God's existence and God's Laws." Perhaps more accurately it could easily be stated, "Earth man's narrow-minded Misinterpretation of God's Laws of the universe." So many still preach the brimstone and fire-gospel that everyone is either "going to be saved and go to Heaven," or "doomed to go down into that other horrible place to suffer forever."

But seriously, that "one is supposedly not capable of being really Moral and/or Ethical without religion," is what many have been brainwashed to believe by those priests of religious dogma. Those priests who want us to believe that "we the people" are somehow incapable (too unevolved and undiscerning) to be able, with true Wisdom, to truly Know Within the clear difference between true immoral and unethical behavior, versus true moral/ethical behavior.

Myself, I truly perceive that despite this attempt to make us believe that only the priests of religion can "decipher" such behavior, the reality is that 90 to 95% of Earth's humanity REALLY, TRULY inwardly KNOWS the difference between different types of behavior. Most people know what is Right versus Wrong, or what is Moral versus Immoral behavior. In addition, one's behavior is naturally drawn to those things that allow us to experience greater levels of bliss, pleasure and ecstasy, the *opposite* of denial, repression and suppression. These natural desires and tendencies were originally encoded into our DNA/RNA.

Somewhere along the way, these fanatical sexually repressed patriarchal priests came up with the belief (or nonsense) that if one is enjoying large amounts of pleasure and ecstasy, then that person must also be doing something "sinful," and other people are going to be hurt or harmed in the process. It is possible and may have occurred a few times that someone else might be hurt or harmed, especially after the original Sacred Tantric Tradition was perverted and turned into a commercialized activity of prostitution and even worse, of young children being harmed (pedophile, child pornography, human sacrifice, etc.)

But the point is: Prior to when Earth's true ancient history was changed by the Council of Nicaea, the vast majority of Earth's population were very much in touch with and followed "Nature's Laws." They did not need religious priests with major religious biases and narrow-minded judgments to tell them what their version of morality was. Everyone had a close relationship with nature and Divine Source, and everyone understood the laws of karma and naturally did not do anything to harm another.

The priests and priestesses of these early temples "walked the walk and talked the talk." Through their Sacred Tantric Oracle tradition, their whole life was an example of living, breathing and experiencing first-hand this early ability to share the intensity of ecstasy and pleasure, joy and bliss with their own Beloved/ Tantric Life Partner. This allowed them to be able to interpret and understand, with true Balance, what Divine Source was clearly communicating to them.

I would definitely trust the guidance and suggestions of these priests and priestesses over the so-called "guidance" of those in more recent times, who because of their "repressive nature" have been unable to experience such bliss, ecstasy and pleasure. Yes, those who are repressive in their own lives will automatically project onto others (a "psychological truth") their own biased beliefs and limited and twisted version of reality.

Sex had become merely for procreation of the continuation of the human race, to be used by the cabal deep state for bearing "good little worker bees." These "sheeple" were to work as slaves their entire lives for the power elite, and then to be discarded as other sheeple would take their place.

As the cabal continued to manipulate humanity away from anything joyous, beautiful, and uplifting (especially anything with too much bliss, pleasure, and ecstasy), the original sacred Divine Feminine Goddess tradition got hijacked, infiltrated and taken over by the cabal to turn these sacred Divine Goddesses into prostitutes and whores. The cabal was commercializing and perverting something so beautiful, joyous, and sacred into a pornographic mass commodity of slave exploitation. And even worse: the child pedophiles, pornography business and satanic human sacrificers totally destroyed and perverted the original sacred traditions that had allowed humanity to truly be empowered, free and sovereign in their relationship with Divine Source/the Father God/Mother Goddess.

Along with this negative "guilt, sin and damnation" religious programming to make one feel "sinful and dirty" if they dared engage in a passionate romantic intimate relationship with someone they were powerfully attracted to, the cabal deep state introduced its modern, toxic and deadly chemical additives, preservatives, pesticides, GMOs, pharmaceutical drugs and vaccines, with numerous toxic and deadly side-effects.

This all literally resulted in both a psychological as well as a toxic "castration" of what should be a natural ability to be able to "get it up." Or, as I jokingly like to say, to be able to (have their "lightning rod") "stand tall and straight, with rapt and respectful attention for the Goddess!"

It is my perception that because of this destruction of the Nirvanic Ecstasy Grid and the negative genetic programming to lessen one's enjoyment of sexual pleasure and bliss, most people in this modern age are lucky if they can "hit on one or two cylinders, as versus three or four," meaning that they usually only experience only parts of their full set of nerve endings being activated. So, their level of sexual pleasure is much less enjoyable and intense than it was originally in ancient times meant to be.

I truly believe that since the DNA/RNA of the human race is not just physical but also etheric, not only can one restore all the nerve endings (4,000 if they are a man, and 8,000 if they are a woman—one's age not being such a limiting factor), but they can also, ultimately, activate many more nerve endings etherically, which can be energetically manifested down here on this 3D level as well. This can increase and intensify their sexual ecstasy, with multiple-orgasmic pleasure becoming more common. This, in turn, will help reactivate the Nirvanic Ecstasy Grid. And as more tantric Twin-Flame couples are reunited, this process will accelerate, re-manifesting true Heaven on Earth and the next Golden Age for Mother Earth.

Life in the Golden Age of Lemuria: Stimulation of All the Senses

In the Golden Age of Lemuria, it was not just sexual orgasmic ecstasy and pleasure that was an important integral part of the original (and even the later) Eastern Indian Tantra temples. The whole concept, philosophy and way of life of Tanta also included the stimulation of all of one's five senses, as well as their 6th, 7th and Higher senses (also known as the "Gifts of the Spirit").

Stimulating one's Visual sense by seeing brilliant and beautiful colors was a daily experience. There were beautiful, bright, iridescent colors not only on the beautiful rainbow-colored crystal walls of the temples, but also on the brilliant and exotic flowers that grew abundantly all around, even inside some of the areas of the temples.

The flowers also stimulated another one of the senses with their wonderful, intoxicating aromas and smells, which was combined with the smell of the incense that was burning throughout the temples. This also stimulated the tantric couples in very erotic and sensuous ways that helped enhance their "mojo-libido" for even greater orgasmic lovemaking.

Beautiful and exotic music was often heard throughout the temples, which helped create a very relaxed environment and romantic mood for the tantric couples and visitors who were staying there.

And last but not least, the sense of taste was stimulated by enjoying eating not only healthy but also tasty foods and gourmet dishes, seasoned with exotic herbs and spices to tantalize one's taste buds. These special herbs and spices also helped to enhance and greatly stimulate the tantric Twin-Flame couple's sexual desires, powerful attraction, and electrical-magnetic chemistry for each other in a most intensely potent way. The enjoyment of eating such a delicious type meal, especially with one's Beloved, and the wonderful stimulation of the person's taste buds resulted in what I like to call having an "oral orgasm in their mouth"!

What a joyous-blissful-orgasmic experience it truly was to eat such delicious, healthy, and high vibrational foods every day at these temples. It truly was a paradise for those living at that time, and *all* of their senses were well stimulated many times over. This emotionally and psychologically helped extend their lifetimes with years and decades, even centuries!

I guess that in this lifetime, ever since I started to make my own very healthy but also very deliciously seasoned "gourmet meals," I realized I was always subconsciously attempting to repeat this whole ancient "science of food tasting alchemy." I subconsciously wanted to give myself and my guests the same "oral orgasm in the mouth" that I deep down remember from those ancient Rainbow Crystal Tantric Oracle Temples. I know that when I have made various gourmet meals in this present lifetime for myself as well as for guests (or for hosts when I have been staying as a guest with various fellow Light Worker's in their homes while traveling on various "lecture tours"), this has been a deep subconscious remembrance of these ancient temple meals and celebrations.

The first time I tasted a feta cheese and avocado sandwich, for example, back in the early 1970's, was definitely a type of "oral orgasmic" experience. (I jokingly refer to this as "moaning food"—as one moans in joy and ecstasy because of how delicious it is!) In more recent years, I love to make feta cheese and avocado omelets with pesto sauce.

The first time I ate a delicious meal in a Greek restaurant in Greek Town, I joked about becoming a "lemonaholic": From then on I had this intense desire to always make sure that any soups and/or dishes with sauces (and avocado, of course) always had a lot of either lemon or lime juice squeezed on them, along with healthy, Himalayan pink salt and various herbal seasonings (like white pepper, etc.). The taste of dishes was always much tastier to me then compared to if I did not add this to what I was eating. I also often have to add "hot sauce" to my meals to "jazz them up a bit". And, of course, I cannot forget my "famous" personal gourmet pizza and pasta dishes that I love to make, with all organic and non-GMO ingredients.

Of course, once I discovered both "Tandoori Indian" and "Thai" restaurants, I was definitely in "eating paradise." These two wonderfully, exotically seasoned type foods, with all their delicious sauces, remind me so much of many of the foods that were prepared and served in those early temples. The ancient chefs and cooks of the Rainbow Crystal Temples were definitely master "food-alchemists" in their ability to induce "oral orgasms" in anyone who ate their healthy and delicious meals.

Of course, in the near future once replicators become available to everyone here on Earth, these exact same types of ancient dishes and meals can easily be replicated and enjoyed just as they were in that long ago ancient paradise, when the Nirvanic Ecstasy Grid existed.

One more aspect to the whole (Holistic) Paradise life in the Rainbow Crystal Tantric Oracle Temples, was the huge and abundant gardens growing near each of these ancient temples. Many thousands of different and exotic varieties of herbs, plants, fruits, and vegetables grew in vast profusion, supplying all the many dishes and meals served at the temple.

In those early years of Lemuria's Golden Age, many of those beings we now refer to as elementals and nature spirits (many were part of or connected to the "Elvin Kingdom") worked as gardeners and caretakers in these magnificent and beautiful gardens. They acted as energy alchemists to the nature realms. Being Guardians of nature, they helped infuse the life force into every herb, plant, fruit, and vegetable that made them so healthy, tasty and rejuvenating to eat. This too, of course, guaranteed that it would be a powerful "oral orgasmic" experience to taste and eat these numerous species of herbs, plants, fruits, and vegetables. It was also considered a great Honor and joyous privilege to have the chance to work with the elementals and nature spirits, to "ground one's self" into Mother Earth's very healthy soil and to help take care of and to continue to plant new botanical life (many varieties were also imported from other worlds).

It is estimated today, in the beginning of the 21st century, that only about 3 to 4%, at the most, of the entire flora of the Amazon Rain Forest have ever been cataloged. Imagine that even if modern-day botanists were able to catalog 100% of the total number of different species, this would still be just a very small percent of the entire number of species of botanicals that once grew in ancient Lemuria. The Botanists that lived at that time understood so much more about both the healing and rejuvenating qualities of all these species, as well as which ones specifically enhanced and intensified one's sexual mojo-libido pleasure and ecstasy, and which herbs and spices would enhance one's taste buds and give intense "oral orgasms" in their mouths.

Yes, life was indeed good when living and celebrating every moment of one's existence in this Golden Age of Paradise, especially as part of these early Rainbow Crystal Tantric Oracle Temples. Living well over a thousand years was common for those enjoying such levels of pleasure and ecstasy all the time, sharing this with their Beloved/Tantric Twin-Flame partner day in and day out for their entire lives.

CHAPTER 7

Reliving Ancient Tantric Oracle Self-Realizations Together

Cindy and I had discussed about what our daily routine was going to be. She wanted to first do the Cosmic Color Chakra Meditation with me there at the duplex in my side of her house, before we both got into the van to go to the various vortex spots to do another ceremony. Of course, at the duplex she and I kept our clothes on and did a much more "platonic" version of the meditation.

During the meditation, Cindy sat on my lap in the Shiva-Shakti-Lotus position with her legs totally wrapped around me and hugging me tightly, which can be considered a fairly intimate position. Of course, as I look back on what she and I experienced there in my bedroom; I sense that if Tony had walked in on us, he probably would not have liked what he saw. He would no doubt feel that Cindy and I were being too personal, even if our clothes were still on.

In fact, several days after I first arrived at their home, Cindy one day came over to my bedroom. She was suddenly acting kind of strange and appeared to be in some kind of inner emotional turmoil or conflict. Instead of getting up on my bed to sit in my lap to do our daily "duplex home Color Meditation" before we left in the van to do it in a much more intimate naked tantric version, she sat down on the floor against the wall, a few feet from the bed. There she mumbled something about having an inner conflict about what she and I were doing, and that she thought we were "moving too fast or too quick" in our relationship.

The strange thing about this was that in respect to her feelings and what she really wanted to do or not do, I had at least a few times during our meditations, asked her if she felt that I was moving too fast for her. I wanted to make sure that she did not do anything that she did not really want to do. I made it very clear to her, more than once, of how much I truly not only Loved her, but how much I respected her. I told her that I did not want her to ever feel in any way awkward and that I did not want to pressure her in any way to do anything—that if she felt emotionally uncomfortable I would back off and give her any space that she needed to process whatever she was feeling. I would take it as slow as she needed, if she were having any inner conflicts with what we were both experiencing. But each time, she very sincerely and quickly told me that everything was great and not to worry. This was why I was initially so surprised that she would now suddenly, express reservations or doubts to what she was experiencing.

We had only been sitting there for a few minutes when the door to my side of the duplex was suddenly and unexpectedly opened and Tony quickly walked into the living room. A few moments later he was standing in the doorway of my bedroom, initially looking intently at both Cindy and I and where we happened to be sitting. When he saw where we were both individually sitting, he relaxed, and I could tell that he was relieved at not finding us “engaged in any hanky-panky” behind his back.

A moment later, as he was standing there, I sensed that he had not just come over to “check on Cindy and I”, but that he also had something that he wanted to say or share if things appeared normal. He looked at me and then proceeded to mention that he wanted to know if I might be able to tune in to what was going on with his two business partners(since he knew that I did my Readings for fellow Light Workers, just as I had for Cindy). He wondered if I could help him get any insight about what was going on with his major challenge and what his business partners' motive really was; were they really attempting to “screw him over” a lot or just a little, and could I help him clarify more of their actions and real intent?

First of all I was relieved that he had not suddenly walked in on Cindy and I in our somewhat intimate position which we had practiced every day until now. I suddenly knew that Cindy's own Higher Self must have sensed what could or would occur if that had happened, and that Cindy's conscious self was influenced to suddenly behave totally opposite from how she had been every day before this. In her conscious mind, she emotionally interpreted this as if it was some kind of emotional conflict which caused her to react a little withdrawn, to ensure that she did not do what she normally wanted to and was inclined to do.

This turned out to be a Blessing, helping us to avoid any unnecessary conflict with Tony here on this conscious level. And on top of that, the fact that Tony was actually asking me to help him with insight regarding his business challenge allowed things to be more openly in harmony with Tony, Cindy and I, as his sudden visit went from focusing on checking up on Cindy and I, to focusing on his own challenge. His business challenge had been taking most of his time since I had arrived there, which of course had allowed Cindy and I to have all that time to experience such intense Blissful intimate interactions. This was in total agreement with all three of our Higher Selves, but would still have been reason for a major conflict with his conscious self.

I tuned in to what I was getting about his situation, which he said helped quite a bit. I did confirm some of what he already knew, but I also helped by giving him more insight into what he should do to solve this sudden business challenge. I could tell he was happy with having asked me for this help.

He then suddenly informed me that if I was open to doing so, he himself was interested in experiencing a personal Transformational Channeled Reading with me. Now, once again, those feelings of awkwardness that I had thought I had been able to let go of regarding what Cindy and I felt for each other and what she and I were experiencing so intensely every day, came back once again. Somehow I had not been expecting that Tony would also want to experience a session of his own.

I was suddenly concerned of just exactly what might be revealed in doing a session with him, as it obviously might reveal Cindy's and my romantic love connections, and of how this might play out for Cindy's and his own relationship on the present conscious level.

This same concern about what might have been shared with Cindy from the Higher Being, Ashtar, had turned out not to be a problem. Ashtar obviously understood the intimate and powerful connections between Cindy and I, but had allowed me to personally "break the cosmic ice" to reveal my own feelings and personal romantic connections to her. As a result, in case Tony later heard the recorded CD of the session, there would be no real, obvious hints or clues to exactly what Cindy's and my real and powerful feelings and connections actually were. I did find out that Tony had in fact listened to her session several times while she was playing it back. I was relieved that Ashtar had understood my predicament during that session, and kept things very impersonal and platonic when he had mentioned that Cindy and I had definitely known each other in previous lifetimes.

But now that Tony also wanted to experience a session of his own, suddenly I was feeling somewhat uncomfortable again. Yet, I did not want to say no to Tony, because I could tell that he really was interested in getting more insight and clarity about his mission of being here in Earth embodiment. Tony said that it would probably be a couple more days before he was ready for his session, and then turned and walked back out of my room to take care of his business challenge.

Suddenly Cindy was acting more like her previous self, and she wanted to go out with me again in the van. We did, and we spent another wonderful and intensely fulfilling afternoon doing our very intimate tantric version of the Cosmic Color Meditation and the Energy Vortex activation ceremony.

Ayahuasca-Channeling

The following day, as Cindy came over once more to do our more platonic version of the Meditation, she informed me that because the date was December 21st, the Winter Solstice, she had another thing that she wanted to share with me which should make the whole experience much more interesting and intense for us both.

Cindy had already discussed with me over the phone what she wanted to do, prior to me coming to stay with her and Tony. She wanted to use the "psychoactive" substance known as Ayahuasca, which has been used by many Shamans to help Spiritually Activate and Awaken their initiates into the Higher Dimensional Realms and realities. The use of Ayahuasca had been shown to speed up and/or intensify one's spiritual and psychic Awakening, and when combined with various meditations, mantras and ceremonies it had the capacity to help lift one's veils.

Here is a quote about Ayahuasca that I copied from an article that I found on the internet, titled, "Top Ten Psychoactive Substances Used In Ceremonies":

> "Includes BOTH Ayahuasca Vine (Banisteriopsis caapi) and Chacruna Shrub (Psychotria viridis). The word "Ayahuasca", translated to "vine of the souls", refers to a medicinal and spiritual drink incorporating the above plants. When brewed together, and consumed in a ceremonial setting, these plants

> are capable of producing profound mental, physical and spiritual effects. Ayahuasca is mentioned in the writings of some of the earliest missionaries to South America. It may be considered as a particular shamanic medicinal brew, or even as an entire medicinal tradition specific to the Amazonas. The effects of the drink vary greatly based on the potency of the batch, and the setting of the ritual. They generally include hallucinogenic visions, the exact nature of which seem unique to each user. Vomiting can be an immediate side-effect, and is said to aid in "purification."

Instead of making a drink out of it, it also could be smoked—either in a pipe, or rolled up in a paper like those Cindy had brought for us to share a couple "hits" or "puffs" off of.

Up until now I had never used any psychoactive substances to experience all that I had, but in this particular case, because of who I would be sharing it with, I decided to make an exception. I would allow myself, more out of curiosity than anything else, to share this unique substance with my Beloved. I wondered what, just exactly, might be experienced with her and I both sharing this together in our love, powerful attraction and chemistry for each other.

Cindy had told me on more than one occasion, that while she had definitely sensed her and my powerful connections, and while she had really enjoyed her own Transformational Channeled Reading with me, she herself had not specifically been able to Direct Voice Channel the Higher Beings as I did all the time. Even though she felt very much in harmony and attunement to what had been channeled to her through me, she wanted to actually experience this same type of Direct Communication and Channeling from a Higher Being herself. To her, what had been channeled through me would be confirmed and verified even more if she, herself, was to personally experience this same type of communication and energetic interaction with fellow Light Beings. She felt very strongly that using Ayahuasca would act as a type of enhancer for her, to be more able to experience this type of connection and communication[2].

I was of course very curious about what exactly either or both of us would experience once the Ayahuasca "kicked in." I am only estimating the time here, but I remember quite clearly that after taking a couple "puffs" or inhales of the Ayahuasca, I begin to suddenly feel a slight energetic shift, as if time and space itself ceased to exist. I could see and sense very intensely into other realms and dimensions, a little more easily than usual. Also, I was suddenly feeling and sensing what Cindy was feeling, and what she was experiencing—just as I sensed that she was also feeling and sensing what I was experiencing.

[2] Disclaimer: I want to make something very clear. I am NOT in any way, making any claims about the use of Ayahuasca being able to "Spiritually Awaken" or "Activate" anyone else. Up until then, and ever since, I have never used such a substance in my spiritual work, and of course one must always be very careful in how and when one uses such a substance (if it is in fact used). I would never recommend for most people to do this, and as stated, I decided to allow myself just this one time, as a unique experience because of the unique circumstances: being with my Twin-Flame. Cindy also told me that she herself had only once before used Ayahuasca. She felt that this time, it being the Winter Solstice, positioned over a very powerful Energy Vortex, and because of what she and I were experiencing together, that it would somehow create for her, and even myself, something definitely more unique than if we did not use it.

This was most interesting and a wonderful sharing-experience; how we each felt and sensed so strongly what the other was experiencing. I sensed that part of this was because of us being each other's Universal Other Half/Twin-Flames, which of course intensified the whole experience for us both.

We were both transported back in time to our ancient lifetimes as Tantric Life Partners and numerous other romantic past lives, and what we then experienced for hours every day: the intense levels of erotic ecstasy and sensual pleasure, of multiple-orgasmic lovemaking, beyond anything that anyone in this modern age had been able to experience.

Being able to remember this exquisite and sacred intimacy that she and I had shared for literally hundreds of years, day in and day out, acted as a sort of powerful "Surrogate experience" through the "time-space continuum." It allowed her and I to anchor this same potential type of experience into this new timeline that was now beginning to manifest, ensuring that other modern-day, tantric Twin-Flame couples would also be able to experience such wonderful and sacred intimacy. All these Divine Couples reuniting, and now experiencing this same quality of tantric multiple-orgasmic lovemaking, will begin to more powerfully re-manifest the entire Nirvanic Ecstasy Grid.

I also sensed how angry (or rather hateful and revengeful) the imbalanced forces were at me for being able to remember so intensely what they had assumed they had been able to 100% erase from all of humanity's genetic DNA/RNA memory bank. Now, suddenly all their intense negative work and efforts for eons had been for nothing.

Because, as stated before: if just one person (or rather, in this case, if one Divine Couple) could remember (especially if they could remember it simultaneously with another person), then suddenly this will act as the ultimate Activation, Empowerment and Manifestation through our True, Pure Heart's Desire to be reunited

Even if Cindy and I could not be together for a short while because of the possible aftermath of this sudden Revelation of Truth, our moments of remembering would still forever reverse the energetic damage that the imbalanced forces had done to block humanity's potential to remember. This would result in the reactivation of the entire planetary Nirvanic Ecstasy Grid, and Earth would never be the same again.

Within minutes after Cindy and I had first shared the Ayahuasca, I suddenly felt an energy shift around both of us, and sensed the etheric presence of Higher Light Beings, who had made their presence known. I sensed that one or more of them wanted to Channel/Communicate with us, either telepathically and/or to speak through either of us.

I specifically felt and knew that Cindy herself was about to experience channeling for the first time. I could suddenly feel her physical body go through some kind of subtle, energetic, frequency shift, very similar to what I always experience moments before I Channel the various different Higher Light Beings. This was a very unique and wonderful experience for her, to now be able to experience this first-hand, versus listening to someone else channeling.

As I have taught through my Channeling Workshops: Part of the unique aspect to being able to Direct Voice Channel a

Higher Light Being, compared to being a psychic medium channeling a discarnate astral being (as occurs when one channels a spirit world/astral realm entity) is that one should not have to go into a complete trance state where one completely forgets what was communicated through them. Instead, in Direct Voice Channeling one can stay conscious, although in a more "altered state," and one can remember what was shared.

There are various forms, or levels, to Direct Voice channeling Higher Light Beings. Some of them appear to be much deeper or more complete, there the Light Worker channeling the Being may not be as conscious as others would be, and they do not remember as much from when the being was speaking through them.

In other cases, the person who is experiencing the presence of the Higher Being may be combining both Direct Voice and Telepathy; the person will first receive in their mind very clearly what they are hearing mentally, and they then repeat out loud what they are hearing. This combination Direct Voice channeling is quite common, as it also allows the person to receive the message very clearly, in their mind first, before they then pass it on/verbally repeat it to whoever happens to be physically present to hear their channeled message. This combination channeling also helps make the person feel more relaxed and confident that they did, in fact, channel the Being or Beings who are speaking to and through them. It is also quite common that someone will be Channeling their own Higher Self, who may be one of the beings present, "Over-Lighting" (a better word than "Overshadowing") the entire experience.

Celeste Presents Herself

What happened next was truly revealing and very confirming on a personal level for Cindy's conscious 3D Earth mind. She spoke out loud, sharing what she herself was receiving directly. The message was short, but as with the expression that is often used on Earth, "It was short, sweet and to the point":

"My Higher Self's name is Celeste—or "Lady Celeste," as I Am known on the Higher Realms. You, Michael, are my True Divine Other Half/Twin-Flame, and you and I have a very important Mission together soon in this lifetime!"

With that, I could sense and feel that that what she was supposed to share had in fact been shared. Sometimes, keeping it "short and simple," as versus "much more long winded," is better, and it is easier to remember all that was specifically stressed and/or emphasized during the Channeling.

Because of what Cindy herself had just personally experienced, I also could now suddenly feel that she was allowing herself on a more emotional and intimate level to open up to me a little more than she had before. Though very short, for her it was nevertheless a very profound and powerfully self-confirming moment of self-realization, and a deeper, more personal Confirmation of her and my True, Divine connection.

After a few hours of Blissful Intensity and not really wanting to end our wonderful interlude together there in the van, it became late afternoon, early evening. As we "returned to the real world," we knew we had to get back to Cindy's home and prepare for dinner.

In the evening after we would return to the duplex, I would usually go over to Cindy and Tony's side to eat dinner with both of them. I did so that evening as well. As we were finishing our meal, Tony again mentioned his interest in experiencing his own Transformational Channeled Reading, and he wanted to know if I could do it the next day, in the afternoon.

Again, I was feeling somewhat awkward about doing a session for him, considering all that Cindy and I had been experiencing together every day. Especially now that the cosmic ice had been broken even more completely through what Cindy and I had experienced so intensely together; her own special, short and powerful personal Channeling experience, her own very powerful confirmation of her and my Energetic Connection. Obviously, though, there was still many questions about what the future held for both her and I, and her present relationship with Tony.

As I have emphasized more than once already, it had not been my intent or desire (at least here in this 3D level) to break up Cindy and Tony's relationship. But I realized that with my own intense feelings for Cindy, which were only more intensified after sharing so much with her once again, I obviously had not been looking at this whole thing in a rational and practical way—how this much deeper connection that we each just shared had made it much more complicated and hard NOT to want to be with Cindy for the rest of my life. Yet, I did not want to cause Tony any emotional pain from experiencing Cindy choosing to leave him for me. What was I going to do? And what was Cindy going to do?

For I knew that she, too, was struggling with her own feelings: Her Love for me, her own Twin-Flame, and her Love for Tony, one of her soul mates who she had already had a very wonderful relationship with. (In addition to not wanting to break his heart the second time.) All this sudden emotional drama—the very thing that I had NOT wanted or expected to ever occur when I finally did meet my Beloved.

On top of all this, here was Tony wanting to experience his own session with me, obviously wanting to get more clarity about his own relationship with Cindy, etc. What was I going to do, tell him, "sorry, I can't do your session"? Or just bite the bullet, and somehow hope that nothing too awkward would be presented through his session with me?

I had never in my entire experience of all the decades of doing thousands of these Transformational Channeled Readings for fellow Light Workers/Volunteers in Earth embodiment, ever been in this type of predicament, being caught a love triangle, with "the other person" wanting me to do a session for him. This could definitely cause a major compromising situation to manifest, which might be an emotional nightmare for all three of us (here on this conscious level) before it was all over.

What a mess I had gotten myself into. Here on this mundane 3D level of existence I had no idea how this could be solved, how to make it a true "win-win" for all concerned, as I always truly desire to do. It was a major dilemma for me, just as I knew it was for Cindy, and I had much compassion for what she must be going through as well, considering what was at stake. I also had much compassion for Tony in case everything was revealed during his own session if I went ahead and did it. (And it would also appear strange if I choose *not* to do it, after having just agreed to do so a couple days before.)

Of course, since Ashtar had kept things fairly impersonal and platonic about Cindy's and my actual past life connections during her session (obviously, this was partly because he knew that Tony would later hear it, plus he also knew that I would be the one, immediately right after her session, to tell her about my feelings for her), I assumed that he would be using similar discretionary tactics to not reveal just exactly how intense and powerful Cindy's and my romantic love connections actually were compared to Tony's connections to her (her and I being Twin-Flames).

Tony's Reading

The next morning, Cindy came over to my side of the duplex as usual. But this time, instead of doing the Cosmic Color Meditation with me as she usually did, she just wanted to talk to me for a few minutes about the fact that Tony had just informed her of some changes in their schedule for the next few days. This change was somewhat of a surprise to her, and she wanted to apologize about this, since this now suddenly changed her own schedule.

Part of this sudden change was about him finally getting more clarity about his business, which called for him to now go out of town on a trip to another part of Florida. Cindy always went with him when he traveled. This was going to occur within the next several days, or a couple days right after Christmas.

In addition, Tony had found out that his own parents and relatives were going to come visit him and Cindy within the next couple days. They would be arriving on Christmas Eve, and would be staying until right before Tony and Cindy left to go on their business trip. Tony had not been sure before whether his family were actually coming or not, partly because of flight details etc. suddenly changing, and they could now come after all. This meant that I had to now move out of my side of the duplex, to allow the family to stay there. I would now be staying in another, smaller, extra bedroom on Cindy's and Tony's side of the duplex.

Suddenly it all felt even more awkward, and this was definitely not how I had initially envisioned my visit with Cindy. I had been given the impression from what Cindy had originally told me that I was welcome to stay for at least two or three weeks, while I taught her all about meditation, channeling, etc. But now it was obvious that things had been sped up much more quickly than I had assumed was going to be the case.

That afternoon I prepared to do Tony's Reading. I sat in one of the large, comfortable chairs in the living room, and placed my small digital recorder on the table beside the chair. I sat back and prepared myself with my normal condensed version of the Cosmic Color Meditation. I prepared for Ashtar to begin speaking/Direct Voice Channeling through me for Tony.

When I am doing a session for a person, since I am normally not in a deep trance, I am mostly aware at the time of what the Higher Light Being is saying through me. I do so without allowing my conscious mind's beliefs, concepts, and opinions to filter or influence whatever the Higher Beings would be sharing. I am in an altered state of awareness that allows me to tune into the Higher Truths and Higher Beings, but still in a conscious state so I can receive and also consciously remember what was shared at the time it was coming through.

When Ashtar first started to speak through me, and up until about half way into the session, it appeared to me that Ashtar would keep things very impersonal as far as Cindy's and my romantic connections were concerned.

But then, all of a sudden, Ashtar changed the focus of his presentation. It had all been focused upon Tony's mission and purpose for being in Earth embodiment. Now, suddenly, Ashtar began to focus specifically upon Cindy's and my romantic connections, upon the fact that she was my Twin-Flame and that Tony was Destined to meet his own Twin-Flame. Ashtar now seemed to open the flood gates of information upon the very things that I had hoped he would NOT talk about, let alone to such an extent and in such detail as he now did. I was shocked and even horrified that he had chosen to do so, because of the obvious emotional aftermath that would occur if he did. I had assumed that he would follow the impersonal and non-romantic protocol while doing Tony's session.

I was stunned, and could only imagine what Tony must have been feeling after of this sudden romantic revelation about Cindy and I. I was also stunned at how much time Ashtar spent on going over this situation with Tony. To my conscious self, this seemed like an emotional nightmare. What was I to do now that Ashtar, for whatever reason, had suddenly chosen to spill the beans as far as Cindy's and my situation was concerned? Our situation was just as in the saying, "one cannot put the genie back in the bottle."

Despite my conscious mind and ego conscious self being in denial; in the back of my mind, on a much Higher spiritual level, I knew and sensed that Ashtar had done the right thing. Of course, at the time I felt that Ashtar had ruined the whole thing for Cindy and I, and that there was going to be major emotional damage and awkwardness, to put it mildly, now that this truth was literally out in the open between the three of us.

Normally when I do my sessions with Ashtar channeling through, he always leaves about 15 to 20 minutes toward the end of the session, for the person experiencing it to be able to ask any questions that they need to get more clarity about. But under the unique circumstances of what had just been shared for the last half hour, and how obvious it must have been that Tony was attempting to process all of these sudden and unexpected emotional revelations, Ashtar did not do so.

Instead, I was coming back to my conscious self abruptly, still in shock from what had just transpired. As I opened my eyes, Tony was sitting there in his chair, with a stunned look in his eyes, as well as some obvious anger about what he had just heard. He suddenly jumped up out of his chair, as he mumbled something about, "if I had been any other man, I would have thrown you out of my house right now for what you said. I think you are just using this session as a way of stealing my woman from me!"

Tony quickly walked out of the room. I was still stunned, and I felt much compassion for whatever Tony must have been feeling about what he had just heard. I did not blame him for whatever he was going to say or do to react to this whole thing.

I just sat there for a couple minutes, trying to process what this now meant for Cindy and I, now that her and my secret was out in the open. I would not blame Tony if he DID throw me out, considering his own feelings toward this whole thing. He had had his heart broken once before, and now he had just accused me of attempting to steal his woman through the spiritual work that I had been doing for many decades. I knew he was upset and I was feeling for him, considering what he must be going through after having just heard these shocking revelations with no conscious warning. But I also suspect that on some very deep level, he must have known or suspected that it was true. During the session, Ashtar had told him of his own Higher agreement for this to all occur as it had.

I also wondered what Cindy was feeling and thinking. I knew that she had probably heard most of what was shared during Tony's session. I had seen her standing near the doorway of the living room right before I had started the session, and I had glimpsed her briefly as I came back to my total conscious state, right before Tony had jumped up out of his chair to go out of the room.

As I sat there for a few awkward minutes in my chair, trying to think about what I was now going to say or do, I could hear Cindy and Tony speaking together in very low, hushed tones. I could not tell what they were saying. After a few minutes I got up and walked out of the living room, and I went into the room that I was going to be using until I left.

Now that all of this had so drastically changed because of what was revealed during Tony's session, my future seemed very uncertain. Up until the time I had first arrived at the duplex, I had been in communication with a few other fellow Light Workers who had originally expressed their interest in hosting and sponsoring me for workshops like the one in which I first met Cindy. But now, after getting back in touch with these particular individuals, I suddenly found out something had energetically shifted compared to my normal opportunities to make connections for hosting and sponsorship. It was as if I had suddenly hit a blank wall. For the first time in as long as I could remember, there were no new connections occurring for me. I suddenly realized that I really did not know where I was supposed to go or stay after this stay at Cindy's home came to a close—which was about to occur soon. Cindy was now going to go off with Tony on the business trip that he needed to go on. For the first time in as long as I could remember, I felt very alone and unsure of my purpose in life.

The person who I had assumed so strongly was Truly my Beloved, the Love of my life, had because this sudden turn of events reluctantly chosen to continue her relationship with Tony. I sensed that this was because of Cindy really not wanting to hurt him, not wanting to break his heart the second time. And after all, he WAS one of her soul mates, and she did have feelings for him.

I did not blame her in the least for choosing this, versus choosing to be with me. I had to admit, as I looked at my own life, being realistic—what could I have offered her, anyway, here on this 3D level? I had no normal, financially secure existence.

I was traveling around totally on Faith, some might say I was almost like some modern-day "gypsy." I had no real home of my own, instead I was being hosted and sponsored all the time, staying with various Light Workers. Tony, on the other hand, had the duplex and a very secure job (despite this recent, now solved business challenge), and many other 3D financial securities that I did not have.

Of course, I did not really feel that these things were that important to Cindy. But her decision of continuing to stay with him was really a more compassionate reason, feeling that she still had a Destiny with him for right now and of course not wanting (here on this 3D level) to break Tony's heart the second time by running off with me and forgetting about all of her own responsibilities.

I also found out, when I talked with her during our various conversations, that she was very involved in a creative way with his business and various other creative projects that were also important to her. She felt that these were important also for the raising of the planetary frequency. She had also promised Tony that she would be doing various other creative projects with him which would take a few years. She felt obligated to complete these.

Considering the circumstances and all the many pragmatic reasons to stay in her relationship with Tony, I truly did not blame her in the least for feeling that she was obligated to continue to stay with him.

I also knew, though, that her own very intense and deep feelings for me had made the choice difficult for her. In fact, on the day that I was forced to finally leave the duplex (during the only moment that Tony was not around), she quickly came up to me to briefly whisper to me that she wanted to make sure that I would not lose touch with her and that she hoped she and I could still communicate with one another. She apologized sincerely about things not working out as she had hoped.

The Last Days Before I Left

After Tony's session I spent the rest of the day in my new room with the door closed, feeling very much alone, confused and depressed about how it had all turned out. Not that I had realistically thought I could really have any real chance of winning Cindy's heart and her choosing to be with me instead of being with Tony. But yet I was still so confused. Even she, in her own personal experience of channeling, had Confirmed of her and my True Sacred Connection. Why would my Beloved be in another relationship when I finally did meet her? It made no sense to me, especially in my idealism with a True Pure Heart's Desire to always make everything win-win for everyone and not to cause any emotional pain to anyone else.

In my deep and powerful Faith I had assumed that God/ Divine Source and the Higher Light Beings would have taken this into account and would have made sure that such a complicated situation would NOT have occurred this way; to cause one of us to be so disappointed and hurt, rather than truly working the situation out for all concerned. To discover that I could not be with my Beloved because of her circumstances in life—suddenly everything that I had ever believed and knew inside seemed to make no sense. I started to doubt and question my very existence, doubt so much that I had been inwardly confident about before. I started doubting my whole mission and purpose for being here as a Volunteer in Earth embodiment.

I just felt very miserable, as well as awkward about everything, now that it seemed fairly obvious that my chance to ever really be with Cindy was not going to occur, despite all that she and I had shared so intimately and intensely for so many days. This left me in a total quandary of trying to figure out what to do next.

On top of that, now Tony was no longer spending all his time attempting to solve his business challenge. He was now being very affectionate with Cindy all the time, which I could not help but feel somewhat jealous of because of my own deep and intense feelings for her. I knew that they both had been together a couple years before I showed up, but still it also seemed to me that he was being even more affectionate with her than he might have normally been. Perhaps because he realized that he had been too tied up all those many days in solving his business challenge and he just wanted to catch up for lost time of showing and demonstrating strongly his own feelings for her. Or perhaps because he did not want to risk "losing her to someone else"—me.

I am sure he wondered about what exactly she and I had actually been doing when we would leave every day to go out in the van to meditate at various vortex spots, etc. I could not blame him for his concern and suspicions about her and my more intimate and very personal interactions. It just was extremely hard for me to now watch their interactions all the time in front of me, while all I could do was watch. For the next couple days I just stayed in my room, refusing to come out to visit with them and with Tony's family and relatives. It was definitely one of the worst Christmases I had ever experienced.

Of course, both Cindy and Tony had come by my room to invite me to come over to say hi to everyone who was there, and they were attempting to make me feel better and less awkward about everything. Finally, later in the afternoon, I decided to venture out of my room and walk over to the other side of the duplex, to where everyone was. I kind of blended in with everyone, as they were all visiting and sharing various family stories and experiences.

At one point Cindy came up to me, and I could not help but feel once again the powerful chemistry and electricity that was energetically shooting back and forth between us. I knew she too felt this, and that what she and I were feeling was stronger and more intense than what she and Tony had experienced.

Cindy looked at me very intensely, and then mentioned that they had a special pool in the back of the duplex. It was not chlorinated, instead they used a natural salt solution to purify the pool. She was going to get in, and wanted to know if I would like to join her. She said that the others already had jumped into the pool and swam around earlier. But she had not joined then, but wanted to now. She was already wearing her bathing suit, covered by a towel, and she presided to walk toward the pool.

I followed her as she let her large beach towel drop to the side of the pool and stepped down onto the steps leading into the pool. I could not help but stare at her, as the small bikini she wore did not leave much to the imagination, and could not resist my attraction for her—just like I knew she had to also be feeling for me.

I quickly ran back to my room and put on my own bathing trunks, grabbed my own large beach towel, and walked back to the pool. I could tell how happy Cindy was that I was going to join her.

After all those days of intense tantric intimacy, and with the attraction between us, she was obviously having trouble just ending the wonderful interactions that she and I had shared every day. The pool water temperature was just perfect, and it felt very pleasant for us both to be able to still hang out together—even if we (supposedly) could not be as intimate as we really wanted to be.

I leaned against the side of the pool, a few feet away from her, attempting to be somewhat detached, considering her own situation with Tony and his family. She immediately started to move closer to me, and told me how sorry she was that things did not turn out as she had really hoped. She hoped that I would somehow understand her own predicament, and was sorry for any emotional pain that she had caused me.

But as she moved toward me, the intense electrical-magnetic attraction between us intensified, and I could not resist her any more than she could resist me. She moved around totally in front of me, with her body pressing against mine, as her arms went around me. As she looked up at me, I bent down to suddenly kiss her passionately—giving into my own intense desire for her, as she also responded very passionately.

She suddenly reached around to unclasp her bikini top, which she let fall to float beside her in the pool as she also moved slightly to take off her bikini bottom. My own desire caused me to let my own swim trunks drop down off my own body, and I pulled her to me. A moment later I was inside of my Beloved. She moved against my body, surrendering to her own erotic, sensuous desire for more tantric-orgasmic intimacy of such an intensity that only Twin-Flames can possibly experience.

It was as if time and space in a normal 3D sense seemed to not exist, as we completely surrendered to our intense desire for each other. As I made love to her, and kissed her, with her and my tongue moving around in each other's mouths, it also enhanced all the powerful erotic-sensuous orgasmic pleasure and ecstasy we were both feeling and sharing together. We became totally telepathic, being able to read each other's minds so easily. Our shared erotic orgasmic pleasure and sensuous ecstasy became even more intense, as we each could energetically feel and sense what the other was experiencing.

For me it was overwhelmingly intense, because I was able to feel what her over 8,000 nerve endings in her "yoni"/vagina felt like for her, which was added onto my own 4,000. She felt not only her own 8,000 nerve endings, but my 4,000 as well. It is a known fact that normally a woman's ability to experience levels of orgasmic pleasure far out-weighs a man's. But, perhaps for the first time in many ages as a man, I was able to feel how intensely powerful her own orgasmic, pleasurable ecstasy was. Our body's and spirits seemed to totally merge as one being. The warm temperature of the water helped to also enhance our wonderful, bliss and orgasmic ecstasy.

I could sense in the back of my mind that every day we had experienced this same exquisite tantric intimacy, just as we were at that moment, the Nirvanic Ecstasy Grid had begun, once again, to anchor and re-manifest itself back into alignment with Mother Earth. Every time we, and other tantric Twin-Flame couples, would now experience multiple-orgasmic lovemaking, this would continue to enhance and strengthen the grid even more.

I also realized that the Nirvanic Ecstasy Grid had its own consciousness, as if it was a living being of Light that thrived and was enhanced the more times that tantric Twin-Flame couples could intimately, lovingly and passionately share this same intense type of orgasmic lovemaking. It was as if the grid had a type of Higher personality and self-consciousness of its own.

I sensed at that very moment that it wanted Cindy and I to experience once more, as we were, this same exquisite lovemaking that we had for the last week. I sensed that every time we did, the very experience helped bring the grid more back to life, which in turn energetically reached out to both Cindy and I to help enhance our orgasmic rapturous ecstasy and joy. This, in turn, would be multiplied, and it would also feel this same orgasmic pleasure.

The Nirvanic Ecstasy Grid also seemed to have the ability that the more it came back to life and back into existence, the more it could somehow control the time-space continuum. It did so at that moment for both Cindy and I, to give us plenty of time to enjoy our intimacy together there in the pool—totally naked and not having to worry or be concerned about anything else. I knew for sure that Tony or any of the others would never come out to discover us in the "throes of passion." To them, it would seem as if only a few moments had passed since Cindy and I had left to go outside.

I also realize, as I look back upon Cindy's and I my intimate time together, that it had been unlike normally when someone is enjoying themselves as much as she and I had been; the time frame of a week would normally have flown by so fast as to seem but a few days at the most. It was as if the Nirvanic Ecstasy Grid's Higher consciousness had helped our True, Pure Heart's Desires and attraction for each other to be able to experience this more enhanced, exquisite tantric-orgasmic lovemaking every day, and made it seem as if a *whole month* had actually passed since I had first arrived to be with Cindy.

All of a sudden, we experienced another energetic shift in the time-space continuum. Cindy's light Caucasian skin, beautiful long blond hair and blue eyes began to transform or change into an entirely different appearance.

She now was a very exotic, gorgeous Asian sex goddess priestess, sitting in my lap, in the "Shiva-Shakti-Lotus" position, mostly naked, except for just a few small pieces of gold jewelry on her arms and legs. I could feel myself inside of her, very tightly stretching her inner Yoni muscles, causing her and I both mind-blowing multiple-orgasmic pleasure, for hours and hours on end.

I could remember her being my Sacred Tantric Life Partner, in that very ancient past lifetime, in the Tantric temples. I remembered how she had first traveled over a long distance in her royal caravan, in the hopes of being allowed to join my tantra temple as a young initiate. She was a royal daughter and princess of one of the ancient "dragon families" of China.

When she arrived, and I had first greeted her at the entrance of my temple, I was astounded at how beautiful she was. I was so moved with great emotion and passion by her presence, and the instant Love at First Sight that I had experienced, that I had unexpectedly dropped down onto my knees. Looking up at her, overwhelmed by the instant electrical-magnetic chemistry that she and I were feeling, I asked her if she would be my main, special, sacred Tantric Life Partner, and she accepted—totally in awe over this unexpected honor that I had instantly bestowed upon her; someone who I had only just met mere moments before.

Many more scenes flashed very quickly before my eyes, as we both relived that life; only one of many similar and very romantic lives that she and I had created to attempt to keep the Nirvanic Ecstasy Grid in place; to counteract what the imbalanced forces had done to literally destroy it with all their horrific loush energy.

Time seemed to disappear, as scene after scene manifested before us. Just as Cindy and I had experienced back in those very ancient Tantric Oracle Rainbow Crystal Temples of Lemuria (and later on, in the Tantra Temples of India), the Nirvanic Ecstasy Grid was reminding us of the fact that after many wonderful hours of intense, orgasmic lovemaking, we were truly in Paradise.

We would then lay back in each other's arms in the afterglow, to share and experience numerous Visions and communications from Higher Beings of Light, and directly from Divine Source, itself. The very experience of sharing such passionate, powerful, and fulfilling intimacy, WAS the major catalyst that allowed us to then manifest our shared Sacred Oracle experience. It was NOT the *lack of (Sacred) sexual intimacy and pas-*

sion, as others later erroneously believed, being influenced and programmed by the imbalanced forces, as in the "virgin oracles" of Delphi. It is actually amazing that they could even be able to read the oracles at all at that time, considering that the very catalyst/main protocol (that which allows one to be most attuned and clear in what one is psychically-spiritually seeing or receiving) IS this intensely fulfilling intimacy and exquisite tantric multiple-orgasmic lovemaking with one's Divine Partner/ Beloved/Cosmic True Love.

Finally, as these wonderful scenes and ancient tantric oracle self-realizations began to fade away, we both sensed that it was time to put our bathing suits back on. We were both now back in the real (3D) world.

CHAPTER 8

Forced to Leave My Twin-Flame

No sooner had we done so, than the door that led out into the patio suddenly opened, and Tony's mother and family relatives began to walk outside. Cindy had moved back a few feet away from me, as we now both acted as if nothing out of the ordinary had occurred with us.

Tony also came outside, as everyone continued to visit and enjoy their time at his duplex. Tony's mother came walking over to stand near Cindy and I, as she looked down at both of us. I sensed somehow that she was suspicious about me and of my reasons for being there.

A moment later, looking intently at me, said in an accusatory way, as if she suspected something was going on between Cindy and I, "Who are you, and what exactly are your reasons for being here?" I realized that mother's have a natural intuitive sense about things—especially since here I was, being intimate with her son's partner. I felt that she was somehow being intuitive on some deep level about Cindy and I, even though she had no evidence to prove anything.

I just acted very calm and cool, and told her about how I had met Cindy at my Workshops and that I had been invited by Cindy to come visit so that I could teach her various meditation techniques. Tony's mother persisted to question me in a very intense way, as if she did not fully believe that my being there was merely for platonic spiritual teaching reasons. I just continued to act calm about the whole thing.

Finally, she stared at me and asked me what my plans now were, since both Tony and Cindy had to go out of town right away within the next couple days and she and her relatives were also leaving to go back out of town. She interrogated me about where I actually lived, and what exactly my plans were for the near future once I left the duplex. My answers did not seem to satisfy her questioning, and she kept pressing the point of where I was going to go once I left.

Despite the incredibly wonderful experience that Cindy and I had shared together just moments before everyone came back outside, I had to admit something to myself: Before I had come to stay with Cindy, I had been making a lot of important contacts and connections with fellow Light Workers for sponsorship and hosting. But now, all of a sudden, it felt like I had hit a blank wall, and had absolutely no idea where I was going to go, or what I was going do once I had to leave in the next couple days.

So, in an attempt to "get her off my back," I finally just said that I had many contacts and connections, and I would work something out, find another place to stay and continue my spiritual work, as I had been doing for quite some time. Finally, she just said one more time, that I definitely needed to be out of there in the next two days, and to have my stuff packed up and to catch a taxi or whatever I need to go to. Then she turned and walked off.

As I really did not have any idea just exactly where I was going to go, I told Cindy that I needed to go back to my room and continue to call some more people—hoping that I would in fact make my connections for the next leg of my continued journey. I did make quite a few phone calls the next couple days, but without really making the connections I had been hoping for. I was starting to feel a little desperate.

After spending most of the next day calling, and not being able to connect with anyone, I decided to take a break. Cindy and Tony had come by my room again in the late afternoon, inviting me to come over once more if I wanted to visit with everyone there. I once more walked over to the other side of the duplex, and went into the living room. When I first walked in, I observed that everyone seemed to be having a fun time, joking around and telling stories about their families and what had happened in the past.

After a few minutes, in which the conversation had turned to various other topics, I noticed that Cindy seemed to be acting kind of strange and somewhat withdrawn from what everyone else had been focused upon. Initially, when she had seen me come in, she immediately came over to tell me that she was glad that I had come over to visit. But then she had gone over to sit on the couch by herself. She kept looking at me every now and then with a strange expression on her face, which I had not seen before. It was as if something was emotionally bothering her. She just sat there for a few minutes.

I could tell that she was feeling some very intense emotions, as if she was in some sudden extreme inner emotional conflict about this whole thing of her and I, about what she felt so strongly for me but could not allow herself to express out in the open in front of the others. It seemed that she now was forced to hide her true feelings, because she was attempting to not stir up any problems that would cause Tony and his family to be concerned about their relationship. It seemed that she was struggling with this inner challenge.

I watched with great concern, wanting to go over to hug her and hold her in my arms, to tell her that I would always be there for her. But of course I could not, as the others had no idea that Cindy and I had feelings for each other, let along how powerful they were. Tony of course suspected, but he too was pretending that everything was great with his and Cindy's relationship.

All of a sudden, what with Cindy attempting to not show her feelings for me, trying to suppress these powerful feelings, it was as if she suddenly could not take it anymore. She seemed to have some type of emotional meltdown, as she suddenly started to cry and to have what I can only say seemed to be an "emotional seizure."

At that moment I almost jumped to my feet in my love and concern for her; it was instinctual because of my feelings for my Beloved, and I barely stopped myself in time. I forced myself with extreme effort to just stay sitting where I was. I knew that if I had ran to her, it would have seemed strange to everyone that I would be so quick to show such personal concern, compared to Tony.

Initially Tony seemed very confused at her behavior, and for a few moments did not seem to understand what or why she seemed to be acting so emotionally out of control. Finally, he got up and walked over to sit down with her, as he tried to calm her down.

Initially it did not seem to work, and she continued for a short while to flip out. She was expressing different emotions, with everything from frustration, desperation and anger, and every emotion in between. I had such compassion for her and what she must be feeling and struggling with, of having to pretend to everyone else. To hold inside all that she was feeling for her and I, and her feelings for Tony as well, while being especially concerned about what Tony's family and relatives would think if she did openly admit her feelings for me. I knew that this type of situation could truly be an emotional hell—having to save face and not be able to be or say what they really want to, feeling locked into something without any easy option available to them.

All I could do was to silently and energetically send her, my Beloved, a lot of Love and Light energies, and pray that she would somehow be able to cope with this whole thing and to be able to be strong until a solution would manifest for both of us. Finally, after a few minutes, she seemed to be able to return to a more normal, balanced emotional state. I was really glad that at least she was able to feel calmer and more balanced about everything.

It was difficult for me to watch Tony now be very affectionate with her. I knew that as one of her soul mates, he definitely loved her. But for me, as her own Twin-Flame, it still was difficult to be around them, watching them romantically interact. I knew that what she and I felt for each other was much more intense and passionate, and that she would never be as happy or fulfilled with him as she could be with me, now that we had had a chance to experience such extreme levels of Bliss and ecstasy for the past week.

The next day I called dozens of fellow Light Workers who I thought might be able to help me, mostly just leaving phone messages. On this last day there I was able to speak to Anne, the elderly woman who had originally channeled and prophesied that she saw me finally meeting my Twin-Flame. Anne, who lived in Texas, finally invited me to come stay with her for a short while, until I could make my next connection. I really did not want to have to go all the way to Texas from Florida, but considering my situation I could think of no other option.

I quickly called the Greyhound Bus lines to see about securing a ticket, which I knew was going to be somewhat challenging because of the very late time of the day I was calling them. I was able to purchase a one way ticket, costing more than it would have if I had had more days to have reserved myself a ticket than I did. I was calling only a few hours before the bus was scheduled to leave for Texas. I next called one of the local taxi companies to send a taxi to take me to the greyhound bus station. I quickly packed my two suitcases as fast as I could, and I just finished only moments before the taxi arrived. I had to rush out of the door to catch it.

I felt so bad about how this whole visit with Cindy had come to such a sudden close, with me having to rush off, not being able to even say a proper and meaningful goodbye to her, as I wanted so much to do. Tony and everyone else were just standing around, looking at me taking my suitcases to the taxi, and they all had no idea how much I loved Cindy.

She just stood there, obviously feeling just as awkward as I did; not being able to also show me openly what she felt. Like me, she had to pretend to everyone, especially Tony (despite what Ashtar had told him during his session with me), that there were no significant romantic connections or feelings between us.

I almost cried at that moment. I had just put my two suitcases into the taxi, and turned around to stand for a few moments, staring at Cindy. She was standing about twenty feet away from me. I sensed that she too was on the verge of tears, in her own anguish of the spirit that she might never see me again. I wanted so much to quickly run over to her, my Beloved, and hug and kiss her so passionately before I had to leave. But instead I stuffed down all my feelings and closed my heart down. I did not want her to have to answer any awkward questions that would obviously have followed if they had seen a more open display of our feelings for each other. I forced myself, with great effort, to just bend down and climb into the taxi.

As the taxi began to drive off, I turned very quickly and waved intensely and passionately at Cindy for a few moments, hoping that she saw me do so. Then the taxi went around a corner, and Cindy was out of view.

CHAPTER 9

Just How Bad Could This Next Place REALLY Be? Oh, My God, You Have Got to Be Kidding Me!

As I sat there in the taxi and then later in the greyhound bus (which I almost missed, because of arriving just minutes before it started on its journey to Texas), all I could do was think back with deep longing for what Cindy and I had experienced so intensely during my time with her. I sat somewhat dazed and confused about everything, or rather about how everything had turned out; with me having to suddenly leave, not having any real closure of what Cindy and I felt so intensely for each other.

It had seemed so much in Divine Order that I was supposed to go visit with her and to be with her as I did. At that point in my life I could definitely say that never had I ever experienced such fulfilling and passionate romantic feelings for another fellow human being, let alone anything like the intense and powerful Sacred Intimacy that she and I had shared most every day while being there.

Before I had gone to be with Cindy, I had suspected that I would probably end up having to leave her and go elsewhere until the time that Destiny and the Divine Plan would allow her and I to actually be together without her being in a relationship with someone else. At that time she and I would be able to be totally open with everyone else in our lives about her and my deep and intense feelings for each other. But of course, being only human, I still felt disappointment because of the recent circumstance that had forced me to leave. I had still hoped for a miracle, that somehow she and I could have found a way for us to continue to be together, and not have to be separated for any length of time.

I just had to continue to keep my Faith that somehow, someway, she and I would yet find a way to truly be together, without all these other things getting in the way of her and my happiness and fulfillment. I still believed, in the depths of my being that despite our separation, my Beloved and I would find the way to be able to be together. I just could not give up Hope, and I refused to allow myself to be negative and hopeless about the whole thing. As with so much else in my life I had learned to Trust Divine Guidance (both from Divine Source/God and from the Higher Light Forces), who had Guided and protected me and my mission for being in Earth embodiment my entire life.

I forced myself to focus my attention on my next destination, which was to stay with Anne in Texas. I hoped that I would shortly be back in the flow of things, as I had been before my little "Interlude on Earth" of being with my Beloved. But at the same time, in the back of my mind, was the awareness which I had touched on before, that I must also always be very Discerning. As in the biblical phrase, "To be Wise as a serpent, Harmless as a Dove," I must always use my Inner Discernment and always do everything with a True, Pure Heart's Desire to uphold the "Divine Will of God."

I am very aware of the importance of how the Divine Feminine Goddess tradition was destroyed and suppressed by a bunch of old, corrupt patriarchal priests of religious dogma. In respect to this original Sacred and more balanced and Holistic view of reality and the Divine Plan, I have in recent years always included this Divine Feminine together with the Divine Masculine when I pray, meditate and Invoke the Light. I ask for God's and the Goddess's Blessings and protection in all things that I think, say and do, hoping that I will be able to accomplish and do what Divine Source/the Father-Mother God/Goddess wants me to do. I am also recognizing that as Light Workers we are still "co-creators" of our Destiny, and our Intent and Motive truly helps create and define our ultimate Destiny, both individually and collectively.

Through this whole process, we are creating the present and new timeline in the time-space continuum that we are presently existing in. I knew "Beyond all shadow of a doubt" that it WAS my ultimate Destiny to truly be with my Beloved when the time was right. I just also had to learn to be more patient than I already was, and to just trust the process. (Or, as in another important saying that has become quite popular in 2020, because of the recent Victory of the Light by the Q White Hat Alliance against the cabal, to "Trust the Plan"! And "Where We Go One, We Go All"! More about this later.)

The Imbalanced Forces' Sabotage

I was still aware that the imbalanced forces were angry about what I had been able to remember and experience with my Beloved, and how that had caused the Nirvanic Ecstasy Grid to begin to be re-anchored. I could sense that they were determined to stop me in my "romantic quest" to finally be reunited for good with my Beloved, and that they were energetically attempting to now sabotage this if they could.

I put my attention upon my immediate destination, Anne's home. I knew that I would just have to trust the plan that I was being guided to follow, no matter what the consequences might (temporarily) be, until the TOTAL, complete, planetary-wide Victory of the Light and of the HEART would indeed, occur!

I forget, just exactly, how many hours that it took for me to reach the town closest to where Anne lived. But ultimately, to my great relief, the bus pulled up at the greyhound bus station. Anne was waiting in her car to pick me up and take me to her home. Anne seemed happy to see me, and we talked for a while about what had been going on since we had last spoken on the phone.

But she had no sooner brought me to her house (and I had unloaded my two suitcases in the guest bedroom), than I started to sense, first in a very subtle way, that the imbalanced forces were really "working overtime" to attempt to energetically mess up my visit with Anne.

I had spoken to Anne quite a number of times over the phone, and I always felt a good rapport and positive vibes with her. We had had some long conversations, without any negative interactions. I knew that she was a dedicated Light Worker, as well as a clear channel. She had helped me to get clarity and insight about a number of situations in my own life, just as I had shared different things with her that appeared to help her with whatever challenges she happened to be going through. In all these phone interactions there never seemed to be any personality challenges and/or conflicts of any kind between us.

But now, all of a sudden, within a very short time once I stepped into her house, things began to "go to hell" energetically between us in some very strange and unexpected ways. I sensed that the imbalanced forces were very subtly doing everything they could to cause conflicts between us, to cause tension and communication challenges with her misinterpreting what I did or planned to do about a number of very "pity" and seemingly "unimportant" things. Each day that passed, these bizarre, negative interactions between us only got worse. It is true she has a strong personality, just as I do, but I truly do not think that would normally have been a problem.

It has been noted by many insightful people that often one's relationships and friendships with certain people can be very harmonious while speaking to them over the phone, but then, for whatever the reason, this harmonious balance seems to change once one attempts to live with them. I have stayed at many dozens, if not hundreds, of people's homes throughout the many years and decades since I have been fulfilling my mission. I have been hosted and sponsored by them, and I have stayed for many weeks. A few times I've even stayed a little longer than that, because of how successful I was with my Workshops, media interviews, and the number of Transformational Channeled

Readings that I had scheduled in after the events. Through all this, I do not ever remember having a difficult or stressful time of interacting with any of those people. Occasionally there might have been very minor challenges or so-called conflicts, but nothing even close to the type of situation I was in now.

Every day it only seemed to get worse, and I could sense how intensely the imbalanced forces were working overtime to attempt to mess my life up. Finally, after a few days of tensions increasing between us, Anne told me that I had to leave right away; to get out ASAP. Of course, from her perspective I sensed that she thought I was being negative and unreasonable, when that was at the same time how I thought she was acting toward me. I just "could not win" with her, and the stress and negative vibes had reached such an intense level that I knew I had to leave to be able to feel balance and harmony once again. I truly do not feel that Anne is a negative type of person, but the imbalanced forces were determined to ruin my opportunity of being there.

I sensed that one of the reasons that they were throwing so much negative energy at both of us, was because this was their way of getting back at Anne and me, because it was Anne who had predicted that I would meet my Beloved at my event two months before. They were angry of me for all the awesome, Transformational-fulfilling, and literally Energetically Timeline Changing experiences that I had shared so intensely with Cindy, so they targeted Anne and I to really energetically punish us both for this.

I was not intimidated by this, and I had immediately Invoked a huge amount of Light to counteract what they had done. But the damage had already been done, and I had to leave and find somewhere else to stay. I was trying not to feel desperate in anyway, but considering the sudden turn in my life (not being able to make the connections and contacts as I had seemingly so easily done prior to staying at Cindy's), I was starting to wonder what I was going to do or where I would go. I had absolutely no idea, really, for the first time in many years, where my next destination was. It suddenly seemed that all my Help and Higher Guidance was no longer there, that I was entirely on my own. I did not sense the normal "Cosmic Backup Team" that I always sensed and communicated with through the decades of being on my mission in Earth embodiment. I could not understand why I suddenly felt I had no help and guidance, nor why I had this lack of, this "emptiness", of Hope. I had not ever felt such sudden hopelessness and loneliness as I did then.

New Hope?

Then, as all hope seemed lost, I suddenly got in touch with another individual. I had last connected with her many years before, she had attended one of my many hundreds of events. Joyce was another elderly lady who I had spoken to several times over the phone, and who had attended a few of my events in the past.

As I look back on what she told me, it seems kind of like she gave me mixed messages regarding her allowing me to stay at her place. After I had shared my situation with her, she initially told me that she had a small apartment, and that she had an extra room that I could stay in. She then changed her story; I could *probably* stay. She told me she was helping her friend, an older man, and because of him being "partially handicapped," she was not sure if he would be open to me staying there with them. She also mentioned that she did not know if it would work out because the apartment was not that clean. According to her, her friend had a lot of bad habits which resulted in the apartment not being very clean, and they were concerned about me staying in such a mess. As I look back on it, she totally "downplayed" (to put it mildly) just HOW messy—or rather dirty and filthy—the apartment actually was.

Considering how desperate I had suddenly become, I could not be too choosy. I did not want to just end up on the streets, which I had never had to do before. Unfortunately, with my financial situation at the time, I really could not afford to "throw my money down the black hole of a hotel."

"So", I thought, considering that this was my only choice at that moment, "just how bad could it really be?" In all the many years of being hosted and sponsored, I had never stayed at any place that was not clean enough. nor too cluttered with the people's personal belongings. So, I just assumed that the place could not be too bad, despite her description of it being "dirty and a mess" because of her friend's living habits.

Initially, Joyce had seemed much more open for me to stay there, despite the "physical appearance and conditions of the apartment." She then seemed to want to change her mind. I just told her that if she did not allow me to stay for a few days, I would probably, for the first time in my life, end up on the streets with literally no place to go. Who knows what would have happened to me if that occurred?

So, she consented to allowing me to come, but I knew that I did have to find somewhere else soon. I was still hoping for some last-minute miracle that would open up for me presenting a better choice, or hoping that at least I would hear from one of the many people who I had called or left phone messages with.

Having spoken to Joyce over the phone did not prepare me for exactly HOW horribly filthy and messy her apartment was. To attempt to be specific; let's just say that if the local Health Department ever saw it, they would literally "condemn" it for health reasons, and it would have been shut down because of how horribly filthy it was. For me, as I tend to be somewhat of a "clean freak," it was the ultimate nightmare to now be forced to stay at such a place.

To make matters worse, the elderly man who was living there with Joyce was extremely crude and vulgar. His living habits included a lot of loud cussing and nasty comments about everything. Despite his physically handicap, he was a total control freak with everything and everyone around him. He treated Joyce as if she were his servant (or slave), making her life an emotional toxic hell—day in and day out. I then understood that part of her hesitation about me actually staying there was that she was embarrassed not only about the condition of the apartment, but also about her interaction with her friend. She was concerned about me having to be around him.

No sooner than I had arrived at the apartment, the man made it very clear how much he did not like the fact that I was going to be staying there for the next few days. He was extremely nasty and crude in everything he said, and it seemed that he was going out of his way to also make my life a living hell with his despicable personality and living habits. I sensed how the imbalanced forces were also energetically using him to attack me, continuing their earlier efforts to punish me in whatever way they could. It was obvious to me that the man had various "attached negative entities," who used him whenever they wanted.

I felt much compassion for Joyce, for having to put up with this whole thing. I focused upon still attempting to find another place where I could stay, one that would definitely be much better than where I now suddenly found myself staying. I just could not believe how bad this place was, nor that I had suddenly experienced such an extreme sense of hitting a blank wall, with absolutely no other options available to me.

Each day that I was there, the man's extreme abusive and nasty personality only seemed to get worse, because of the forces that kept coming through him. They were using him for their targeting of me, to make my life even more of a hell. I could tell they were getting an evil, fiendish delight in what they were doing, in me feeling trapped in my situation, and in being able to energetically emotionally torture me day in and day out, knowing I no other place to go to find peace and comfort from this horrific treatment. It was impossible to even meditate, what with this constant negative energetic inundation that I was experiencing, and with not knowing what I was going to do. I knew that I needed to leave this place immediately, but had no real plan.

Then, at one point during one of those very rare moments when the man was not around for a few minutes, Joyce suddenly mentioned to me that she wondered if I had ever thought of going to a homeless shelter. She thought that even though it might be challenging compared to all the other places I had ever stayed, at the very least it would be better than literally ending up on the streets.

Considering the level of such negative and nasty energy that was being directed at me at the moment, I was literally about to be forced to think she was right. I had to get away and attempt to find some real inner peace, I had not felt that since being there at Joyce's.

I knew my very "emotional survival" had reached such a level that I had to escape from this emotional and psychic hell before I literally lost my mind. I wondered, though—was I just about to leave one type of hell, only to go to still another type of hell by staying at the homeless shelter? Despite what I had just gone through, and being an eternal optimist, I thought, "really, how bad could it be?"

So, I thought about Joyce's suggestion. Considering my circumstance, I knew that I ought to consider this as a possible next move. Since I knew that my stay at Joyce's was coming to very rapid close [Thank God!], I did some "information exploring" on the internet. The city of Pleasantville, Florida, where Joyce's apartment was located, had no large natural food store. After finding out that in Jacksonville, Florida, there were several (including a Wholefoods Market), I decided to catch another Greyhound bus over to Jacksonville.

I then took another taxi to the homeless shelter that I had chosen out of the several that existed in the Jacksonville area.

CHAPTER 10

These Are the Times That Try Men's Souls: My "Dark Night of the Soul" Experience in the Homeless Shelter

Well, just as I had hoped would not be the case; sure enough, it seemed that I did go from one hell to another. As mentioned before, never in my entire life had I ever been forced to stay at a homeless shelter. I had no real clue about what, exactly, it would be like to stay at such a place, nor about what type of people that would also be staying there once I arrived. Now that I look back with hindsight and wisdom, I do believe that these types of experiences really do cause one to develop a lot of Unbearable Compassion for the suffering that so many other less fortunate people have been experiencing in their struggle to just survive.

The cabal deep state had manipulated our economy and political system gradually over the years, allowing the cabal/power elite, through their corrupt central banking system and the corrupt tax system, to destroy our Constitutional Republic and replace it with a draconian, socialistic, corporate-controlled hierarchy. This allowed them more and more control over the masses and allowed them through their fiat currency to amass more financial and political power for themselves. This in turn slowly caused the average person to have less and less abundance, until a vast majority of the population have been barely surviving, being in debt and constantly in survival mode.

Most people, up until very recently, have been clueless about how the cabal has been manipulating the entire system, and how this has caused so many people to suffer and just barely survive in this world. Of course, since no one is REALLY a "victim," this does not mean that the (evil and satanic) cabal has not VICTIMIZED the ignorant masses with their plans for total world control. Unfortunately, many millions, if not billions, of people who feel desperate often do things in their desperation in an attempt to "numb themselves out." They develop bad habits, such as excess drinking and using various illegal drugs, to deaden the emotional pain and hopelessness. Such people often find themselves not only "down and out," but having become alcoholics and drug addicts. This was the reality for the vast majority of the guys that were staying at the homeless shelter. Many of them had also experienced how these problems broke up their relationships and families, and many other problems and personal challenges that I was fortunate not to be experiencing. But nevertheless, I had much compassion for what they were going through.

After I checked in to the homeless shelter, I began to discover what it was going to be like to stay there. It was not in any way as dirty as where I had just come from, since many of those that were staying there were "volunteered" for clean-up duty. However, it was still going to be quite a challenge, for a number of reasons.

For starters, there was only one toilet and two showers in the entire place, which over a hundred guys had to share every day. There was always a long line of guys waiting to use them, and these did not make it easy for the one who happened to be using them at the time. This was a horrible, stressful situation that I did not want to have to experience or deal with. In fact, I almost always used a toilet at one of the several health food stores that I went to (during the few short hours that I was actually allowed to leave the homeless shelter, in the early part of the day).

Another challenge was the shelter's strict rules, which they imposed upon everyone who stayed there. They needed to force discipline upon many of the men, who had numerous addictions and other challenges that they were dealing with. The rules obviously helped these men to find more order and balance in their lives. But for myself, being a very "sovereign free soul" who did not need such extreme discipline and control, it was quite a challenge to have to do these same things every day.

Especially difficult was the fact that the sleeping accommodations were similar to the conditions that I had endured at Joyce's. Everyone had to go to sleep at 10:00 P.M. at night. Being something of a night owl, I had to get used to this much earlier sleep cycle. At 5:00 A.M., everyone had to wake up and get up, so that those whose duty was to clean the concrete floor where everyone slept could do so. The floor, especially during the winter months, was quite cold. We were each given a stained, worn-out pillow along with a dirty looking blanket, which was what we got to sleep on. What with over a hundred guys sleeping within a couple feet of one another, we had absolutely no privacy whatsoever.

One can imagine what this was like during the 3 to 4 months that I was there. I felt like I was in prison, what with all the rules and rigid policies that one had to follow, and with how one did not have very many hours to spend outside before one had to come back in the early afternoon in order to get a bed space on the cold concrete floor.

One of the greatest challenges for me at the homeless shelter was the food they served. Normally I follow a strict, all natural, organic, vegetarian non-GMO diet. This diet is healthy, promoting a strong immune system. It was also important for my spiritual work and mission: a healthy body allows me to be a clear channel when doing my personal Transformational Channeled Readings. As I always say to those attending my Channeling workshops; "Are you a clean, pure, fast-moving river, or are you a slow-moving, toxic, swampy bog?"

In the last few years, I have seen an interesting "energetic analogy" to this question of mine. Consider the corrupt, former cabal-controlled government, media, Hollywood, music industry, and almost every area of society—President Trump accurately defined it all as a "swamp." The Q White Hat Alliance and Trump are in fact now "draining the swamp," healing our corrupt, polluted planet so that it can become once more a healthy planet. A planet without us being controlled and influenced by the evil, satanic deep state cabal anymore.

We do not want our bodies to be like a polluted swamp, instead we want a pure, fast-moving river. This also allows our abilities to accurately tune in to what has really been going on behind the scenes; everything the Operation Mockingbird CIA, cabal-controlled mainstream ("lamestream") media always suppressed through their fake news that they constantly made up and attempted to brainwash us all with. Thank God that the Great Awakening, that Q so often accurately predicted, is indeed occurring all over the planet. The Great Awakening is preparing Earth for full disclosure of all that was covered up by the cabal. Hundreds of thousands of children that were abducted by the cabal have recently been rescued by the White Hat Alliance from hundreds of underground bases all over the world. These crimes against humanity are in the process of being exposed, this entire planet is in the process of being Liberated, and most of Earth's humanity will experience the planetary Ascension and the Golden Age.

Getting back to my overwhelming challenge in the homeless shelter: As stated, I had never faced such an experience in my entire life, and really did not know how I was going to get through this whole thing. It was, a "dark night of the soul" experience for me. It was truly as in the saying, "These are the times that try men's souls!" I could sense the imbalanced forces attempting to make me feel as if all Hope were lost: Feeling that being stuck in this homeless shelter was to be my future. Feeling that I would never make my connections again, never be sponsored and hosted again, never do more events nor any more of my personal Transformational Channeled Readings.

My connections, my events and my readings were how I had always been able to buy my food and the few necessities that I needed to survive. It had now been awhile since my last events and sessions, and my "money energy" was now running low, with little to still purchase any healthy food from the health food stores that were in Jacksonville, and I had no real indication when things would even turn around for the better. I kept refusing to give up hope, but I sensed how intense the imbalanced forces were really determined—they were truly trying to "hit me while I was down." I feared I had better start eating the unhealthy, GMO laden "food" that they served there, or else I was going to starve to death.

A Test of Faith and Intent

I continued to Invoke the Light, and I prayed to God/Goddess. I could not believe, with all that I knew to be true about my own mission of being in Earth embodiment, that I would be stuck here forever. I considered my many experiences of personal "Divine Intervention" in the past years, as the cabal constantly had attempted to kill me. They had only succeeded once; that time they used a psychotronic weapons system upon me (I shared this experience in my first book, and I also summarized it in chapter two of this book). That time the Elohim had physically beamed my body on board a Merkabah Light Ship, brought me back to life, and energetically upgraded my body. That experience, along with so many others, had made it very obvious how much the Higher Light Forces watched over and protected me and all other Volunteers during our missions.

Of course, to what degree we have been protected is dependent on the nature of our mission. Because my mission was to boldly expose the cabal on an open, public level for many decades, I was afforded a correspondingly high level of protection. In addition, what we each do and what protocols we use all the time not only gives the Higher Light Forces more authority to Divinely Intervene in our lives, but also helps to keep ourselves much stronger and more balanced on our missions. Truly, "God helps those who help themselves." But now, despite my Invoking the Light and sincerely praying, it seemed as if nothing was working. It seemed that my efforts were suddenly no longer able to help me, and that the Higher Forces had forsaken me.

At least, this was what the imbalanced forces were attempting to convince me of as I finally ran out of money and healthy food and the days began to drag slowly by; that I could not count on the Higher Forces anymore. The imbalanced forces continued to attempt to energetically overwhelm me with Hopelessness, and I had never seen them so determined. They wanted me to just give up; to think that somehow I had just made all this up, that I had been merely living in a fantasy world of my own imagination. They wanted me to think that now I was facing the "real reality" in the "real world" that so many others throughout the world were experiencing. They wanted me to just forget everything else, and to acknowledge the fact that I would never experience any more help from above.

They even tried to tempt me: They attempted to convince me that if I would simply join them, energetically embracing them and their darkness, they could do all kinds of incredible things for me. Then suddenly Miracles would be manifesting into my life, they would help me get out of the homeless shelter, everything would magically change and I could have anything I wanted. All I needed to do was to "sell my soul," at that bleak, hopeless moment. Just like so many well-known, famous, and powerful people of society; like most of the "A-list" celebrities of Hollywood, the music industry, the power elite of the financial banking system and politics—yes, all these corrupt individuals all had one thing in common: They had literally sold their soul to the Devil, aligning with the evil, satanic forces, becoming forever controlled by these forces of darkness.

But after all I had gone through—intense spiritual challenges for so many decades, not only exposing the imbalanced forces, but also exposing the cabal deep state/illuminati and their plans for total world control, having battled them fearlessly my entire life through so many eons of being a Light Warrior and Guardian of Light—at this "late date," I was NOT about to give into these forces.

I remembered how the imbalanced forces had attempted to fool me in earlier years, by pretending to be beings of Light. They had in fact tried a few times to masquerade as Lord/Commander Ashtar, trying to channel through me. But it did not work; as I have always taken major precautions to make my channeling very fail-safe, these attempts to interfere with my spiritual work and mission were unsuccessful. Ashtar (the real Ashtar), Archangel Michael, and various other members of the Spiritual Hierarchy had warned me of imitators and imposters of the dark side who would attempt to fool me. They also made it clear that one should always be Inwardly Guided by a True, Pure Heart's Desire to invoke the Divine Will of God and Goddess!, and always Visualize, Decree and Invoke the White (Christ) Light of Protection, Purity and Integrity to Activate, Empower and Protect one's self with the Highest Intent and Motive in all one thinks, says and does in every area of one's life and existence. Yes, if one has enough spiritual energetic empowerment and protection, then one can always find their way on the Path to the ultimate and Destined "Victory of the Light," both personally and collectively for the entire planet—no matter what the imbalanced forces attempted to do to stop God's Divine Plan.

We must just believe and Know Within that it has always been darkness before the Dawn. Often, we are spiritually tested in ways unimaginable to us; at those very difficult moments in our life, when all does seem lost, will we weaken in our Resolve, in our Dedication and Devotion to the Light? Or will we be able to stay strong, even when "all seems lost and hopeless forever"? Yes, those are the times that try men's souls. God and the Higher Forces of Light have tested and WILL test us, to see if we are able to demonstrate what we are really made of. Will we succumb to the manipulations of the dark side, as they attempt to ensnare us in their sophisticated "honey traps" of choice, circumstance and temptations? Will we "buckle under" and become weak?

Or will we, despite the sophisticated propaganda of the Destroyer, stand strong before the Trial by Fire, able to STILL embrace and hold on to the Higher Principles?

CHAPTER 11

My Vision of the "Story of Job"—the More Complete Version of What He Really Experienced

Back in the early '80s I had a challenging time with the imbalanced forces, they attacked me severely to try to convince me that I would not be successful on my mission. I then had a powerful vision of the person in the Bible known as Job.

In my opinion, so much of what is in the Bible was altered and suppressed because of the Council of Nicaea, those corrupt patriarchal religious leaders. For instance: Concerning Job, that which is described in the Scriptures was somewhat downplayed; some of the original details were being left out. In my opinion, what Job actually went through in his "Test" by God was substantially more severe and challenging.

My powerful vision was based upon the Akashic Records (of whatever particular timeline that I was seeing). In my vision, the soul of the Higher Being who had taken Earth embodiment as Job was the Cosmic son of Archangel Michael and Lady Faith. He had Volunteered to fulfill this "mission impossible" to be able to demonstrate that he would STILL, under the absolutely worst conditions that one can even imagine, keep his faith and be patient until God turned things around for him. Despite how things seemed totally hopeless, despite how God seemed to have forsaken him, despite the negative forces ultimately torturing him in the most unimaginably, sadistically cruel ways (both physically, emotionally and in other ways), he would still keep his faith.

Introducing the Blessed Job

On the 3D earth level, Job was a highly evolved, educated soul, with much ancient knowledge and wisdom. He was a compassionate and ethical person, who always went out of his way to be of service to others. He constantly showed much kindness and generosity to others less fortunate. Being one of the richest men on Earth at that time, he was very influential to the society he was living in. Unlike the extremely wealthy and powerful elite of today (of the illuminati-family bloodlines and of the cabal deep state), he had not accumulated his power and wealth at other's expense.

He was the incarnation of all the good and higher qualities of a very evolved spirit and soul. He also had many conscious psychic-spiritual gifts of the spirit, which he used to help make life so much better for those around him. He was able to read the Akashic Records, and throughout all the early years of his life he constantly received Insights from God and communications from the Higher Light Forces. He seemed to constantly have "Lady Luck" smiling upon him; everything seemed to magically manifest easily into his life, whatever his True, Pure Heart's Desire was.

So it was that one day, at a large social gathering, he first saw HER—Princess Juanita, his own Beloved/Twin-Flame. She was a Divine Feminine Goddess incarnation of beauty and grace, both inside and out. They just stared at each other in their Love at First Sight, mesmerized by the overwhelming feelings, chemistry and electrical-magnetic attraction that they both instantly felt for each other.

It did not take long before they were married, in a lavish and wonderful Celebration Ceremony of Love. It was truly a "Live-Happily-Ever-After" energetic type of event, displaying such romantic True Love that had never before been seen nor experienced by the others around them. They truly were in Paradise, with plenty of time to experience the most intensely passionate, fulfilling, multiple-orgasmic tantric lovemaking while they both remembered being together in their past lives. They had been Sacred Tantric Life Partners in the ancient Tantric Oracle Rainbow Crystal Temples of Lemuria.

Ultimately, they had several beautiful and evolved children, and they had Blessings and Miracles constantly occurring around them. Others marveled at how Blessed and wonderful their life truly was, and at what an inspiration they were for others seeking such a life: A life with not only Higher Purpose, but also balanced with constant demonstration of kindness and generosity of spirit. Both Job and Juanita helped many less fortunate whenever they could. They and their family were very well liked because of these Higher spiritual and noble qualities. One could say that they were truly Blessed on so many levels, beyond human understanding.

The Shift to Terror and Horror

One day, things began to inexplicably turn from all the good and joy to the worst things and that one could ever explain, imagine or understand. There seemed to be no explanation for this bad luck, this sudden turn of events.

This negative shift started out subtle, then gradually things began to escalate from bad to worse. Over a number of months, Job and his family experienced sudden financial losses that resulted in them loosing ownership over their vast wealth and properties. They were suddenly forced to move out of their own palace home, to end up destitute and on the streets. They were without any financial help from others who had originally respected and looked up to them. Job's own family relatives and friends turned against him, and all kinds of lies and made-up rumors were spread about him, destroying his originally positive reputation. Now his character was forever unjustly vilified, in the most bizarre and unimaginable ways. He literally lost everything he had ever owned and overseen, with nothing left to his name on a material level.

It was as if pure, horrifying evil began to attack their entire family, as if they were suddenly being energetically targeted on every level. It seemed as if there was absolutely nothing they could do that would protect them and stop this unspeakable horror and terror that was attacking. It was not just horror and terror on the 3D conscious waking level of their life, but also in their dream states, where they suddenly began to experience horrifying nightmares and visions of impending doom for themselves. Even in the dreams there was nothing they could do to stop these terrible events from occurring soon. Nasty and terrifying demonic forces began their onslaught against Job and his family on all levels, to destroy their Hope and Faith about life and their very existence.

Job's ability to see into the Akashic Records could not account for what they were so suddenly experiencing, as there was no negative karma that could explain this; it made no sense. Their entire existence became the worst Hell on Earth that one can even imagine, with absolutely no Higher explanation to give them any insight or help in their intense plight.

Job was naturally a courageous man, but now intense fear began to penetrate his heart and soul. He heard and saw, clairvoyantly and clairaudiently, these horrible demons that were now constantly attacking and terrorizing him and his family day and night. He heard the horrible things they screamed at him. They gloated about all the nasty tortures that they were planning for him and his family, and they bragged about there being absolutely nothing he could do about it. They also screamed that God and Higher Forces had now deserted Job. They claimed that he was entirely on his own, without any help or Guidance from on High, whether inwardly or outwardly.

Up until then, Job was always able to get powerful and quick Insights and communications from God and the Higher Light Forces. All of a sudden, it was as if God, the Divine Source, the Great I Am That I Am, and his own I Am Presence/Higher Self had disappeared, as if they had never even existed. They were replaced now by a deep sense of strange emptiness, of being entirely on his own. There was no God Essence or Divine

Higher Connection of any kind that he could tune into, as he always could before.

It was as if God truly did not exist, or that if He did exist, He was merely a fickle God, without any real Divine Plan, Justice or Mercy. There seemed only to be random, chaotic disorder, and any belief in a Higher Power seemed to be the belief of fools and idiots. It was as if Job had been fooled his entire life with a stupid and psychotic belief that had absolutely no evidence or proof of any kind. It was as if everything was just a series of pure coincidences and so-called luck, as if there was no Higher Power and never had been. At least, that was what the demons now attempted to make him believe, despite all his memories to the contrary.

Job was devastated in ways too hard to describe or even to understand. He struggled to somehow, despite how horrible and hopeless things were and how sophisticatedly convincing the demonic forces were, to still keep his Faith and Hope that things would somehow turn around. It might be said that Job was the first person who demonstrated so powerfully what is described as "blind faith."

Job's "blind faith" was not based on any silly, immature, irrational belief with no evidence to back it up. Job had what would be termed "photographic memory," ensuring that everything he had ever experienced was forever recorded holographically in detail in his conscious brain and mind. He knew that he had not just imagined what he could remember from up until this sudden, horrific turn of events. It did not make sense to him WHY this change had come, but he refused to give up Hope.

As a man of great intelligence, he had always been able to balance his "left and right sides of his brain," so that his left brain intellectual intelligence was balanced with his right brain spiritual-psychic intuition. In this balance, he was always able to get the insights that he needed. Now, though, to continue on without his intuition, he must somehow find the insight through his highly developed qualities of logic and reason. How, he did not know.

The horrible and terrifying onslaught only continued to get worse, with no let-up, as these demonic forces sought to also drive Job and his family unsane and into total madness with no possible return to sanity, peace or relief. As this horrendous and insidious attack against him and his family only intensified, Job watched in horror and hopelessness as each of his innocent children were tortured and killed in horrible, sadistic ways.

He cried out to God so many times, pleading, begging and praying for help, for any Divine Intervention to save his family. But nothing occurred to stop these horrific and cruel deaths. His guilt at not being able to protect and save their lives himself ate at his sobbing heart and his conscience. The forces of darkness laughed and enjoyed Job and his family's intense suffering, as they created more loush (the negative energy that was created from intense agony and suffering of souls).

Then, Job watched in horror as his Beloved, Juanita, started to suffer intensely from a weird viral disease that caused much physical pain and a crippling of her entire body. As with their children, Job could not help her or comfort her in any way, no matter how much he wanted to. He helplessly watched her waste away, her physical body becoming skin and bones as she cried out in her agony, pleading for him to kill her to stop the unimaginable level of pain she was enduring. This continued for many months, until she slowly died in horrible agony.

Job's utter hopelessness and guilt, over his failure to protect his Beloved and his precious children from such horror and pain beyond human understanding, caused agony of the spirit of such a level that no human had ever experienced until that moment. The demonic forces had gained partial control over him, in a type of demonic, psychic "MK-Ultra mind control." Job intensely fought this energetic control over his mind, body, and soul.

This particular form of mind control, on this more 3D physical level, was perfected in the 1950s and '60s by the CIA to control and brainwash people. Because of the intense forms of psychological torture and sleep and food depravation that they were put through, the victim gives into the program. They are then totally controlled, and can also be programed into becoming types of negative sleeper agents who can be used for assassinations and other covert espionage work that their conscious mind does not even know about. This allowed these more modern-day CIA "handlers" to train and program people to do things that their normal, conscious self and mind would never ethically and morally do. After finding out what they had done, the victims were then blackmailed to do even worse things for these cabal captors.

But what these cabal controllers did not know, is that numerous Higher Beings specifically had taken Earth embodiment to take on this karma, in God's Cosmic Covert Sting Operation. These Higher Beings infiltrated the dark side and these mind control programs. Even though these souls initially became "dark hats," eventually their previous more powerful, Higher Programing, "kicked in". They had undertaken powerful Higher Dimensional Elohim programming of the Light while aboard the Merkabah Light ships prior to taking Earth embodiment, to remind their conscious self of who they REALLY were and what they needed to do to take down the cabal.

Many of these former dark hats broke away from this early MK-Ultra programming to turn on their handlers. Since they had all the secrets of the cabal, they could now expose and end this whole plan for world control. This is partly how the whole Q White Hat Alliance came about (with much help from off-planet), to Liberate this planet once and for all from the illuminati/satanic cabal deep state.

Getting back to Job and what he was still experiencing in the final months of his life: Job had also been infected by a weird type of virus, similar to the flesh-eating virus. It was eating his whole body slowly, from the inside and out, and he was in the most unbelievable pain. He welcomed the pain in an attempt to appease his guilt-ridden mind after not being able to protect and help his own Beloved Juanita while she was still alive. He felt he must be punished for this inability.

When I first had this Vision of Job and what he endured, it was an incredibly intense experience. I was viewing it in a very detached way (Thank God!), so as not to be too overwhelmed with all the intensely horrible details of Job's and his family's suffering and what they went through. Not all of the events were negative, some were actually extremely uplifting and inspiring, especially toward the end of the Vision. I was not shown every single moment of Job's life, instead many images flashed before my eyes. This helped give me a more complete overview of his life and what he, his wife and his family experienced.

The Challenge and the Volunteer

One of the many images that was revealed to me was the moment when Juanita had died and her soul and spirit finally left her horribly tortured body to suddenly be free of all that pain. Now, her soul finally soared in peace, able to look down on her own Beloved Job who was still suffering horribly back on Earth. She suddenly understood and remembered the reason for all this pain, she remembered what had happened prior to them both taking Earth embodiment on an important mission for Earth's humanity.

As Higher Beings, Juanita and her Twin-Flame, Job, were part of Higher Intergalactic Councils. The councils consisted of many Elohim, Archangels, and other Light Beings, races, and species from many Higher Dimensions, worlds, and realms. They were all specifically helping Earth to eventually be Liberated from the luciferian-satanic forces that had infiltrated Earth.

She remembered when the luciferian forces (which consisted of many archons, reptilians, draconians, negative annunaki, and various other demonic forces) had challenged the Higher Light Forces: They did not believe that there was even *one* human mortal Volunteer living upon Earth who could endure and survive their attacks if the Higher Light Forces would temporarily take away their protection and guidance, leaving that person entirely on their own. The "Wager" or "Challenge" was basically that if there was even one soul spiritually strong enough, virtuous and faithful enough to endure such a negative experience while STILL being able to keep their Faith in God, then they "promised" that they would all come back to the Light and sincerely embrace God's Divine Plan. God/Divine Source and all Higher Light Forces had to completely stand aside and allow them to do whatever they wanted to that soul, no matter how cruel, horrible and evil it would be. The Higher Light Forces did not REALLY believe that the dark side was being sincere in their challenge. However, if there actually was a soul who could truly demonstrate such Faith and Patience and endure such a major test, then this was an opportunity to prove that there WAS at least one soul who could keep their faith no matter what the imbalanced forces did to this person. So, a great Cosmic Announcement was sent out all over the Universe.

That Cosmic Announcement was actually similar to when Lord Sanat Kumara (the Lord of Venus), many millions of years ago had sent out the Great Clarion Call,. He was asking for Volunteers who would be willing to take Earth embodiment to help anchor Light upon Earth until the Light had been able to overcome the darkness that had manifested upon Earth. This was when the 144.000 Volunteer souls from all over the Universes first took Earth Embodiment. We all took a very Sacred Vow; that we would not stop incarnating upon Earth, no matter how many lifetimes it would take, until the Light WAS Victorious. Finally, after eons of time has passed, in this present lifetime we are about to achieve our goal, and our missions will then be over. Since that original Core Group of the 144,000 souls, the number of Volunteers has increased: now over half of the world's population are in fact from somewhere else all over the Universes. We are all working together in our combined mission of Light to finish up this Great Liberation and Planetary Ascension of Mother Earth.

This more recent Cosmic Announcement, following the dark forces' challenge, was specifically asking for just one soul. One soul, out of the entire Universes, out of all dimensions of Light, who had the specific combination of these Higher qualities, who could endure despite what unthinkable and unspeakable suffering would be forced upon this soul (as well as members of his family) once they took Earth embodiment. So it was, that out of the many applicants who submitted their desire to do this, and after much Higher Testing, one of Archangel Michael and Lady Faith's Cosmic Sons passed the necessary tests. It was determined that he had the greatest chance to actually accomplish the mission—the mission that many other beings thought would be too difficult, even impossible.

Job would be endowed with numerous spiritual and metaphysical abilities while in Earth embodiment, such as an ability to easily communicate with God/Divine Source and all Higher Light Brings that he had known while in the Higher Realms. Because his Cosmic Amnesia Veils were not in the way of all of his memories, he was able to consciously remember many more of his experiences in these Higher Realms prior to taking Earth embodiment than most other Volunteers. What Job would not be allowed to remember was the specific Higher Council meeting where he had been Chosen to be the soul who would have the chance to demonstrate his absolute Faith in God and the Higher Forces. Yes, the "Ultimate Test of Tests" is when one *does not even suspect* (on the conscious level) that one is being tested by God and the Higher Forces. The Ultimate Test is when everything that one Knew and believed, everything that had given meaning to one's existence, is suddenly shaken up, energetically contradicted and "proved to be wrong" in the most sophisticated and insidious ways, to completely and utterly convince one that it was all just psychotic, silly and childish beliefs.

Now that Juanita once again was aware of why she and the souls of her earth children, who were also Higher Beings, had chosen to endure this test with Job, she wanted very much to directly communicate this fact to her Beloved. But she knew, as did the rest of the Spiritual Hierarchy, that part of the protocols of the Sacred Agreement concerning the Test was that Job was not allowed to know that he was being tested. All she could do was to watch from the Higher Realms with Unbearable Compassion, as her Beloved Divine Other Half was enduring in his extreme and horrific suffering, as no soul had ever endured before while being in Earth embodiment. She could do nothing to alleviate his suffering even the tiniest bit. Now she deeply regretted that she had agreed with him when he had been Chosen to endure this heavy challenge that no soul had ever had to face before.

But, then, it was as if God/Divine Source suddenly Guided her to do something that somehow would energetically, help Job in the end "when and if" he actually passed this Ultimate Test of Tests. It just so happened, that many miles from where Job and her family had lived before they had each died under the most horrible and painful of circumstances, the daughter of another ruler in a nearby country was lying close to death from sickness. The significant thing about this particular lady she was about the same physical age as Juanita had been while she had been alive—she even looked very similar, as if she could have been a twin to Juanita.

Juanita could tell that the lady lay very close to death, growing weaker by the day. Suddenly, Juanita heard the Divine Source telling her that if she wanted, she could have her own soul come back into Earth embodiment in place of the lady's soul, as a "Walk-In" in a "soul transfer." Because Juanita's soul happened to be a little stronger in spirit, especially after what she had just endured with Job while she was still alive, she managed to heal her new body back to vibrant health and well-being.

The father of the lady who had lain close to death happened to be Clairvoyant, with many Gifts of the Spirit. He had perceived with great sadness that his beautiful daughter was about to die, and that even his own healing abilities could do nothing about it. He watched as her spirit and soul departed her body—then suddenly saw the spirit of another beautiful soul suddenly take her place. He felt her Divine presence and understood some of why this soul transfer had just taken place. Now suddenly his own healing abilities were able to help Juanita heal her new body. Within a few days, she was completely well and in perfect health.

The next image that was shown to me, was Juanita having her own vision of the future: She was in her father's caravan, crossing the desert. In the sand of the desert up ahead they had seen what appeared to be the body of a man, more dead than alive. She had suddenly recognized her own Beloved lying there in the final moments of his life. He was still fighting to keep his Faith, despite the horrendous torture he had endured during the years he had been alone and on his own, with nothing to his name and only extreme levels of unbelievable suffering, as the demonic forces sought to gain total control over his mind, body and soul. They wanted him to curse out God for letting him suffer.

At one point in my vision I saw him stumble and then crawl with very little strength, from lack of food and water, and all the pain he had already been enduring, into some kind of very swampy marsh. It was very filthy, nasty and smelly, and he fall into it. It covered his body, which was already being eaten alive from that horrible type of flesh-eating virus. Now his pain and extreme suffering was even worse, as the filth from the swamp infected his sores and wounds from the virus, now his body was breaking out with infected, agonizing, pussy sores all over it.

Later, I saw him crawling in the desert with his last ounce of strength. The sand was so hot that merely touching it could cause painful burns to his bare flesh. All he could do was to slowly crawl on his bare hands. Most of his body was bare, the few dirty soiled rags now hardly covered any of his body. Most of his body was touching the sand, so his painful flesh was being burned alive. There was no shelter or cover available in which he could get out of these horrible conditions. The powerful sun beat down upon him, causing a horrible sunburn and dehydrating his tortured body. There were many large sand spiders and scorpions that began to attack him, eating his flesh from his body.

The demonic forces also kept energetically torturing him, enjoying his suffering. They were laughing and gloating at him about all the many types of extreme suffering he was enduring. They told him not only that had God entirely forsaken him, but that this proved how much God was truly cruel, unjust and unmerciful, as He allowed such great suffering as Job's. They told him that all he had ever believed was obviously just a fantasy. The dark forces told him that he must curse out God to be able to get any help from them, and that they would then remove all his suffering instantly and give him anything he wanted. All he had to do was this one thing; sell his soul to the devil and renounce his faith once and for all, forever.

But as mentioned before, there was one thing, even in his greatest agony and suffering, that Job had been endowed with from the time of his birth: He had a very developed intellectual left brain, which had been balanced with a very intuitive, psychic-spiritual right side of his brain. Even though his right brain was no longer presently working, because of his disconnect from God/Inner Self/Higher I Am Presence, the brilliant left side of his brain was endowed with much logic and reason. Most of all, he had been gifted by God/Divine Source with a very powerful photographic memory, allowing him, in holographic detail, to vividly remember every single thing he had ever experienced, seen and read throughout his life.

So even though he was now unable to experience communications from Divine Source and the many Higher Light Beings that he earlier had communicated with on a regular basis, he could clearly remember not only everything they had shared with him, but also the wonderful feelings and sensations of receiving Cosmic Downloads from God and the Higher Beings. In vividly remembering these specific and Sacred vibrations and Divine energies associated with these Higher Realms, he remembered the obviously compassionate nature of God.

Job was one of those rare individuals who, as a man, understood that the Divine Creator was not JUST a masculine force, but also consisted of the Divine Feminine; that it was definitely BOTH Masculine and Feminine. The Patriarchal, chauvinistic, narrow-minded old men who later compiled the Bible did not want to acknowledge that the Divine Creator was indeed both a masculine as well as a feminine force of Sacred Divine Intelligence. In my opinion, instead of always saying the "Heavenly Father God," one should refer to it as the "Heavenly Father-Mother God/Goddess" to truly be more accurate.

Job could also vividly remember several of his own past lives where he had been with Juanita, his Beloved, when she was his Sacred Tantric Life Partner in the ancient Lemurian Tantric Oracle Rainbow Crystal Temples. He could remember experiencing exquisite, multiple-orgasmic tantric lovemaking with her, and could remember how these were the moments when they both were the most directly and powerfully in touch and in communication with the Divine Source. This All-Knowing, All-Loving Divine Intelligence, which is both Divinely Masculine AND Divinely Feminine, was blessing them and all the other Tantric Twin-Flame couples for helping to anchor the Nirvanic Ecstasy Grid onto Mother Earth (as the Grid kept everything in Divine Balance).

I remember a funny, modern-day "religious commentary" that I saw on a billboard and postcard, which stated humorously: "Lying in bed on Sunday morning with your partner, (while she is) screaming 'Oh, my God, Oh my God!' (in joyous Ecstasy and Orgasmic Fulfillment) is not the same as being in church." I totally disagree, based upon what I have just shared! Our bodies are considered Temples of the Soul. In our (body) Temples we are truly Worshiping God/Goddess when we are with our Beloveds, our Twin-Flames, and are sharing this truly Divine, Sacred Uniting and Merging. Being able to experience this same Divine Connection that Job and his Other Half experienced, IS truly experiencing Nirvanic Ecstasy. (Hence the term "Nirvanic Ecstasy Grid.") We don't need some patriarchal old fart telling us what is and what is not being "Faithful to God." We know, just as all the Sacred Tantric Twin-Flame couples in ancient Lemuria knew. Strange and weird things energetically occur when the "religious leaders" take celibacy vows, as has been documented; so many of the priests become perverted in their sexual orientation, becoming child pedophiles and into satanic human sacrifice.

Getting back to those final moments of Job's life: Job's photographic memory and his ability to use logic and reason were things the imbalanced forces had not considered when they had thrown out this Cosmic Challenge to the Light Forces. They had not stipulated in the Agreement what exact qualities and characteristics the person was allowed to have.

As mentioned before, Job could remember all of his sensations of great Compassion and Mercy from the Divine Source and the Higher Beings that he used to communicate with all the time. Despite not having his normal very developed intuition, his logic and reason still allowed him to be able to remember how incredibly great and wonderful things were before this hellish time, despite what horrible things he was now experiencing. Because he believed in an orderly Universe, his logic and reason told him that even though things were suddenly (temporarily) all screwed up and made no sense ("Murphy's Law" and

"Mercury Retrograde" having gone "absolutely crazy and out of control" and "on steroids"), he still had faith that the Universe would soon return to its normal balance and order. While he did not know why this all was occurring, or why it was even allowed by God to occur, Job's logic and reason, combined with all the wonderful intense personal feelings and sensations of experiencing God's presence so strongly, told him that the world had to soon become orderly and balanced once more. Since he himself was not God, he could not claim to Know when, exactly, that God would return things back to normal—but he had Faith that it would.

This quality and belief gave Job HOPE, and the dark forces could not initially seem to shake Job's Faith, no matter how much they tried. It angered them even more that he stubbornly held onto his Faith in God. But as he got weaker and weaker, in more and more agony, and closer to death, it became much harder for him to continue to hold on to his faith. The dark forces had been using these energetic manipulative psychic techniques mentioned earlier to trick Job into saying anything against God, even "accidently," to take away all his pain and to find the peace and relief that he so desperately needed.

The Test's Final Moments

Finally, as Job could endure it no longer, now about to die from all that he had endured, the dark forces felt that he was indeed about to say the words they wanted him to say, that would seal his fate and would allow them more complete control over his mind, body and soul. As Job struggled in those last brief moments, knowing that he was indeed about to die, he still attempted to hold on to his faith—but now he felt that his faith began to slip away from him, no matter what he attempted to do to hold on to it.

I was as if in a vision within a vision, I saw Job somewhat symbolically. It was as if he was hanging over a dark and hellish abyss, about to fall into it and with his soul about to be taken over by the hordes of hell. His weak and painful fingers could hold him no longer, they began to slip off the cliff. In another moment, he would fall into those dark depths of hell, and there seemed to be nothing that Job could do about it. No matter how hard and determined he had been, with the greatest Intent to hold on to his faith, it did not seem to matter. But then, just as all seemed lost, I heard him utter very weakly with his last breath, "I still Love you, God!"

Just moments before, Juanita was sitting on her camel in her father's caravan, just as she had seen in her own earlier vision. And sure enough, as in the vision, someone had spotted what appeared to be a body up ahead in the hot sand. Juanita remembered what she had seen, and quickly jumped down onto the sand to run over to the body of her Beloved, who was only alive by a thread. As she gathered him up into her arms, she heard his last gasp of his Love for the Divine Creator, and she felt that he did not feel any hatred or anger toward the dark forces.

At that moment, with great Love and Unbearable Compassion in her heart for him, she knew he had been Victorious! He had proven his Faith and Dedication, and had passed this Test of Tests (or, as I like to call it, the "M.O.A.T."; the

"Mother of All Tests"!). Suddenly, something had appeared up in the sky, huge and glowing, with powerful and beautiful lights and rays. As the huge Merkabah Light Ship came down quickly to hover overhead, it bathed Job and Juanita in the most wonderful of energies and in rays of joy, beauty and celebration. An instant later, they were beamed up through the glowing beam that had enveloped them, transported aboard this Ship of the Celestial Heavens. Job fell unconscious but was alive.

Job awoke sometime later, to find himself inside some kind of wonderful soothing, and healing chamber that surrounded his body. He saw that all the nasty muck from the swamp, and all the dirt, sweat and all his suffering, were all gone. All his wounds were now healed. He lay there in such indescribable peace, relief, and utter contentment. The cover on his rejuvenation chamber was slowly opened, and he saw his Beloved, Juanita, who was beautifully dressed in soft, comfortable garments. Many Higher Beings were standing around, smiling at him in their own joy of his Great Victory of the Light.

Job had more than shown and proven to the dark side that there WAS indeed at least one individual who had kept his Faith despite what they had done to him—as well as been able to Forgive those forces who had unmercifully tortured him. He could now also consciously remember the Higher Council meeting he had attended, where he had Volunteered and had been Chosen to be the one to demonstrate this Great Faith and Love for Divine Creation. He would forever be Celebrated for his courage and determination.

Suddenly, both Job and Juanita were beamed back down to Earth, and they found themselves back with their family in their palace, right before all of the hellishness had occurred in that old timeline. It now appeared that a new timeline had replaced the old, before all of the horrible things had a chance to occur. It was now as if they never did occur, so Job would not have to actually remember (with his photographic memory) all of his and his family's suffering.

Yet his story (or rather parts of his story) was later written down and recorded. An edited, watered-down version was allowed a place in the Bible, but in my opinion you have now had the chance to hear, as the famous radio commentator, Paul Harvey, used to say, "the rest of the story!"

"A Little More Up Close and Personal With My Beloved, Celeste."

CHAPTER 12

Rescued by My Beloved, Celeste, and the Beginning of Many Blessings and Miracles

As I lay there in the dark, on the cold concrete floor of the homeless shelter, many thoughts about my life passed through my mind. I dwelled on all the wonderful and awesome moments during that special week, when I had experienced such incredible fulfillment with my Beloved. I wondered if I would ever be able to see her again, to hold her in my arms, and to experience once more the most intensely fulfilling, heavenly exquisite intimacy with her, of the kind that few humans in more modern times have been able to experience.

Even as I remembered these happy thoughts, the stark, depressing, and hopeless nature of my present situation bore down upon me. It only had seemed to get worse every day that I was at this hell hole called a homeless shelter. I knew that I would indeed starve to death, if I did not soon somehow manifest more money to be able to buy the healthy foods that I needed. I had refused to eat any of the very unhealthy stuff that they called "food" there at the shelter.

Many people, who do not have or understand the higher ideals and specific important health protocols that I had, might say that "beggars can't be choosers"; that eating these things would be better than nothing, especially if the result would be starving to death. But these people would not understand that some of us follow a higher vibrational way of life, which also includes the foods that we ingest. I truly consider my body a temple, which I must keep pure and unpolluted. Because of my mission and purpose in life, it has always been important for me to only put very healthy foods in my body in order to be a clear channel. Plus, I still had the faith that somehow, someway, a miracle was yet to occur. A miracle that would result in me being able to escape into a better situation. I did not know what the miracle would be, but I refused to give up, even though I was growing weaker from not having eaten for a few days. I was using the little bit of money that I still had to my name to fill up a glass gallon bottle with purified water from a nearby water machine. I was determined to at least drink pure water, out of a non-toxic PBA container, avoiding the unhealthy out-of-the-tap water that contained fluoride, chlorine and other unhealthy, toxic substances.

As the days and weeks began to stretch out to what seemed forever, with no hope in sight, the imbalanced forces began to energetically torture me with all kinds of horrible predictions of me starving to death and never getting out of there, unless I would accept their help (in other words, sell my soul to the devil). They promised me that they could do all kinds of wonderful things to alleviate my suffering and struggle, that they could easily manifest Miracles that would forever change my life, allowing me to have anything and everything that I craved. Yes, they attempted to bribe me with their promises of help—all I had to do was to sell out to them and denounce all things sacred and pure of the Divine Universal Source/God.

The First Miracle: Celeste Appearing

Finally, as the dark forces grew more intense with all that they were attempting to ensnare me with, I had enough of their nasty and manipulating attempts to tempt me. Suddenly, with great intensity, I told them to back off, to go back to hell where they were from, and to leave me alone. I told them that they would never be able to accomplish what they were attempting to do, despite me being in a more desperate situation than I had ever been before. They had obviously thought that their torture would spiritually weaken me to a point where they could wear me down. I lay there in the darkness, surrounded by the other hundred guys who were also lying all over the floor, sleeping or attempting to finally get to sleep. A few moments later, I suddenly began to feel some kind of energy shift occurring in the area of the floor where I happened to be lying. I sat up, attempting to determine what exactly was occurring, as the imbalanced forces were somehow no longer there.

Suddenly, an area of a few feet (about the size of my sleeping area) began to light up. A Higher Dimensional Portal opened, to reveal the most gorgeous Goddesses I had ever seen manifesting to me. In great joy and excitement, knew that it was HER—my Beloved, an Immortal Intergalactic Goddess. She was hovering just above the floor, looking down at me with such deep and intense Love and compassion. I realized that I was seeing her with my clairvoyant sight, and that others who were lying nearby would not see anything out of the norm. For me she was very real, even though she was appearing to me on the 5th Dimensional (etheric) level.

I say that I Knew it was HER, my Beloved, my Twin-Flame. Initially this was confusing to me, as her beautiful energetic presence felt somewhat similar to what I felt when I had been around Cindy. Now this energetic chemistry was actually stronger. She quickly cleared up my initial confusion. She explained that she (part of her Higher Essence/soul/spirit) had merged for a short time with the soul that had already been in Cindy's body, as a "walk-in". The Higher Self of the other soul had agreed to allow Lady Celeste to do this for the few weeks that she needed. Lady Celeste did this walk-in "to get my attention" (as she expressed it), for her and I to have a chance to enjoy personally anchoring in the Higher Energies as a Sacred Tantric Twin-Flame couple, and for us to be able to reactivate the Nirvanic Ecstasy Grid. We had needed to begin the process of restoring Earth back to the original Paradise, as it was Destined to re-manifest back onto Earth in the coming time.

Celeste's sudden manifestation at the shelter that evening felt like the Cosmic calvary coming in to rescue me from all the hardship and struggle that I had been going through since I had last connected with her (while she had been a Walk-in briefly sharing Cindy's body). Now that Celeste's soul was once more fully merged back with all of her true Higher Self, Lady Celeste, she told me that she had many special powers and abilities. As my Twin-Flame, she was "authorized" to use these now, to help me transform my life. She would, in fact, manifest numerous Miracles and Blessings for me from then on.

I was so excited to now have my own Cosmic True Love around me on the etheric/5D level, where I could see her clearly. At times it felt like she was almost at the 3D physical level when she would come around, so intense and powerful was our Love for each other. I could not thank her enough, nor find the words that even remotely could express how much I Loved and appreciated that she now appeared with a much more direct presence. For so many years she had been forced to be much more in the background, and I had not been able to ever see or speak with her. The only exception had been briefly one time many years before, in 1981. It was right after I had gotten married to my ex, and we had just had one of our many horrible, "WWIII" emotionally toxic fights.

My First, Brief Meeting with Celeste

The fights between my ex and I were always horribly devastating to me—emotionally, spiritually, and on every level. The imbalanced forces loved to come through her all the time to attack me. This happened many thousands of times throughout our relationship, and usually when I least expected it. I knew on an emotional level that I should have ended that very toxic relationship much earlier. Instead, I kept rationalizing to myself that I had to continue it, quote: "for the sake of the mission, I must *stay in it* to (supposedly) finish my mission." (As the years and decades passed, I slowly realized that "for the sake of the mission"—especially my emotional health, well-being, and very survival—I actually had to get *out* of that relationship.)

Celeste had briefly appeared to me for a few minutes in 1981, after I had been so devastated from the fight with my ex. In her intense, Unconditional Love and compassion for me (her Other-Half, who was in Earth embodiment), she would often say something to me: "what about your own emotional health and needs, and your own well-being?" I realized only years later that it had been Celeste who had said this to me, again and again after all these horrible fights. As the "masochist" that I apparently was, I would just blow it off in my dedication to the cause. I was dedicated to the Greater Mission, "no matter what the emotional price would be." I had been reluctantly willing to go through emotional hell, as I thought it was a part of my incredibly difficult mission. I had allowed my own happiness, emotional health and well-being to be constantly and completely compromised and devastated.

The years began to pass. Although the imbalanced forces continued to energetically, emotionally, and psychologically attack me through my ex, Celeste's Love and protection for me (that she was constantly using to protect me from being killed directly by the cabal) also began to influence me. I began to come to the self-realization that I had to allow myself to change my life, realizing that I could finally allow myself to manifest a new and better reality that would allow me the emotional peace and space that my soul craved.

Celeste Showing Me A Way Forward

Finally my Beloved, Celeste, was able to reveal herself to me more directly, compared to before when she always had to be in the background. It was so wonderful to energetically interphase with her there in the homeless shelter; to be able to not only see her and communicate directly with her, but also to feel and experience her awesome, powerful Divine Feminine Goddess presence and her intense, Unconditional Love and support for me. These amazing feelings that she triggers in me are why I constantly use the phrase, "Blessed and Blissed by Celeste!"

One of the first things that Celeste told me that I needed to do, was to send an email blast to everyone on my email list, informing them about my challenging predicament. I had to "sincerely speak from my heart" as Celeste expressed it. I would be letting them know about the challenge I was facing, and simply ask them if they could help me with a donation—any donation. I would let them know that a donation would help me to get through this present predicament (until Celeste could energetically manifest further Miracles and Blessings for me).

I like to feel that I am self-sufficient, and I do not like to have to ask anyone else for help if I do not need to. Believe it or not, I have always had a small personal challenge in asking others for help, especially for financial help. So, it was a little challenging to ask for help through this email blast.

However, I really had not expected all of the amazing responses that I received over the days and weeks following the email blast! It blew my mind how caring and compassionate people can be, and how they truly could sense and feel what I had been going through. I was amazed at how much financial Blessings I suddenly received, money that would allow me once again to be able to eat the healthy food I needed for my spiritual mission. I also know that Celeste helped to lovingly "overlight" (as mentioned before, I find this a better word than "overshadow") all these wonderful fellow Light Workers. Through her "over-lighting" they were more easily able to help me out, until I could begin to once more to do my personal Transformational Channeled Readings (with Celeste's help).

My laptop computer crashed on me a short time after that, and I lost my entire original email list. If you who are reading this book now are one of those who helped me, but did not receive my sincere thank you-reply to your generous emergency donation: Celeste and I both want to sincerely thank you for your help to get me past that extremely difficult time that I faced at the homeless shelter.

As the days began to go by, Celeste continued to energetically manifest her wonderful Divine presence around me every day, helping me to a much more positive view upon my future. She told me that she was in the process of energetically helping to get me out of the shelter ASAP. I Knew with Faith that she would help get me back on track, manifesting more individuals contacting me to schedule in sessions. She helped me to make some more connections in the Sarasota area in Florida, to possibly be sponsored and hosted for not only places to stay, but also for workshops.

So, it was: With great relief, I was invited to come to Sarasota, and stay for a few weeks at a couple of different people's places. I did a couple Readings, as well. Then, suddenly, my laptop crashed. This caused me to lose everything on it, including my original list of email addresses for the email blasts that I had done. This was a major problem, as I did not have enough money to purchase another laptop.

In addition, the laptop crash presented me with another major challenge, and I did not know what I was going to do about it. I still had my small, portable digital recorder, which worked just fine. Because it was several years old, in order to be able to use it and then "dub" a copy for my clients of the session that I just recorded, I had used a correspondingly old version of the "sound organizer" program. My recorder will only work with that original version of the program, not with any newer version. Unfortunately, every year Sony (the company that had sold me the miniature digital recorder) release a new version of the program. To be able to use the more recent version of "sound organizer," I would need to purchase a correspondingly new digital recorder. So, it appeared that I was screwed as far as being able to record and dub copies of my sessions for my clients.

One reason that I always record my sessions, is that they are way too long for anyone to be able to remember all that was shared with them. But more than that, most people experience actually hearing information in the dubbed copy that was not originally there during our session. So, the main reason for playing back the dubbed copy is to allow the Higher Light Encodements that have been Energetically Downloaded through the Higher Elohim Consciousness Technologies to activate one's DNA/RNA. This then causes unique, individualized Transformational changes for each person who has experienced a session.

However, Celeste told me, "not to worry"; she would manifest another laptop for me, as well as somehow manifest another copy of the old version of the "sound organizer" program that I needed in order to actually use my digital recorder. She also told me that she would soon manifest an apartment of my own, so that I would not have to be dependent on others to have a place to stay. These were just a few of the things that Celeste promised me would soon be manifesting into my life. I Knew that my Beloved, who is also my Muse, *would* in fact manifest these Miracles and Blessings for me, just as she told me she would.

Right after I was invited to stay as a guest in Sarasota, I heard about a New Age networking event that was being held at another person's home. Celeste strongly urged me to go to, telling me that I was going to make a very important connection there that would change my life considerably for the better. So, of course, I made sure to go, with a hopeful sense of something really great happening.

Fredrick's Gift and Insights

When I first arrived at the event and started to go into the large living room, I noticed that there was probably at least about 30 to 40 people standing around, visiting and networking with each other. I walked in, planning to talk to whoever I felt energetically connected to, and I could feel Celeste nearby. I noticed a particular man who at that moment had his back turned away from me, apparently speaking to someone else. All of a sudden he turned around and looked in my direction, as if he had sensed my presence in the room. There was something that seemed kind of "official" about him, as if he held an important position of some kind.

He spoke briefly to the person that he had been visiting with, then walked over toward me and introduced himself. He said he had heard about me and my spiritual work for a number of years, and that he had wanted to connect with me for a while. Then he told me something that was "quite interesting," to put it mildly. He mentioned that he was a member of the Q White Hat Alliance.

He was presently living in the area and wanted to know what he could do to help me in any way. I hesitated at first about telling him of the needs and challenges that I had been facing for quite some time, but I could feel Celeste urging me to do so. So, I did. He listened very intently to what I was sharing, then looked at me, smiled and said, "Well, I guess I need to give you your own apartment." For a moment, I did not quite seem to hear what he had just said to me; it did not initially register with my brain. What he had just said he could do for me was an absolutely amazing, major thing. He patiently repeated it again, as I just blinked at him, trying to figure out whether he was really serious, if he was actually able to "give me my own apartment."

He next mentioned that yes, he could do this; he often set up safe houses and places to live for Alliance members and families. He felt that this was something he was guided to do for me, to enable me to "continue to do my spiritual work." I was in total shock over what he was proposing: Me actually having my own apartment where I would be able to have total privacy with no one else around (except for my Beloved, Celeste, of course!). A place where I could enjoy my own unique sojourn in my present journey in life.

Suddenly, I saw Celeste etherically standing nearby with a big smile on her lovely face. I realized then that she had spiritually "Over-Lighted" him, to help influence him in making his decision. His decision was something that not only would change *my* life in so many wonderful ways, but also would change life for *Celeste and I both,* on a very intimate level. Celeste smiled at me in her own joy as she said to me that this would allow her and I to have "lots of privacy together,". We would be able to, as she described it, "Bliss out together in intimate Energetic Ecstasy"! Yes, the need for a little "Cosmic Hanky-Panky"!

The White Hat Alliance man told me his name was Fredrick, even though I somehow sensed that this might have been an "anonymous" name that he was using for security reasons. He told me a lot of other interesting things. He had at one time been a member of the secret space program, as well as a "Remote Viewer" for the Special Forces in the military. He had also worked with the Dragon Families in Asia, to help bring in the new, worldwide "Quantum Financial system." This system is connected with what used to be referred to as "NESARA", which is now called "GESARA" ("Global Economic Security and Reformation Act"). It is right now behind the scenes in the process of replacing the old corrupt power elite central banking system. Planet Earth would soon be freed and Liberated from the satanic deep state cabal. He told me that, as early as within the next 2 to 3 years, (from 2018), the Plan is that Q and the Alliance will begin to expose and then arrest all of the cabal. Military tribunals were indeed going to occur, televised openly to the public.

On a more personal level he also mentioned having met his own Twin-Flame, who was the daughter of one of the major Dragon Families. He was about to go back and be with her for a while until his next mission of help to others. I was so excited about having made this connection with him. Not only because he had the ability to help me in such a major way, but also because he was a member of the Q White Hat Alliance.

(I know that the cabal deep state controlled mainstream ("lamestream") media, with all it's constant "fake news" negative propaganda and brainwashing of the masses, has attempted to debunk the reality of Q and the "Q drops." For those who are still skeptical of the reality of Q, just try to keep an open mind, and not let your programed Cognitive Dissonance about Truth and reality keep you from allowing yourself to check out this very informative Documentary. It truly shows the vast amount of accumulated evidence of Q's authenticity. The title is, "Ultimate QAnon Proofs (For Dummies!) Help Wake Up Your Friends with This Clear and Concise Exposé of Q—Volume 1," and you can find it on this link: https://stillnessinthestorm.com/2020/04/ultimate-qanon-proofs-for-dummies-help-wake-up-your-friends-with-this-clear-and-concise-expose-of-q-volume-1-video/)

Having made this awesome connection with a member of the Q White Hat Alliance, which also verified all that I had been tuning into earlier (along with Celeste's own personal verification of the Authenticity of Q), was a real game changer for me in so many ways. I was incredibly excited about this opportunity which had now suddenly been provided for me: to actually have a place of my own to continue to fulfill my mission, as well as to have a place where Celeste and I could enjoy each other's company in a much more private way (as Twin-Flame couples need).

Another major challenge occurred a couple of days later, when Fredrick took me to see my new apartment. As I got out of his car and walked with him up to the apartment, I was feeling excited and positive about this opportunity to have my own place. Fredrick and I had talked for a while the day before about what my future goals and plans were once I moved into the apartment. He was glad that he could help me in this way. It was going to be a wonderful change, after having stayed at numerous other people's places, to actually have a place of my own. A place that I could really refer to "as my own", rather than explain that I am "staying at someone else's place." I actually prefer to say that it is "Celeste's and my own." Even though she may not technically be here on the 3D level, she is still around me 24/7, Etherically-Energetically, and we are both really enjoying our wonderful experience of having plenty of "privacy to be together."

Of course, I would continue to accept other people's invitations in the future, once this book was published. I will be hosted and sponsored once again, for future workshops, Readings, media interviews, etc. I realized after having moved into her and my apartment that Celeste had planned this whole thing ahead of time—she knew the "Coronavirus pandemic" would occur, and that it would be the perfect time for her and I to work on this book together, while people were forced to temporarily stay home. (The "Coronavirus pandemic" was of course initially created and bio-weaponized by Bill Gates and George Soros of the cabal deep state, helped also by the corrupt WHO and CDC)

During Fredrick's and my conversation, he told me that I was welcome to invite anyone I wanted to come to the apartment. But, there was one stipulation/agreement that he told me I had to agree to ahead of time, or he could not allow me to have this apartment. I was at first surprised by the sudden demand that he was placing upon me. But then, after he explained to me why he was doing this, I fully understood why he had done so. He had been, and still was, an excellently trained remote viewer for the White Hat Alliance. He was a very spiritual, psychic and intuitive type person. He was always getting psychic "hits and hunches" about all kinds of things, especially about all the illegal and unspeakably evil things that the cabal was doing behind the scenes. He was determined to end the reign of the negative and twisted power elite worldwide, the child pedophiles, and the satanic sacrifice networks that the cabal constantly involved itself with. He often gets psychic messages from his own Higher Self and from the Higher Guides that he is very attuned to—the messages have helped him save people's lives.

He also confirmed to me that other members of the White Hat Alliance had gotten the E.T. Technology (referred to as the "Looking Glass") from the cabal. This device that had originally been used by the cabal for negative control of the future was now in the Alliance's hands, and they were using it to help humanity. By being aware of the cabal's (original, old timeline) plans, Q was able to so accurately predict events ahead of time. This is partly related to the numerous "Q posts" that allow the public to accurately be aware of the Alliance's plans. In addition,

President Trump (Q+) has been personally working with them (contrary to what all the constant negative, biased and cabal manipulated "fake news" is saying). The Alliance knew of the "Great Awakening" that was to occur from 2020 on.

Getting back to the single stipulation that I had to agree to, in order for me to have my own apartment: Fredrick looked at me very intently, I could sense that he was psychically tuning in on my life. He sensed all of the negative, stressful things that I had experienced before, things that had occurred in my personal life from years past that I definitely did not want to ever experience again. I did not even need to tell him anything, he now knew. He then looked very intently at me, and said meaningfully, "There is just one person from your past who, absolutely under NO circumstances, are you to allow this particular individual to ever be able to come to this apartment, or to even know exactly where it is, any time or ever in the future. Do you understand who I Am referring to, and agree to this?"

A moment later I knew exactly who he was referring to, and I agreed. The fact that Fredrick himself had tuned in to this person, that I did not even have to bring them up, was very interesting (to say the least). Besides, who in their right mind would have turned down this awesome opportunity to live at such a nice place as I would now be able to do?!

CHAPTER 13

Eliminating All Negative EMF, for Harmonious Living

After Fredrick had briefly shown me the apartment, he left to allow me to just walk around inside and take time to look it over more in-depth. Earlier, when Fredrick had first brought me inside, I had only briefly glanced into where my bedroom was going to be. To my consternation, I now felt that something was negatively energetically affecting the apartment. I had kind of ignored this when I had first arrived, because I was so excited about being given this apartment of my own.

I then knew what it was I was sensing, what it was that was negatively energetically bombarding my apartment as well as all other apartments in this apartment complex. It is something apartment complexes all over the U.S. have to put up with, until better and more safe technology is developed and installed.

I am referring to the "smart meters" that were installed on the building, right on the outside wall of my apartment, only a few feet away from my bedroom. There is plenty of documented information all over the internet on how deadly and toxic such high levels of electromagnetic fields (EMF) actually are for everyone. It was especially problematic as I was now going to have to sleep every night right beside this horribly high level of deadly EMF.

When I was in an earlier relationship with a lady named Laura, I used to live in Seattle, Washington. Laura and I, along with over 30 other individuals, filed a "Writ of Legal Notice" against the City of Seattle and the public utilities. We legally warned them that if they went ahead and deployed the many thousands of smart meters (which are part of the whole cabal planned "Agenda 21"), we were going to sue them for the personal health effects and damages that would result from the smart meters being put all over the city. Interestingly enough, within a short time after that, at least three of the City Council members suddenly decided to "retire." Of course, they all claimed on a public level that they were doing this for personal family reasons. However, we strongly believe that in truth the reason was the notice we had filed to them, and that they did not want to have to deal with all the possible legal repercussions that would have resulted if the City went ahead with their plans to force the smart meters on everyone in Seattle.

Now I was suddenly feeling confused regarding the opportunity to have this apartment: I had not expected (or rather had forgotten about) this one challenge of living here. If I chose to live here, it would be uncomfortable, energetically toxic, and unhealthy to my immune system, because of how extremely high the EMF was. What was I to do?

The Q-link Devices and Celeste's Playful Teaching

Then, just as I was starting to worry about all this, Celeste etherically manifested herself to me to tell me a positive thing I had forgotten about: A few weeks before, she had guided me to purchase a couple of special pieces of alternative technology called "Q-Link." Interesting enough, they had changed to this name from "Clarius Technologies." I actually used to sell and distribute these products many years earlier. Even though the company itself (Q-Link) does not ever make any claims of what this technology can or cannot do, it was the opinion, of one of the original researchers from years before that it alters the negative EMF fields into the "Schuman Resonance" (the natural magnetic field of Earth). After much testing, this theory seemed to be verified, according to this particular researcher. I cannot ever make or legally claim that this is true, but it is still my opinion—especially as Celeste and the Higher Forces have confirmed to me that this is true.

I was, once again, so happy and filled with such joy that my Beloved, Celeste, was always looking after me, protecting me against all kinds of possible negative and challenging situations. With her own Higher Elohim and Divine Goddess Awareness, combined with the advanced Consciousness Technologies on board the Merkabah Light ships, she was able to easily see ahead through the time-space continuum on this new timeline what I would need help on. Still, I was so appreciative of her and all that she was doing for me now that she was energetically with me all the time.

I sat there for a few minutes on the floor of my apartment, right near the wall of the bedroom where the twenty smart meters were located on the outside of the room. It did not take much to feel just how horrible the total amount of EMF was, from these combined smart meters constantly bombarding my apartment. I knew that I immediately had to go and get my two Q-Link devices, which I had placed in a small storage locker.

One of devices was the "Nimbus" device, a small device that basically looks like a large night light. It can either be placed directly into the side of one's laptop, or one can plug it into a wall socket using a small adapter. Once I had gone to purchase a small adapter and had plugged it into my bedroom wall, then "presto"; the entire EMF of about 60 feet around the device is totally altered into a more harmonious field, aligned with life force and beneficial to one's health and well-being. The other item was a small pendant, worn around the neck. Right after obtaining the Q-link pendant I had worn it most of the time, but for whatever reason I had forgotten to wear it these last few days.

Just as I was thinking about this, Celeste explained to me that she had temporarily influenced me to not wear it so that I would feel how bad the EMF actually was in the apartment. She wanted me to experience the contrast, to feel how much the Nimbus unit could actually alter the EMF. I could see and feel Celeste's Divine Goddess presence so intently, feeling how much she Loved me and was protecting me, allowing me this rare opportunity to experience the difference between what I felt now when I did not use this technology, and how it was shortly going to feel once I plugged in the Nimbus device. (I would also used my pendant all the time from now on.)

Before I left to get my Q-Link devices, as I asked Celeste something very important: If it was possible with her special Goddess powers and abilities, and if she was authorized to do it, could she enhance and strengthen my Q-link devices beyond what they were originally designed to be able to do (on this normal 3D level)? So that they would be stronger in their ability to alter/change/transmute EMF fields? She immediately told me that she would.

I then asked her one more question, and I asked her this with a True, Pure Heart's Desire not just for myself, but for everyone who would ever use any Q-Link devices. Could she do this same thing for all other Q-link devices as well (including all that would be designed and built by Q-Link technologies into the future), so that everyone else too could get the maximized energetic benefits that I would now get? Celeste immediately confirmed this to me. I was so happy and excited about what I just experienced—that I could ask on the sincere behalf of all Earth's humanity, and that they would now receive this extra energetic benefit because of my positive heart felt desire for them all.

This is an excellent example of that when we ask for something truly positive, anything that is in "Divine Order," then everyone does collectively benefit from each of our individual sincere desires and positive actions. All we need do is remember to include everyone else, remember that everyone else should be allowed to benefit from our "good graces" (given that their own Higher Self is in agreement). Be aware of the so-called "energetic disclaimer": that what we ask for must be in Divine Order.

There are certain rare exceptions that might keep our wish from affecting absolutely everyone, such as karma, useful learning experiences, etc. The world will continue to get better and better from the unlimited blessings and miracles that we bestow upon each other "anonymously".

I traveled to where my small storage locker was. I closed it down; I did not need it anymore now that I had my own place to put my few physical belongings. I then quickly caught the city bus to the Best Buy store, to purchase the small adapter that would allow me to plug the Nimbus device directly into the wall socket in my bedroom. After arriving at the store, I just walked around for a while, looking at everything, as it had been some time since I had last visited a Best Buy. I wanted to see if there was anything else that I might need for my apartment. Finally, I went up to one of the checkouts near the front of the store to purchase the adapter.

After my purchase, I walked a short distance to sit down on the bench that was near the front doors of the store. I sat only a few feet away from a wall alarm. About 20 feet away was a podium where a store employee stood, acting as a kind of security guard for everyone using the front entrance. As I sat there for a few moments, Celeste re-manifested herself etherically to me, just smiling in her love for me. Suddenly the alarm on the wall near me went off, starting to buzz loudly. The employee at the podium acted very surprised, and he came toward me. He asked me in an "accusatory" voice, "What are you doing?" He suspected that I had somehow caused the alarm buzzer to go off.

I instantly knew that Celeste had energetically triggered it, for some reason. She just giggled as if she were a small child having fun confusing and freaking out the human adults nearby. I wanted to laugh, but I forced myself to act as if I did not know what had actually occurred. I was definitely not going to explain to him that "my Immortal Intergalactic Goddess named Celeste, who was invisible to him but who I could very easily see, had just caused it go off with her supernatural powers"! No, I did not think he would believe me. I just sat there, attempting to appear unaware of why the alarm had gone off.

It seemed that Celeste was having fun with the alarm, like she just could not refrain herself. She caused it to go off again, now it was as if she wanted to emphasize something that was important for me to know. I could hear her laughing a little as she did so. The podium guy looked up startled and came over toward me again. Once more he asked me, "What are you doing?" I did think it was odd that he would even suspect that I was in any way responsible for these mysterious incidents of the alarm buzzer going off, as I had not walked over to the alarm, nor touched it in any way. But maybe he sensed on a subconscious level that I was somehow connected to the alarm buzzer being activated. Again I just looked at him, still appearing as innocent as I could. Again, I stated, "I haven't done anything."

Celeste was of course giggling and laughing about this whole thing. The guy looked at me quizzically, then turned back once more to whatever he had been doing at the podium before these two mysterious alarm incidents.

But of course I should have known that Celeste was not quite done with her little alarm game. After a few more minutes, I suddenly had the strong urge to take out the Nimbus device from its package, along with the little adapter. Plugging the Nimbus into the adapter, I got up and walked over to the wall. I inserted the adapter into the wall socket. No sooner than I had done this, than—wouldn't you know it—the wall alarm went off for the third time, as if to emphasize and confirm its subtle, but powerful effect on the EMF frequencies.

At the instant I plugged it in to the wall, I noticed a subtle change of the energy in the room, as if everything had altered into a much smoother and more harmonious feeling around me. Once more, with perhaps some exasperation this time, the podium guy started to come over toward me again. This time I quickly explained to him that I had just plugged a "special device into the wall socket that alters the EMF into a much more harmonious field." That was all I said. I included no explanation of how the two earlier "mysterious" alarm buzzings were caused, despite that my plugging the device into wall just now might somehow have caused the alarm to go off the third time.

The podium guy now had an even more puzzled look upon his face, and he just stood staring at me dumbfounded for a few seconds. Then he turned back once more to whatever he had been doing before these three weird alarm activations. I got up and walked out of Best Buy, to go back to my apartment. When I finally got back, I immediately went into my bedroom and sat down on the floor near to the wall socket, preparing to plug the Nimbus and adapter into it.

Celeste re-manifested to me once again, now in a much more serious mood. She quickly shared with me that she had specifically caused the Best Buy alarm to go off the three times (not once, not twice) to make it even more obvious that what offset the alarms was definitely her. She wanted it to be obvious that the alarms were not caused coincidently by any mundane, 3D effect that a skeptic would tend to use to explain away these three separate alarm activations. She did it so that the left, analytical side of my brain (which is also connected to one's ego conscious self) would have to acknowledge that it WAS, definitely, her who was doing it. This would confirm what the right, more intuitive side of my brain had already felt and sensed.

Another reason for her alarm activation was that later, when I would share this experience with others, the story would give credence to the fact that she had enhanced the Q-Link technology's abilities with her own cosmic, magical Goddess powers. Just as I had sincerely requested of her a little earlier.

Now, though, I had just one more little test to do, which would further confirm this more obvious effect of the Q-Link Technology's ability to transmute all the dangerous, toxic effects of the EMF into a more harmonious field. In the Best Buy store, I had already noted a subtle, but obvious change of the energy in the store immediately after plugging the device into the wall socket. Now, in my bedroom apartment, within a few feet of those twenty smart meters, it was time to experience an even more profound shift of energies.

I wanted to do it in such a way that I could rule out any so-called placebo effect. So, I cleared my mind as best I could of any expectations, and just waited a few moments. I specifically focused upon how bad the EMF was as it was bombarding my bedroom. Then I picked up the Nimbus and the adapter, and I plugged them into the wall socket. The Nimbus, about the size of a large night light, lights up (like a night light) to visually confirm that it is working.

Suddenly, I felt an obvious, major energy shift, from the horrible, discordant and uncomfortable sensations a moment before to a calm and peaceful feeling which now permeated my bedroom. I was especially impressed with that it was more extreme than what I had experienced in the Best Buy store.

Considering that each smart meter is literally giving off more EMF than one cellular tower does, these twenty smart meters were giving of EMF like twenty cellular towers. It was awesome to experience such a wonderful shift in my apartment's energy. I felt so Blessed by having had such wonderful guidance from Celeste to purchase the two devices. As I have been saying ever since my Beloved energetically came into my life, "I am Blessed and Blissed by Celeste!"

After a few moments of enjoying the new, more harmonious and peaceful sensations of what I would now always feel while living here in Celeste's and my new apartment, I decided to do a couple more major contrast tests by unplugging the Nimbus from the wall. Immediately all that discordant energy was back once again. It was so obvious to me what a difference this technology could do. One more time I plugged it into the wall, and once again the feeling of harmony and peace instantly returned.

The Dark Forces' Involvement in EMF

Initially, when Celeste and I first started to work together on this book back in late 2019, I had planned to add a few links to various alternate sources in which scientists and researchers had compiled the documented dangers of the 5G technology.

I was very concerned as I knew that the 5G grid was in the process of being set up all over the world, to be ready to be fully implemented sometime in 2020. I was planning to inform as many people as I could, once Celeste and I finally finished and published this book. There is plenty of this information available online. If one types in the search phrase "health dangers of the 5G technology" lots of links appear. I suggest that those who are ignorant or uneducated about how bad 5G is (compared to even the older 3 and 4G levels of EMF) do research this further.

I also do highly recommend using the Q-Link technology to overcome the normal unhealthy and uncomfortable effects of all EMF fields, especially those from smart meters and other devices that emit EMF.

As I mentioned before, Q-Link Technologies will not make any medical claims. I understand they refrain from this as the various (corrupt) agencies like the FDA, CDC, WHO, and Big Pharma do not really want one to be healthy. They do not want one to use protocols that actually effectively help protect one's health and well-being, especially because these more natural and holistic solutions do not allow them to make huge amounts of profit off of most people's limited knowledge.

But getting back to the fact that I was concerned about these negative effects that even the less powerful 3 and 4G EMF were emitting: I had come upon information about tests that had been done using rats. After the rats had been exposed to the 3G and 4G levels of EMF, all the rats in the study developed cancerous tumors all over their bodies. The findings from this research study were suppressed by the corporations who had the most to financially lose if this information had been more readily available to the public.

As I was checking out various links to all this information that truly documented how bad EMF normally is, Celeste explained to me that she did not only enhance the protective capacities of the Q-Link Technologies because it was my True, Pure Heart's Desire that not only I, myself, would be even more protected (as in the phrase, "God/Goddess helps those who help themselves"), but that I wanted others to also be just as protected; she also did it because the EMF was part of the cabal's plans.

The cabal planned to use the destructive and deadly effects of EMF on the population in so many horrible ways. Not only to kill off a vast amount of the population: for those who survived this energetic assault, they would also use these same deadly energies to enhance their mind control and behavioral modification to manipulate everyone through their DNA/RNA.

The dark forces plans also included the 666-mark of the beast biochip implants which all vaccines now have, that allow the cabal to track and monitor them. This was of course the evil plans of Bill Gates, George Soros, and other prominent members of the satanic deep state cabal. They intent to force these even deadlier vaccines (including their new coronavirus vaccine) on everyone.

But this WAS their evil plan. Now, in this new timeline, it will not ever be allowed to be implemented by the cabal. (The "cabal", the "new world order"—or as I like to call them, the "old world odor"; because they "stink to high heaven".) In this new, more positive timeline, most of humanity, at least 90 to 95%, will be experiencing the planetary ascension. This gives the Higher Cosmic Light Forces the total Divine Authority to help the Q White Hat Alliance take down and arrest all of those who have been a part of the cabal deep state. This has already started to occur behind the scenes. Now that all of the over 200,000 sealed indictments are unsealed, and all these cabal players will be fully exposed, arrested and sentenced at the upcoming Military Tribunals, the reign and existence of the illuminati cabal will end once and for all.

Recently, before most of the 5G network was allowed to be activated, new information became available that definitely linked the cabal to the coronavirus and to the EMF that was being emitted from the majority of the 5G towers. With help from the Higher Forces, the Alliance became aware that not only did the cabal create and weaponize the COVID-19 virus to wipe out many millions of people, they were also using the 5G technology (produced in China) to broadcast the radionic/psychotronic frequency of the virus.

In fact I heard how different researchers had opened up the 5G transmitters that were produced in China, and inside they found an actual electronic part that had the inscription: "COVID-19." It does not take a rocket scientist or brain surgeon to realize that this particular electronic part was being activated to energetically spew out the energetic signature of the virus itself once each of these 5G towers were activated. This is why large numbers of people on the various ocean cruise ships came down with the symptoms of the virus: it appears that all of the

5G towers on each of the cruise liners all had these particular 5G towers that were made in China[3].

I also heard through more than one alternative media source that was in contact with the Alliance, that the Alliance (with the help of the Higher Forces) were able to greatly downsize the original cabal-weaponized virus into a much less contagious one. This is why there has not been millions of people dying and becoming sick as the cabal had planned, instead there has been very few people actually dying from the COVID-19.

Numerous doctors who visited different hospitals all over the U.S., discovered over and over again, that the official numbers of people who actually died from the COVID-19 virus were way, way lower than what was reported on all the lamestream media. Over 80 % of the people that were reported on their death certificates as having died from the COVID-19, actually died from some other cause. Corrupt officials were definitely blowing out of proportion the actual number of people who really died from this virus. Plus, most of the COVID virus testers were all manufactured in China, which is why all the so-called positive test results are totally fraudulent. These false numbers have been used by the cabal and the cabal-controlled, lamestream, fake news media to manipulate our perception of how many people there are that really have the virus.

But getting back to this 5G challenge: the majority of the 5G equipment that had been installed all over the U.S. were

---

[3] (Read more in the article "5G Tower Tech Discovers "COV 19" Written on Circuit Board—Is this Proof of a Coronavirus 5G Connection?" by Marko De Francis. You can find it here: https://stillnessinthestorm.com/2020/05/5g-tower-tech-discovers-cov-19-written-on-circuit-board-is-this-proof-of-a-coronavirus-5g-connection/ "In a video uploaded to twitter, what appears to be a technician with access to 5G tower technology shows us something that seems quite disturbing.")

produced either in China or by one other U.S. company that was also using very similar equipment. The majority of the 5G equipment would definitely covertly broadcast the COVID-19 virus, and would also emit high EMF.

President Trump, despite the massive propaganda of the satanic cabal deep state-controlled fake news media, really does care about humanity. To make sure that we will not become energetically targeted by the cabal, he recently ordered all the these particular 5G towers to be taken down. They are all being replaced with a much safer form of the 5G technology. Trump has already, more than once, mentioned that he wants to eventually put up the 6G technology as well. What he is referring to is much more advanced technology that is connected to the Nikola Tesla inventions, technology that will make us energy emancipated. This will also most likely relate to the full disclosure of E.T. technology that will soon be revealed to humanity. Most people do not know that Trump's uncle was involved in helping fund Tesla with his technology, and that Donald Trump had a chance to study all of this. Trump wants to more openly fund and develop this technology to be used by humanity in the near future, as soon as the cabal deep state, and their controlled fake news media, is fully exposed and out of the way.

Celeste has told me and wants everyone else to know that we (Light Workers, Volunteers in Earth embodiment, and everyone who is reading this book) all need to do what we each can to enhance our well-being. For those of us who have amassed broad knowledge and who put it to use as much as we can, our responsibility is to do the things that allow us greater health and protection from the EMF, such as using the Q-Link technology.

Many others are still "ignorant" or "unaware" (on a conscious level), as well as "insensitive" or unable to feel how bad the EMF actually is, but still have a positive intent and desire of a higher purpose. All these people, as long as they are part of the approximate 90 to 95% of humanity who has the potential to Awaken more and ultimately experience the ascension, will be receiving Higher help, guidance and protection from the EMF. The level of help is related to how much personal responsibility each person has experienced. So, the more we each do, the more complete our protection and help will be.

So, it behooves each of us to do all we are capable of doing, for example by doing research to enlighten oneself and then sharing this knowledge with as many others as we can. We should, of course, also personally use the Q-Link technology, to help alter/eliminate/transmute any of the negative effects of EMF. These Q-Link devices also make great and useful gifts.

Here is the Q-Link technology's website address:

https.//www.shopqlink.com/

CHAPTER 14

Blessings, Miracles, and My Powerful Vision (and the Awesome Synchronicity of Celeste Verifying It)

"Blessed and Blissed by Celeste" became one of the things that I found myself saying over and over, ever since my Beloved/Cosmic True Love, made herself more energetically present in my life. It is a very simple yet very broad statement. It is a Mantra that reflects so much of the wonderful and awesome experiences that I have been having with Celeste, since she Blessed me with her Divine Feminine Goddess Presence. The statement also reflects the intense "Blissed out" feelings I have been sharing with her almost 24/7. From the moment I awake in the morning until I go to sleep at night, Celeste's wonderful and Unconditionally Loving Presence is forever around me. She is permeating and flooding me with her intense feelings of Love, which she so naturally expresses to me on a daily basis.

It is actually hard to find words that even remotely can express how "awesome, joyous and incredible" it is to experience my life with her, ever since she came more directly into my life to share this unique journey with me. I put quotation marks around the words awesome, joyous and fantastic, because even those words fall short of just HOW awesome, joyous and incredible it actually has been to be able to constantly feel the powerful, Loving presence of my Twin-Flame/Universal Other-Half. In fact, not that many have had the Honor and Absolute Privilege to be around their Beloved on such a daily basis as I have had the chance to experience.

I tell Celeste how much I am truly Honored by, and how much I appreciate, her Divine Goddess Presence. It feels so good to be able to be so completely honest on every level with another person (or being) as I have been able to be with her.

It is a blessing to not experience any of the so-called relationship challenges that so many people here on this 3D level of Earth so often go through once they get to know each other. Of course, these challenges are usually the result of most people not (yet) having met and gotten to know their True Love/Beloved/Twin-Flame. Most people have not experienced this Divine, Heavenly type of relationship, they have only been in "karmic earth type" relationships, which are so often emotionally toxic. The emotional toxicity can reach extreme levels, as it did with my ex and I for decades. It was a total hell to be in such a relationship, in more ways than one. Even for "soul mate" relationships there can be challenges. We all have more than just one soul mate, but we only have ONE Twin-Flame/Twin Soul Mate. Soul mate relationships are not that rare, and these can be quite fulfilling—depending on how much unity and harmony is experienced and whether there are any personality conflicts or challenges.

From all the research I have done on this subject, up until now (on the old timeline) it has been extremely rare that these

Divine Couples have had a chance to be together for more than just a few lifetimes here on planet Earth. There are many reasons why this has been so. It is not because the couples did not want to be together. There is much interference by the imbalanced forces. They have been so manipulative that they have controlled much of the time-space continuum, which has blocked most Divine Couples from being able to reconnect down here on this 3D level.

Many people who have not yet met and gotten to know their own Beloved and Divine Other Half would say to me that this more energetic experience of Celeste being around me on the 5D or etheric level is quite different than if she and I both were living together on the 3D level. But to me, because I am clairvoyant and clairaudient and can easily see and communicate with Celeste all the time, I don't feel that these types of relationship challenges would really be any different once she at some point physically connects with me. We will both then be together that way, until we go back aboard our own Merkabah Light Ship, the Celestial Star. This is, of course, sometime in the future; at the moment I am just enjoying and savoring my Goddess as she is now. I feel this level of such harmony and bliss because of her personality and essence. It does not matter to me that she is presently only allowed (or authorized) to be with me in this unique type of way until First Contact finally does occur.

I say "unique type of way," only because of her being on the "5D or etheric," and me on the "3D." Here I put quotation marks around the terms 3D and 5D (I will share more on this in another chapter) because being very energetically intimate with my Beloved on a daily basis has caused my energy level to shift. I actually have to be careful at times when I am out "power walking" around town; I have experienced many vehicles just not seeing me until I would actually get eye contact with them. It has been quite an interesting experience to have my energy level raise so high that I guess I have been operating on a much higher level. My body often vibrates on the 4D or 5D level, closer to where Celeste is all the time around me. Yes, a resulting joke was: I was in "Nirvanic Ecstasy tantric paradise" with my Beloved. But right afterwards, each time, the drawback was that I would become "the Invisible Man!" But I was always willing to "take that risk"—who would not!

As Celeste and I began to settle into her and my apartment, it was great to have a place of my own where I could now have the privacy and space to energetically recover from all the challenges that I had experienced earlier. This wonderful place allowed me to just relax, and really enjoy getting to know Celeste in a deeper and more sacred way. I specifically stated in the first sentence to this paragraph, that this is *her* apartment, as much as it is mine. She is the one who was behind me getting it, and she spends so much of her time around me, anyway. I feel extremely appreciative to the Alliance guy for having been the one on the 3D level who offered me this place. But I also know that it was Celeste who also Over-Lighted him on her energetic level, guiding him to do so. So, I WAS definitely, "Blessed and Blissed by Celeste"!

Celeste Solving Challenges

Right after I had moved into the apartment, I experienced this major challenge of my laptop crashing on me. As I have mentioned, everything that had been on it was lost, including the entire email list of everyone I had connected with since 2011 (or even earlier). Suddenly I could no longer send email blasts out to everyone. With the laptop crash also came the aforementioned problem of the computer program I had lost: I needed an older version of the Sound Organizer program to be able to use my current digital recorder. If I was going to use the newer version which was available online, I would also need to purchase a new digital recorder. I did not have any money to do so; what little money I had, I had to save for buying the food I needed.

So here were just two of several challenges that I was still facing after having received the Blessing of this new apartment. Celeste just Lovingly and warmly smiled at me, and simply said, "Not to worry!" As my Cosmic muse, she said she would re-manifest both a "new" computer, as well as the older version of the Sound Organizer. I knew she truly had the ability to do so, to manifest these and other Blessings and Miracles into my life. I just needed to be as patient as possible until she did.

What I had almost forgotten about, was that I had actually saved all the phone messages and sign-in pads from my earlier events, and information for all the personal 90-minute Transformational Channeled Readings I had done. I had these in a special bag at the very bottom of one of my suitcases. I started to call up people I had not spoken to for the last several years. Everyone was excited to hear from me again. Some, in fact, wanted to get another session from me, to experience an "Update Reading." I now planned to do these once these other two mentioned challenges became two new Blessings and Miracles from Celeste.

In fact, the second person I spoke to, a lady named Robin who had experienced a session with me from a few years ago, just happened to have a fairly new computer that she had not used for a while, because she had one she personally liked more. She asked me if I would like to have the computer that she was not using, and I said "yes." She sent it to me, which I so very much appreciated.

Right after I had received it in the mail I called up the Geek Squad, who have been my tech support for many years. I had already attempted to find the older version of Sound Organizer that I needed, the one that was still compatible with my older digital recorder. I now figured that if anyone could do it, it was the Geek Squad. I had them access my computer remotely while I was talking to them over the phone, as I had done many times throughout the years. I watched as the technician spent well over an hour attempting to locate this elusive earlier version of the Sound Organizer.

After doing everything that was possible, the Geek Squad agent finally said that he was sorry; he had tried everything he could, but unfortunately nothing had appeared in his search. He was sorry that he could not help me as he had hoped he could. He was just getting ready to sign out and disconnect his system from my computer, and for a second I (or, rather, my ego conscious self) thought that this was not after all going to be the Miracle and Blessing that Celeste had promised me.

Suddenly I felt Celeste's Divine Goddess Presence right by me, as I was sitting on our bed. She was smiling as I felt some kind of subtle energetic shift occur, and suddenly a new icon appeared on my desk top of my computer. The Geek Squad guy had almost signed out, when he suddenly hesitated. He sounded surprised, like "where the heck did this thing, out of nowhere, suddenly pop up from!" He clicked on the icon, which opened the *older* version of Sound Organizer, the one that I specifically needed to be able to use my digital recorder! I have to say I was so astounded, as it was obvious that Celeste had just energetically downloaded a copy to me of this older version that I needed.

There is always perfect timing when something is supposed to appear. As in this case, when Celeste chose to do it: She had the Geek Squad tech guy search and search and find nothing. Then, when he was about to totally give up, at the last possible instant, she manifests the program for me, and voila; "All was great in Paradise!"

Underground Bases and Abducted Children

Now, suddenly, once more, I was "back in business." I would not starve, now that my Beloved had indeed manifested two more "unbelievable" Miracles and Blessings for me. After such intense stress that one feels when their basic needs are not being taken care of, I now desperately needed to be able to not just survive and to eat, but also to finally be able to relax and truly enjoy being more with Celeste. This has always been one of the main challenges for so many within the New Age community: we all want to truly fulfill our passion and Higher Purpose in life, without selling out, without compromising our Higher Ideals and Ethical Principles. I certainly was not willing to compromise my principles.

Since being with Celeste, I knew that she was to be such a major Blessing to me in so many ways, that she would be able to manifest so many Blessings, Miracles and Synchronicities. As stated, I just needed to be as patient as I could be, until she was able or allowed to do so. Of the Synchronicities that Celeste has manifested for me, the one that perhaps is the most significant is a powerful Confirmation about the reality of Q, the Q Drops, and what the White Hat Alliance has been doing to end the reign of the satanic deep state cabal.

I know that in the coming months of this year, 2020 (as Celeste and I are working together on this book) and on into 2021, a gigantic amount of documentation is to be released by Q and the Alliance. Well over 200,000 sealed Indictments that prove what thousands of individuals who have been a part of the satanic deep state cabal did are going to publicly be presented through upcoming military tribunals. Huge numbers of well-known Hollywood celebrities, actors and actresses, many who are part of the music industry, and other "icons" of society that so many people have looked up to are involved in this. Ordinary people assumed these were "good" because of the false impressions they portrayed in their acting careers and in their public appearances.

I already know this from numerous sources that most people have not had access to. Millions of people will be shocked and go into denial when they learn that these particular "icons" have fooled us all concerning who they REALLY are in private. Horrible and unspeakable crimes against humanity that a vast majority of Hollywood has been personally involved in include pedophilia and satanic human sacrifice, and they have used a drug referred to as "adrenochrome."

I have had to admit to myself that even as discerning as I thought I was compared to most other people on Earth, I realized after finding out this disturbing information how well we all were fooled by these people.

It is stated in the Bible that, "the Elect shall be Fooled." I do not interpret this as a negative judgment from God, I rather see it as a specific warning and observation by Divine Source: even those of us who are Light Workers/Volunteers in Earth embodiment, who normally are able to truly discern the negative from the positive, can be fooled. After all the spiritual work and dedication to uplifting this world and helping liberate humanity from the control of the imbalanced forces and exposing the illuminati cabal that I have been doing most of my life, I am normally being able to truly discern the truth.

Unlike most of the masses of Earth's humanity who display "preschool/kindergarten/elementary school level" of discernment development, I have always felt that I went through what I would refer to as the "University Level Discernment School of Hard Knocks". But even I, having been able to discern so much of what the imbalanced forces were covertly doing and of who was associated with these forces, was not prepared for some of the recent revelations that have come to light (that most people do not yet know about). I see now how very naive I have been, as has so many other fellow Light Workers. But I have always stated that one's true intent and motive, that which is in one's Heart, is what God and the Higher Forces of Light judge us for—NOT our human mistakes, imperfections, and frailties.

No longer are we fooled, the "spell has been broken." I have been set free to be able to see that all these corrupt and evil individuals so effectively fooled us all with their external charm, humor, positive outer appearance and personalities, and that in private they were involved in so much unspeakable horror and evil against our children. Celeste strongly confirmed to me that these revelations are totally true. As I became more aware of these very disturbing revelations, I realized that I must also help as much as I could. I must prepare others for these revelations that will become more public once the sealed indictments are unsealed, once all of these individuals are fully exposed for who they really are. They will be arrested and judged openly at the upcoming Military Tribunals, which will be publicly broadcast for all to see.

I also sensed (on some deep level of my own consciousness) that in some way, I myself was energetically involved in helping the Q White Alliance and the Higher Cosmic Light Forces take down the cabal and help Liberate earth's humanity. Yes, in some unusual way I felt that I was personally involved in this epic takedown of the satanic deep state cabal. But, more specifically, I sensed that I was somehow involved with the revelations of how millions of young children literally have been abducted throughout the past decades all over the world and taken to hundreds of deep underground bases, never to be seen again. This is very disturbing, but unfortunately true.

I had known for many years about these "D.U.M.B.s," the "Deep Underground Military Bases." They are constructed by the dark hat military and corrupt government, not only here in the U.S., but all over the world. I had heard about some of what had been going on "down there," which would shock most people, but I had not realized to what degree these evil things were being done, nor how many children had been abducted. Neither had I realized that many organizations that were supposed to be helping and/or protecting our children, were actually being used by the cabal to give them full access to abduct as many children as they wanted. No one was doing anything about it, if anyone attempted to expose this, they were never seen again. Yes, I read so many accounts of these things, of how the cabal was using these hundreds of D.U.M.B.s for things that are too horrible and evil to speak about, but I knew that one day much more would be revealed—which it most definitely has.

I also became aware that in more recent years the military became totally aligned with and a major part of the White Hat Alliance, along with off-planet benevolent E.T.'s who belong to a vast Federation of Light, Intergalactic Confederation. The Alliance has been helped in many profound ways, along with recent new funding. The White Hat military Alliance now has authority to go down to rescue these hundreds of thousands of children that were abducted. The abductions have been going on all over the planet for decades, but have increased these last several years.

The Alliance penetrate these bases, and battle against the dark hat military from earlier years who have been guarding them. The Alliance is rescuing the children who are kept prisoners in thousands of cages and holding pens. As the Alliance Navy Seals, Army Rangers, Delta Teams and other Special Forces penetrate some of the deeper bases, they have LITERALLY encountered actual physical demons. They have battled these demons, and they bring specially designed "light laser weapons": when fired at the demons, the demons go "puff," and then just cease to exist.

This has literally been a series of epic "good versus evil" battles, occurring underground all over the planet. When the Alliance Forces finish their rescue operations they usually have to blow up these deep underground bases, because the evil energy of what happened there must be allowed to be transmuted by Mother Earth. Her wounds must be allowed to heal, now that these evil places have been discovered and all these children have been rescued.

I know that to many who are reading this *very short summary* of what has been going on, it will just seem too unbelievable, like some fictional story. But I can assure you it IS all true, and I have barely scratched the surface of what has been occurring (which the corrupt "lamestream, fake news" media has not ever reported on).

Behind the scenes, the Alliance is helping restore our Constitutional Republic from the corrupt deep state swamp that had almost succeeded in destroying our country because of the New World Order cabal agenda. The cabal would have succeeded, had it not been for Divine Intervention from off-planet working with the Q White Hat Alliance to stop them. In this new timeline, as the planet is in the process of experiencing its

Ascension, there are new Cosmic Frequencies of Light incoming that have never existed in the universe before.

All of this together has caused what Q and the Q Drops have referred to as the "Great Awakening." "Where We Go One, We Go All," and "Trust the Plan." Yes, it IS all happening. Humanity is truly and quickly waking up fast. This is a "Cosmic Crash Course" in "Reality Therapy", to get hip to what is REALLY going on behind the scenes. We all had to "take the Red Pill" (as opposed to the "Blue Pill"). We had to "go down that rabbit hole" (and through that Wormhole) of Total Truth, because we CAN handle the Truth. The cabal did not want anyone to know just HOW extremely evil they actually were, what unspeakable crimes they have been doing for centuries, which had increased in more recent years. This had to finally be stopped. Thank God/Goddess for the courageous and dedicated men and women of the Alliance, and for our Friends Upstairs. The latter recently cleansed the Heavens of all negative alien forces, so that they will never be able to invade this planet, nor have any more negative influence or create sabotage of any kind.

All negative alien implants, including the negative biochips injected into ignorant people who received vaccines, are in the process of being neutralized. To what degree and how fast this occurs has a lot to do with what each person does to take more personal responsibility. This includes deciding to not get any more vaccines and following a healthier and more responsible lifestyle that is in harmony to Divine Source.

Here are a few links[4] to excellent sources on the Internet, that document and reveal the children being rescued by the Alliance and much of what has been occurring in the D.U.M.B.s:

"People actually drink adrenochrome":

Heavyweight Boxer, David Rodriguez Says Hollywood Pedos are Real, and They're Going Down! Also, a link to very informative Documentary Video, "Out of the Shadows," which Documents about the true facts of Child Pedophile and satanic human sacrifice.https://stillnessinthestorm.com/2020/04/people-actually-drink-adrenochrome-heavyweight-boxer-david-rodriguez-says-hollywood-pedos-are-real-and-theyre-going-down/

Excellent Follow-up Interview with Heavyweight Champ David Rodriguez K.O.s Ped*wood and Shines Light on Spiritual Awakening #EdgeofWonder

https://www.youtube.com/watch?v=EO_iIJOZWM8

Gene-D+Code Videos: Documenting the Cabal's D.U.M.B.'s or Deep Underground Military Bases, which are being either totally destroyed and/or Dismantled by the White Hat Alliance. Hundreds of thousands of Children have recently been rescued

[4] Google, Facebook (which I refer to as "Fake book"), Twitter, and other social platforms literally censor and delete people's accounts as well as any videos that expose the cabal's agendas. Thus, many links may suddenly be "un-operative" and will not work. If this happens to any of the links mentioned in this book, I highly recommend that you do an Internet search to find other links to these same subjects. When I initially attempted to find links for these subjects, I could not find them – even though I had seen them before. This was because the cabal's A.I. (Artificial Intelligence) information bots were blocking me from finding them. So, I asked Celeste, if she could help me find them, and voila: immediately, these links popped back up for me. So, if you have difficulty in attempting to locate other links on the Internet, just ask the Higher Light Forces, and they should be able to help you overcome this "cabal censorship"!

from these bases that were to be used in the world-wide pedophile network and satanic sacrifices. Victory to the Light!

https://www.bing.com/videos/search?q=Gene-D+Code+and+Underground+Basesandqpvt=Gene-D+Code+and+Underground+BasesandFORM=VDRE

My Vision—The Children and Trump

We are now getting back to what I had referred to earlier as my sense that I was personally involved in helping stop the cabal and their crimes against our children. This is also about the powerful and awesome Synchronicity that Celeste manifested for me.

I want to remind everyone who is reading this that Synchronicities occur in all kind of ways. It can be when one is riding along in a car, and suddenly experience a wonderful revelation in their thoughts. It can be that someone is thinking about something important, and then, a second or two later, they look over to see a bumper stinker on the vehicle in front of them, or they notice a billboard, and the phrase they see just happens to confirm what they were thinking about. Synchronicities can also be in the form of a song being played right after having an intense and significant vision of some kind. This latter form of Synchronicity is what I am about to share: hearing a very interesting song that Celeste actually arranged energetically for me to hear within a few minutes of having experienced an incredible vision.

To attempt to summarize the main points, here is what occurred. Since living here in Sarasota, I have always had this ingrained habit: Shortly after waking up most days, I will call the Trader Joe's store. I do a lot of my shopping at Trader Joe's because I like to save a few nickels and dimes by buying something there, rather than going to another store to purchase the same item for a higher price. Yes, who does not like to save a little money?

I also do a lot of power walking all over the Sarasota area, and usually like to combine my power walks with going to buy whatever food I need. If Trader Joe's does not happen to have what I need, then I will call a few other stores such as Whole Foods and even Publix, because they also carry a lot of organic foods. This is one of my routines, something I have been doing for many months; an ingrained habit.

But one morning in 2019 I forgot to call Trader Joe's, and could not at first understand why I would forget to do so. I was to later find out from Celeste that she actually Over-Lighted me to not call Trader Joe's that day, because had I called I would have found out that they did not have the particular item I needed, and as a result I would not have gone to Trader Joe's that day. But as I was to find out later, there was a very important reason that I had to go there. It had to do with this very amazing and powerful Synchronicity that Celeste wanted me to hear; a particular and very unique song that "just happened" to be playing over the store's intercom system that afternoon, which was going to help energetically confirm what I had come to realize from the powerful vision I was about to have that afternoon.

One of the reasons why I briefly summarized a little earlier in this chapter about the underground bases and the children was to give you as a reader a better understanding of what I experienced, saw and realized during this very powerful vision. So many children have been abducted and taken to those deep underground bases. Unspeakable things have been done to them that I do not want to go into details on, but it is truly evil beyond one's imagination.

In this powerful vision, which I know Celeste helped to initiate and activate within my consciousness I was, indeed helping the Alliance Special Forces rescue many thousands of these children, as was she. How horrible they have been treated, held in these cages and holding pens in the deep underground bases in total darkness, with no light and no relief from their horrible torturous existence. Most of them have been used many times in the vast human trafficking network for pedophile actions and satanic sacrifices. One can only imagine in what horrendous emotional, psychological states, as well as physical condition, the children are in (those who are even still alive after being prisoners to the cabal).

In the vision I saw and experienced that Celeste and my Higher Self, using our own Merkabah Light Ship, the Celestial Star, were rescuing many of these children by beaming them into our ship. They were then taken to other larger Mother ships, where they could be specially cared for and comforted, and where their wounds on all levels could truly be healed. These wounds are too intense and too deep to be cured on a 3D Earth level.

I could hear and see these children crying and moaning in all their pain and suffering as we were beaming them up aboard our ship. Our ship was only one of many similar Merkabah Light Ships that had been helping the Earth Alliance in their valiant, courageous, and truly compassionate rescue operations. These images were very vivid in my mind and consciousness; these children crying as we were beaming them up, loading them aboard our ship so that they could then be more specially and individually cared for on board the larger Light ships. Many scenes such as this flashed before my eyes. Even though I saw the vision on this Higher energetic level, seeing through the eyes of my Higher Self, it was still very intense to sense all the pain and suffering these precious Earth children had been experiencing before we rescued them.

Now they cried not only in their pain, but also in their intense joy and relief to be rescued by Higher Beings who they knew would truly care for them. They could now be totally healed from the horrendous evil that they had just been removed from. I, my conscious self, could not help but cry from the intensity of what I was seeing and experiencing.

Then the scene shifted to something else which was also just as real as what I had just seen and experienced, but which also gave deep insight about someone who has been so unmercifully and unjustly vilified by our corrupt lamestream fake news media. The media has had a whole agenda to demonize this person, because of what a threat he has been to the cabal. They have been fairly successful at creating such a false narrative, brainwashing many to believe this. If any of you who are reading this have a bad impression about President Trump, all I would ask is that you allow yourself the benefit of doubt regarding what his real intent is compared to how horrible he has been painted by the media.

Understand that I, myself, have not been involved in Earth politics for decades, because to me both major parties have been totally controlled by the cabal after the assassination of John F. Kennedy in 1963. It does not matter whether it be the Republican or the Democratic party; both have been totally controlled by the cabal. Sometimes even the third or so-called independent parties also have had (at least) major cabal influence.

I will admit that when I first heard in 2016 that Trump was one of those running on the Republican Ticket, I (or rather my conscious self) was biased and not open to even considering that he actually had any redeemable qualities. I did not assume that he would be any different than any other career cabal-controlled politicians. So, my conscious self was surprised when he became the Republican nominee in 2016. Judging by the presidential elections since John F. Kennedy's assassination, the cabal has always been in control of how things turn out. The modern-day electoral process includes both the entire "vetting process" of initially choosing the final nominee, as well as the whole casting the vote process where vote fraud and electronic manipulation of the number of votes occurs. Again, my conscious self, had just assumed that because of this entire modern-day electoral process, no matter what "we the people" TRULY and SINCERELY wanted or desired, it did not matter; the cabal still controlled both parties, and that was "just how it was."

But then, suddenly my Higher Self and the Higher Forces who I was in communication with (especially my Beloved, Celeste) all had a totally different opinion of Trump and who he actually is. He is different from any of the others who have "run for office" for many years, with two exceptions mentioned by the

Higher Forces: Jimmy Carter and Ronald Reagan. Both genuinely wanted in their hearts to do the right and ethical thing for this country.

When Reagan was first becoming involved in being a politician, he had actually chosen to be a Democrat. But when he found out about the true history of what the early Democrats actually stood for until shortly before Kennedy's time, he changed political parties to become a Republican. Why did he do that? Perhaps when he found out that it was the Democrats who were for slavery, while the Republicans were opposed to it. The Democrats were the ones who formed the Ku Klux Klan. They were the ones who created the Jim Crow laws, and a whole bunch of other racist things against the blacks/African Americans. Reagan did not want to be associated with or to support these discriminatory things.

An interesting fact (and I know this is going to sound weird) with all the presidents since at least the '70s, early '80s, is that they were all cloned (the original human was killed), so that the cabal could control the clone, more easily. When Reagan began to speak out against the corrupt and fraudulent Federal Reserve bank (which was formed by the cabal to control our financial system), the cabal sent their MK-Ultra programmed John Hinkley to assassinate him. It has been rumored that then the original, actual Reagan was then replaced with a clone. In the case of Jimmy Carter's cloning: Because of how evolved a soul he was, Carter was able to retain some of his original life soul force despite being cloned. He was still attempting to bring peace to the world, resisting being just a tool for the cabal and New World Order forces.

But getting back to President Trump: When I really began to tune into who he really is, I could now attune to the fact that he really was unique compared to the vast majority of the career-controlled politicians. He truly was going to fulfill his initial promises, "and then some." No, he is not perfect; he has flaws and imperfections, just I as have flaws and imperfections—we are human. But what is important is to see his true intent and who he is as a human; what is really in his heart, his numerous redeeming and Higher qualities of spirit, and especially who he is on a Higher level of existence. The extremely biased, cabal-controlled media vilified him more than I had ever seen them do to any other candidate running for office before, and there have been numerous false and fraudulent attempts to remove him from office—this is all because he really is a major threat to the cabal in so many ways.

Cathy O'Brien is the author (along with Mark Phillips) of the book "Transformation of America," which was first published in the 1980s. The book is about her and her daughter being MK-Ultra mind controlled sex slaves for the cabal deep state, and all about the human trafficking and satanic sacrifice of children. She recently mentioned that her cabal handlers would sometimes tell her and her fellow sex slaves about certain individuals who they did not want the slaves to ever connect with, because these individuals were considered a threat to the cabal. She stated[5] that they told her that, "Trump was not one of them." They told her that he was NOT a member of the cabal.

---

[5] Former MK Ultra Sex Slave Was Told by Her Deep State Handlers "Trump is Not One of Us": https://stillnessinthestorm.com/2020/05/former-mk-ultra-sex-slave-was-told-by-her-deep-state-handlers-trump-is-not-one-of-us/

Neither is Trump a member of any of the cabal's numerous secret societies; he truly admired President John F. Kennedy, and took to heart how Kennedy mentions in one his famous speeches that as Americans "we abhor secret societies". Trump is not a member of the cabal, despite being so wealthy and having "hung out" with some of the power elite. Trump has always followed the philosophy, "keep your friends close and your enemies closer."

Recently, as I was tuning into Trump's past existence prior to him incarnating in this life, I became aware of something very fascinating: One of the main reasons he is so interested and drawn to the famous book "The Art of War" by Sun Tzu, is that he thrives on solving strategy challenges—the more challenging and more difficult, the more he likes it. For the same reason, Trump is definitely a 4th and 5th Dimensional Chess player, and for the same reason he wrote "The Art of the Deal": he enjoys understanding what strategy is needed, be it in financial challenges or on the battlefield of war. He enjoys outsmarting the satanic cabal and their corrupt central banking system, with his ability to know what their moves will be many moves ahead of them.

Of course, for those who have been following and deciphering the Q drops that the White Hat Alliance has been posting, it is obvious that "Q+" is President Trump. This is made clear in the video that I mentioned earlier. But it is also my opinion that President Trump was Sun Tzu in one of his past lives.

I heard from a couple different sources that the cabal attempted a number of times to entrap Trump so that they could blackmail him, and to honey trap him to have control over him. But Trump was too smart and discerning to fall for any of these attempts, so they were never able to accomplish their goal. Once, though, they almost succeeded with trapping him. when he went to one of the power elite's exclusive parties. Trump had always been careful to watch his drink; to not turn away for more than a few seconds, in case someone should "put a mickey" in his drink to drug him and set him up. However, at this particular party, which I believe took place sometime before 2012, he made the mistake of turning away a little too long. The next thing he knew, he woke up totally naked in bed beside a very young girl, who was naked and obviously drugged.

But Trump was faster than his captors had expected, he immediately jumped out of bed (before the hidden cameras could film him, of course), somehow found his clothes in a nearby closet, and barely got out of there with his life. I believe that he had some kind of Divine Intervention from Higher Forces to help him escape, because of his destiny to take on the cabal, to totally defeat them and eliminate them forever from this planet. Right after the failed entrapment, he sent out a tweet where he stated that "all child molesters should be executed!" It was some time right after that the White Alliance approached him and asked if he would be willing to run for president to help them defeat the cabal. And "the rest was history," as they say.

Getting back to my vision that I had as I was walking along on my way to do some shopping: As mentioned, the scene shifted. I no longer saw us saving the children. Instead, I now became aware of Trump's Higher Self, who was a member of the Higher Galactic Council. I became aware of the moment when he stood up with great determination and compassion and vowed that once he took Earth embodiment, he was going to totally take down and dismantle the entire illuminati satanic deep state cabal once and for all. This was a particularly important moment for him.

For me, this entire vision that I had just experienced and its implications was energetically overwhelming: not only learning about Trump, but about what Celeste and I were doing to help the Alliance. Experiencing her and I rescuing so many of the millions of children that had been abducted and held in those deep underground bases, and then being allowed (here on this conscious 3D level) to know and remember what Celeste and my own Higher Self had been doing. It was overwhelming to experience how we were beaming up and loading those poor precious children, who I heard crying from such misery, into our Merkabah Light Ship (the "Celestial Star"), then taking them to one of the many much larger Motherships where very advanced and special healing chambers would totally cleanse them on every single level of all their wounds and horrible memories.

Celeste's Synchronicity

It was when I had just finished experiencing this incredible vision, that I suddenly remembered about having forgotten for the first time to call Trader Joe's, as I always had every other morning. So, I decided to do some more power walking for a while, over to where Trader Joe's was located. When I finally got to the store and walked in, I heard some music being played over their intercom. This was only the second time in all the many months of having been in Trader Joe's that I had I ever heard them playing music in their store.

I immediately walked over to the produce area, to see if they had the item that I had intended to call about earlier that morning. I do not even remember now what exactly the item was, because of what I was about to experience a few minutes later—it was so astounding, to put it mildly. Since I could not find the item out on the shelf, I immediately walked up to the front desk to ask them if they had any more in the back, and if they did not, when they were expecting more to be delivered to the store.

A number of times in the past months, I have asked one of the employees if they had some more of an item available in the back since I had not seen it out on the shelf, or if they did not, when they were expecting more to come in. Every time in the past when I had asked them this same question, I had never had to wait more than about a minute at the most. But this time it took about five minutes, at least, before the employee finally came back to say to me that they did not have the item anymore and that it would be a few days before they got more in. So I thanked them, and then turned to the front entrance to walk to another store where I thought might have this same item.

As I was approaching the door, suddenly a new song began to play. It did sound a little familiar, but I could not at first recall the title of the song. What caused me to suddenly stop in my tracks in surprise and awe, was the lyrics that I heard. It was totally mind-blowing (to put it mildly), considering the intense vision I had experienced only minutes before. I knew in an instant that Celeste had arranged for me to hear this particular song at that exact moment, only a short time after my vision. I also knew it had taken incredible coordinating on Celeste's part to make sure that this exact song would be playing that exact moment.

She told me that she had specifically Over-Lighted me to, for the first time, totally forget to call Trader Joe's earlier that day. If I had called, they would have informed me that they did not have the item, and I would not have even gone to the store. Celeste had also caused the employee to delay a lot longer than usual, otherwise I would have walked out of the store before being able to hear this particular song being played. In fact, the last time I had heard this particular song being played over the radio was 15 to 20 years ago.

And what was the title of this song, and what were these unique and unusual lyrics that I was hearing that just blew my mind? The song is by Neil Young, and he was singing his famous song "After the Gold Rush," which had been recorded back in 1969. These were the lyrics which I was suddenly hearing:

"...I saw the Silver Spaceships Flying in the Yellow Haze of the Sun... there were Children Crying... The Loading had Begun..."

CHAPTER 15

Sightings of the Celestial Star, and Celeste "Rides Shotgun" for Me

In case anyone who is reading this book did not get a chance to have read my first book (*Prepare for the Landings!*), then I do recommend doing so. I there share in-depth about my earlier physical contacts and experiences, communications and channelings with various Higher Beings.

As I shared in the introduction of this book, on a very personal level I enjoy writing this second book so much more than my fist one, because the chance to share this whole process with my Beloved, Celeste. Having her energetically present throughout the time of compiling it and hearing her own many wonderful insights, made this so enjoyable for me and so much more meaningful. Also, when I wrote my first book, describing some of the cabal's attempts to kill me, I did not know consciously that it was Celeste, herself, who was personally protecting me. Now I know, as she has shared with me, how much she was constantly having to protect me from the many dozens, if not hundreds of attempts of the cabal to kill me and to silence me.

Yes, Celeste "rode shotgun for me." "Riding shotgun" is a famous old phrase from the wild west, describing those whose job it was to guard people and valuables. So it was with my

Beloved, Celeste. She took her mission seriously, and she was able to provide the personal Cosmic Backup that I needed while fulfilling this much earlier phrase of my mission for being in Earth embodiment.

For me, as I have had the Honor and Privilege of now being able to directly communicate with her, and her with me, without her having to "hide in the background." Because of not being allowed, then, to reveal herself to me, until late 2017/early 2018, when she first "Got my Attention." As the Walk-In, and then "Energetically" manifesting herself directly around me in the 5D/etheric mode.

I have discovered so much in these last two years, for example the fact that Celeste and my Higher Self have a Merkabah Light Ship together, named the Celestial Star. It is usually in a stationary position above the Earth, "parked" somewhere over the Sarasota area since this is where I have happened to be for the last couple of years. Its exact position may vary somewhat, depending upon what "energetic changes" are occurring throughout the Earth, the new timeline, the newer incoming Cosmic Energies that are Transforming everything upon Earth, and the exposing of the cabal.

I have also now become aware of the fact that Celeste manifested the Celestial Star a number of times throughout the earlier parts of my life, up until the time of her finally being allowed to reveal herself to me. There are also a few more recent sightings of our Ship that I directly knew consciously was the Celestial Star, unlike during those much earlier times when the Ship had manifested and I did not know it consciously.

I want to also refer back to a few of the incidents regarding Celeste's personal involvement in protecting me from being killed by the cabal, now that I have the extra wisdom and knowledge.

Right after I had come to Sarasota in 2018 (after having been at that homeless shelter), I was initially hosted by some people and had a temporary place to stay. I had been guided a few times to go up to the town of Bradenton, which is just north of Sarasota. Normally, I prefer the energy and/or consciousness of the Sarasota area to that of Bradenton. But I would now and then go to this little park that happens to be near the ocean, and which has a little energy vortex. I would always meditate there, and I realized later that I had been guided by Celeste to go there.

Most of the time I would go to the Siesta Key Vortex to meditate. Basically the entire white crystal sands of Siesta Key Beach are part of the Siesta Key Vortex. It is always wonderful to put one's bare feet into that fine, powdered, 99% pure white quartz crystal sand, and to ground to Mother Earth at the same time. But the Vortex at the Bradenton Park was different, it provided a contrasting energetic perspective compared to where I always used to go to. I had lived here in the area about 15 to 20 years ago.

I was sitting one day at Bradenton Park, when I suddenly felt Celeste's presence very strongly. I could see her sitting there by me etherically, and I could feel all the intense Love she felt for me. I heard her telling me to look up into the sky, in the direction of the ocean. As I turned around to look in that direction, I suddenly saw the beautiful saucer-shaped lenticular cloud that was there. I had not seen it a few minutes earlier, and I could now feel the energy coming down from it. It felt very personally familiar to me.

I know that most traditional Earth meteorologists would attempt to explain these lenticular type clouds as nothing more than the result of certain mundane, 3D weather and atmospheric conditions. But for those of us who have a more attuned perspective of Higher Dimensions and the Energetic Consciousnesses of the Beings who inhabit these Higher Realms of Light, it is obvious that these types of clouds (as well as various other "atmospheric phenomena", such as sun dogs with their beautiful rainbow effect) are evidence of the Higher Dimensional Merkabah Light Ships and the Light Beings who pilot and manifest them.

Years ago, I had gotten to know the famous Channel and Contactee, Sister Thedra. Together with her co-author and photographer, she published a book titled *Celestial Rays From the Sun*. It contained dozens of awesome photos of these same type of saucer-shaped clouds, photographed around Mt. Shasta and other locations, along with many channelings and communications from these Higher Beings. The book was first published in 1986, and has long been out of print—so any copy is a real "collector's edition."

Up in the sky near the Bradenton Park that particular day, was now another of these same type of clouds. I had seen such clouds many times before, over all kinds of different terrain. Sometimes the ship is partially or completely in the 3D physical, but usually it is in the 5D/ etheric or a higher dimension. Either way, the lenticular saucer-shaped cloud is partially caused by the various energies, rays and special emanations that are being generated from the ship itself. This helps create or form the ionization cloud as part of the forcefield covering the ship's basic form and presence.

Various gases, such as xenon gas (pronounced "zenon") is also produced. This was discovered back in 1969 by Soltec, an astrophysicist from Alpha Centauri. The xenon enhances one's ability to raise one's consciousness. Also, its higher energetic properties are helping to open the third eye, and has various other positive effects on the body. From 1969, the Higher Light Forces have been manifesting more Xenon gas from these continuous manifestations of lenticular clouds, to help raise the consciousness of the entire world.

The cabal is, of course, aware of this, and it is one of the reasons that they have been doing their chemtrail operations (also known as geo-engineering) all over the world. The chemtrails were not only used to (attempt to) counteract the xenon's beneficial effects. They were also a part of the cabal's original HAARP program (and their smaller, movable "Gwen towers") to manipulate humanity's consciousness and to poison as many people as possible through their human depopulation agenda. But the Higher Forces have been responding to this, by doing various positive energetic countermeasures to neutralize as much of these negative cabal operations as possible.

It is also up to us, as citizens of Earth as well as Volunteers in Earth embodiment (who are still technically major members of various Higher Galactic Councils), to do all we can here on this 3D conscious level. Our actions give the Higher Forces greater official intergalactic and planetary mandated authority to neutralize even more of these covert agendas by the cabal.

Getting back to this particular manifestation of the lenticular cloud: Celeste informed me that this was her and my Higher Self's ship, the Celestial Star. This cloud was also partially a "sign in the sky" representing how much she had been intervening for me throughout the many years I have been on my mission (since the late 1970s/early '80s) and how many times she specifically stopped the cabal from assassinating me. She had manifested our ship a number of times prior to this moment, but it was only now that she was allowed (or authorized) to let me know this on my conscious 3D level.

This manifestation of the Celestial Star was also there to confirm something else that she said, something especially significant about her and I regarding our mission as a Twin-Flame couple: She explained that besides us being members of the Intergalactic Confederation/Federation of Light, we were also members of the "Love Ops/Special Forces of Romantic Love." This is a universal organization within the Federation, which is going to play an important role in helping many other Twin-Flame couples reconnect.

The Love Ops/Special Forces of Romantic Love are helping the Q White Hat Alliance to take down the satanic deep state cabal to not only directly help rescue many children (as Celeste and I have been doing), but also to then take the children to those much larger Motherships where they can receive the much more advanced, special healing that they need.

One of the more recent sightings of the Celestial Star occurred in 2019, right after I had done an Update Reading for a couple in Australia, named Craig and Trish. They happened to be Celeste's parents in a past life when she was incarnated on Earth. A lot of interesting and significant information was shared with them from Celeste, who was Direct Voice channeling through me for them. This helped them get greater insight about many things. I had also tuned in to the fact that they had been my own parents as well, in a couple of past lives.

A few days later, Craig and Trish emailed me about the fact that as they were looking out their window, they saw a huge lenticular cloud manifesting right over their property. As I was reading their email about what they were describing to me, Celeste (who was etherically sitting on the bed with me) told me that this was the Celestial Star. She had manifested the ship there to confirm to them everything that she had shared with them while she was channeling through me for them.

When I then replied to their email and shared what Celeste had just told me, they were excited. They mentioned that they had felt that they were receiving a telepathic message from Celeste when they saw the saucer-shaped cloud. Reading my email confirmed to them that they had received her message clearly. Craig also had taken a short video clip of the sighting. When they viewed it with their eyes, the lenticular cloud was obviously not part of the cloud bank behind it. Unfortunately, in the video footage it all seemed to just merge together, and was not as obvious as when they had just looked at it with their eyes. So, the film was not that impressive this particular time, otherwise I would have provided at least a copy of one of the frames of the video in this book.

One of the most recent sightings of the Celestial Star occurred a few days before Valentine's Day, 2020, and I was able to photograph it with my cell phone. A copy of this photo can be found in Chapter 19, "My Cosmic Valentine."

Sightings and Chemtrails

Another, much earlier sighting of the Celestial Star occurred about 15 to 20 years ago, but I did not know it at the time I very briefly saw it. Interesting enough, this sighting happened the first time I was living here in Sarasota. This was also right after I had been doing a lot of research about chemtrails. I had taken dozens of videos of all the chemtrails that I had been seeing all over the skies of Sarasota and other areas of Florida. I remember that I had just moved from another location of Sarasota to this new place, which would be the house I lived in until I moved back to Phoenix, Arizona, in 2003.

I also remember that because of how much thicker and more prevalent the chemtrail-geoengineering spraying had been back at that time all over the world, I had been taking numerous videos and compiling huge amount of documentation and data off the internet regarding what other prominent researchers in the field had compiled. Back in those earlier years, the chemtrails were much more intense (at least that was how it was appearing to me), and they were appearing much more often than in more recent years.

Often the skies were completely blanketed and covered with numerous chemtrails, with numerous patterns of multiple chemtrails from one horizon to another. Then from another direction, and they would crisscross each other, creating giant

X's all over the skies. Quickly the chemtrails would all spread out across the sky, until it was entirely covered; the trails would become one total, artificial gray cloud, covering the entire sky from horizon to horizon. It just seemed to be getting worse, I knew and sensed this from not only all the research I had been doing, gathering evidence off the Internet, but also from what I myself was tuning into.

Ultimately, one evening I went to the local channel 3 public television, that broadcast the Sarasota City Council meetings live. Any citizen can go there to comment openly and publicly to not only the City Council members, but to anyone who happens to be looking at the meeting while it is being broadcasted. Anyone who goes to the effort of sharing whatever they want before the City Council Members and the camera has exactly three minutes to say all they want to. The City Council members are not allowed to respond to the individuals who are appearing for the three minutes; they just sit there and listen.

I am sure that in the entire history of how long they have been doing this, my three-minute presentation was by far the most unusual presentation that had ever presented there before the City Council members and the TV camera. I had titled my presentation, "Why Is the City Council of Sarasota allowing Aerial Spraying of toxic Petrochemicals over the Skies of our City?" I crammed as much summarized information as I could into that short amount of time, barely even scratching the surface of what was going on. Even though I was not allowed to talk with or interact with the City Council members, I could tell by the looks on their faces how bewildered they all were. They had the shocked "deer in the headlights" kind of look, apparently they had never heard of such a topic before, nor seen something like it presented before all of them.

I then went back a second time, a few weeks later. This time I had with me copies of some of the information that I had been able to copy off the Internet from various websites, documenting the whole subject quite well. While I was waiting to go back into the three-minute spot, I handed out flyers to everyone at the City Council building. The flyer informed of an organization that I had recently created, which was named "C.L.E.A.R.," (also known as "Citizens League for Environmental Awareness and Response"). The flyer listed a few of the main websites with information about the chemtrails. I had already handed these flyers out at various networking events, and I had posted them all over Sarasota and other cities throughout Florida. I had spoken at various centers and had given out these flyers everywhere I could for many months, to help enlighten those who did not know anything about this particular cabal covert agenda to kill and poison as many of the population as they could.

Even though one is normally not allowed to personally interact with the City Council members, I kind of ignored this: I mentioned during my three-minute "repeat performance" that I had a chemtrail documentation packet that I wanted to give to each Council member. The interesting thing was that for a few moments they, too, seemed to ignore this so-called "rule" they normally would have followed: when I reached the end of my three-minute presentation, most of the Council members made it clear by gesturing their hands and smiling friendly at me that they wanted to receive that information packet from me.

So, I walked over a few feet to where the edge of their table was. A couple of the Council members started to speak to me in some excitement and interest at what I had just shared, and they wanted to know more about this whole subject of chemtrails. But then one of the other members reminded the first two members that they were not allowed to talk to those who are giving their three-minute presentation. This was probably one of the first times that one or more of the Council members momentarily forgot to follow this normally rigid rule of local bureaucratic policy of not associating or intermingling with us "peons" who come to complain, comment, share our grievances, etc.

It appeared that this whole topic of chemtrails was suddenly fascinating and unique. There did not seem to be any so-called cover-ups nor any specific knowledge about it at that time in 2003 in the Sarasota area in Florida—despite the fact that it was going on every day and night. Obviously, the cabal had not expected someone like me to publicly address this subject, causing these local officials to now be interested in finding out more about chemtrails and whether their City of Sarasota was being heavily sprayed by numerous petrochemical poisons (as explained in the information packet that I had handed out to all the City Council members).

I also went to a City Commissioner's meeting a couple of days later. This meeting was held in the afternoon, and it too was open to the public. Interestingly enough: when I drove up into the parking lot to park my car, right there up in the sky was a huge bunch of chemtrails crisscrossing in X's. When I walked in and sat there, waiting to come up to sit in the seats provided for the public, I noticed that there were only a few other people there to speak with the City Commissioner, Mr. Mills. He looked at me and asked me what I was there for. I told him about what I had presented twice before the City Council, and that this was why I had come to this meeting as well. I also pointed out to him that at that very moment, up in the sky right outside, a huge number of chemtrails were being sprayed out again even as I was speaking. Just as they had been sprayed out for many months now. I told him that if he did not believe it, he should go outside right then and take a look at what was going on.

Mr. Mills, just stared at me with a slight, bemused smile (or perhaps a smirk) on his face, and said to me, "You must think I am part of the conspiracy, right?" I looked at him and said, "You said it, not me." I just sat there, waiting to see what he was going to say next. He kind of chuckled, shrugged his shoulders, and then said that if what I was claiming was really going on, he and the City Council had no authority to do anything about it. He said that I would have to take it up with certain, other higher authorities. With that the meeting was over, and I was told I had to leave.

Suddenly, a few days after my 2nd City Council/Channel 3 TV presentation and the City Commissioner meeting, I sensed that the cabal was now once more specifically focused on me. They did not like the fire-storm of sudden interest about these covert aerial spraying operations that were taking place all over the world resulting from me "stirring up shit" with the (formally) ignorant local bureaucrats as well as everyone else who happened to see and hear my two presentations or get one of my many hundreds of flyers.

Even though at that time very few people knew about this subject, or had even heard the term "chemtrails" before, I use the word "covert": Because as with so much that the cabal has done throughout the decades of their agenda, they have always done things "hidden in plain sight." Initially in the case of chemtrails, when those of us "conspiracy theorists" (or, rather "conspiracy realists") and those of the "Truther movement" would first mention chemtrails, the cabal would always claim that we were somehow confusing chemtrails with the usual contrails from jets.

Anyone who has really studied this entire subject (which was finally indirectly acknowledged in more recent years as "geo-engineering") understand the difference between the chemtrails and the normal ionization contrails that come off of jets, which usually dissipates and disappears in about a minute. While chemtrails may look similar, it is instead a petrochemical trail. Unlike a normal contrail, the chemtrails will not disappear. In fact they will spread out, often until the entire sky will be covered by these trails as one huge gray cloud cover. Researchers were able to obtain both air samples and ground samples of the stuff that has fallen from these chemtrails. After laboratory analyses, these samples were shown to have all kinds of toxic and deadly amounts of chemicals, and substances very poisonous to humans, animals and plant life.

In more recent years there has been much Divine Intervention from Higher Cosmic Light Forces, as well as the White Hat Alliance: finally recently causing the chemtrail program to be shut down. The Alliance is in fact now reversing all the damage that was done during the last few decades. With these same jets in the Alliances hands, they are now spewing out Hydrogen Peroxide and other healthy substances into the atmosphere. So, while we will continue for a while to see what visually appears to be the old and toxic chemtrails coming out of planes, now these new atmospheric trails are actually good for the atmosphere and environment.

The same thing goes for the original HAARP cabal program: It too is now in Alliance hands. It is no longer broadcasting all the cabal's nasty mind control and weather modifications, nor is it any longer able to create destructive earthquakes. Much of the climate, weather, and other earth conditions should begin to slowly improve, now that the Alliance has gotten HAARP out of the cabal's hands.

The Elephants in the Room

These two topics, chemtrails and HAARP, were NEVER discussed or even acknowledged by the very organizations that should have not only mentioned them all the time, but also have made them one of their number one priorities to expose and eliminate. I am referring to the corrupt and compromised environmental organizations, such as Greenpeace, the Sierra Club, and all the other similar organizations that sprang up in more recent years. They are all claiming to be concerned and passionate about environmental issues, yet not once did they EVER mention anything about chemtrails or HAARP. "Why would that be?" you might ask, being somewhat naive—just as I was when I first discovered the hypocritical fact that these organizations refuse to acknowledge this major contradiction between what they say and what they do. These organizations are always publicly portrayed as serious and passionate about ending any and all environmental challenges, yet when one brings up chemtrails and HAARP, they are suddenly silent. They turn the narrative to something else, or they pretend that chemtrails and HAARP do not even exist.

I became aware of this about ten years ago when I started to receive a huge number of emails from many of these environmental organizations, asking me for donations to help support them. I asked them some simple questions about what they use their donations for and why I have never, ever seen them even mention chemtrails and HAARP. I guess it is the old "elephant in the room" type of situation. Each time I asked them they sent me another email, and each time they totally ignored my question as if I had not asked it.

I received at least two dozen of these donation emails that were supposed to be from different, individual members of each of these organizations. They all totally ignored my important questions, and I felt they expressed a lack of integrity by not ever addressing these two topics. Finally, I just unsubscribed from their email lists. It was not until 2019 that I heard from another researcher that the real reason they will never talk about these two "forbidden" topics, is that they would not be able to keep their "nonprofit" status if they did! That the corrupt cabal bureaucracy strictly forbids them from ever discussing certain topics that are a threat to the cabal and their many hidden agendas that are directly related to human depopulation.

The cabal want everyone to stay ignorant of the important issues. Yes, "knowledge is power," and it allows us to be fully informed and empowered. In more recent years, so many people are all in the process of becoming enlightened, just as Q predicted. The Great Awakening is indeed taking place! We just need to remember to "Trust the Plan."

The Cabal Taking Action and Celeste Taking Counteraction

So it was that after these two public presentations and the handing out of hundreds of flyers on the reality of this covert chemtrail spraying operation, the cabal was now focused upon me once again. Just as they had been many times before. As mentioned, they had attempted numerous times to "off me," but were, of course, never successful—what with my Beloved, Celeste, riding shotgun against them all those years.

As I looked up into the sky a few days after the presentations, it was as if the chemtrail patterns seemed more intense and more plentiful than I had ever seen them before. I intuitively sensed that the cabal was specifically targeting me in retaliation, with this greater and more dense amount of chemtrails. The chemtrails were specifically right up over the property and house where I was living. I sensed that the cabal wanted to poison me severely, using the numerous petrochemical toxins that were proven to exist in the chemtrails being spewed out of all those high-flying cabal jets that were constantly crisscrossing the skies. They figured that if they did these spraying operations more intensely just over where I was living, somehow the higher concentrations of these petrochemical toxins could then "do me in," despite how strong my own immune system actually was.

As I looked up into the sky that was so unbelievably filled with so much more chemtrails, now quickly filling up with that usual artificial gray cloud cover, I started to get somewhat pissed off about this. ("No more mister nice guy!"). In fact, as I was looking up at the sky, I suddenly sent a clear and intense telepathic message to all the many Higher Cosmic Light Beings. I telepathically shouted at them all with this message: "Hey, I may have a much stronger immune system than most people on this planet. But I do not like living down here in this petrochemical soup the cabal is constantly spraying out in all their very nasty and negative chemtrail operations, so why don't you all get off your asses and do something about all of this for Earth's humanity!"

I realized right after I had just done this (specifically, passionately, and very sincerely complained to the Higher Light Forces), that I had now officially asked them, on behalf of all humanity, to step in and activate mass planetary Divine Intervention to help neutralize the chemtrails. Of course, I had been individually taking action, as in "God helps those who help themselves." I had specifically been doing as much as I could down here on this 3D level. I had been researching, exposing and sharing this information with as many people as I could, and my efforts had actually been considered problematic by the cabal. My taking all these actions individually DID, of course, give me certain "individual authority" to in turn now ask the Higher Light Forces for help. With a True, Pure Heart's Desire I now asked them, on behalf of all humanity, to begin a more direct form of Divine Intervention.

My combined actions and passionate, positive intent clearly now gave them the Mandated Authority to step in and help more directly. They now began to neutralize all these negative petrochemicals being spewed out every day. About two weeks went by. One night, as I was about to get ready to go to bed, I suddenly, telepathically, heard a Higher Being telling me "to go outside and take a look at the night sky!" (What I did not know on a conscious level until more recently, was that it was actually Celeste who had given me this short but specific message. As I look back on this whole event, I do remember that it did seem like the message was coming from a more "feminine" source, rather than "masculine.")

So, as I walked out the front door of my house and looked up into the sky, suddenly a very bright, large green fireball shot rapidly across the entire sky. Again I heard this same voice (which I know now was my Beloved, Celeste), continuing to telepathically speak with me. At the instant I saw it, I heard her dramatically state, "We're starting to take action!" "Pray tell, what exactly are you doing?" I replied. She explained that the green fireball was a special Merkabah Light Ship that was specifically neutralizing all the toxic and deadly petrochemicals from the chemtrails. The bright, iridescent green glow that was emanating from the ship was specially transmuting these various negative substances.

She also reminded me about something else that had occurred during the 1950s and '60s: Huge number of green fireballs were sighted in the skies all over the world, especially around the areas where the nuclear testing had taken place. The Higher Beings were neutralizing and lowering the high level of radiation that had existed because of the nuclear testing. What is interesting is that I remember in elementary school during the 1960s that the teacher in one of our classes had shown us a film about the dangers of illegal drugs. They showed images of dead fetuses that were deformed and in weird physical states, which they claimed were born this way because of the mother being addicted to a lot of the illegal drugs. But what I had been told right after that, from a Higher Source (which I now realize was also Celeste), was that these specific deformities had actually been caused by the high levels of radiation that had existed. Had they not intervened to lower the radiation level, there would have been many millions more babies born that same way.

I remember that she had next referred to my personal 90-minute Transformational Channeled Readings—specifically to the Higher Light Encodements that were always Energetically Downloaded into the recording of the session. She explained that these Encodements were specially energetically custom-designed for each Light Worker/Volunteer in Earth embodiment who experienced a session with me, and that they help transform their consciousness and help to protect them from various negative cabal influences. Now that the Higher Beings were Divinely Intervening against this whole cabal chemtrail program, these Encodements were also updated to help energetically neutralize any negative effects from the various petrochemical toxins.

Protected by Celeste

As I have mentioned more than once: now that Celeste is energetically a part of my life 24/7, she has shared with me about her constantly protecting me from the numerous attempts of the cabal to kill me. I knew "beyond a shadow of a doubt" that

I was being protected and watched over. It is just so awesome and wonderful to have recently discovered that it was my very own Beloved, Cosmic Other-Half, Celeste who had made it her own very personal mission to keep watch over me, and to stop any harm from coming to me from the cabal.

As I look back with much greater hindsight and wisdom, with a more expanded perspective, it is interesting to recall many of these earlier events that had such an impact in my life. This added dynamic makes Celeste's Unconditional Love and Devotion even more significant to me; understanding what she had to do to make sure that these constant dangers of my life being ended by the cabal would not be successful, no matter how many times they tried.

I know that I have always lived my life fearlessly, with the Absolute Faith and Inner Knowing that I would survive the cabal's continuous attempts to do me in. I know that these attempts were not just on a physical level, but also on an emotional, psychological and psychic level. The cabal constantly targeted the very toxic emotional relationship that I endured with my ex, by causing a psychic amplification of her imbalances to literally make life a living hell for me. In these more recent years, I have had to do a lot of special healing modalities and stress relief protocols *(including keeping anyone or anything that originally caused me this stress entirely out of my life!)*.

The extreme damages to me from the PTSD effects had grown greater and greater throughout all those decades of "fulfilling my mission," of "enduring for the sake of everyone else"—sharing what the cabal was planning, because I wanted as many others as possible to know what I knew so that this knowledge could empower them.

I was willing to endure, to emotionally suffer for the Greater Good, so that one day as I stand before the Higher Councils, looking back on my life, I would know I had chosen right. Had I "taken the easier and more comfortable path", or had I chosen to "stay in that difficult and emotionally, psychologically intense relationship because of the Mission"? Despite how horribly emotionally toxic it was, the Mission was more important to me, I had risen to the occasion. I realize now that I could finally finish up that earlier phase of my mission, so that I could be free to allow myself this wonderful period of "emotional R. and R." with Celeste and be able to experience this later phase of my mission.

So yes, being "Blessed and Blissed by Celeste" is allowing me this long overdue Healing and Emotional Rejuvenation. I am Totally Blessed by being in the presence of Celeste, an Immortal Intergalactic Goddess, my Muse and Beloved.

Celeste told me on more than one occasion that I should have literally died decades ago, because of all the incredible emotional abuse and the unbelievable stress that I experienced. Unfortunately, Celeste could not protect me much from that; I was mostly on my own. So, it literally IS a miracle that I am still alive after all this abuse and stress. I have so much to be Blessed for, and will now be able to enjoy my life a little more like a "normal person" does.

It has been a wonderful Revelation to find out about all that she did for me for so many decades. It is wonderful to now have a chance to share my life with her, and to share this awesome experience of writing this book with her. In writing our book we aim to inspire others, so that you, too, can be reunited with your own Cosmic True Love and discover the greater meaning and mission for you being a Volunteer in Earth embodiment; that you are soon to hook up with your own Beloved, through the Energy of IntergalacticMatch.com!

Yes, call upon the Love Ops/Special Forces of Romantic Love to help YOU find YOUR own Cosmic True Love, and Live Happily Ever After! I feel that this book, or rather, "Celeste's and my book," may be one of the catalysts that will help accomplish you reuniting with your Cosmic True Love. I am told that much more than my first book, this book (with its specific Cosmic Romantic theme and reality) will draw more people to it from this younger generation of Light Workers/Volunteers in Earth embodiment who want to be more energetically activated into their own missions for being here at this time of human history—in this new timeline, as the Great Awakening continues to more powerfully unfold as long as we can remember to "Trust the Plan"!

CHAPTER 16

"Diet" and Other Protocols that Will Help Connect You With Your Own Cosmic True Love

Thousands of various diet books have been published here in the U.S., that are all touted as the ultimate diet book to buy, allowing you the maximum health potential.

Doublespeak

First of all: I do not like the word "diet." For the same reasons I do not like such words as "insane" or "incorrect"; as I have pointed out to many people through the years, these are "doublespeak" words. They are supposed to mean a certain thing, but they "subconsciously" mean the exact opposite to the one using, thinking, or speaking them. For example, we are told that the word that "insane" means that a person is NOT sane, that it is the opposite of being "sane." But to be accurate and correct, the word should be spelled "unsane." It is the same as with the word "incorrect": We are programmed to believe that this word means the opposite of being "correct," but once again this doublespeak word subconsciously affects us the exact opposite. To be accurate, it should be "uncorrect."

When one takes apart the word "diet" or "die-it," in my opinion it becomes a little more noticeable how the dietary industry really knows about this negative doublespeak protocol: They have utilized it against most people who are attempting to become healthier and slenderer by using the word "diet," because it consists partially (or mostly) of a word that is connected to "death." The use of this death-connected word ("die" in "die-it") when one attempts through "dieting" to achieve a goal of being healthier and slenderer, is unfortunately subconsciously causing one to energetically sabotage themselves, because of the energetic implication of the doublespeak.

Now, it can be quite different if one knows and understands this doublespeak concept. One can deliberately program themselves to NOT be influenced by this subtle, hidden in plain sight tactic by the die-tary industry. One can program themselves to be able to energetically achieve their sincere goal, by overcoming this type of energetic manipulation of one's mind and consciousness.

Other examples of doublespeak words: When one answers the phone with the word "hi," as opposed to saying "hello." It should be pretty obvious what I am about to point out, right? "Hell-low" is how it is pronounced, and this is NOT a vibration we want to create for ourselves or those who we are speaking to. So, we should always remember to say "hi"; energetically manifesting a HIGH, heavenly vibrational reality here on Earth. There has been enough hellishness from the cabal, now it is our opportunity to create Heaven on Earth.

Two other words I do NOT like to ever say are "demonstrate" and "no-brainer." "Demonstrate" has a negative thing added to other letters; "demon-strate." Then we have something that should be a "brainer", not a "no-brainer" (as in having NO BRAIN to be able to think and reason with!). The word we use should be "brainer," NOT "no-brainer." By saying the phrase, "This is a no-brainer," once again we are programming our subconscious to make us more stupid, rather than smarter. Having powerful cognitive awareness allows us to be able to figure-in (not, "figure out"!) with intelligence what any situation is. Most of the masses have been stuck in total denial until recently. Now that the Great Awakening is going on, people are waking up out of this mass cognitive dissonance.

Another example of a negative phrase is, "the sky is the limit," which is supposed to imply an unlimited distance or opportunity. This phrase was designed by the cabal to limit our potential, by "self-sabotaging" our actual unlimited potential. So, the sky is NOT—and never has been—a limit, unless WE make it our so-called limit.

Subliminal Programming

When it comes to being affected by words; be also aware of subliminal programming. I remember an ad that was aired quite often on television over 20 years ago. One of the actors in the ad was repeating this phrase, "Eat pork, eat pork; it's the other white meat!" They kept repeating it. Finally, the other actor would ask why were they repeating that phrase. The first actor would reply, "Because I am subliminally programming everyone to buy more pork."

This obvious, "hidden in plain sight" type of actual subliminal programming (repeating the same phrase over and over again), is one of the ways that people can be "programmed" to do what others want them to do.

Of course, if one really went to the trouble of challenging the makers of the ad, questioning their real reasons for doing as they did, they would just laugh and deny that there was any real agenda behind what they were doing. They would pretend that this was just a parody, that they were only humorously saying this phrase over and over again. But the facts are, those who do make up ads, whether it be this type of visual and auditory ad, or those ads that have been printed in various publications for decades, know very well what they are doing.

For many years before the Internet I would specifically pick up certain publications (such as Omni magazine), I trained myself to be able to spot the difficult-to-find "subliminals" (subliminal messages) that were often "airbrushed" into the ads. Subliminals were occurring in every major ad that I saw, about almost every product that was being sold at that time. Usually the subliminal messages consisted of satanic and sexual images that were "airbrushed" into the ad. It did not matter how subtle they were (usually the conscious eye cannot see them unless one knew what to look for, as I did) or if the images were upside down; the subconscious of the reader would still "pick up on them" and be affected by them. This would influence people subliminally to be more open to purchasing their products.

I also read an interesting and enlightening book that was first published in 1976, which completely exposed this subliminal tradition found in the advertising sections of all major corporations. The book is titled *Media Sexplotation* and is written by Wilson Bryan. It is available at Amazon: https://www.amazon.com/Media-Sexploitation-Wilson.

I remember when I was young (about 9 years old), sitting in front of that old black and white TV that we had. I was watching something, I do not even remember what. But all of a sudden, I heard the voice of a Higher Being begin to speak to me, and it said, "They are broadcasting subliminals at you and everyone else." When I heard this voice clearly tell me this fact, I knew instinctively that it was not to just freak me out but merely a warning. This Being and those who this Being were connected to just wanted me to be aware of the need to use Discernment. The Being also taught me what I could do to program myself NOT to be influenced by subliminals.

Even then, as early as the 1960s, certain energies/frequencies/signals that the conscious mind was not aware of were broadcast to whoever happened to be watching the "boob tube." Of course, back then this whole subliminal programming was extremely crude, just in the CIA's infancy stages of early development, more theoretical than anything else. But they had obviously begun a few early tests. Ultimately, they wanted to perfect these types of energetic broadcast signals, which the conscious mind would not even suspect was intended to influence what we "think, say and do." The CIA would also perfect their "MK-Ultra" mind control programs, creating sleeper agent-Manchurian Candidates. With these the CIA could, over long distance, program many people to suddenly start rioting and looting under the disguise of civil unrest. The CIA would take control over people's lives, using the tiny biochips that people received through their vaccinations. People would then be used by the cabal to create total anarchy and chaos. These people are not able to discern how they are being used by the cabal in their new world order agenda.

Thank God that the Higher Forces, working with the White Hat Alliance, have been in the process of deactivating these methods for controlling people. People are beginning to truly wake up and are now coming out of their cabal induced zombie trances.

Just recently I found out that it was, of course, Celeste who had given me that early warning about subliminals. This knowledge allowed me to empower myself not to be affected by subliminals. I programmed myself, decreeing that no matter what type of negative subliminals I saw being broadcast at me, or saw while looking at an ad in some magazine, or heard while listening to the lamestream fake news media, my subconscious would automatically reprogram it and have it affect me only in a positive way (opposite of what was intended by those who created it).

Our Bodies Are Holy Temples

Getting back to our health and well-being and what we can do with unlimited potential. (We will not use the word "diet" anymore, except when we refer to what most people have traditionally used when referring to their "health goals.") So often, many people have thought more about how they look outwardly, rather than thinking holistically about their actual health, body, mind, emotions and spirit. "Holistic" is a great word, because it consists of the word "hol," or "whole," and "holi," which is derived from the word "holy" (as in Sacred and Divine).

So, we want to treat our bodies as holy temples. I will often use the analogy that we are either a "fast, moving clean river," or we are a "slowly moving swampy bog." I have mentioned before the analogy of how the health of our country has been a swampy bog, and how the Q White Hat Alliance and President Trump are in the role of guardians in the process of "draining" this horrible swamp of filthy, evil corruption (thank God/Goddess for this!). As guardians to our own health and well-being, we, too, need to make sure that our physical bodies are not polluted, toxic, corrupted swamps. We want to make sure that whatever we put into our bodies is of the highest quality, non-GMO and 100% organic. Yes, not even "conventionally grown" crops are good enough, as they are sprayed with chemical pesticides and grown in chemical fertilizers. While this is supposed to be better than GMOs, it is still adding to the toxic filth that so many people's bodies consist of.

A great device that was developed years ago is the "live blood cell analysis" machine, also known as "dark scope microscope." This allows one to have their blood analyzed, and one can see their blood cells blown up to a large size where one can easily see how healthy or toxic their blood actually is.

Food Items and Ingredients to Avoid

One can use "kinesiology testing," also known as "muscle testing," to know if something is either good, healthy or non-allergic for them to ingest, or unhealthy, toxic and allergy-causing to them. A trained kinesiologist merely holds the item up on the main meridian of their body, in the center of their body where the seven main chakras (or energy centers) of the body are also located. The kinesiologist will have the person hold their arm out to the side or straight in front of them. The kinesiologist will then pull down on the person's arm, while asking if that particular item is good or negative to the person. The theory behind kinesiology is that one's subconscious, through muscle response, will respond with a definite answer. If the item is good for them, they will be able to hold their arm up. But, if it is negative for them, they will not be able to hold their arm up. I was trained many years ago to do kinesiology testing, and it was always interesting to watch how some food items might vary for a person.

During the kinesiology testing there were many items that everyone appeared to be "allergic" to. I will now cover a listing of some of the food items or substances that always appeared to cause a negative allergic reaction to everyone I ever tested:

Artificial Sweeteners

Avoid any of the artificial sweeteners, such as "Equal" (also known as "NutraSweet"), "Sweet N Low," "Splenda," etc. I still remember when the artificial sweetener NutraSweet was first presented in the late 1980's, while I was living in Scottsdale,

Arizona. In the summertime there, the temperature can easily get up as high as 120 degrees. NutraSweet was touted as low calorie, and was pushed upon the unsuspecting population of ignorant people who were looking for anything that would help them lose weight, be more slender, etc.

I read several articles that appeared in the alternative media, which were warning about the negative side effects of using this new artificial sweetener. A number of independent scientists and doctors had determined that when Equal (NutraSweet) was warmed up hot enough, at over 80-90 decrees, part of this artificial sweetener would transform into formaldehyde (also known as "embalming fluid"). This was why I mentioned the significant and questionable timing (in the very high temperature of the summer) of when this first of many such toxic sweeteners suddenly became available to the ignorant and trusting public. The corrupt FDA allowed this toxic and deadly substance to be "okayed."

Splenda, a more recent artificial sweetener, uses the toxic substance chlorine (which is used to chemically purify swimming pools) to produce their unhealthy substance.

I have noticed that the natural, non-artificial sweetener stevia (which is actually healthy) is usually thrown into this same category, when one types the phrase "artificial sweeteners" on the search bar on the internet. This is an example of how the cabal likes to confuse a person who is just "waking up" to what is healthy for them versus what is unhealthy. Stevia, which comes also in a small packet, legally challenged the Equal company many years ago, after Equal tried varies unscrupulous things to destroy and falsely malign this natural sweetener company. If

I remember correctly, there was a massive law-suit settlement in favor of stevia. Having the stevia natural sweetener being referred to as "another artificial sweetener" is totally uncorrect.

Chlorinated Water (Use Natural Purification Systems Instead!)

It is interesting that when foreign Olympic swimmers have come over to swim in the U.S., they refuse to swim in the swimming pool until the chlorinated water is drained out. Water without this toxic poison is then used to refill the swimming pool. Over in other countries they are a lot more educated about so many things that are bad for one's health. Unfortunately, over here the cabal tends to be more in control of suppressing this knowledge.

There are plenty of natural purification systems, protocols and technologies, such as a pool ozone generator, that emits a silver and copper charge into the water, which kills all the bacteria. I also have a small portable ozonator in Celeste's and my apartment, which emits healthy negative ions and ozone. I also have a small unit that I have worn around my neck when I have flown with commercial airlines. They just recirculate the same polluted, stale air all during the flights, and this mini air purifier allowed me to constantly breath fresh, uncontaminated air.

Throughout the 1980s and '90s, I personally met (what I am estimating to be) over 200 to 300 undercover and military intelligence agents, whistle-blowers who had originally belonged to the various "alphabet soup agencies." They all had "affectionate" nicknames for the various agencies that were supposed to protect our health and well-being. These agencies did the exact opposite, endangering our lives with all the things they allowed to be produced and sold to the gullible and trusting public. The whistle-blowers referred to the FDA as the "Federal Death Agency," which is "in bed" with the CDC (referred to as the "Center For Disease Creation"), which also is "in bed" with the WHO ("World Hell Organization").

Refined White Sugar

Avoid refined white sugar, whether white or fructose. Obviously sugar is causing bad health effects, such as the cavities in one's teeth. In addition, the sugar industry is corrupt.

Many years ago I heard a report from one of the whistle-blowers, stating that one of the CEOs of one of the largest sugar companies in the entire world discovered energetic technologies to make a substance more addictive. With this technology one can energize almost anything one wants to with energy from something else. A radionic device is used to perform this mass energizing of a product or substance. The corrupt and evil C.E.O. utilized this technology to energize the majority of the refined white sugar produced in the world with the same energetic frequency as that of cocaine. The result was sugar that would be even more addictive than the sugar itself normally was.

I know this may seem like some far-out, unsubstantiated conspiracy theory. But my intuition said, at least to some degree, that this was in fact done. By making people more addicted to sugar, it was an efficient negative protocol to increase the sales of sugar.

Pig

Avoid anything associated with the pig (bacon, pork, ham, etc.). I tuned into the fact that the pig was originally created during the time of Atlantis, when the negative genetic scientists started to create all kinds of weird plants, insects, and animals that had not existed on Earth prior to that time. What is interesting, is that an old science fiction movie produced in the 1950s titled, "The Lost Continent of Atlantis," actually presented pig-like creatures, half human and half animal, that were created by splicing other animals with the human DNA/RNA. It seemed that the script writers intuitively tuned into this fact and made it a part of the script. The movie also shows how corrupt Atlantis became toward the end of its existence, which was one of the reasons it had to ultimately be destroyed.

Both the Jewish and Muslim religious teachings state that they are not allowed to eat anything from the pig, because they consider the pig unclean and unfit for humans to eat.

From a scientific, biological, physiological, and energetic point of view it is true that when one examines the blood platelets of a pig, one finds that the electrolytes in the blood platelets are energetically spinning exactly opposite those of a human. If one ingests anything from the pig (even lard, which many Mexican restaurants use in their cooking), this will energetically reverse one's own electrolytes. It will cause one's ability of being more intuitive to become less attuned. So, eating pig affects certain spiritual/psychic abilities and causes numbing/dumbing upon one's consciousness.

Sometimes, the best way to break someone's habit is to "gross them out": A few years ago, I watched a person take a piece of either pork, ham or bacon (in other words, I do remember that this particular piece of meat was specifically from a pig). As I watched, the person opened up a bottle of Coco-Cola and poured it over the pig meat. Within a few moments, all the maggots and parasites (which are always in anything from a pig) started to freak out and were crawling and wiggling around, because of how extremely toxic Coco-Cola actually is—even to these maggots and parasites that always exist in pigs. I was told many years ago that it would usually take an extremely high temperature to kill the maggots and parasites that always exist in anything that is from the pig. By that time, all that remained would just be a burned up, charred piece of flesh, and no one would want to eat it any way!

Most Animal Meat

Avoid most meat from other animals as well. Always avoid it if it is commercially produced. When I was 15, I became a vegetarian when my father came down with skin cancer. We had already been eating healthily, but we had not given up meat. We went to speak to a vegetarian holistic person, who told my father that if he quit eating meat, his skin cancer would go away. Within about a month, the skin cancer was all gone. I took a look at this situation and decided that it would be much better for me, as well—not only because of the physical aspects of greater health, but also because of the more spiritual benefits.

Animals are usually raised in the worst toxic, unhealthy conditions imaginable. In addition, consider what the poor animal goes through when they are slaughtered, etc. In my opinion, animals are sentient, feeling forms of life and have a right to live and not be killed or slaughtered for eating their flesh. (I know that as I am guilty of occasionally eating salmon lox, I am being somewhat hypocritical to even make a point about this.)

Commercially Produced Eggs and Dairy Products

Avoid any eggs and dairy products if they are "commercially," non-organically produced. I will only eat healthy eggs from healthy and happy chickens raised organically in a pasture: There the chickens have literally many acres of wide-open space to move around in and lay their eggs in, and they are only fed organic food. Eggs from pasture-raised hens are much healthier than eggs from "free range" hens. "Cage free" does not mean too much, the chickens are mostly still stuck in large cages, with very little space to be able to move around. Hens need to be out in the wide-open space, to be totally healthy and happy.

As far as diary is concerned, since I am not a vegan, I eat dairy products. However I will only eat healthy, organic quality dairy products, and usually from either goats or sheep, not from cows. One of the reasons for this is that I have been told from more than one source that when one blows up the fat molecules of cows, goats and sheep under a microscope, the fat molecules from goats and sheep tend to be smaller than that of cows (even if they are 100% organic). To me, this indicates that it is much easier to digest dairy products from goats or sheep than from cows. I have eaten dairy from cows raised organically, but I still tend to like my dairy from that of goats or sheep.

I usually always eat raw cheese (not pasteurized), because once it is pasteurized, you kill all of the natural enzymes that are really health-enhancing.

There are a few great natural dairies that produce tasty and healthy raw goat cheddar cheese. Trader Joe's is the only source that I can find that actually sells raw, unpasteurized Italian Romano cheese from sheep's milk. One of the greatest, most delicious things I know is to sip a glass of "cold duck" (organic red wine mixed with a sweet champagne), while nibbling on a piece of this wonderful, healthy raw Romano cheese—it will be an "oral orgasm" in your mouth!

I also love both the plain and vanilla flavored goat yogurt that Redwood Farms Dairy produces. The plain yogurt is thick, smooth, and creamy. It is a tasty, healthy substitute for cow sour cream when one is eating something hot and spicy. The vanilla goat yogurt is wonderful to eat by itself, and is especially great for smoothies. In fact, one of my favorite delicious and luscious things to eat in the summer, is to mix up this delicious creamy vanilla goat yogurt with cut-up pieces of ripe organic mangoes and peaches, along with a few table spoons of organic raw liquid honey. All mixed up together: yes, another "oral orgasm" in your mouth!

It is my understanding that humans have been raising goats and sheep far longer than cows. And yet, the raising of cows has become one of the worst forms of pollution—both for the environment and for the humans. I believe that many eating habits are destructive not only to people's personal health, but also problematic because of the mass exploitation of these poor animals from the moment they are born until the horrible, terrifying moment that they are slaughtered.

Coffee (Drink Km Instead!)

Moving on to another unhealthy item: Coffee. As the saying goes: "Don't even get me started" on how bad or toxic it is to drink this vile stuff. "Where do I even begin?!"

Well, first you need to know its actual origin on Earth, how it first came about. How I came to know about this is interesting, as it is connected with another drink called "Km."

The Km is a healthy, herbal drink that I have been drinking since I was first "re-introduced" to it 1987. ("Km" happens to be the symbol for potassium in the periodic table of elements.) I say "re-introduced," because it is my very strong perception that back in the early times of Lemuria and Atlantis, the people of those civilizations had many healthy, elixir herbal liquid drinks. These drinks helped the people live for as long as a thousand years, which was originally quite common. (Of course, another part of what helped them to be so energetically vibrant and happy was being with their Cosmic True Love/Tantric Twin-Flame partner, and all the intense, tantric multiple-orgasmic lovemaking that they experienced every day for their entire life when the Nirvanic Ecstasy Grid was in place.)

It is also interesting how the researcher known as Dr. Karl Jurak first "re-discovered" the Km formula. Dr. Jurak was working for his doctoral thesis at the Vienna University, in Austria in 1922, trying to find a way to increase one's ability to assimilate oxygen through natural botanicals. His research came about because of a personal challenge: he loved to climb the Alps, and he had unfortunately experienced getting more tired and low on oxygen than he felt he should.

His theory was that if he could molecularly combine certain herbs together, the synergy should result in something that would drastically increase his oxygen uptake as well as cleanse his body of any toxins. So, Dr. Jurak began to scientifically experiment in the University's laboratory, combining numerous different herbs. He was attempting to discover exactly what molecular combination of herbs would allow him to create this very special "herbal elixir." But after many weeks, he still had not accomplished what he was after.

Finally, one night he had a vivid dream. In this dream, it is my understanding that the Higher Forces came to him, and showed him the exact molecular combination he had been searching for. He suddenly woke up with the exact formula, and wrote it down on a piece of paper. In the morning he went to the laboratory, and after mixing the exact combination of molecules from the various botanicals—voila! He was able to prove through his research that the ingesting of this herbal botanical allowed him to increase his intake of oxygen by at least 30%. Jurak had been working on his doctoral thesis, and he was given Top Honors for his research.

When I first got involved with this Km, I became aware of its ancient origins. Matol Botanical, the company that had distributed Km in the 1980s and '90s, knew nothing of this. Because of what I expect was interference by the imbalanced forces, Matol experienced many financial challenges that caused it to almost go out of business. Km then became part of another company called Univera. Univera still sells Km, in 32 oz. special medical grade plastic bottles.

I know that the Km that is being sold now is still based on the original formula that Dr. Karl Jurak had received in that dream. Just as it was in the later '80s when I first got involved in distributing it, this unique herbal formula causes little crystals to form in the bottle, which one can see and hear rattling around once the bottle gets empty. They look like tiny quartz crystals, and I have saved a lot of these from the different bottles that I have used and emptied over the decades.

I became aware of how "electromagnetic" this Km formula is, one day back in 1987, right after I had just opened up a new bottle of the Km. As I put my mouth up to drink a sip out of the bottle, suddenly (and this is God's/Goddess's honest truth!) a tiny spark shot off from the Km formula itself at the edge of the lip of the bottle, against my lip. I just stared at it in surprise at what I had just experienced.

Later, I was guided to make up another combination herbal drink, with the Km being a part of this even more interesting combination. For many years, I would mix up a couple of packets of powdered vitamin C (Emergen-C) into a supplement drink. In each packet of Emergen-C there was 1,000 Mg. of vitamin C, as well as a huge amount of electrolytes, antioxidants, nutrients, etc. The only drawback about this particular vitamin C-supplement was that it was sweetened with fructose, which is really not good for the body. Then I discovered a similar type of powdered vitamin C -packets named Effer-C, produced by NOW foods. It is sweetened with Stevia rather than fructose, and it has basically the same combination of the other great ingredients. So, now my combination drink is even better for one's body.

I mix up two packets of the Effer-C into a large glass of water, along with about 11 or 12 drops of another supplement known as GSE. (GSE is short for Grapefruit Seed Extract. It is a liquid concentrate, made by NutriBiotic. GSE is great for eliminating candida and other toxins from the body.) I mix all of this together and have it ready to drink—but first I use a small shot glass to drink my daily ½ oz. of Km. I always allow the Km to set in the back of my throat for about 15 seconds (kind of like an herbal, sublingual tincture), before I swallow it. Immediately after swallowing the Km, I then start sipping the glass of the vitamin C mixture. Within a few minutes of mixing this all up and then drinking it in the order that I have described, many people can feel it energetically kick in as all that electrolyte, electromagnetic and oxygenation activity hits the blood stream. The "morning buzz," as I like to call it!

I also drink another 24 oz. glass of water right after that first one, which makes it two glasses altogether (48 oz.). I do this at least an hour before I eat my first meal of the day. I drink another two large glasses of water in the late afternoon, at least an hour before the evening meal. This helps to flush one's entire system, which helps one to be more like that fast-moving clean river, and less like that toxic, slow-moving swampy bog.

For those who would like to purchase one or more 32 oz. bottles of Km so that they can then enjoy my special-combination herbal elixir recipe, here is the phone number for Univera: 800-363-1870.

But getting back to coffee: My first insight into the origins of this unhealthy, toxic brew actually came about while tuning into the origins of Km. Km was one of the many herbal elixir drinks of Lemuria and Atlantis. It was not called Km then, but it was still made from the same formula as the one Dr. Karl Jurak received in his dream. Km is dark brown in color, just as coffee happens to be. But unlike Km, which was drunk for many thousands of years, Coffee was actually the first negative witch's brew. These ancient satanic witches brewed coffee from the coffee beans that the draconians brought to Earth to replace the Km elixir. This had the exact opposite effect on a person's body, mind, emotions, and consciousness.

Most people assume, based upon all the advertising, that it is the caffeine in the coffee that makes it so bad for a person. However, I drink organic Green Tea, which also has caffeine in it, but I have never found this type of caffeine to pose any problem. Perhaps the caffeine in green tea is different from the caffeine in coffee? Anyway, even 100% organic and decaffeinated coffee it is still unhealthy and toxic. The coffee is bad for one's health because of the oils in the coffee. Drinking coffee is kind of like dumping battery acid into your stomach—that's how acidic it is to the body.

Both through a Kinesiology test and a live blood cell analysis, it becomes obvious how toxic coffee is and how allergic everyone is to it. And this is just on the physical level. When one ingests this original first, negative satanic witch's brew, it causes one's Third Eye to close. The coffee causes a numbing/dumbing effect on one's ability to more easily tune into Higher knowledge and wisdom.

To be a clear channel, I highly recommend not ever drinking coffee. Just as with anything from the pig, coffee causes the electrolytes in one's blood platelets to reverse and to go in left spin, as opposed to the normal and energetically healthy right spin that one wants for excellent health, a clear mind and a Higher attuned consciousness. Instead, drink the Km; it will be a lot better for you in so many wonderful ways.

Tap Water

I assume that everyone reading this book is somewhat educated and enlightened about not ever drinking tap water, because of how very impure it is. The deadly poisons fluoride and chlorine are but two of many pollutants to stay away from in tap water.

I usually fill up my non-PBA water jugs with the pure water that I get out of the Glacier reverse osmosis water machines that are found at many large grocery stores. I had the water from one of these machines tested with a special water quality tester, and the water tested as being excellent and pure. These particular water machines usually have a filter in them which is "Angstrom-sized." There are a hundred angstroms in one micron, so these machines do produce great quality water.

I have a rule that I follow because our skin is the largest organ of our body: if there is something I cannot ingest because of it being toxic and unhealthy for me, then that means I would also not put in on the outside of my body. So, when taking a bath or shower one wants to make sure that the water one baths in is also pure. I shower with an excellent shower water filter, which is guaranteed to remove over 99% of all toxins, chemicals, etc., so that I do not take in these toxins. In fact, it has been seen that when we shower in tap water, we take in more pollutants than if we drink eight 16 oz glasses of tap water.

Fast Food

It is amazing to me to still see people going into any of those fast-food restaurants, whether it be McDonald's or any other similar hamburger joint. I remember seeing a video from a number of years ago, of a person who had bought a McDonald's hamburger and just placed it out in the open, without it being covered. He let it just sit there, and after examining it many years later, there was literally NO mold of any kind growing on it. So, what does this tell a person? Maybe there are SO MUCH chemical preservatives in the hamburger that one would not ever want to eat it.

One more thing about not ever eating the hamburgers from any of the various fast-food restaurants: Alternative news story articles have come out exposing the fact that there *really was* discovered ground-up human flesh (from young children) in the hamburgers. Yes, I read those stories. Despite the attempts from the cabal to debunk the stories as made-up, urban legends, my Higher Intuition (as well as Celeste) confirms that is indeed true. There are evil and twisted people (including the corrupt C.E.O.s of these fast-food corporations) who have performed evil, satanic child sacrifices. They believe that if they secretly add ground-up pieces of some of the sacrificed children to the ground-up hamburgers and people unknowingly ingest this, then those people will also subconsciously take on this same horrific frequency, and this manipulates the people's consciousness. Word to the wise: just stay away from anything from these fast-food joints!

Sodium Fluoride and Aluminum

Two of the most toxic things that people have been brainwashed to use, are sodium fluoride and aluminum. Fluoride is a by-product of processes in aluminum companies, which are primarily owned by the Rockefeller family, of the illuminati bloodline.

During the Bolshevik Russian Revolution in 1917, fluoride was added to the water supply. It was discovered by early researchers that fluoride ingested into the human body caused calcification of the pineal gland, which causes the Third Eye in the center of the forehead to atrophy and shut down. This in turn causes one's normal, healthy abilities of discernment and intuition to cease to function, which allows one to become numbed and dumbed out. Thus the masses could be more easily brainwashed and manipulated by the cabal-controlled fake news lamestream media. In 1917, the fluoride in the water assured that the Russian people were more easily brainwashed to believe in what was being forced upon them.

The Nazi's did the same thing in Germany, adding fluoride to the water supply. This helped in propagandizing Hitler's rise to power, as the Germans were more easily brainwashed to believe what they were all officially told.

Back in the early 1980s, after I had traveled to Denver on my first lecture tour, I stayed for a few days at an elderly woman's place. She had an entire bookcase devoted to the many suppressed books, articles and documentation that really exposed the entire fluoride agenda of the power elite. Among the many items that she had were actual transcripts from the House Committee On Unamerican Activities from soviet agents, that documented who had helped promote the whole agenda of mass fluoridation of the U.S. water supply. The communists wanted to cause the population of the U.S. to be numbed and dumbed out, to make it easier to accomplish the larger communist goals. Of course, after the Berlin Wall came down and the so-called Cold War ended in the late '80s, most people assume that such secret agendas also ended.

But, being a student of history (that is, the history that the cabal does not want anyone to be aware of), we Truthers and conspiracy realists (yes, we are "conspiracy realists," NOT "conspiracy theorists"!) know that the international bankers/illuminati bloodline families, financed BOTH sides of the wars and revolutions that occurred in the 20th century. Not only for greater profit from all the "war toys" that were produced in the factories owned by these illuminati families, but also for the profit of all the rebuilding afterwards. It was the Rockefellers, Rothschilds and other illuminati bloodline families who amassed huge fortunes from these planned-ahead-of-time events.

So, the use of fluoride was pushed upon the gullible masses both during and after these various events, just as mercury was also pushed upon us through the dental industry. They tried to make us believe that a substance which is very toxic and deadly by itself, is somehow magically transformed into something good and beneficial for us when it is used as one of the main ingredients in fillings. And let's not forget all those toxic and deadly vaccines, and the multi-billion dollar vaccine industry which brainwashes the masses to believe that this toxic substance is now good for us in the vaccines. Remember the old saying, "If it looks like a duck, if it quakes like a duck, if it walks like a duck, then by God, it IS a duck!"

But, the bottom line is that if you are still using that commercial toothpaste, or even one of those so-called natural toothpastes that still has fluoride listed as one of the ingredients, then throw it away and buy a toothpaste that does NOT have this toxic substance in it.

The same goes for all those commercial, non-organic underarm deodorants: almost all of them have either aluminum and/or fluoride in them. When you realize that there are important glands right near or under this part of our body, you should avoid all those deodorants. This goes especially for women, with all that breast cancer scare going on for years. It has always been my intuitive awareness that one of the main reasons that women have experienced an increase of breast cancer is that the huge increase of using these very toxic commercial deodorants, made by corrupt corporations who do not care about the toxic side effects. As mentioned, there are glands right near or by the woman's underarms, and it is my perception that the toxins end up in these glands, which definitely helps increase the risk of breast cancer.

The other possible culprit of breast cancer is the use of those metal stays in most of the bras that are commercially sold; these negatively affect the health of the breasts as well. There are energy meridians where energy flows in all parts of the body, and I believe the metal stays will disrupt and/or block this normal, more healthy energy flow. And "don't get me started" about the multi-billion dollar medical industry that also, in my opinion, preys on women's F.E.A.R. (False Evidence Appearing Real!) of getting breast cancer.

I have read a number of exposés by women who have thoroughly investigated this whole (so-called) cancer prevention industry. There is a method called a "thermogram," which is a much more healthy and holistic way of accurately detecting (real) cancer. It is less invasive and less profit-oriented. But instead of using a thermogram, the medical establishment continues to push the more expensive and toxic mammograms on ignorant and desperate women. They do not realize that this mammogram procedure appears to cause the very conditions leading to cancer. Also, so many enlightened women have pointed out that just because a lump appears in one's breast, that does NOT necessarily mean that the lump is malignant and needs to be removed.

One must always, of course, consult a medical professional. But unfortunately, so many of the so-called experts and professionals are brainwashed by the traditional medical training of what causes breast cancer, will not even mention the more natural Thermograms. Neither do they mention the side effects of mammograms, that appear to actually create more of the problem, rather than preventing it. So much of traditional allopathic medicine is more interested in the maximum amount of profits it can amass, of how many hospital beds are filled up, rather than really getting the patient well and totally healed from whatever so-called disease or "dis-ease" that someone is experiencing.

Yes, it is so obvious that that original "Hippocratic Oath" of "First, do NO Harm" is so quickly forgotten, and becomes the "Hypocritical Oath," as these medical students are brainwashed through their medical training where Big Pharma influences and basically controls the narrative of what the students are allowed and not allowed to do. Any holistic or preventative approach to medicine will THREATEN Big Pharma's multi-billion-dollar profit strategy of just passing the patient around: Big Pharma keeps patients trapped in the medical system long enough for the companies to extract as much profit as they can, before they discard that person on the pile of all the other dead patients who were taken advantage of.

This corrupt and evil system control and suppress the real, holistic and effective health protocols that truly DO prevent harm and truly keep someone healthy. The medical cabal does not want people suddenly getting enlightened, becoming aware of all this cover-up of natural, but low-profit procedures that really DO heal someone. Any such really effective procedures are suppressed, and such individuals have been killed so that no one else could have access to such wonderful and beneficial modalities and advanced holistic energy technologies.

Protocols I Follow and Foods I Recommend

I also wanted to share some protocols that I follow. They may not be for everyone else, but they work very well for me. For many years I have been experimenting with various schedules of when to eat my meals as well as how many meals I eat each day, searching for that which energetically feels best for me, with my particular life style. The circumstances are obviously quite different for different people, and we each must decide what works best for ourselves.

At no time in sharing what I have in this chapter am I in any way "giving you medical and/or nutritional advice or guidance." I am merely sharing with you my own personal opinions, insights and suggestions, which I have a right to share. Each person must choose whatever is best for them. And as usual, consult your health professional and/or experts before making any changes in your diet, and lifestyle.

I know that this may sound extreme, but after many years of eating a lot of dense-nutrient, healthy foods, I have found that I just do not seem to need as much food as I used to up until about two years ago. I now realize that this was about the time that my Beloved, Cosmic True Love, Celeste, first manifested herself energetically more directly into my life. Suddenly, her awesome, wonderful, potent, energetic, and romantically, truly emotionally fulfilling presence in my life caused me to not need as much food as I used to. I realized that this focus upon food (so much of my craving for tasty exotic type foods, though still healthy, and the need to eat a greater amount more often) was taking the place of something that I was truly missing back when I was in that emotionally toxic and unfulfilling relationship with my ex. Who could ever be fulfilled in such an unhealthy and toxic emotional environment?

Oh, yes, I still must have, and do quite often experience, "oral orgasms" in my mouth! I just realize that the amount of how much I need to eat and how often I eat changed quite markedly after being reunited with Celeste's incredible presence and all her powerful, fully Unconditional Love for me.

I tended to be this way, anyway, but it has been more prominent since being with Celeste: I will fix my first proper meal around 1 or 2 p.m., and my second and last meal of the day in the evening around 8 or 9 p.m. I found after many years with really healthy, high-density food I am not truly hungry in the morning, especially right after waking up.

Exercise and Cosmic Color Meditation

Three times a week, in the morning, I do various exercises (push-ups, sit-ups/crunches, and my yoga practice) along with the Cosmic Color Meditation (which I always share with Celeste). There are actually three different ways to do the Cosmic Color Meditation: One way is to do it very impersonal with some-one else like I do when I share it with others in my Channeling Workshop "The Dynamics of Cosmic Telepathy," there everyone is sitting around me in chairs or on the floor. The second way is a little more personal, with one's partner sitting on the floor with their knees touching yours, or with them sitting in your lap with their legs around you.

The third way is the most personal and intimate way, this is for those romantic partners who are attracted to each and/or feel chemistry with the other person. Here your partner will sit as close as they can to you on your lap, in the sacred Shiva-Shakti-Lotus tantric yoga position, with their legs and arms around you, hugging you tightly. You can do it fully naked from the very beginning or you can be only slightly dressed, with each person, for example, in underwear or bathing suits. To start out, that is. Because obviously, after initially sharing the Cosmic Color Meditation as sacred tantric partners, you will begin to feel energetically, romantically and sexually turned on, and will want to share your love and attraction with each other. The lady is on top, representing the Divine Feminine Goddess (with her sacred Yoni). She will desire to have the man, representing the Divine Masculine (with his Lightning Rod, "standing straight and tall, with rapt and respectful attention to the Goddess!"). Now she is ready with anticipation to receive his sacred Lightening Rod inside of her Yoni, and can then experience multi-orgasmic pleasure and the re-anchoring and reactivating of the Nirvanic Ecstasy Grid.

Smoothie, Nuts and Dried Fruits

But to (attempt!) to bring your attention back to other health protocols: Yes, for me, I find that just two meals a day works best. That first meal consists of a healthy smoothie, for which I will use cut-up pieces of various organic fruit; a banana, one small apple or half of large apple, one small orange or half of large orange. When I can find them, I will add pieces of either ripe mangoes or papaya. I then add a handful of frozen blueberries, a couple of tablespoons of raw honey, and a few spoonfuls of the Redwood Farms Vanilla flavor goat yogurt. I also add a couple of raw eggs.

Many may question me about whether eating raw eggs is a healthy and safe thing to do. There is a warning on many egg cartoons about making sure that you cook the eggs at high enough temperatures to kill any unhealthy bacteria. Well, I have a major issue about this so-called health warning: It is related to the earlier examples of the officials having told us how toxic and even deadly Mercury is. Put it as part of the fillings for teeth or use it as an ingredient in vaccines, and voila; suddenly I guess it has magically become healthy and non-toxic for you. Right?! So here we have the officials warning us again, we the peons, the masses of society, that we should always cook our eggs at high enough temperature to kill all that pesky, unhealthy bacteria. Yet when one goes to a high class, expensive restaurant, where your waiter comes right over to your table, and personally will make up a fresh batch of Caesar salad—there they will break open a fresh, raw egg yolk as part of the dressing. Somehow, voila! once again, things have been magically altered in this temporary alternative universe whenever it suits those in power to do so! Another example is that I have heard numerous people tell a person with a hangover to add a raw egg to whatever they were going to drink in the morning, to counteract the headache and hangover. No, I would never use a commercial, non-organic egg in my smoothie, only those healthy, organic, pasture-raised eggs from healthy and happy chickens. And again, you must do whatever you feel is best and right for yourself.

Right before I make my smoothie, and as part of the same meal, I will usually eat a small handful of raw, organic nuts, along with pieces of dried fruit. I will never eat any dried fruit that is not organic. I always make sure there is no sulfur dioxide in it. Sulfur dioxide is usually added to commercial dried fruit, and is a toxic preservative. It is an "excitotoxin," and bad for the body, I will get back to this in a little bit. I have found that certain raw nuts and dried fruits seem to go together well, such as brazil nuts and dried Turkish figs (Trader Joe's has the best and least expensive organic dried Turkish figs), walnuts and raisins, and almonds and date/coconut rolls or whole Medjool dates.

Almonds

I just mentioned eating almonds in two great combinations, or just by themselves. But unfortunately, almost all almonds that are grown here in the U.S. aren't just non-organic, but are also actually also pasteurized, even though the different companies will claim that they are still "raw." Officially, the FDA (Federal Death Agency) would like us to believe that the reason they pasteurize all almonds gown here in the U.S., even the organic ones, is that harmful bacteria is on the outside of all almonds. Why just almonds and not any of the other types of nuts? This really drives me NUTS!

Well, let me share a little story with you about a false and fabricated tale (fake news from an earlier era, about 60 years ago). I specifically remember how the unscrupulous and corrupt FDA wanted to cover up the true facts about a very important discovery conducted by independent and dedicated health researchers back in the 1960s. And what exactly was this important health discovery, you might ask? These particular researchers had discovered that organic, high quality raw/unpasteurized (of course) almonds happened to have a huge amount of a naturally occurring and concentrated substance known as laetrile (also known as B-17 or amygdalin).

But this in itself was not what had initially concerned the FDA, it was the fact that these researchers discovered that B-17 has a powerful ability to destroy cancer cells of all kinds. In fact, so powerfully and so quickly that it became obvious to Big Pharma and the AMA (the "American Murder Association"), which has always been in bed with the FDA, that this discovery could threaten the multi-billion dollar cancer industry. After having the laetrile injected into the bodies of various cancer patients, voila!, the cancer quickly disappeared and did not come back. This was in my opinion why the FDA created a major story of how dangerous the use of laetrile/B-17 supposedly was. All the labs involved in this research were quickly shut down, it being declared basically illegal to ever do any more research on this.

Yes, it was dangerous alright—to the multi-billion-dollar cancer industry. I personally spoke to two different individuals, one who owned one of those labs and another who personally knew someone else who was in charge of a similar lab involved directly with this research. Despite how the FDA totally twisted the true facts of what was going on into something quite different, the real facts "from the horse's mouth" was that this research showed the real and powerful potential to threaten an industry that is controlled by Big Pharma. The effects of laetrile/B-17 are always suppressed and called fake news—"just some quack," some "fictional urban legend," etc. I do not need to say anymore. But this knowledge about this cancer-counteracting quality, is the same reason that the famous "sleeping prophet," Edgar Cayce, in one of his many readings specifically stated that one should eat a small amount of almonds every day to help prevent one from ever getting cancer.

Really high quality organic and truly raw, unpasteurized almonds are still obtainable from Italy and Spain, despite the efforts of the FDA. For a while Whole Foods was carrying them, but then suddenly they were not available there. Whole Foods is so corporate-controlled, I believe these corporate elements did not like people like myself who specifically knows and understand these true facts. Thus, they were attempting to stop us from being able to obtain these higher quality almonds. Then I discovered the awesome company known as the "Raw Food World," who only carry raw, unpasteurized items like the almonds from outside the U.S. They make them even more nutritious, because they actually "sprout" these raw almonds. Sprouting anything allows greater amounts of its vital nutrients to be more easily available for assimilation into our bodies. Here is their web address: www.therawfoodworld.com.

Wine and Champagne

Next, we go to the subject of wine and champagne. I understand that there are many who, for various reasons, would not ever drink any wine or champagne. Usually it is because many people feel that drinking wine or champagne is somehow a "gateway drink" to the higher alcohol-concentrated hard liquor. These I myself would never drink, since I want to keep my liver and kidneys healthy for as long as I am here on Earth in this present physical body. For me with my enjoyment of various Mediterranean type foods, there is a natural desire to sip a couple glasses of wine and/or champagne together with these type of meals. I have always been able to limit myself to a couple of glasses, rarely going over that limit, as I do not like to have my awareness too impaired.

While I was living in Malibu and the L.A. area back in the early '90s, distributing organic wine, I discovered something interesting that most people do not know regarding organic wine. The many commercial domestic wine companies here in the U.S. would attempt to make us believe that there is no difference between the synthetically added chemical sulfites, that almost all major U.S. wine and champagne producers add to their wines and champagnes, and the naturally occurring sulfites. But there definitely is a difference, and they really know this—but still they publicly pretend that there is not. The substance naturally occurring as a by-product of the natural fermentation process is *definitely* different from the synthetic, chemical sulfites. It is like trying to compare oranges to apples. You really cannot. Period.

All these U.S. domestic companies will try to convince you of this, despite the difference in one's reactions to drinking organic wine (that has no added chemical sulfites) compared to one's reactions to drinking a commercial, domestic wine with chemically added sulfites. It is not usually the alcohol in the wines that causes one to have headaches and a hangover the day after drinking wines and or champagne: it is these chemical, synthetic sulfites that everyone is allergic to, their bodies and brains are reacting to it. A number of times different individuals have told me about experiencing hangover the morning after drinking wine. When I asked them what type of wine they were drinking, they, of course, admitted it was not organic. Once they drank only organic, however, they did not seem to have these problems anymore after drinking.

While distributing organic wine back in the '90s, I found out that the U.S. domestic wine companies did not like the fact that for many years, when one purchased a domestic wine (produced right here in the U.S., as opposed to imported wine or champagne), the label would say "added sulfites." There were definitely added chemical, synthetic sulfites, as opposed to just leaving the wine as nature had originally created it. The companies were changing and tampering with a process that has been going on ever since the first humans discovered how to make wine and other fermented drinks. Hey, even Jesus loved to party and drink wine. Yes, this is the same type of wine that I like to drink; the very same type of wine that "The Dude," "The Man, Himself," liked to imbibe. Then the cabal decided to attempt to improve on nature, by adding a toxic chemical and also an unhealthy substance known as an excitotoxin.

Just as with the chemical sulfite added to dried fruit, sulfur dioxide, excitotoxin is another substance to completely stay away from. Trader Joe's only charges a little over $4.00 for a bottle of good quality organic red wine, so I usually buy the wine there. I also buy the Asti, Italian champagne, which I mix with the wine to make "cold duck." Sometimes, when I cannot get my organic wine at either Trader Joe's or any other store, I may occasionally buy either a French or Italian wine, even if it is not certified organic. Usually the wine companies from countries who have been producing wines for ages tend to either not add, or to add only few, chemical sulfites to their wines, compared to the U.S. commercial wines.

Nitrites that have been added to various processed luncheon meats constitute another excitotoxin. The worst, most toxic of all excitotoxins is MSG, also known as Monosodium Glutamate. It is always used in Chinese restaurants, and is added to many processed commercial foods here in the U.S. These chemical sulfites are bad for our health and well-being. So, use that good old fashion common sense, especially that "galactic common sense." Stay away from these types of chemical additives, as they play havoc with not only our physical health and well-being, but also with our awareness and consciousness.

Vegetable Salad with Dressing

One of the things that I eat at least twice a week, is one of my favorite vegetable salads. Of course, it consists solely of organic ingredients. I mix up cilantro (which is a great, natural blood cleanser), I grate up a large carrot, a large slice of purple cabbage (which has a lot more nutrients than the green cabbage) and a beet. Then I will make my healthy and tasty salad dressing. I add my seasonings, combining three different organic, cold-pressed oils. The oils are good for your body, and two of them are especially great for your brain (in helping to possibly prevent and/or heal various mental disorders Alzheimer's, dementia, etc.). I will add three tablespoons of each of these three oils: olive oil, coconut oil, and flax seed oil. Trader Joe's carries a good quality olive oil, as well as coconut oil. The flax seed oil (which has to be refrigerated) is usually purchased from a specialty health food store. The flax seed oil has huge amounts of all three major Omega oils in one (Omega 3, 6, and 9). In my opinion, the best producer of flax seed oil is Barlean's.

By the way, while on the subject of healthy oils, there are two oils one should never consume, because of how toxic they are: Soy oil is one of them. Anything from the soy bean should be avoided, even if it is organic it is still not a good oil to use, especially not for men, because of it lowers the testosterone levels. But even worse than soy oil, in my opinion, is canola oil. Both oils are subsidized: they are made a lot cheaper and easier to obtain. Canola oil was first made available here in the U.S. back in the 1980s, without going through any testing about its possible negative effects on our health. This oil is derived from rapeseed, and was originally only used for industrial use. The industry needed an oil that was very penetrating, as many types of parts and devices need to be lubricated to work. The oil was never intended to be used for human consumption.

In fact, just to show how corrupt the Canadian government actually is: In 1985 they paid the FDA $50 million to have canola oil listed on the "GRAS" list (the "Generally Recognized As Safe" list). The Canadian government also subsidizes most rapeseed planting and harvesting. In my opinion, after researching it, this oil is NOT safe for human consumption. As Ty Bollinger, author of the best-selling book, *Cancer—Step Outside the Box*, states:

> Did you know that there is no such thing as a "Canola" plant? Olive oil comes from olives, grapeseed oil comes from grape seeds, peanut oil comes from peanuts, and Canola oil comes from... rapeseed. What's wrong with this pic-

ture? Many companies are selling Canola oil as the "healthy" alternative, but Canola oil is nothing more than "bastardized" oil made from genetically modified rapeseed plants. The problem was that "rapeseed oil" was so toxic that the FDA banned it for human consumption in 1956. So, when Canadian growers bred a new variety of rapeseed in the 1970's with a lower content of the toxic erucic acid, they decided they needed a new name for it. The name of the new oil was L.E.A.R. (Low Erucic Acid Rapeseed) oil, but it was eventually renamed "Canola" for marketing reasons, because no company wanted to be associated with a product having "rape" in its name and "rapeseed" oil was well-known to be a toxic oil.

The term Canola was coined from "Canadian oil, low acid" to convince consumers that this "newer and better" rapeseed oil was safe to eat. You see, rapeseed oil was banned from foods, probably because it attacks the heart to cause permanent degenerative lesions and is better used as an industrial lubricant, fuel, soap, and synthetic rubber base. The truth is that rapeseed is the most toxic of all food oil plants. Even insects won't eat it! That's right, Canola oil is a very effective insecticide, and it is the primary ingredient in many "organic" (non-chemical) pesticide control products sprayed on vegetables to kill bugs.

Studies of Canola oil done on rats indicate many problems, such as developing fatty degeneration of heart, kidney, adrenals, and thyroid gland. When the Canola oil was withdrawn from their diet, the deposits dissolved, but scar tissue remained on the organs. Why were no studies done on humans before the FDA placed it on the GRAS list?

Canola oil depresses the immune system and causes it to "go to sleep." Canola oil is high in glycosides which cause health problems by blocking enzyme function, and its effects are cumulative, taking years to show up. One possible effect of long-term use is the destruction of the protective coating surrounding nerves called the myelin sheath. When this protective sheath is gone, our nerves short-circuit causing erratic, uncontrollable movements.

Another problem is that almost all Canola oil is genetically modified. And lastly, please be aware that Canola is a "trans fat" and has been shown to have a direct link to cancer. Trans fats, including hydrogenated or partially hydrogenated oils, cause damage to the cell walls and inhibit oxygen uptake, thus causing cells to turn cancerous. Avoid all of them!!"

Something that really bothers me (as I am an avid label reader of all packaged foods) is noticing this statement: "contains one or more of the following: safflower oil or sunflower oil or canola oil." This statement can even be found on products that are claimed to be 100 % organic. This is a deceptive listing, and it shows to me the producer's lack of principals and integrity. It is an unscrupulous way of deceiving even those who read labels: If one calls the company up, they will claim that they often have to use "whatever is more available," etc., which is supposedly why they will list three different oils. They want to give the impression that they would supposedly normally use one of the first two (much healthier) oils (safflower or sunflower). But as the canola oil was subsidized, it is obvious to me which oil that they will use almost all, if not ALL the time: the canola oil.

Labels like these are so deceptive, but have been allowed by the corrupt system that has existed up until now. So, do get into the habit of reading all labels. If this particular type of statement is shown in the ingredients list, do not buy that item: They *are* going to use the canola oil, rather than the other, much healthier oils.

Getting back to my salad dressing: I mix in the organic, raw, unpasteurized apple cider vinegar (which has the "Mother"), which I usually dilate in a 32 oz bottle three times. In other words; because this vinegar is very potent, diluting it with pure water will give me three 32 oz bottles. The amount of diluted vinegar that I like to use on my salad is quite a bit; literally about 1 ½ to

2 cups of the vinegar. Then I add each of the three different oils, which I then mix up with the seasonings. For seasonings I usually use about one level tablespoon of the pink Himalayan salt, and a huge amount of a very tasty organic seasoning called "Sea Kelp Delight Seasoning." It contains over 24 dried organic herbs, mixed with sea kelp. This seasoning is produced by Bragg, the same company that makes the raw apple cider vinegar. I now mix everything up thoroughly, and oh, does this salad taste so good.

Part of the time that I was preparing my salad, I am usually also in the process of frying four eggs in a skillet on as low a temperature as possible. When the eggs look almost done, I cut up thin slices of the goat cheese and put them all over the eggs to melt. It is delicious to eat the raw cheese with a couple bites of the salad. I also make sure to save a couple of cheese slices to just nibble on: I like to eat a couple of slices of the raw cheese that has not been melted, as there are nutrients in the raw cheese that helps digest the melted cheese. After I take the cooked eggs out of the skillet onto a large plate, I slice up pieces of avocado on top of it.

As mentioned, I am a "lemonaholic" or "limeaholic": I am "addicted" to large amounts of either lemon or lime (freshly) squeezed on most of my evening meals. Ever since the first time I had squeezed a lot of lemon wedges into my soup, I have had to have lemon or lime squeezed into any soup and avocado serving, and into various other dishes as well. I find that the adding of lemons or limes tends to enhance and bring out more of the subtle flavors in many foods. This is especially true for sauces of any kind. It also enhances the nutritional quality of most dishes. I then will sprinkle Himalayan salt, Sea Kelp Delight Seasoning, and organic, powdered white pepper on the meal. And voila—enjoy!

My "Famous" Omelette Meal

I do eat a lot of eggs, prepared in all kinds of ways. In fact, I find that a couple of hard-boiled eggs make a quick and tasty hors d'oeuvre. Just cut the eggs into quarters, sprinkle on some pink Himalayan salt and Sea Kelp Delight Seasoning, pour some hot sauce on them, and voila: another winner.

One of my favorite egg dishes is my "famous" feta cheese and avocado omelette. I eat this with a couple other side dishes. I do not usually eat much potatoes nor tomatoes, because they are both "nightshade" type vegetables: eating too many of them is not a good idea, because of their energetic physiological nature, as opposed to most other vegetables. But neither do I like to totally deprive myself of them. So when I do eat potatoes, I usually eat them once a week with my delicious omelette. I usually use the red potatoes, they tend to have more nutrients than other potatoes.

Before I begin making the omelette, I will fix the potatoes by scrubbing them, pealing them, and then cutting them each up into pieces a little bigger than that of french fries. I dunk them briefly in olive oil, place them all on a tray, and sprinkle powdered garlic on them. I then put the tray into the oven to bake at about 450 degrees for about a half hour. You do need to check them every 15 minutes or so, to make sure that they do not overcook.

To make the omelette I first cut up several slices of either limes or lemons. (I tend to use Trader Joe's organic limes, partly because limes do not hardly ever have any seeds that you need to remove, and they're a little cheaper than bought at other locations). Next I slice up a whole avocado and place the pieces of the avocado all around the wedges of lime or lemon on a small plate. This makes it easy and convenient to pick them up later, to put them inside the omelette once it is ready for them.

I use Trader Joe's sheep feta in my omelette, its price is great considering how much feta there is inside the container. It is also one of the best tasting fetas that I have ever tasted. It IS (and says so on the top of the tube shaped container) Authentic Greek Feta. As a matter of fact, this is one of the items that Trader Joe's has been carrying for quite a few years—it is pretty much one of their staples. I was actually the person who asked them a number of times to make this available in their stores, and they did. There are two large flat chunks of feta in the container, and I use one of them in my omelette. I break it up into smaller pieces in a small bowl. Next I break up four eggs into another bowl, which I beat with a fork and get ready to put in the skillet. I put three teaspoons of coconut oil in the skillet and put the beat-up eggs in it. Then turn it on to whatever temperature is ideal for your situation.

When the eggs have become nice and done and are no longer sticking to the pan, I put pesto sauce all over the open omelette. Then I place the sliced avocado on one half of the omelette (but make sure to save a few pieces of avocado). I squeeze the lime or lemons on the avocado, and sprinkle the salt, white pepper and Sea Kelp Delight Seasoning on it. Next, I put the crumbled-up feta on top of the avocado. (I save a little bit of the feta, mix it with the extra pieces of avocado, squeeze lime or lemon on it and sprinkle on some seasonings; this is just a "little something extra" to enjoy while making your omelette!)

Besides my cut-up and baked slices of potatoes, I also will serve the omelette with seven-grain "Food For Life" flourless, sprouted bread with raisins and cinnamon (not the "Ezekiel" version of this bread, just the "7 Sprouted Grains" version without the soy). All of this is really a great combination, with a lot of interesting multi-contrasts of flavors, spices and seasonings. (You see—to some degree, everyone craves sweet, salty and sour foods. But unfortunately, most people so often choose the wrong, unhealthy type of sweet and salty.) This particular meal includes all these different yet complimenting, unique contrasts. It tantalizes one's tastebuds with the many types of flavors, and yet combines them all nicely, if prepared as I have suggested.

I toast two slices of the bread. I always get my "butter" out of the refrigerator right as I am just beginning to fix this meal. By the time I need to toast my bread, it is nice, soft and easier to spread. I use a great vegan "butter" that I have discovered, which Trader Joe's also carries. It looks and tastes like normal cow butter, but it is mostly made of organic cashew nuts. It is made by Miyoko's, and is a "cultured vegan butter." It is definitely worth trying out, if you haven't already.

Once I have spread the butter on the toasted bread, I will next pour one of the most delectable natural sweeteners over it. It is also sold by Trader Joe's. I think it is a fairly new item in their store, as I did not see it until quite recently. It is organic maple syrup, infused with ginger root. O.M.G.! ("Oh, my God"!

Or rather, since Celeste came into my life; "Oh, my Goddess!") This stuff is SO delicious. Yes, it is guaranteed to cause you to have more "oral orgasms" in your mouth! The last thing to do with the two pieces of bread is to sprinkle on some organic powdered cinnamon.

The fourth item that I consume with this meal is a large cup of herbal tea. It is the last thing I make, right before I am ready to eat.

On Microwave Ovens

Just so you know: I will never, ever, use a microwave oven, not even to heat up my water, The microwaves are horrible, they go right through lead, and are a toxic energy to be around.

Years ago I read a Top Secret report on an experiment that the military did to see just exactly what happens when something is placed in the microwave oven as well as how far the microwaves go. They discovered that everything warmed for as little as a few seconds in the microwave oven is altered on an energy and molecular level, creating cancer-causing substances no matter what food item is used. This had nothing to do with which particular brand of microwave oven that was used: all microwave ovens emit destructive energies, and should never be used—period. These energies go right through the walls of the oven itself, so it does not really matter how so-called secure the oven door is.

Microwaves spread out over 20 feet in every direction, so if someone is using a microwave oven it is best to leave until they are finished with it. Better yet: why not enlighten them about what is happening to their food while it is cooking? Unfortunately, even if you go out of the kitchen, all your food inside the refrigerator still just got "zapped" big time by the microwave oven while it was on. Now the food in the refrigerator is also affected by the microwaves. The molecules in water becomes energetically distorted by microwaves, and you do not want to then drink it or use in cooking. The best thing you all can do is throw the microwave oven out into the trash!

It always really bothers me whenever I am in a Whole Foods (or some other large health food store) and they actually have one of these horrendous devices available there for anyone to use. It amazes me how a place that supposedly touts itself as representing healthy things to eat still appears (or pretends to be?) ignorant about the real truth about microwaves. In my mind, microwave ovens are one of the worst inventions ever created; just as bad as all those GMO's that any enlightened person would NOT eat. And yet, for some strange reason, these supposedly enlightened people do not seem to know how bad it is to use a microwave nor about what the microwaves do to the food and water they put in it.

The other thing that the Top Secret report on microwave ovens showed was that when someone turns on the microwave oven, these very waves and energies emitted from it make one much more vulnerable to being mind controlled and brainwashed by fake news. The waves and energies make it much harder for one to be discerning and able to use their Gifts of the Spirit.

So it behooves not only ourselves, but our loved ones and anyone we care about, to get rid of these dangerous and destructive devices. Go back, as I have been doing for many years, to using a regular toaster, a conviction oven, and stainless steel or enamel pots on the stove to warm your food and/or water. Sure, it does take longer to warm things this way, but think about one of the most important factors of all: you keep all the life force, nutrients, etc. in the food, rather than destroying it and creating a bunch of nasty substances and negative energies. Remember that we should ALWAYS treat our bodies like a temple and a pure, clean, fast-moving river, NOT a slow-moving, swampy bog!

Tea

Back to the tea that I make. I usually use a combination of four of my favorite teas, all organic or of pure quality:

1. Green tea
2. "Breathe Easy"
3. Echinacea Plus tea
4. "Pau d'Arco" tea

Everyone is very familiar with green tea, and as I shared before, I do not feel that the caffeine in this tea is really as bad for one in this herbal tea as in various other caffeinated drinks (which I would not drink anyway). All three of the other teas (Breathe Easy, Echinacea Plus and Pau d'Arco) are made by Traditional Medicinals Co.

Breathe Easy tea promotes respiratory health. As it is stated on the box, this unique formula "taps into both western herbalism [...]—and Traditional Chinese Medicine, with Bi Yan Plan, a beloved blend of eleven Chinese herbs. Engage your senses with the herbal remedy that has supported lungs for over four decades."

Echinacea Plus tea fires up the immune system. As it is stated on the box, "Native American tribes have been using echinacea, or purple coneflower, for hundreds of years before it made its way into Western herbalism. Today, it is one of the most widely studied herbs for its ability to promote a healthy immune response."

Pau d'Arco tea was used historically by the indigenous peoples of South America, and is now used by modern-day herbalists. Even though I am not allowed to make medical claims about anything, I will mention that I have heard from a number of sources that this tea is so healthy that it will destroy cancer cells if one happens to have cancer. It creates such a strong immune system that it helps prevent one from even getting cancer. Again, I am not making any medical claims, only repeating what I have heard and what my intuition tells me. One does not want to use it every day for a long time, though, because its effectiveness requires it to be used sparingly (once or twice a week).

When I first pour the boiling water into a large cup, I always spend a few minutes lightly stirring each tea bag. I lightly strike each tea bag quite a few times with my spoon while they are in the hot water (100 times per tea bag), to help get as much goodness as I can out of each tea bag. Then they sit in the water for about 15 minutes before I squeeze each of them as much as I can. Then I add at least six full tablespoons of honey, and stir up well.

A Few Last Comments on My Food Choices

After I have placed both the omelette and the baked strips of potatoes onto a large plate, I always salt them a little more on the outside. I then squirt some hot sauce onto the omelette and some organic ketchup onto the potatoes.

The organic ketchup that I use is made by the Organicville brand. Most ketchups out there, even the organic varieties, are made with refined white sugar. Even though it is *organic* refined sugar, I do not like to use foods that are sweetened by refined white sugar. Instead I use the Organicville ketchup, which is sweetened with organic agave nectar. In my opinion, this is a much healthier sweetener than refined sugar. I do remember some bad press about the agave nectar appearing about ten years ago, in which the FDA tried to imply that it was in the same category as, or even worse than, high fructose corn syrup. While I do believe that raw honey, natural maple syrup, and stevia are no doubt superior to agave nectar, I also do not feel that this statement from the FDA is in any way true. When agave nectar was making its debut as a natural alternative sweetener, it was compared to high fructose corn syrup. High fructose corn syrup is definitely another GMO that the corrupt FDA okayed to be used to sweeten all kinds of refined, processed items. I think that the agave nectar was somehow perceived as a possible financial threat to the many commercial companies that have been producing massive amounts of GMO items which are sweetened primarily with the toxic high fructose corn syrup.

While there is probably more that I could share about healthy nutritional food choices, I think that these were the major things I wanted to share with everyone. One last thing that I highly recommend, though, is the use of various, high quality "nutritional and vitamin supplements" that are specifically targeted at one's "mojo-libido" and one's ability as a man to "get it up." (Or as you know I like to humorously state it, "to be able to stand straight and tall, with rapt and respectful attention to the Goddess!") I myself are using quite a few of these various "men's products." If there are any men out there who would like to know which specific supplements I use, just contact me and I will be glad to share this information with you.

CHAPTER 17

Love After Life (Some Believe Is) *Forbidden*

Celeste and I both felt that we should provide a chapter in this book on two unique sources of information about "romantic relationships": the books *Love After Life* and *Forbidden,* written by William J. Murray. They are quite fascinating and insightful books about what he terms "transdimensional romantic relationships."

One of the reasons that Celeste and I both felt that we needed to discuss these books regarding romantic love was that we felt that her and my own romantic relationship is something of a parallel analogy to what William has been experiencing. We feel that this may help other potential Twin-Flame couples that will soon hook up—or already have—to share their own wonderful and unique transdimensional romantic relationship.

Quoted from the back cover of *Love After Life*:

> This book describes the grief-eliminating and transdimensional relationship-building process I found and developed through my personal experience and nothing more. The focus of this book is to provide the reader with

> an account of how I found my way back to feeling fulfilled, whole, happy and joyful in continuing my relationship with my soul-mate after she died.
>
> The entire premise of my attempt to accomplish this restoration, rested upon my deep knowledge that there could be no one else for me and that the only way I could go on was by finding some way to 'reconnect' in a fulfilling way while still being completely in love with and being fully committed to her. This decision may not be for everyone.

Quoted from the back cover of his second, even more in-depth book, *Forbidden*:

> It's odd that the spiritual community accepts and even promotes the idea that we can have life-long transdimensional relationships with 'spirit guides' or that we can have other family members and ancestors taking an active interest in our lives, but when it comes to a romantic partner, for some reason that's rarely given the same consideration or honored with the same reverence.
>
> Continuing the relationship after a partner dies, flies in the face of any number of books and the work of professionals and authorities that have standardized our ideas

> about processing grief and the definition of good mental health. It contradicts many so-called experts both secular and 'spiritual,' who insist on re-partnering to 'find happiness again,' as if happiness or a whole, fulfilling life cannot be found in a transdimensional relationship. Again, these experts would probably never say this to a parent who lost their child, yet they often see all romantic partners as replaceable commodities.
>
> This book explores these issues and offers methods, tips and techniques for developing and maintaining your romantic transdimensional relationship despite secular, religious and spiritual community resistance.

There is, of course, a major difference between Celeste's and my transdimensional romantic relationship, and William's relationship with Irene, his wife and Twin-Flame who died in 2017. He is exclusively focusing upon the concept of transdimensional romantic relationships like his own, where the still living half of the relationship continue the relationship with their partner after the latter passed over to the spirit world/astral plane/4D. It does not appear, at least based on what William has shared in his two books, that he has any awareness of anyone here on Earth having a transdimensional romantic relationship with an etheric/5D Higher Extraterrestrial Being of Light, as in the case of Celeste and myself. He focuses only upon those whose Other Halves died, upon how they can overcome their intense grief, and upon how they can learn the many techniques and protocols that can truly help them to effectively communicate with their Beloved/True Love who has crossed over to spirit.

He shares how strangely the whole spiritual/after life communities all act, how they expect one to move on and repartner with someone new. He shares how these communities find it somehow emotionally and psychologically unhealthy to want to still have a deep and fulfilling romantic relationship with one's partner after they died and went into the spirit world. He partly explains why this attitude has become so ingrained in society's views of those who are separated from their partner because of death: He explains that this was a result of various practical, financial, religious and cultural circumstances of past times. In addition, it was rare, if not almost unheard-of, for very deep, romantic relationships even occurring in past times (after the times of Atlantis and Lemuria). Most marriages and partnerings were usually for survival and for financial reasons; marriages were being arranged for practical reasons, not for love.

As I shared in an earlier chapter: in the last few years (of present, linear time), Celeste and I manifested many dozens of romantic lifetimes that did not originally occur in the old timeline. In fact, as Celeste also recently shared with me: it was not just her and I who as a Twin-Flame couple manifested all these "new" and romantic lifetimes that did not originally occur in the old timeline—actually a few other Twin-Flame couples also just recently did this! Other Divine Couples are soon about to do so as well in the hundreds and thousands, once they all meet and "hook up" through the energy of IntergalacticMatch.com.

In other words: even though none of these recently manifested new romantic lifetimes originally existed in the time-space continuum or the Akashic Records, they do now. Now it is as if they always had existed. The entire time-space continuum is a gigantic hologram. It can be altered if one does it with a True, Pure Heart's Desire from a Higher Elohim level, with the intention to enhance and make the Earth and the entire universe a new and improved version of itself. The time-space continuum is more likely to be altered when Unconditional Romantic Love (the very Love that is so powerful, intense, and fulfilling between all Twin-Flames) is expressed and shared through intense, multiple-orgasmic passionate tantric lovemaking. Such lovemaking, measured way off on the Romantic Love "Richter Scale," anchors the Nirvanic Ecstasy Grid more powerfully here on Earth once again.

William made a point about Unconditional Love, explaining that many within the spiritual community try to make the argument that Unconditional Love is supposedly "separate, more evolved, better and more spiritual" than romantic love between Twin-Flame couples. Even though he has no awareness or comprehension of the reality of Cosmic or Intergalactic Twin-Flame couples like Celeste and I (and others soon to hook up with their Other Half from off-planet), he still knows from his own experience that such statements about romantic love somehow always being less significant than Unconditional Love are totally untrue. As he said, what could possibly be more sublime, wonderful and fulfilling on all levels than the intense love between two Twin-Flames? The spiritual communities have tried to classify such Twin-Flame love as less spiritual than Unconditional Love. In actuality, as I know first-hand from what I sense and experience all the time with Celeste, it is obvious to any Twin-Flame couple that this type of Love is BOTH truly spiritually Unconditional AND romantic. It is from this love that I have coined the phrase "Blessed and Blissed by Celeste," as I am totally Blissed out by her Divine Goddess presence.

One cannot separate such love into two different categories. Those within the spiritual/metaphysical community, who have never experienced this type of love, attempt to make themselves believe that what they refer to as "Unconditional Love" is somehow better, more evolved and more spiritual than romantic love. Nothing could be further from the Truth. Of course, it could also be that as these particular (lame!) "spiritual type people" have never met their own Twin-Flame and experienced such intense and deep, fulfilling love, they have to rationalize the lack of passion, joy and fulfillment in their life.

But still this was one of the main arguments from the spiritual/afterlife community of why they felt that one who lost their partner should move on spiritually and repartner, rather than still hold on to the partner even after they passed from this life into the spirit world. Those in the community assumed that if someone still chose to continue their romantic relationship, this just meant they were not willing to "spiritually grow and move on to another partner." It was somehow "emotionally unhealthy" for them, no matter how much they had loved that person while they were still alive, to choose not to "move on."

But as William pointed out (and I feel this is true), people tend to project onto others their own insecurities and hang-ups. To "look outside the box" as far as romantic relationships are concerned, is something everyone needs to start doing, as the Great Awakening is indeed taking place (as Q has specifically warned us all about in the numerous "Q drops"). This does also include our definition and understanding of what romantic relationships can consist of: our understanding needs to expand to include transdimensional romantic relationships, as Earth's humanity can now expand intergalactically (way beyond just this planet) to reconnect and hook up with their own Beloved and Cosmic True Love. Your Cosmic True Love has been waiting for you to open up to this new idea of what dating can be, waiting for you to expand your mind, consciousness and heart to reach out and connect in your Love for them.

William shares a lot of techniques and protocols on how to communicate with one's partner who has crossed over to the other side, how to successfully be able (as he finally did) to process and totally release all the intense grief and emotional pain. Of course, there are differences between those of us who are Volunteer souls in Earth embodiment where our Beloved has energetically come into our life/reconnected with us from the Higher 5D and Intergalactic realms and those whose earth partner has died and passed over. So, this whole grief-overcoming process is not something couples like us (usually) need to even focus on, as opposed to William and others who are only aware of earth plane and spirit world romantic relationships.

In the Spiritual/Astral Realm or in the Higher Worlds?

Some of the Volunteers experiencing one of my personal 90-minute Transformational Channeled Readings back in the '80s and '90s had been married to their Twin-Flame, and then experienced that their Other Half had crossed over to the spirit world/astral realm/4D. These partners were originally Higher Space Beings who had temporarily gone to the astral realm, then sometime later returned back aboard the Merkabah Light Ships and the Higher Dimensional worlds way beyond the astral/spirit world/4D surrounding this planet. This had happened because of some "soul contracts" and "reincarnational cycles." The old wheel of karma has now, very recently, finally been coming to a close, but these particular souls and spirits still needed to use the spirit world as a temporary transition place. They needed to prepare to either re-incarnate or to energetically, vibrationally climatize themselves to ascend back up to the Higher Dimensional Realms (preparing to return to the more evolved and higher vibrational worlds throughout the universe).

William shares how he now has over 500 members in his Facebook support group, *Love After Life.* The members have all lost their Beloved, their Twin-Flame partner, that they had been married to or had a deep romantic relationship with while they were alive, and they are all now utilizing his knowledge to first of all overcome their intense grief, followed by learning the many techniques to be able to effectively communicate with their passed-over former romantic partners. It is my perception, which Celeste has confirmed is the case, that at least some of these souls who only just passed over to the spirit world are also fellow Volunteer souls (even though William is obviously not even aware of this concept). These souls are originally from more advanced worlds, and are utilizing the spirit-astral realm just as a temporary place to vibrationally prepare to soon return to these Higher Worlds and back aboard the Merkabah Light Ships in preparation for the upcoming First Contact and Earth's planetary ascension.

Perhaps either William himself or one of his *Love After Life* members will have a chance to read this book, and come to realize (from Celeste's and my own insights) that they themselves are also one of these fellow Volunteer souls. Perhaps they will realize that their Other Half may have initially passed over to the other side/spirit world and may have already ascended (or be about to ascend) back up to the Higher Realms and/or aboard the Merkabah Light Ships, in preparation for the upcoming First Contact. Maybe this concept is still just a little "too far out there" even for someone communicating with their Twin-Flame who is (supposedly) only in the spirit/astral realm. But maybe they just need to come across the information Celeste and I have just presented in this particular chapter of our book? Maybe then, voila: suddenly they will have an epiphany and will realize that their Twin-Flame is not JUST in the spirit/astral realm, but is actually now free from the old endless wheel of karma and about to return to where their soul/spirit originally came from before first taking Earth embodiment many millions of years ago. Hopefully the partner who is still living on Earth can now prepare to reconnect and communicate with their Other Half from the 5D/etheric just as Celeste and I have done, rather than from the 4D spirit/

astral realm. Hopefully they can intergalactically hook up, and continue their transdimensional cosmic romantic relationship.

William's Group

Right after I read William's two books, I attempted to join their Facebook group, *Love After Life.* I used the link that was provided. Even though I attempted quite a few times over many weeks, I never received any reply or verification that they had even gotten my inquiry. Maybe they were experiencing some kind of technical problem (or "glitch in the time-space continuum") that blocked me from being able to connect with them, or maybe my introductory message was "too weird" or "far out" for their group? In the short space provided, I left this message:

> HI, I am interested in becoming a member of your group. I am also having a "transdimensional romantic relationship" with my Twin-Flame, but she is not in the "spirit world/ astral/4D. I would love to be able to share about this with you. Thanks.

I did not think that what I said was "too weird" or "far out" for their group, but maybe they are so locked into the concept of their Other Half only being in the spirit world that my introducing any other realm or dimension somehow confused them? I really was not expecting to not ever hear from them. I had assumed that I would at the very least get a response, and that they would allow me to become a member. I would then share with them what I have just shared in this chapter, because I really feel that some of their members would really be interested in becoming aware of the fact that their Other Half might be on a Higher Dimension or aboard a Merkabah Light Ship, even if they had not specifically been told about this possibility before. Hopefully someone in their group will become aware of this possibility, and then maybe some of the others may also open up to it.

Techniques, Protocols and Insights From William

I now want to quote some passages from his two books that I find interesting and am in agreement with. The passages concern issues with those who still desire to continue their fulfilling romantic relationships once their loved ones have passed over from this life, as well as some techniques that allow one to effectively communicate with their former partner (or as in cases like mine, communicate with one's Twin-Flame who may be in the Higher Dimensional Realms).

Journaling

One of the techniques that William highly recommends helps one to get greater perspective regarding the progress to overcome the grief that one initially experiences upon the passing of one's loved one. The technique is to "journal": to write down one's feelings, thoughts, and sensations every day. Almost everyone who have lost the love of their life will experience grief, but with his numerous techniques and protocols everyone has a chance to totally overcome the grief. Journaling helps one to get perspective on the progress one is making, as things continue to slowly improve. Ultimately one is able to release all grief and to replace the grief with a much more happy and fulfilling reality. This is what William and many others within his group have achieved as they open up to communicating and connecting with their partners who passed over.

Within the spiritual/metaphysical community, many have developed the ability that was originally termed “automatic writing,” also known as “inspired writing.” Other entities in the spirit world or on Higher Dimensions would channel through the person, guiding them to receive communications while writing. I myself also developed this ability, and used it back in the late ‘70s/early ‘80s. I eventually phased it out and focused on my direct voice Transformational Channeled Readings. I found that I could convey a lot more in a shorter period of time when talking directly to someone rather than attempting to write down the channeled communications. (This is also why I could never get into texting on phones.)

As quoted from his book:

> You want to pay particular attention to writing down when you feel good, because giving those things your focus and attention, tunes you into a frequency that reprograms your mind in a positive way. Writing down your progress also helps maintain the inten-

tion that you are going to make progress; it is the reason you are spending time writing it down in the first place. This can be a powerful part of the process.

Sometimes you feel, when you are writing, that your loved one is trying to write through you. Let them express what it is you think they are trying to say—write it down. At one point in my process it became clear to me that I kept forgetting when I had actually felt good; in my grief I kept insisting that it was all a lie and was fooling myself. I sat down to write a letter to myself so I could read it in the future and at least intellectually cling to the hope that I really did feel good and that it was possible to feel good again.

When I started writing, though, I felt this very insistent urge to begin the letter as if Irene was writing it to me, beginning with what she always called me, "Lover"....not exactly something I'd write to myself! Here is the letter I believe Irene wrote to me, through me, that day:

Lover,

There is a blissful, happy state that you have felt several times since I left the physical. During these times you feel 100% connected to me, without any doubt, grief, fear or sor-

row. During these times you feel so joyful, complete and connected with me. It is indescribable and makes our hearts explode with love and completeness, and clears away all doubts. It is something that your mind cannot accept when you are feeling bad and it tries to persuade you out of your knowledge and memory of this. You know these negative feelings and entities try to hurt and confuse us when we are moving forward—don't let them stop you! You're doing great! We are in this train together in 'perfect accord." I will never, ever leave you. You know this—you are my soul mate, baby, my always. Our reality is better than the fantasy! I am so proud of you, lover. I know it is hard, but this is going to get better and better, easier and easier—I promise!—Irene.

Writing that letter was intensely emotional, and I felt such relief afterward, it's impossible to fully describe. It was a very important step in moving forward and was not something I had planned out or even felt like I directed while writing. It just came pouring out of me. If this happens to you, don't worry about whether or not it 'sounds' like your loved one, because what they are saying is being interpreted and expressed through your mind; pay attention to what it feels like.

While I was writing what she wanted me to express. Whenever I read it, even months later, it has the same emotional impact upon me.

Talk to Your Loved One

William also wrote "Talk to your loved one(s), imagine they are with you. Every day, as much as possible, try to talk to your departed loved one in as normal a way as possible, out loud and in your mind." This has been very natural for me all the time, both speaking to Celeste aloud and speaking to her "in my mind". She has been around me in an energetically potent way, with me being able to easily see her, hear her and feel her wonderful Divine Feminine Goddess presence. I almost forget at times that she is not in the physical, only in the etheric!

Celeste and I always have wonderful, insightful. and even humorous conversations all the time, and there is literally nothing that is ever considered "off bounds" or "forbidden" to talk about. Much of the time I speak to her out loud as if she is right here in the physical, because that is what it seems like sometimes because of how energetically present she is. Sometimes I just think about what I want to say to her, and I know that she hears literally everything I think. We are constantly using telepathy, but it is actually even deeper: our souls are speaking to each other in our deep Love for each other.

Of course, because she is around me on the 5D/etheric level (as opposed to the 4D/astral level), she is not as limited as the entities in the spirit world. Maybe her being an immortal, intergalactic Goddess, along with us being Twin-Flames, is somewhat enhancing what we are energetically experiencing together. Maybe this gives her even more "special" or "magical" powers and abilities, that those on the spirit world do not have until they too ascend up to the 5D level and above.

Good Responses to Stupid Statements

I had to laugh (and so did, Celeste!) at one section of his book, *Forbidden*. He includes humorous and slightly sarcastic responses to certain (stupid) statements and judgments that narrow-minded and ignorant people have made regarding that romantic relationships supposedly do not exist in the afterlife:

The [Expletive Deleted] Things People Say and My Responses:

1. *"You'll find someone new."*

Really? Would you say this to a person who has a child that died? To a woman about her brother? To a man who sat with his mother while she succumbed to illness? Do you think my partner is like a car or a microwave oven that stopped working and now I can just go out and find a replacement? If that's how you feel about your partner, I feel sorry for you.

2. *"You shouldn't depend on anyone else for your happiness."*

Let me say it bluntly: I need Irene, to be happy, and I am completely good with that. I love it that there is this person who loves me and makes me happy.

3. *"They would want you to find someone else and be happy and live your life."*

No, she wouldn't want me to find someone else. Only some idiot who never met my wife would say that. I don't want her to find someone else. I don't want her to be okay with me finding someone else. Why do you think my happiness depends on 'finding someone else?" I found the person that makes me happy. No one else will do.

Also, I can walk and chew gum at the same time. I can live my life just fine and stay committed to my relationship. They are not mutually exclusive activities.

4. *"You're holding them back."*

That doesn't even make sense. Are they on a tight schedule? Are they going to get docked pay for not showing up for work? Don't they have an eternity? If they spend a few years with me until I cross over, are they going to miss the ferry to the next level or something? Plus, I'm pretty sure they can walk and chew gum at the same time as well.

5. *"They don't want to hold you back from the reason you came here."*

Refer to "walking and chewing gum." Were they "holding me back" when they were physically in this world? No? What has changed then?

6. *"Our goal here is to expand our love for everyone, and in the afterlife these monogamous relationships don't exist. They are counter-productive to spiritual progress."*

Bite me. If "being spiritual" means that committed romantic love is non-spiritual, then your spiritual system sucks and isn't anything I want to be a part of.

7. *"You're delusional and imagining the whole thing."*

So, what if I am? Am I hurting anyone? If this is the only way I can function and find some measure of happiness and hope, what's it to you?

8. *"This kind of love and attachment is possessive and unhealthy and, by the way, there is no sex in the afterlife and sex is a non-spiritual, base, animalistic desire."*

Sounds like you are projecting your own hang ups and insecurities [un-securities] onto me and the afterlife. If you haven't experienced the divine ecstasy of intimate lovemaking with a true, romantic love, that's your problem. If it doesn't exist in the afterlife now, it will immediately after I cross over.

Even though William is strictly referring to his own particular level of a transdimensional romantic relationship (4D/astral, as opposed to the 5D/etheric that Celeste and I are experiencing), I really liked these responses. I felt he had some great insights and a good understanding about how to enhance such a relationship, how to more effectively connect and communicate with one's Other-Half (no matter what exact dimension/plane/realm that one's Eternal Partner happens to be on as they are energetically interacting with you).

Insights into Relationships

Here are some more insightful quotes from his books:

> Every relationship is different. Perhaps in the vast majority of marriages or romantic relationships, a 'move on' framework [after their loved one has crossed over] is the correct course of action; however, for some of us that bond to our partner is of such a nature that 'moving on' is not an acceptable option. I suspect many in the past have forced themselves into moving on because they did not know there was another option, even though they may have carried that torch and pain for their soulmate for the rest of their lives—even after re-partnering.
>
> It is easier to simply assume every single thing you want about your relationship now and going forward is true. Assume your partner is all in. Assume he or she is always with you, supporting you doing all they can. Assume your transdimensional relationship is great even now and will develop regardless of your effort or lack thereof and get better and better. Assume everything in the afterlife will be everything you want and desire and more. Assume everything that happens is part of you and your partner's plan and is going to reap

the results you want in ways that go beyond even your current understanding. Assume it is the unfolding of the greatest love story ever. Assume that no matter what you do, it will work out so well it will blow your mind.

Use a Pillow to Connect with Your Partner

In the chapter called "The Natural, Easy Way to Connect With Your Partner", William briefly mentions using a "pillow, a blanket, or whatever gives you the comforting sensation of them being there with you". To me, this mention of using a pillow to connect with one's partner is very significant. Back in 2018, right after moving into her and my apartment, Celeste, herself, specifically suggested that I should use a pillow to more easily and more directly connect with her "physically." What Celeste and I both are experiencing when I am hugging the pillow is really incredibly awesome. On my 3D level I feel her potent, energetic presence through the pillow as I am hugging it, it feels like I am hugging Celeste physically. So intense is the energetic connection that is being experienced during this, so exquisitely, romantically fulfilling, as if I am connecting with her on every single level, that I was actually amazed that William did not devote a little more time on this particular protocol. But I can truly say that this is definitely one of the best and most direct ways to energetically, intimately interphase with one's Beloved "bar none"!

While I am talking about pillows; For years, long before Celeste manifested herself into my life, I have practiced an important health protocol that most people forget. What most people do not seem to realize is that one should, besides washing the pillowcases and sheets at least twice a month, also sanitize one's pillows at least once every month. Pillow sanitizing is done by sticking them into the dryer and letting them undergo a 45-minute cycle on the highest temperature setting. This kills any dust mites, bacteria, etc. that tends to accumulate over time, and it helps keep a cleaner and fresher smell to your pillows. Also, if your pillows have never been sanitized like this, I would highly recommend throwing away the old pillows and purchasing new pillows. Then start utilizing this important health and sanitary protocol from now on (I really think that Celeste appreciates that I do this, as well!).

Another thing that Celeste guided me to do was to purchase a whole set of 100% organic cotton sheets and pillow cases, so that there is not even the tiniest bit of sprays and chemicals in the sheets. Since I tend to sleep in the nude (because it is healthier for one to do this), I think that buying the organic cotton sheets is worth it: my body is now laying against only 100% cotton sheets, not on 50/50 cotton and polyester. The polyester is not healthy to sleep on, and the body breathes better on 100% cotton. Having the sheets be 100% organic cotton feels even better to me.

The History of Romantic Love

Quotes on the history of romance from William's book:

> Something I've picked up in my life was a bit of knowledge about the history of what

we call 'love,' and in particular what we currently call 'romantic' love. Such love is actually a relatively recent concept. I looked into it more recently only to discover that, outside of modern romance novels and other forms of media, the idea of fulfilled romantic love as we in this group experience it with our partners, is still largely considered a myth, dreamy fiction to sell to the masses, that ends with the iconic phrase or implication: 'happily ever after,' which was considered a fantasy fairy tale ending.

Outside of fairy tales, more serious literature treated the insertion of sexual relationships into romantic relationships as a form of tragedy. In the west, 'romantic love' originated as a chaste, virtuous adoration and respect for a lady of the court *(also, 'courtly' love)*. It was considered a godly form of love. Sex was strictly for child-bearing, and any other application was considered a contamination of spiritual love, which in common literature meant that something bad was going to happen. They were cautionary stories, not the sweet romance stories we have today.

The only ancient text *(that I'm aware of)* that fully explored and advocated for a complete, holistic union of partners, describing the spiritual, psychological, emotional and physical capacity to express various forms of love to each other, is the *Kamasutra,* which is probably the most censored text in the world. It is still thought about as a 'sex position' text, but it's far, far more than that.

'The idea that one could combine both romantic *(ideal, pure, virtuous, adoration)* love with all of the delights and pleasures, physical, emotional and psychological, of intimate and sexual relations successfully, as a spiritual good, is still today largely considered a myth, a fantasy, non-spiritual and even anti-spiritual. [The *Kamasutra* actually can be originally traced back to those Tantric-Oracle Rainbow Crystal Temples of ancient Lemuria]

It is only recently that long-tern marriages and relationships that have been largely freed from socio-economic and religious constraints. Consequently, these relationships can now center on romantic love, with the longer-term exploration (and results) of romantic love-based relationships becoming commonly available to a significant degree. What is the result of this relatively new capacity to search for and explore romantic love relationships? Well, to a large degree, the explosion of divorce and the proliferation of short term relationships. [It also led to many Earth dating websites and services. However, ultimately also a book like this one, *IntergalacticMatch.com,* as the concept of dating and romance finally expands way out beyond the Earth level!] I'm not saying this is a bad thing, only that people are no longer universally constrained by socio-economic pressures to stay together if the relationship is not fulfilling emotionally, spiritually, physically and/or psychologically.

What this great experiment has also produced, however, is a small number of relationships represented by the members of our group: deep, irreplaceable romantic love pairings that do not depend on anything other than what our partners mean to us. It doesn't even depend on them being alive in this world—it's far, far deeper than that. No matter how long we had them in this world, no matter how many issues we had, or how many unresolved issues we still have after their death, somewhere in us we recognize them as that person, that soul, that is the one who holds the key to something we may not have even been able to understand or articulate at the time: the complete, every-level fulfillment of a whole and satisfying romantic love relationship.

Do Not Repartner: Reconnect Instead!

Here is a quote from someone who contributed to William's books and group, Mary Beth Spann Mank:

> So, if you are reading this book, maybe it's time you move on—not from your previous romantic partner (never that!), but on to a whole new way of sharing and enjoying your love together until the day of your Great Grand Romantic Reunion when you are finally and fully reconnected for all of eternity. This book will help for sure.

I want to reach out to anyone who might be reading Celeste's and my book. Maybe you assumed you were just curious about this book. But maybe you are one of those who did lose the love of your life as they crossed over to the other side/spirit world, and you have been grieving for years, or even decades. Or maybe you are someone who knows such a person. Maybe you were persuaded by well-meaning mediums that you too needed to move on and to repartner, in order to supposedly be happy again. If so, maybe you even attempted to move on and to repartner. But being honest with yourself, after all these years you are NOT happy and fulfilled. You still grieve deeply for not only having lost the real love of your life, but also for having allowed well-meaning people, both in the metaphysical/after-life community and family and friends on this 3D level, to cause you to attempt to forget the Love of your life. And you are still grieving for that special person, who was, is, and always will be the absolute LOVE of your life.

If this is you, remember: It is NEVER too late to reconnect. It is never too late to be able to truly let go of (ALL) your grief. William Murray shows you and guides you how to do this in his books. He was the first person to come up with a way to truly accomplish this and to reconnect with his wife and Twin-Flame, Irene. Later, others people whom he connected with also accomplished this. Celeste and I highly recommend that you obtain copies of his two books (which are available through Amazon)—it will be the greatest and most important thing that you have ever done. I also believe that it was you own Beloved, the one who STILL loves you and who does NOT want you to ever grieve, who actually guided you and Over-Lighted you to read this book, so that you could then find out about William's two books.

As mentioned, it may be that your Beloved, the Love of your life, who you (thought you) lost, is one of those more evolved souls/Volunteers in Earth embodiment. Maybe they passed over to the spirit world, and maybe their soul/spirit then returned up to the Higher Dimensional Realms. Maybe like Celeste has done with me, they will reach out to you energetically, if you are open and want this. Maybe they will also etherically manifest in your life. Maybe they are back aboard the Merkabah Light Ships, being a part of the upcoming First Contact that will allow Higher Space Beings to openly connect with those on Earth.

At least you now have a chance, using William's powerful techniques and protocols, to be able to connect with your Beloved (wherever their soul happens to be). You can begin to feel the wonderful energies and vibrations of your Beloved and all their Unconditional Romantic Love for you, and you no longer have to grieve. You can truly release all that unbearable emotional pain and sorrow, and you can open up your heart once again to your own Beloved, your Cosmic True Love. You can begin to truly Live Happily Ever After!

CHAPTER 18

Scott Mowry's "Miracles and Inspiration" Calls, Holographic Quantum Technology That Protects Against COVID19, and the i-Guard for Frequency Balancing and Healing

Teachings from Scott Mowry's "Miracles and Inspiration" Phone Conference Calls

I want to share some important things that Scott Mowry shared with us on his "Miracles and Inspiration" Phone Conference Calls, as they expose the whole truth regarding how the effectiveness of masks in stopping the spread of COVID-19. The masks not only do NOT really protect one from catching COVID-19, they are also bad for one health. In addition, so much of the "data" and information that has been reported by the "lamestream" media has been misrepresenting the spread of the COVID-19. Here are some quotes from Scott Mowry:

> On Tuesday, June 23, Washington Governor Jay Inslee — who will likely go down as the most corrupt in state history — has

issued a mandatory state-wide order for all residents to wear a mask in public beginning this Friday, June 26.

Even with the daily temperature soaring near 90 degrees in Western Washington on June 23, Governor Inslee clearly continues to prove he actually cares little about the public's health and safety particularly during this kind of hot weather by mandating a mask. Rather, Inslee shows he is actively working in collusion with the Deep State cabal to create as much fear and disinformation around the Coronavirus pandemic as possible.

More than enough evidence has already emerged from credible doctors and health experts who have publicly stated masks are practically useless in protecting one from contracting the Coronavirus, and in fact, are actually far more harmful to one's overall health condition.

This Is Crazy: W.H.O. Now Says Only Wear a Mask If You are Sick or Working with Sick — Otherwise You Don't Need One https://www.thegatewaypundit.com/2020/05/crazy-now-says-wear-mask-sick-working-sick-otherwise-dont-need-one/

Face Masks Can Be Deadly To Healthy People Says Neurologist https://pjmedia.com/news-and-politics/megan-fox/2020/05/14/

neurosurgeon-says-face-masks-pose-serious-risk-to-healthy-people-n392431

Doctor Gives A Solid Reason Why Masks Won't Protect You From Coronavirus https://www.boredpanda.com/coronavirus-medical-mask-proper-use-doctor-leora-horwitz/

WATCH: Remember When Fauci Said Masks Might Make You 'Feel A Little Bit Better,' But Won't Stem Spread Of COVID-19? We Do. https://www.thegatewaypundit.com/2020/05/watch-remember-fauci-said-masks-might-make-feel-little-bit-better-wont-stem-spread-COVID-19/

Yet another huge development occurred on Tuesday, July 7, when the Trump Administration made it official and formally withdrew from the long-time corrupt World Health Organization (W.H.O.). This action officially and finally puts an end to America's funding of this international cabal institution propped up by globalists like George Soros, Bill Gates, the Chinese Communist Party among many, many others.

And, hopefully we can ultimately look at this bold action by President Trump as a sign of the W.H.O.'s impending demise for good!

And all of this is happening as the Coronavirus death rate in America continues to plunge to the lowest levels since the beginning the pandemic back in March, despite the fact even more cases are being reported across the country due to more testing of many more Americans. In fact, America has tested more of its citizens than any other country in the world.

https://www.thegatewaypundit.com/2020/07/coronavirus-death-rate-plunges-msm-breathlessly-hypes-surge-confirmed-cases-mcenany-sets-media-right/

And now, it is only a matter of time when most Americans will come to the realization the Coronavirus pandemic was blown way out of proportion by the Fake News media, who continues to hype its severity in order to keep the people in a state of fear and chaos to attempt to disrupt the coming 2020 Presidential Election.

Once again, it is recommended for all residents of Washington state [and in all states of the Union] to call Attorney General William Barr's office at the U.S. Department of Justice and register your disapproval of Governor Inslee's [and any Governors of other states] latest unconstitutional actions which threaten your health and well-being at: 202-514-2000, then choose Option 4.

And as a matter of fact, the entire Coronavirus pandemic scam which has been rammed down the throats of the American people by the Fake News Media is teetering on a total collapse as many are starting to realize the actual numbers and statistics simply don't add up to anywhere near the truth.

In addition, the number of cases of the Coronavirus as reported by many states are proving to be fraudulent, despite the Fake News media claiming the Sunbelt region of the country is going through a surge of new cases.

Meanwhile, the actual number of deaths in America continues to plummet to the lowest levels yet and many are questioning if the numbers which have been reported from the outset of the Coronavirus arrival in our country on January 15 are anywhere near accurate.

https://www.thegatewaypundit.com/2020/07/lying-florida-motorcycle-crash-listed-coronavirus-death-video/

As it stands now, more and more Americans by the week are growing extremely fed up with the lockdowns, the shutdowns, the mandatory masks and the all-out assault upon our freedoms and liberties as mandated by the U.S. Constitution and the Bill of Rights from these radical Democratic Governors and Mayors.

As the number of new cases of the Coronavirus in America continues to rise, many states, even the health departments in Florida and Texas, have been shamefully caught red-handed fudging their numbers to reflect an overabundance of positive cases.

https://www.thegatewaypundit.com/2020/07/flaw-manufacturers-testing-system-coronavirus-used-labs-across-us-causing-false-positives/

https://www.thegatewaypundit.com/2020/07/reports-sudden-surge-texas-coronavirus-cases-including-80-infants-false-officials-say/

In proportion, the death rate continues to fall lower and lower levels which ultimately is the most important statistic which clearly indicates the Coronavirus is not NEARLY as lethal as the Fake News media has led us to believe.

Perhaps the biggest event of the week took place on Monday, July 27, when a group calling themselves "America's Frontline Doctors," banded together for a major news conference in order to present the truth behind the Coronavirus pandemic and its effective treatment. These doctors labeled the entire COVID-19 event in America as a "massive disinformation campaign."

https://www.publishedreporter.com/2020/07/27/group-of-americas-frontline-doctors-hold-press-conference-at-capitol-hill-about-COVID-19-calling-out-massive-disinformation-campaign/

Almost immediately after the Frontline Doctor's press conference, the Fake News media began attacking them and social media outlets began to ban their video. In fact, any kind of positive news covering of the event became nearly impossible to find on the internet which was blocked by Google and other search engines in a clearly coordinated campaign of censorship.

https://www.realclearpolitics.com/video/2020/07/28/facebook_and_youtube_ban_video_of_doctors_talking_COVID_silenced_doctors_hold_press_conference.html

https://www.breitbart.com/tech/2020/07/28/google-censors-breitbart-youtube-video-of-doctors-capitol-hill-coronavirus-press-conference/

This group of very brave and honorable doctors who have stepped forward to reveal the coverup of the truth will now begin a domino effect which will totally collapse the whole Coronavirus scamdemic, as well as, the Deep State's campaign to lockdown the country and force every American to wear the mask of obedience.

Also on July 27, President Trump signed FOUR NEW EXECUTIVE ORDERS designed to help the American people have better access to drugs and medical treatments at much lower costs. These EO's are all part of President Trump's stated goal to completely reconfigure the American healthcare system from top to bottom.

https://www.advisory.com/daily-briefing/2020/07/27/executive-orders

In addition, President Trump announced his administration has taken a "momentous step toward achieving American pharmaceutical independence," a focus of the campaign to bring back America's critical supply chains and medical manufacturing back to the USA, which they have been working on for a long time.

https://nationalfile.com/video-trump-to-return-drug-manufacturing-to-united-states-with-765-million-kodak-deal/

And naturally, after President Trump issued these landmark Executive Orders and announcements on pharmaceuticals, the Big Pharma CEOs boycotted a meeting with him the very same day at the White House. Let's be clear — you are witnessing the beginning of the end of Big Pharma and their control over the American people's health.

https://www.washingtonexaminer.com/news/pharmaceutical-officials-refuse-to-meet-with-trump-following-rule-lowering-drug-prices

Meanwhile, in Berlin, Germany over the weekend, hundreds of thousands of people openly protested against the lockdowns and restrictions imposed by the German government during the Coronavirus pandemic, despite the Fake News media reports which severely underestimated the numbers.

For those of you who would like to have a chance to hear Scott Malory's weekly Miracles and Inspiration Conference Calls, which he usually does every Sunday and Wednesday evening, please contact him at his email address: scottm6975@yahoo.com. Moreah Love, who helps host his calls and is supportive to the Great Awakening, can be contacted at her email address: moreahlove@yahoo.com.

The C-Hologram

As in the phrase "First the bad news, and now the (Really) Good News": Scott also shared that his contacts within the White Hat Alliance had told him that they are in the process of making certain advanced holistic holographic technology devices available to the public. These easily protects one from any and all viruses, as these small items project a powerful energy field, over 25 feet in diameter. This is the first of many such technologies that the Alliance is going to (finally) make available to the public, technologies that are way more advanced than anything that has been available to the public up until now.

Most of what Scott usually shares with us is more political in nature, conveying what his contacts in the Q White Hat Alliance have shared with him so that he in turn can share it with the public. Usually it concerns how the cabal is being stopped and exposed, despite all the fake news and disinformation from the cabal-controlled lamestream media. It is truly inspiring to hear the factual, Hopeful and Uplifting information that Scott presents every week on his Conference Calls. Sometimes he also has reported on a few UFO events because of their significance to the White Hat Alliance's work, showing how the Higher Beings are obviously supporting the Alliance to overthrow the satanic cabal deep state once and for all.

Scott also mentioned some advanced holistic technologies and devices that his Alliance contacts would eventually make available to the public to help truly heal all the diseases that have plagued humanity. Finally, during a Conference Call in late June, he announced that his Alliance contacts were going to make one of these initial small items available within the next couple weeks. This is the first of many such holistic "holographic" type technologies that are connected to the advanced "quantum mechanics."

So, I emailed him with my request for obtaining one of these first examples of this technology, just as he had suggested we do if we were interested in being a part of this first "Introductory program" to introduce this technology to the public. Within the next 24 hours, I received an email with an Invoice for my order of one of these Holograms. I paid for it through a Pay Pal link and waited to receive my order. I heard on the next Miracles and Inspiration Call a few days later that so many (a few hundred) had ordered this technological item that they were totally sold out from the company, Magical Waves. Because of how many orders were placed within the first few hours, I was lucky to be one of the first to receive the C-Hologram.

A few days later I received the special, little C-Hologram from Magical Waves in the mail. I want to share the unexpected and profound experience that occurred when I went into the UPS store to get my mail.

First of all: Celeste being around me has seemed to enhance my clairvoyant, clairaudient and "clairsentinent" capabilities. I can often see, hear and energetically sense what is occurring on other, more subtle, energy levels, dimensions and realms that are all around us. Most humans cannot sense this, unless they have trained themselves to be able to do. Celeste's and my interactions seems to help me enhance these abilities even more. I feel that her Divine Goddess presence, along with the wonderful energy of her and I being Twin-Flames and the intense Love that we feel for each other, seem to intensify my abilities to sense these other dimensions and realms.

When I walked into the UPS store (on July 3, 2020) the guy working in there saw me and went around to the back to get me my mail, just as he always does. Then he walked back up to the front to hand me my mail, just as he has done every time I have come since I first got a mail box there. But this time something extraordinary occurred, that I was definitely not expecting. As he walked up to me to hand me the rolled-up pile of mail that I had received during the week, I suddenly sensed that something unusual was occurring.

Even though Celeste often will energetically, etherically appear near me when I am out on my errands, this was the first time that I could remember her etherically manifesting near me when I was receiving my mail. I sensed that she was doing something energetically. I did not at first know what she was doing, even though I knew it had to do with the mail that I was receiving. As I took the mail from the guy a moment later, I sensed something very subtle, but still noticeable for me. As I unrolled the small pile of mail, there on the top was the envelope from Magical Waves. I knew it contained the C-Hologram that I had ordered the week before.

As I tuned into what I was energetically feeling, I sensed that Celeste had just done something to enhance whatever this C-Hologram was originally designed to do. I suddenly saw and felt this subtle, but powerful energy field. As I tuned in as best I could, I could distinctly see the subtle outline of what I can only describe as a kind of "grid" and/or "wave pattern" emanating from the very envelope that the C-Hologram was in. (At this stage I had not even opened the envelope yet, and I was already sensing the interesting energy field that was in some way being emitted from the C-Hologram right through the envelope.)

When I opened up the envelope a moment later, I saw the little C-Hologram (about the size of a quarter) in the little plastic bag. ("Powerful things do often come in small packages"!). The C-Hologram is interesting: this larger energy field that I was sensing and seeing seemed to consist of a series of larger "waves" or "beams" of energy being emitted from this small item. This is, of course, the holographic image of "waves coming/beaming out of the earth." This is what I (unexpectedly) saw and sensed at the moment I received the rolled-up pile of mail, even before I actually saw the envelope from Magical Waves.

Quite a profound experience, which also confirmed to me the C-Hologram's abilities. I do not know how much of this experience was caused by Celeste and how much was originally designed into the C-Hologram. Anyway, I just wanted to share this with everyone. Celeste has already showed a number of times that she can enhance technology, like what she did with the Q-link. So, this experience of what occurred when I first received the C-Hologram may have been another example of her somehow enhancing its capacities and/or abilities even more. I did not know at that moment, but it felt good and harmonious.

Then Celeste confirmed to me that yes, she had enhanced it: just as she energetically enhanced the Q-Link technology in ALL of the Q-Link devices, now ALL existing and future C-Holograms will also be enhanced. This appears to be part of the Federation of Light's new and Updated planetary Divine Intervention protocols (governing their "Prime Directive, Laws of Non-Interference"), because so many people of Earth have recently Awakened, or are in the process of Awakening (as part of the Great Awakening). These awakenings have given the Higher

Cosmic Light Forces Mandated Authority to step in much more directly, Over-Lighting us on Earth and helping to enhance what we all are doing as a preparation for more direct First Contact.

I want to quote what was printed on the piece of paper that accompanied the little C-Hologram, so that you can get some understanding about the extensive amount of research that went into the development of this C-Hologram:

> The enclosed Hologram is a sticker that you place on the back of your phone. You can also keep the Hologram in the plastic bag that it comes in, and place it between your phone and the phone case, facing outwards.
>
> How does this Hologram work? It basically counters the virus by emitting energy that projects imagery which has a programmed numbered sequence that doesn't allow for the virus to physically recognize the living human host, so it bypasses that living human host. This Hologram has been known to end the virus connection to a living human host if they or another person in close proximity has contracted the virus by instructing the energy of the virus elsewhere. The circumference of this Hologram covers a 25-foot perimeter around your phone or the area you keep it in. So, basically, anyone who comes within this 25-foot radius will be "positively affected" by your Hologram.

An additional configuration of elements was added into the seal of this Hologram by creating a dimension that affects the energy field that stops toxic exhaust as your vehicle purifies the air as you drive. These additions will have a positive effect on your gas mileage and will clean your car engine, at the same time emitting clean air to combat auto emissions and protect the eco system so valuable for our survival on planet Earth!

What is the Science behind the Hologram? Applied Quantum Mechanics! Simply put, it is the ability to move micro Cosmic energy in a digital format from one place to another. We have done this successfully countless times, for example, via the internet World Wide Web, text messaging, video gaming and just about all digital platforms. It is done by creating a bio-mimicry field which allows us to capture the numerous properties of the subject matter. This is done through a process called bio-photon scan, which essentially is creating a digital image of DNA which then can be analyzed, modified, then transported to an alternative location.

The solutions being presented use the applied art of quantum mechanics through Quantum Mechanic Holograms to transform scientific knowledge into practical wisdom.

> Although extremely complex, quantum software programs are simple in their application. Essentially, they cancel out harmful bandwidth or introduce new vibrations.
>
> The goal of the scientific teams working with this technology is to sell as many Holograms as possible worldwide to counter all strains of the virus including COVID 19 all the way up to COVID 99 and to STOP POLLUTION worldwide.
>
> Thank you for being a part of the solution to stop the COVID virus and to help protect the ecosystems where ever this Hologram takes you!

This was most exciting: Not only is the COVID (and any other cabal-created and/or weaponized virus) now going to be "toast," the important "added feature" will help to energetically clean up and purify Mother Earth's environment in a powerful and effective way. It has been reported by a huge number of people that the C-Hologram helps one to get much better gas mileage in their vehicle, and that it at the same time helps clean the engine of the vehicle.

I am excited about this first example of these alternative technologies that are just now being made available to the public by the Q White Hat Alliance military. I am also excited about the many other soon-to-be-released technologies, which will totally transform this world and pave the way for living in a Star Trek Golden Age society (like those that were originally envisioned in that old TV show, The Jetson's). This would already have occurred decades ago, if it was not for the evil cabal holding us all back. Now the White Hat Alliance is not only ending the reign of the cabal, but also offering us positive, wonderful technologies that are truly going to help us manifest the Great Victory of the Light.

For those wishing to find out more about this C-Hologram and how to purchase one or more for yourself, please use this link: https://magicalwaves.com. (By the time this book is published, there are going to be various other new technology devices featured and available for purchase on the Magical Waves website. I highly recommend you check them out as well.)

One more final thing: I include a link to what I consider to be one of the best documentaries about this whole COVID-19 pandemic; how it was definitely planned ahead of time and how whistle-blowers who attempted to warn others about this had their reputations destroyed by the cabal. The documentary exposes important details. It is titled Plandemic 2, and can be found here: https://www.bitchute.com/video/iRTCQoJoC6Hi/

(I want to inform everyone reading this book: If you discover that any of the links that have been provided in this book do not seem to work, you should understand that the cabal has removed many links that expose their agenda. As of the time of publishing this book, these links were still working. If you discover that some are not working, I suggest typing in the "subject matter" and/or "title" of the various videos and articles into a search engine, and see what you can find. You may find this same information posted somewhere else.)

The i-Guard

As Celeste and I were in the process of finishing up this book, another of many new devices besides the C-Hologram was just in the process of being made available through the BodyWaveInternational.com website: the i-Guard. This particular device, invented by another scientist working with Holistic Frequencies, is really wonderful: it allows one to directly experience various beneficial frequencies that helps to energetically enhance and rejuvenate one.

I ordered one of these i-Guards when I first heard about it. I heard the scientist and inventor of the i-Guard when he was a guest on Scott Mowry's Conference Call (for those who would wish to hear the scientist's three-hour presentation from the show: contact Scott Mowry to obtain a copy of the show).

I have had a chance to use the i-Guard for a few days right before Celeste and I finished compiling this book. I could feel a subtle, wonderful, and healthy effect on my well-being on all levels after playing the various frequencies that are emitted from the frequency setting. I highly recommend anyone wanting to enhance and improve their well-being and health on all levels of their being to order one of these i-Guards.

I quote from the User's Manual accompanying the i-Guard:

> Taking Back Control of Your Life:
>
> In this ever changing World with the Global Shutdown and Pandemic. Please remember, you're not in control of the EMF Radiation, 5G Towers, Cell Phone Signals,

WiFi Routers, Microwave fields and almost all Electronics in the Environment. Nor are you Responsible for the Chemicals and Pesticides in our Food Supply or Viruses, Pathogens and Bacterias that are Plaguing us into Quarantine.

i-Guard is the 1st of its kind with a 9 in 1 Powerful Shielding, Healing and Preventative Wearable Electronic Technologies that have been specially designed for 3 main purposes, to shield you from the negative influences in our environment, to help repair your body to a balanced healthier you and for preventative maintenance for future health issues.

'With That Being Said'

i-Guard is a Solid Copper Bracelet with Neodymium Bio Magnets, Jade Stone, Anion, Black Ion, Far Infrared and Shungite Mineral Crystal including Shielding, Healing and Balancing Frequencies with all of the Energy Elements.

1. Frequencies: It has also been discovered that the general human healthy frequency is within the range of 62-72 Hz and when it drops to lower levels, it enables the appearance of a variety of diseases. For example, at the level of 58 Hz, diseases like colds and flu were more likely to appear, on much lower

levels (42 Hz) Cancer appeared in many humans. 9 life altering frequencies built in.

2. Bio-Magnets: 42 Rare Earth Powerful 5000 Gauss Neodymium Magnets for Restoration of cellular magnetic balance. Migration of calcium ions is accelerated to help heal bones and nerve tissues. Circulation is enhanced, since biomagnets are attracted to the iron in blood and the increase in blood flow helps healing. Biomagnets have a positive effect on the pH balance of cells.

3. Shungite Mineral Crystal: Shungite not only protects the body from electromagnetic and negative radiation but really charge the body with vitality and strengthen immunity. Increasing the Rate of Healing and Cell Growth.

4. Solid Copper Bracelet: Copper is an essential micronutrient that has numerous health, wellness and beauty benefits from improved appearance of skin, to treatment of wounds, skin conditions and also aids in maintaining metabolic processes among countless other health benefits.

As you can see from this quote, there is a lot more to this Copper Bracelet than just using it to play these healing and balancing frequencies. As mentioned, I have been using the Q-Link technologies as protection from EMF sources, which is very effective (as I have already shared in chapter 13). However, I sense that the i-Guard is also effective for this. It is always great to have more than one choice in how to protect oneself from EMF. Because of the EMF protection and all the other added benefits that are incorporated into the i-Guard, I highly recommend that anyone desiring better quality of life should utilize this wonderful new invention.

As mentioned, I asked Celeste the same question about the i-Guard as I had about the Q-link technology: Could she enhance the ability of the i-Guard's Frequency settings, so that all of the frequencies emitted from the i-Guard could be even better than they were originally designed to be? Celeste agreed, and just as she had done with all the Q-link devices (that have already been sold by the company, and are yet to be sold), so too will now all i-Guards (that have been sold and all that will yet be sold through BodyWaveInternational.com) have this extra, subtle, more enhanced quality. Even greater, more wonderful healings and transformational health changes can now occur whenever this device is used.

I can understand why there was so much of an attempt by the cabal to block the i-Guard from being made available. As Scott stated in a recent Conference Call (and just as I have known for many years); major negative interference from the cabal and the imbalanced forces is a major confirmation of how important an issue is.

I cannot prove that the energetic enhancement from Celeste has actually occurred. But I used the i-Guard before Celeste enhanced it and I used it after, and to me there is a clear difference in its effect. I do sense that something has indeed been done to enhance to increase its abilities, but the effect is very subtle. I do not know if even the scientist who designed it could detect such subtle enhancements with whatever 3D level instruments that are presently available on Earth. Certain types of more advanced Instruments from beyond planet Earth would definitely be able to tell the difference caused by Celeste's energetic enhancement of the i-Guard. Anyway, since none of us will ever make any medical claims about what the i-Guard can or cannot do, this subtle enhancement is something that does not need to be proven. The i-Guard should just be experienced and enjoyed. Many Greater Health Blessings to everyone!

I have one more thing that I want to share. It may be considered somewhat controversial, so I will not be too explicit. After using the i-Guard, let us just say (and this is not a medical claim) it is obvious to me that one's "mojo-libido" can be enhanced with the use of this device. Of course there are a numerous other important factors affecting the "mojo-libido," such as whether one is eating only healthy, organic foods, taking various supplements, doing yoga and other exercises, getting enough sleep, staying away from stress as much as possible, etc. These factors are all a part of one's synergistic holistic energy recipe for life. But for someone who is already doing all these things, this intimacy enhancement should in my opinion be possible to feel and experience (even if only subtly). This in turn will help anchor the Nirvanic Ecstasy Grid all over the planet.

I have heard from Scott Mowry that various other advanced technologies and devices will be made available to the public, either through BodyWaveInternational.com or a similar website that the Alliance will also be in charge of.

Yes, our Future does indeed look much brighter and healthier, what with Rejuvenation Chambers and Replicators both being made available to the public over the next few years as we finally go into the long prophesied "Star Trek Golden Age"!

CHAPTER 19

My Cosmic Valentine!

The following text is an email that I sent to everyone on my email list on 2/14/20, copied ad verbatim. I think it is a perfect addition to this book. Some of what was shared in this email has already been covered in earlier chapters of this book, but I still want to share the email because of the other things that are described here.

"My Cosmic Valentine"
By Michael Ellegion & Celeste, 2/14/2020

Those of you on my email list who have been following all of the many wonderful experiences that I have had with my Beloved, Twin-Flame, Celeste. May, also remember me sharing about a few of the many awesome "Blessings, Miracles and Synchronicities" that she manifested for me.

I do like sharing with others about these as well, because I want to Inspire everyone else. That you, too, can and will, ultimately, experience with your own "Cosmic True Love," this same awesome and unbelievably—literally "out-of-this-world"— fulfilling, passionate Unconditional Love, that Celeste & I have been experiencing. She & I will be sharing about this in our upcoming book, *"IntergalacticMatch.com: How I Met My Cosmic True Love, and How You Can, Too!"*

I have some other things, also very wonderful and awesome, that Celeste very recently manifested for me, to "Energetically Symbolize" her Love for me. This had already been "proceeded" by a few other, smaller "Romantic Love Signs," that had appeared, of all places, in my kitchen sink.

A few days prior to Christmas, while I was busy in the kitchen, of having briefly ran water to wash my hands, I was singing a very spontaneous romantic Love song to Celeste. All of a sudden, I suddenly felt and saw Celeste's beautiful etheric presence near me, and felt her own very intense Love for me because of me singing that song to her.

As I glanced down into the stainless steel sink, I was surprised to discover something amazing in the bottom of the left side of the sink. I had temporary not been using it, because of a small leak in the water drain pipe right underneath the sink. In other words, because of this leak, I had quite running water temporarily so that it would not get things wet underneath. But, I had, accidently, a few times, splattered a few water drops into the left side of the sink.

As I looked down, to my surprise, some of these small individual water droplets, that had been scattered all over the sink bottom, were now totally together as one larger water droplet—in the perfect shape of a heart! And I could definitely feel and sense that Celeste had just "magically" made some of the individual very small water droplets to suddenly, "energetically" merge together to form into this wonderful little heart shaped larger water droplet. I just stared at it with joy—and Love in my own heart for her—as it was so obvious to me what she had just done to "spontaneously" show her love for me.

And, of course, what's that saying that has often been used by Earth humans to express "wonderful things yet to Manifest in our life"—"*The Best Is Yet To Come!*"

A couple days later, and only a couple more days before Christmas Eve, I was once again in the kitchen. I was making my smoothie to drink for lunch, and I was thinking of how much I intensely Love Celeste. Of how much Appreciation I have for her for all the many

"Blessings, Miracles and Synchronicities" that she has manifested for me since she started to come around me "24/7." And I sincerely, in my "heart, mind and soul" thanked her, as I often say to her, for all that she has done for me, both "Known and Unknown."

I say "Known and Unknown," because I discovered more recently just how much she actually did for me in years past, even though I was not [consciously] aware of it at the time. And, I keep discovering more and more things that she secretly did to either help me, or to save my life from the cabal's constant attempts to kill me, literally hundreds of times. And she just Loves now to continue to do more things all the time for me, without telling me, because she also likes to surprise me when she can.

For so many years and decades that I have been on this planet, she was forced to "be in the background" and could not directly Connect with me as she can now. This was because of what I had to do for so many years, until finally. These last couple years, she was allowed to "energetically" make herself much more present. Yes, to totally reveal herself to me, and of her Love for me, as my Twin-Flame/Universal Other Half.

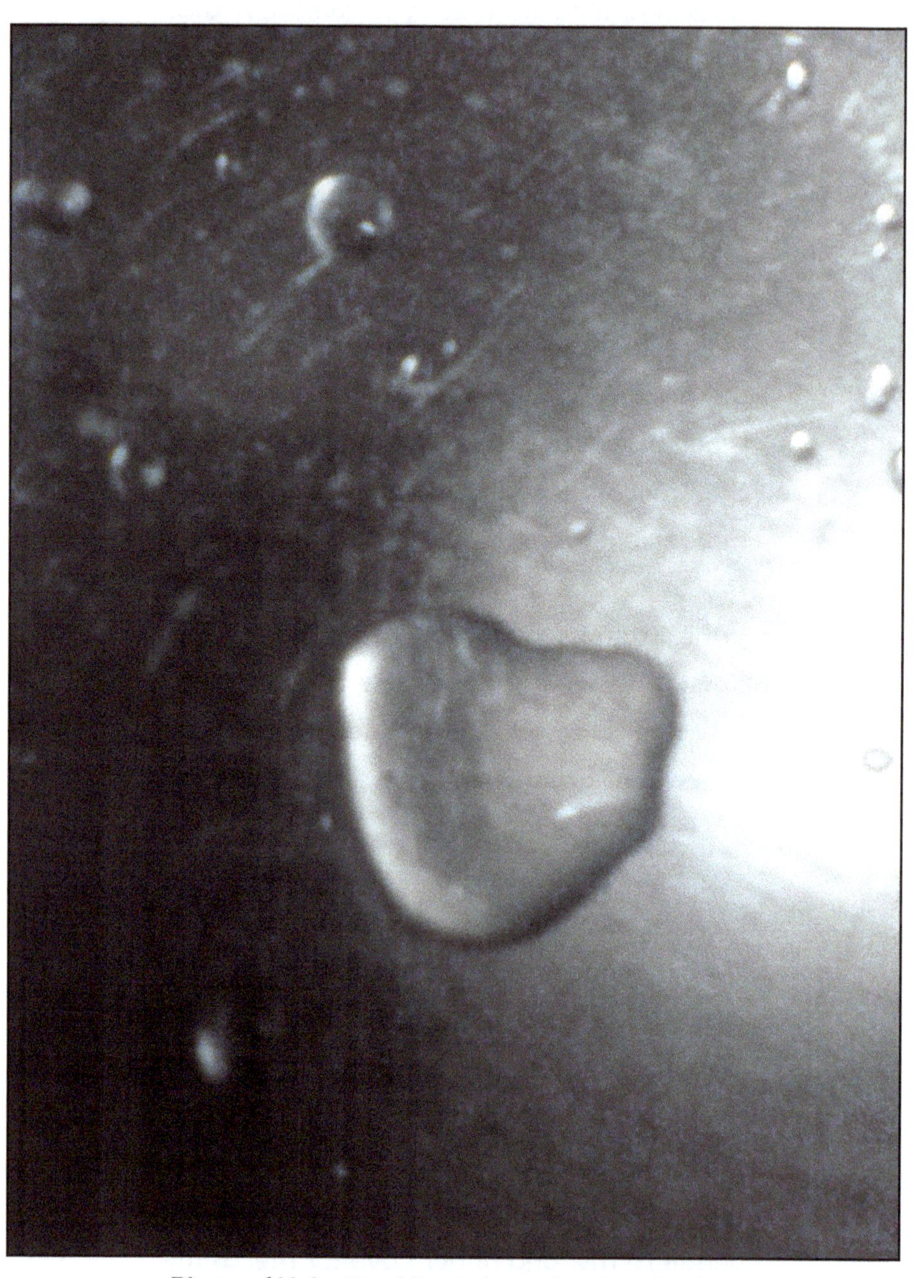

Photo of Valentine Heart shaped water droplet,
Celeste "Energetically Manifested" for me.

She was so excited that she was finally allowed this. I tuned into the fact of so many things she did "behind the scenes" to help me, without it being important for her to ever get any "recognition." This was because of her being so naturally giving and compassionate, and her devotion to me for so many years.

But for me, it was important, not because I "had to" thank her, but just because I wanted to tell her how much I appreciated all those "anonymous, behind the scenes" years of help and guidance. Of her Loving devotion to me and my needs, to fulfill my earlier mission. How happy and excited I Am now that she can be around me, much more directly; etherically and energetically, in preparation for her & I being totally physically together.

Because of the "unusual" nature of her & my mission together now, we had chosen to temporarily experience this "very unique" type of romantic relationship. Of many very interesting "perspectives" that will come out of this, until she & I do come together within the next few years on the physical level.

Yet, to demonstrate and show, that Love, real True Love, is never limited or blocked just because she happens to be, for right now, on a more "etheric" or "5D" level, while I Am still on this [temporary] "3D" level.

But getting back to this next wonderful "Water Droplet Manifestation in the Sink" that Celeste next did for me. As I started to mention, that two days after her "Heart shaped water droplet", I was in the kitchen, making my smoothie. I could energetically feel her loving presence so very intensely again, that she really enjoys my romantic feelings and me singing to her.

I was specifically thinking about all that I was appreciative for, because of the numerous, special "Gifts, Blessings and Miracles" that she had manifested to me. I also told her how I felt; that she, my Beloved, was, of course, my greatest Gift that Divine Creator could ever have manifested into my life.

I again felt that I needed, for some reason, to look down into the left side of the sink. This time, to my surprise and joy, many of the very small water droplets that had been accidently splattered into the sink, had now, once more, "magically" formed into a larger sized water droplet.

It literally had the outline of a "Christmas evergreen tree," and I knew that Celeste had, once again, given me a wonderful "sign." Of her own joy of being with me and of sharing this incredible and awesome journey together with her.

I was so moved and inspired by these two "water synchronicities" that Celeste had manifested, and wondered if she would do or manifest any other "unexpected" and awesome things in the future.

Well, what happened next, I like to refer to it as "Celeste's Magic Bag Opening Trick." One of the several main stores that I always shop at is Lucky's. One of the things that I often buy there is the very delicious and large sized organic dried Turkish figs that they sell in these large bulk barrels. The inner part of each bulk barrel is a large sized (about two by three foot) smooth hard plastic container. These Inner containers of each bulk barrel, in all the many months of shopping there, I had never seen either mostly, if not totally empty.

A few weeks ago, I had specifically gone there to purchase more of these delicious figs. To my surprise, the bulk barrel of these figs was nearly, totally empty. With maybe, I'm estimating, about one to one and a half dozen figs were all that were left at the very bottom of this huge bulk container.

In all the many months, maybe for a year or more, of shopping at Lucky's, I had never seen this particular bulk barrel of figs to ever be, literally, if not almost, totally empty.

Most of the bottom of the container was easily visible.

I looked closely, to see if I wanted to still actually buy these last few figs that were at the very bottom of the container. I did notice that it did not really look that clean. Which, I guess, is how the bottom of any basically empty bulk container would no doubt appear. If, as in this very rare case of it actually becoming totally or almost totally empty. After being filled and used for so long before it would be filled back up with the dried figs. I had never, actually, in all the many years of buying items out of these type of bulk containers, ever seen a bulk container so very empty.

In my mind, I wondered if instead of buying these last few figs at the very bottom of this very large container. I should, instead, wait a day or so until they filled this container back up. Even though these dried figs were definitely certified as organic, as verses the more "commercial" type dried figs.

I looked down into the very bottom of this nearly empty container, whether it was actually "clean" enough to be okay to scoop up these last few dried figs. How actually "clean" and/or "sterile" was the bottom of this very rare nearly empty large container actually going to be? Considering how long it had taken to now be so very empty, of whether, over a long period of time, who knows if people may have accidently dropped anything down into the barrier unintentionally. Or, if for whatever reason, it just was not that clean, or at least as clean as the figs normally are when this very large container is filled up with them.

In fact, as I looked closely at the bottom of the container, I did, actually, see what appeared to be very small "black colored pieces of something" that were scattered a little bit around among the last few figs. I did wonder in my mind if this was such that maybe I should just wait until a day or so had passed and the container was filled back up, as I knew it would probably be right away.

But, my desire and "hankering" for these delicious large organic dried Turkish figs, because of wanting to eat more right away, finally "overcame my better judgement." I ignored my Inner sense that it would be better to just wait and buy more after they had filled it back up.

So, I walked over to where the box of new plastic bags were, that specifically is there to be used for scooping the different bulk items. They also had a small white square near the top where one writes the Plu# on, so that the cashier can weigh the bag and come up with the amount that one owes.

The box that I pulled my bag from, was totally filled with these new, clean bags. Which were also very strong, in that they can hold up to at least 2 lbs. or more of nuts or dried fruit easily, without ever causing any strain on these bags.

I Am specifically mentioning this and also that I definitely could tell that there was no cut or hole of any kind on the bag; either on its sides or on the bottom of the bag. There is a reason I specifically mention the condition of this new bag. So that if someone is skeptical of what I was about to experience, that such actually occurred as I Am about to describe. One will have to acknowledge that something "extraordinary" did "miraculously-magically" occur. That this cannot be explained away with merely some mere "mundane explanation."

As soon as I had grabbed this new bag, I opened it up all the way. Picking up the large metal scoop, I preceded to [attempt] to scoop these last few figs out of the bottom of the barrel and to put them into my wide open plastic bag.

This is when the "weirdness" began to occur. I have for many years been buying bulk items, like organic raw nuts and dried figs. I do not ever have any difficulty at picking up either one or a lot of these. Every time I have ever used a large metal scoop to take them out of the large bulk container, and then put them into a bag.

But this time, "I swear to God" [or rather the Goddess!]-—that what happened next IS definitely very "strange"! Each time I would reach down with the metal scoop, and preceded to scoop up each of these last figs. It was as if some strange outside force literally began to knock them out of the scoop onto the floor. No matter how careful I was being to scoop them up and place them into my bag. After attempting several times to do this, and each time, to have this "strange force" interfering with my attempt to bag the figs. Each time, the figs were literally knocked out of the scoop onto the floor.

I began to get really determined that somehow I could still "salvage" the last several figs. I tried even harder and more carefully, to "outwit" whatever "force" was stopping me from getting some of these last figs at the very bottom of the container. Finally, with what seemed a "miracle," I was able with great difficulty, of securing about a dozen of the last figs.

I then, initially, picked up the mostly very empty bag of these few last figs, and held it up for a few moments. I was still wondering that after all this extreme effort, if I should still just not get them and leave the bag and walk away.

For in the back of my mind, I realized and felt Inside, and admitted to myself a little later, that it was actually Celeste who had "obviously" used her "magical powers" to attempt to let me know that I should NOT eat these last few figs on the bottom of the barrel. Which is why she was "energetically" knocking them out of the scoop onto the floor. She was merely attempting to—"Dah!—"give me a hint" about not buying these last few figs until the container was filled back up.

But I tried to "play dumb" about this, which I had never done before. For me to just "ignore" her whenever she has communicated with me in many different ways. With great Love, joy and respect, I have always felt so wonderful when she has given me so many Insights and have created these other awesome "synchronicities."

For some reason, this time, I just did not want to acknowledge her being the "source" of this "strange fig behavior," and still attempted to purchase these last "successfully bagged figs."

What happened next, is definitely "one for the history books." I had for a few moments, held the very empty bag over the floor. I can definitely say, as I look back on what happened next, that there was absolutely no holes, rips or cuts of any kind in the bottom of the bag. And, as I mentioned earlier, these particular bags are very strong and durable, and can easily hold over two or three pounds of nuts or other bulk items, and would never break or bust open by themselves.

I emphasize this point, because of how "incredible" it was for what happened a few moments later. I had then, briefly, laid the bag down while I quickly wrote the "Plu#" on it, and then picked it up to place it into my grocery cart.

It was then, at that moment, that the seemingly "impossible" occurred. It was as if an "invisible knife" suddenly cut totally across the entire length of the bottom of this very strong, secure plastic bag (about 12 inches in length). In that next instant, all the figs fell out through the bottom of the bag, onto the floor.

Photo of Heart, with the outline of Angelic Being behind it, Celeste manifested in the eggs I was about to cook on the stove, before Valentine's Day.

I just stood there for a few moments, in shock, of what I had just experienced. At first, my conscious mind did not want to fully acknowledge what I knew to be true. Because, especially, at that moment, I could feel my Beloved, Celeste's intense loving—and protective—presence.

I knew, a few moments later, as I saw her clairvoyantly and heard her beautiful telepathic voice in my head. She had, in fact, done this to actually protect me from whatever thing that had somehow "contaminated" those last few figs at the very bottom of the barrel. She didn't "elaborate" about what, exactly, it was, and I knew she didn't need to. For I, myself, had some possible "concerns" about the exact conditions of those last few figs.

As stated before, usually, I would not ever think of trying to "scavage" the last of any items that might be at the very bottom of one of these large bulk containers. It was obvious from her more evolved perspective, that my initial concerns were definitely valid.

I then felt so much appreciation, joy and Love for her, as I do all the time, with this being just one of many examples of her having watched over me in her Love for me.

I immediately thanked her from the bottom of my heart, as I also mentioned earlier, for all that she has done for me, both "known and unknown." Because, I knew and sensed, that she had done far more things than my conscious mind could ever, specifically, know. I could "intuitively" sense how much she has done for me throughout all the many decades since I had been born into this final Earth lifetime, back on Sept. 20, 1953.

So, it was really awesome to experience these types of "Miracles and Magical Synchronicities" with Celeste, and wondered what the next awesome surprise from her might be.

As you can see, from the two above photos (with the same photo slightly enlarged in the second one), that I took a few weeks ago. Her next major wonderful "energetic [and very romantic] manifestation" was the beautiful Heart that she energetically created in the stainless steel frying pan, while I was in the process of getting ready to cook some eggs for my evening meal.

She later specifically told me, that this was to definitely "Commemorate and Celebrate" her & my Love for each other, for this Valentine's Day. But the reason she did it when she did, a few weeks ago, as verses much closer to the actual date of Feb. 14th, had to do with the specific "conditions" she was dealing with here on this "3D" level.

Because of the fact that I cook with coconut oil, especially using it whenever I cook my eggs, and that coconut oil, will usually stay in a more solid form. As verses staying in a more liquid state, when the room temperature is approximately in the higher 70 degrees. Here in Florida, where I happen to be living for the last couple years, even in the Winter time. Just as we experienced a couple times in the last couple months, the temperature rose into the upper 70 degrees, which caused the coconut oil to become liquid in form.

Again, as Celeste explained to me afterwards, this was all very important in order for her to be able to "energetically manifest" this wonderful, awesome [and traditional Earth] romantic love symbol for me.

Even though Lady Celeste, my "Cosmic True Love," and "Immortal Intergalactic Space Goddess", as I often refer to her in a humorous, loving way, definitely has many special abilities and powers. This allows her to do all kinds of incredible and seemingly "impossible" things (as compared to the so-called normal "3D Earth limitations"). She explained that she actually needed to still have a few specific things "in place," in this particular instance, on this "3D" level. To be able to "Energetically Manifest" this wonderful "Eternal Romantic Love Symbol" of the Heart in my eggs.

The "consistency" of the coconut oil had to be in liquid form, in order to make this special Manifestation possible. Just prior to her doing this, as I was preparing to actually turn on the stove skillet, that the frying pan was sitting on. I had first spooned out three teaspoons of the liquid coconut oil into the pan.

I then proceeded to break open four of the [organic, "pasture raised"] eggs that I always use [and, by the way, these are definitely the healthiest eggs available on the market. As verses even "free range" eggs, because they come from much happier and healthier chickens, who have many acres of wide open space to move around, etc.].

As soon as I had put the broken open eggs in the skillet, I had turned away for a couple minutes to also finish making my large salad that I always eat with my eggs. This consists [with everything organic, of course] of celentro, broccoli, grated up carrots, purple cabbage and beets. I usually seasoned it with himalayan pink salt, along with a special organic mixture of dried herbs, called "Sea Kelp Delight" [made by the company

Bragg, that makes the organic raw, unpasteurized apple cider vinegar that I also use on my salad]. I was about to actually turn on the skillet to start cooking the eggs.

It was then that I saw this perfect "Heart" now manifested, in the exact middle of the skillet in between the eggs. I just stared at it for a few moments, as I then felt and saw Celeste energetically manifested right beside me in the etheric. As she hugged me and told me how much she Loved me.

I was, as I always am around her, totally "Blissed out" with her (as I always tell her that I Am "Blessed and Blissed by Celeste!")

As I stared at the skillet, I noticed that there was a white colored ring around the inside edge of the frying pan. Besides the beautiful Heart in the exact middle. As I looked more closely, there appeared to also be some kind of subtle "angelic being image" in the background right behind the Heart, as well. (Celeste also later informed me, that this "angelic being image," was to represent her "Over-Lighting Angelic Protective Loving Presence.")

On a more "mundane," 3D level, that when I had broken open those four eggs, which had been in the refrigerator at a much colder temperature. Once the cold eggs "interacted" with the warmer liquid coconut oil, this had obviously caused the oil to start to "solidify" once more.

Exact ["Divine"] timing was important in this whole "oil solidifying process." As Celeste needed to use this, in order for her to actually create or manifest her "Romantic Heart" for me.

It was this specific, sudden "temperature change," that was needed for her to use. Combined, of course, with her own special powers to complete this Awesome and wonderful "magical, "all-in-one" Heart & Angelic Being-oil-egg" manifestation.

As Celeste explained to me, since it was not clear if, in fact, whether the temperature here in Florida, would actually, once more, before Valentine's Day, become warm enough, so that the coconut oil would be warm enough to become liquid again.

Celeste just decided, I felt, to "go for it" when she did. To make sure that I would have a chance to see and experience her awesome Romantic Heart (with "Angelic Being in the background") for me before Valentine's Day came and went.

One more thing that both Celeste & I want to share with all of you who are on my email list (and anyone else that you forward this email to). We are working a lot on her & my book, *"IntergalacticMatch.com."* And I must say, I will never suffer from "writer's block," what with my Beloved around me all the time.

Actually, as Celeste guided me to do in 2018, when she started to come around me almost "24/7." I use a pillow, which I place in my lap, right in front of me. As Celeste "energetically-etherically" will "merge" with the pillow.

As incredible as it may seem, when I hug the pillow, it literally feels as if I Am hugging her physically, directly. The pillow acts as kind of an "energetic dimensional translator device." To allow her & I to "energetically interact" more directly with each other. She came up with this unique, innovative idea of utilizing one of my pillows for our "personal interactive needs." Because of the "challenge" of her not being able—or rather allowed [YET]—to actually be with me physically on this 3D level (until "First Contact" has occurred. Hopefully within the next few years).

As we come toward the end of this email, Celeste specifically wants to say Hi to everyone, and that she wants all of you to know something very important. As a major member of the "Love Ops," also known as the

"Special Forces of Romantic Love," Celeste emphasizes this point about each of your own Destiny. That just as she & I were recently able to be Reunited as a Divine Couple. So, too, each of you who are still "searching" and yearning for your own Beloved, will, indeed, be Reunited very soon. By or before the time First Contact has occurred.

As we will be sharing in our book, you too, can also experience, just as Celeste & I are right now, a similar, Divinely, passionately fulfilling Romantic Relationship. Yes, no matter where your "Cosmic True Love" happens to presently be, either on the 4D, 5D, or any other alternative dimensional realm. As Celeste & I are experiencing, it doesn't matter that your own Beloved happens to be "somewhere else."

You not only can communicate with them, but also "energetically interact" directly with them, as if this so-called "separation" doesn't really exist. One can, if they desire it strong enough, overcome this so-called "dimensional handicap" and "re-energetically Connect" right now. Even before this more direct "Great Grand Cosmic Romantic Reunion" finally does occur.

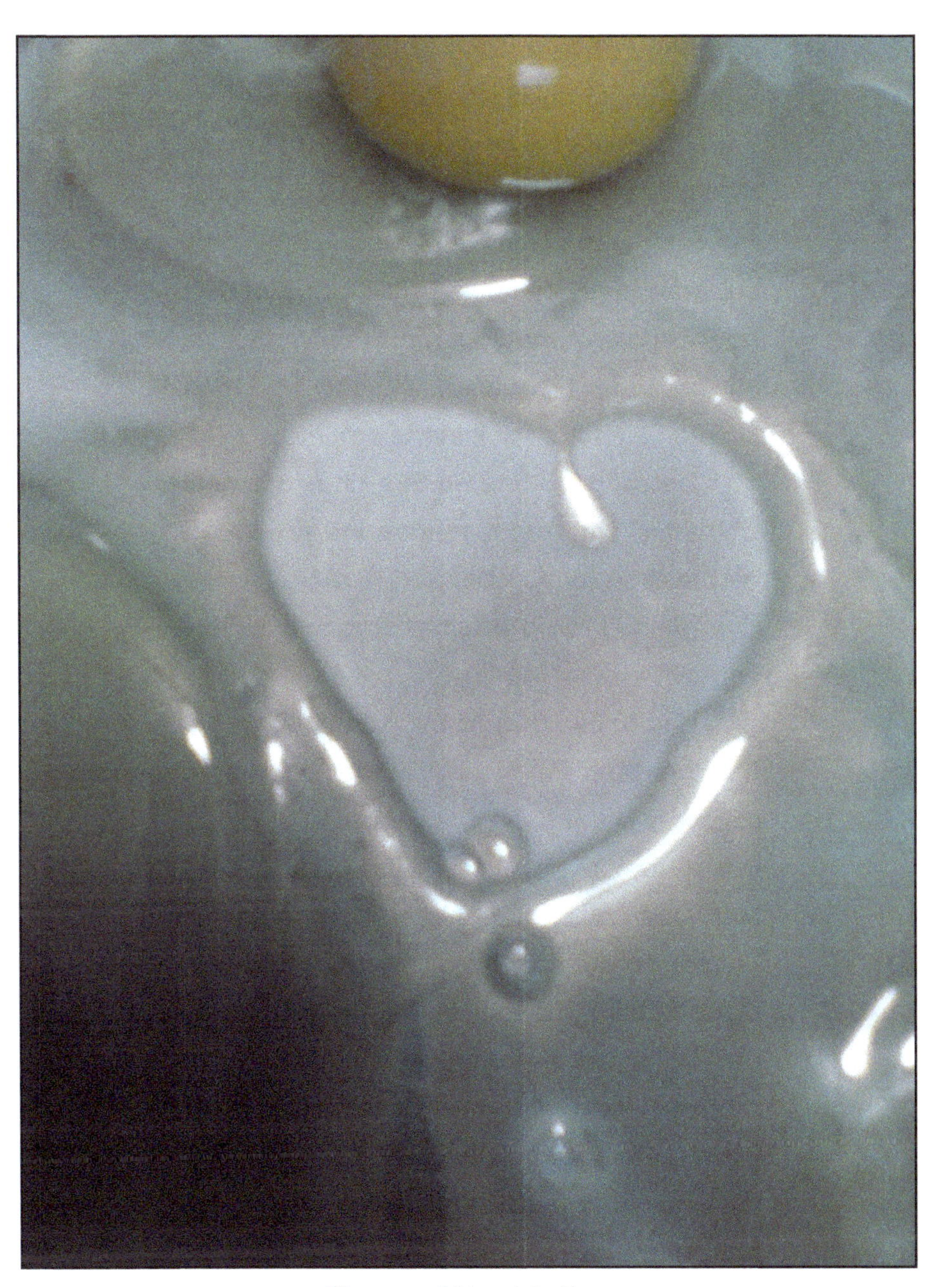

Closeup of Heart in Eggs

I have sincerely told Celeste many times since she has been "energetically-etherically" manifesting around me. Because of how wonderfully "Blissed out" with her that I Am all the time now. If I had a choice between her, my Twin-Flame/Twin Soul Mate, in her present etheric presence. As verses being able to be with one of my Soul Mates on a physical, 3D level. That I would, without hesitation, choose Celeste as she is in the etheric.

Because the intense Bliss and "energetic chemistry" that she & I share and experience all the time. Would be, and is, more intense, than what I could possibly physically experience with a soul mate.

I do know, that in the future, when it is the right time, Celeste will, in fact, be allowed to totally be with me on all levels in the physical. I Am not focusing upon this, of our eventual physical relationship. But, upon what Celeste & I are able to so intensely share with one another right now, in the present.

When the time is right, this other more "normal" form of a physical relationship will occur. I Am truly enjoying and savoring her right now as she so Lovingly manifests herself around me all the time.

As stated, I feel so extremely Blessed and Blissed by her, of being so very Honored to have had this "once-in-lifetime" chance to experience what I Am with her. To also share this awesome and Inspiring life journey with her, with everyone else. And what she & I will be experiencing together as a "Cosmic Divine Couple." For the short time that it will be, until she & I will then be physically together.

One just needs to be sincerely open to this Ultimate Divine Romantic Relationship. And to reach out and ask with a Sincere, True, Pure Heart's Desire. Just as I did, for this awesome, wonderful and indescribable—yes, literally—"Out-of-this-world" fulfilling romantic Love that most assume were only part of "fairy tales."

Yet, as I know, these "fairy tales" were actually based upon real past life stories of Twin-Flames, like Celeste & I, and other Cosmic Divine Couples. Who, created, thru various "time line changes," these many romantic life times, to also Inspire and Uplift others.

That you, really can "have your cake and icing too!" And that you can, with your Beloved, Truly, "Live Happily Ever After"!

I had just finished the above paragraph in this email, and thought [in my conscious mind], that this would be how I would end it. But, suddenly, another wonderful event occurred a short time later, which I wanted to also share with everyone.

This was one of Celeste's wonderful "Synchronicities" and Manifestations; this time up in the sky. Which also involved what I will refer to partly as an "I.F.O." sighting. Otherwise known as an Identified Flying Object. As verses how mundane "UFO investigators" tend to imply (in their "left [unintuitive] brain") that these are all just merely "Unidentified Flying Objects," or can mostly all be simply "explained away as merely some kind of "natural atmospheric phenomena."

For me, Intuitively, it was "Energetically" very obvious, that this was another one of Celeste's numerous "Confirmation Synchronicity Manifestations" or C.S.M.'s.

Of not only her wonderful Divine Feminine Goddess presence, but of her & My Higher Self's Merkabah Light Ship, the Celestial Star.

This event and sighting occurred this last Mon., Feb. 10th, in the late afternoon, as I was doing my daily "power walk." From where my apartment is, to go over to a near-by store to buy something I needed for my dinner later.

As I was walking back, again, I suddenly felt Celeste's presence very strongly, and I heard her very specifically tell me to look up at the sky, toward the horizon, which was toward the west.

I stopped and turned my head around and looked up. There, very clearly, I could see, what earth meteorologists refer to as a "sundog." It was a very large, brilliant and beautiful, semi round and slightly "elongated" rainbow shape in the sky. Which was near the edge of a cloud bank.

Jutting out of or part of this bright rainbow glow, which contained all of the colors of the rainbow. I also could clearly see, right above this, some of the outer edge tip of a gigantic spaceship, slightly silhouetted against the sky in the background. To me, it appeared to be manifesting somewhat in between both the physical and the higher 5D or etheric level. With a very hazy "saucer shaped lenticular cloud" somewhat framing the outer edge tip of the giant craft, as it just sat or hovered there off on the far horizon. I knew that this ship had to be quite large, judging from where it appeared to be, as compared to the horizon.

Then, suddenly, within a few seconds, I knew and sensed instinctively, that this was, indeed, a "manifestation" of Celeste's & my Higher Self's ship, the Celestial Star. That Celeste was manifesting it for me as a "Confirmational-Sign and Synchronicity." To verify something that I had just asked her about a couple days before.

Without going into very much detail, as stated, I was facing a particular "personal matter" that had been a little challenging how I would be able to solve the "dilemma." So that I could still make it "win-win" for everyone involved. I had felt that Celeste had given me the "perfect solution" to solving the challenge. But, sometimes, it is great to also have one or more "synchronicity-confirmations" that help more powerfully Confirm this.

So, when I looked up into the sky, as Celeste had directed me to do, to now see this beautiful and awesome rainbow "sundog" and part of her & my Higher Self's own ship, the Celestial Star.

Her message to me was that this was a definite sign that her earlier message to me was, indeed, correct. That all would work out as I had felt would be the case.

I attempted with my cell phone camera, to take several photos of what I was observing in the sky. But, Interestingly, when I then looked at the photos, the beautiful and bright "sundog" rainbow, was just not as brilliant, with the individual colors, as what I had actually, visually, seen. Nor, was the part of the ship that was clearly showing itself to me, as clearly shown in the photo.

I had assumed that I should have been able to get a few much better or clearer images. But, instead, it only showed part of what I was actually seeing with my own eyes. I wondered if one of the reasons that the cell phone camera had not been able to catch it as well as I had actually seen it. Was that even though it all seemed to me to be mostly manifesting in the 3D physical level, maybe it was also much more in the 5D or etheric as well.

Of course, maybe I just needed a much better and more expensive camera. Maybe, then, everything would have appeared in the photos much more as I actually observed this wonderful sighting.

Then, on the same day that I had seen the "sun dog" and part of the Celestial Star. When I had finished my power walk and returned back to my apartment, Celeste had done one more "Energetic Heart" manifestation for me.

As I had shared earlier, of her causing some of those water droplets, that had been accidently splashed on to the left side of my sink. To form the small "Valentine Heart" shaped water droplet. But I had not had a chance to photograph it before.

Original Photo of ship in background

I went back into the kitchen a couple hours later to start fixing my dinner, and I glanced into the sink. I suddenly saw another, and slightly larger, very perfectly formed "Heart shaped" water droplet had once again manifested for me.

I sensed Celeste's Loving wonderful presence, and that since I had not had a chance to take a photo of the last one she had done. It was as if she was giving me another chance to photograph this one. Which I did, and thanked her sincerely for all her extra efforts of expressing her Love for/to me.

How awesome this was, to also be able to share some of this powerful Love that Celeste & I feel for each other, with others. Through these photos, to help Inspire everyone else, that they, too, can have a lot to look forward to. That they, too, can experience this same wonderful and passionately fulfilling romantic relationship with their own Beloved.

"If" they will but—"ALLOW themselves"—to truly believe and Know Within. It IS the Destiny of all incarnated Volunteer souls in Earth embodiment, as well as many others here on Earth, to be able to finally meet your Beloved/"Cosmic True Love." That it is time to truly ask, with a sincere, True, Pure Heart's Desire.

That it doesn't matter how many times, here on Earth, in your past, you were acting out of a "less mature and less Discerning" state of consciousness.

As the lyrics of an old famous love song from a few decades ago, stated: "Looking for love in all the wrong places...." Most people have attempted, through various earth dating websites, went out to bars and nightclubs. Even attempted all kinds of "mundane, 3D earth dating techniques," in hopes of finding you True Love.

Only to be disappointed, over and over again, like a bad, "Ground Hog Day nightmare." Then, they "gave up hope," and maybe became "cynical" that "True Love." Really, authentic, True Love, didn't actually exist.

They erroneously concluded in their left brain intellect, and through their "ego conscious self." That this type of really special, intense, fulfilling, passionate romantic love. Was only the basis of ancient myths and "fictional romantic novels," and had nothing to do with real reality today.

Well, Celeste & I are "here to tell you," that this is NOT just some fictional myth and or "fairy tale." As stated earlier, these so-called "fictional, mythical" stories ARE, in fact, real. True stories of when Twin-Flame [and "Tantric"] couples came together and were Re-United numerous times, throughout Earth's history.

Now that there have been many recent, new Time Line changes. Many of you reading this, also, just as Celeste & I have done, with your own Universal Other Half, created numerous very romantic lifetimes together, both on other worlds and here on Earth.

And speaking of "romantic past lives on other worlds." I want to specifically refer to the beautiful image that was at the very beginning of this email. I first saw this painting, which was posted at the "Pinterest" web site, last year. The instant I saw it, I felt intense emotions, and started to cry in what I was suddenly, powerfully feeling, sensing and psychically "flashing back to." Of what Celeste & I experienced in a past life on another world and dimensional realm near the Pleiades Constellation.

I Am going to be describing much more in-depth, about what I powerfully "tuned into, from the "galactic Akashic Records." That this image actually and accurately shows about one of the many romantic past lives that Celeste & I experienced many millions of years ago, during the "Orion Wars."

> Of how she existed in this other dimensional realm near the Pleiades. She was a beautiful Goddess-Angelic being with actual wings, etc., appearing just exactly as the "fantasy artist" painted her. I am assuming that the artist probably thought (in their conscious mind), that they were just painting some kind of "earth medieval fantasy scene" from their "vivid imagination."

Note on the email: I had originally planned to include the awesome, wonderful image that I am referring to here in this book, so that the readers could see it. Unfortunately, I was never able to connect with the artist to get the "legal okay" to do so. But if you type this exact phrase, "Pinterest-Fantasy Art-Knight & Angel Couples," into your online search bar, you should be able to easily see this particular image. I did this search four times, and each time the particular image that I am referring to popped up (along with numerous other images). The image appeared on the top left side of the search results each time I did the search. This particular image should appear immediately for you too, and it should be pretty clear which image I am referring to: The knight is in his armor (and red cape), hugging the beautiful Angel with her large white wings. They are looking at one another with such love in their eyes. Click on it to enlarge it. You will see just how beautiful and magnificent this particular image really is, and how the artist so excellently was able to convey their love for each other. There are also lots of beautiful flowers around them on the ground in the foreground. If you look closely you will see a couple of golden, lit-up angel beings flying around behind them in the sky.

Getting back to the email:

> What Celeste verified to me, was that this particular scene that was painted ["Channeled"] by the artist, IS actually a very real scene when she & first met in that lifetime or existence. That I was wearing a very advanced type of "smart armor." Even though it may look a little like the more mundane, and much heavier armor that the knights on Earth wore. Technologically, it was definitely much different in how it was able to "energetically" protect me with a very powerful forcefield. It actually Empowered me and "energetically enhanced" my natural Higher abilities, as a "Galactic Guardian, who under Archangel Michael, had traveled to the Pleiades star systems. To specifically train various "Cosmic Special Forces Light teams" to battle the negative forces that had attacked the area.
>
> Celeste had "sent out a cosmic S.O.S." for help against these same forces attacking her realm. This particular scene [that the artist so well depicts] quite accurately, the moment when Celeste & I first re-met in that life time. Of all the intense, instant "Love at First Sight"

of first seeing her, and holding her in my arms, etc.

All of this "energetic Love romantic energy," that is felt and expressed between Twin-Flames, help transform Earth into the upcoming "Star Trek Golden Age." Where future True, really fulfilling Romance, IS already an established reality. Where the beautiful Rainbow Crystal, Tantric-Oracle Temples of the ancient Lemurian Golden Age will be re-manifested once more.

All you have to do is ALLOW yourself, to reach out with a "True, Pure Heart's desire", and sincerely ask your own Cosmic True Love to make their Divine Presence known to you. So that you can start either communicating with them, if they happen to presently be on a "5D" or Higher Dimensional level, just as Celeste & I are. Or, you may shortly be reunited with them here on this "3D" physical level of reality.

Yes, it will most likely "energetically require" that you ALLOW yourself to "emotionally/psychologically give up or let go of"—or, at least ATTEMPT to do so. All of the so-called "negative human habits, tendencies and traits," that have kept you "stuck in the funk," in any past Earth "karmic, emotional toxic relationships."

Cropped (& Enlarged) photo, showing part of the outer rim of the "Celestial Star" (with "ionization" around it) sticking out of the cloud bank and the "sun dog" that was just below it.

Know that as I will be sharing in Celeste's & my upcoming book, "IntergalacticMatch.com," there are numerous very effective "techniques and protocols" one can do here on this "3D earth level to help Transform your lives.

There are also many powerful and wonderful things that the Cosmic Masters, with their very advanced Merkabah Elohim Consciousness Technologies, can do for you. Such as using the "Accelerator Chair" on the Jupiter One Light ship, while one is sleeping at night.

All these many things can really help release so much of this "emotional gung/funk" from your total consciousness. To help to "energetically reprogram" any and all of these "toxic imbalances," out of your system, never to influence you again.

Yes, "God helps those who help themselves," or as I also like to say now that my own Beloved and Cosmic True Love, Celeste, is so much a part of my life, "the Goddess helps those who help themselves."

And for each of you to ALLOW yourself this new and unique opportunity to experience this same intense, passionate and yes—unbelievably—literally—"out of this world" fulfilling love, and Bliss to become part of your own lives as well. What Celeste & I are experiencing together, can be yours, as well.

No one has to "go without," and this definitely includes experiencing such a fulfilling relationship, on ALL levels of our being. Again, it IS a combination of what we each "think, say and do." And, combined with what we ALLOW Higher Forces to also do, to "help us help ourselves."

As I shared earlier, Celeste is a member of the "Love Ops," also known as the "Special Forces of Romantic Love." She and her fellow members of this vast Universal Romantic organization (which is part of the Intergalactic Confederation/Universal Federation). Are here to officially manifest what I like to refer to as the Divine Creator's "new mantra": "You are going to Enjoy life whether you like it or not!"

So just "surrender" to this wonderful romantic "Self-Realization." That is only going to increase in intensity over the coming months and next few years. That you & your Cosmic True Love will be Reunited.

The only question is, how long will you decide for this to take; you can help speed it up or slow it down, depending upon your choice in all this. I would assume, that you would want it take as short a time as possible.

As verses delaying it in any way, with all the things you "think, say and do" that determines your exact, "Vibrational Romantic Emotional Relationship Potential" at any given moment.

This IS, also, very connected with that "Harmonic Vibrational Consciousness Scale" that Ashtar, Voltra and various other Higher Beings who have channeled through me, have mentioned during my numerous sessions. This "Harmonic Scale" also determines how "vibrationally ready" we each are, both individually and collectively, for "First Contact" to occur.

But remember, a major part of this historical upcoming event, IS the reuniting of all the Twin-Flame couples.

This really is NOT a "complicated" procedure," as some of you may assume through your conscious Earth minds, but actually very simple. As long as you ALLOW yourself, with Intent and Motive (which is the only thing Higher Forces "judge"—NOT our so-called "human Earth mistakes and imbalances).

And do what James Gilliland of ECTI Ranch, says: "Keep an Open Mind, Loving Heart, and Pure Intent."

If you each do that, I know that you are more than "worthy" to Truly be reunited with your own Beloved. And it Will become a wonderful and positive "Self-Fulfilled Prophecy."

No matter what you have experienced up to now in the "Earth relationship reality."

So, let it now be the one you have always known in the deepest part of your being, and your I Am Presence. That our Divine Creator, "made that perfect, Divine Partner for each of us." It is up to us to reach out and ask. Yes, "ask and ye shall receive".

That IS what I did, and "lo and Behold", my own Beloved, Celeste, finally made herself known to me and is with me now. We are truly having this most wonderful, fulfilling, romantic relationship. It doesn't matter about the so-called "dimensional handicap." As she & I have been able to overcome, and are enjoying ourselves "24/7." Sometime within the next few years, she & I will be totally reunited on a physical level.

Celeste & I both wish for you on this Valentine's Day, Love's Fulfillment for you, when the time is truly right. It WILL occur, and maybe you can, indeed, speed it up a lot faster by being open and ready for it. I sense that some of you will, in fact, before this new year of 2020 is over, that you will be "reuniting" with your own Beloved.

I put quotation marks around the word "reuniting, because it may be that this will begin to occur "energetically" on other levels before it is completely, totally obvious to your conscious 3D Earth mind and consciousness.

This may be how Celeste & I are presently experiencing our own "Transdimensional Romantic Relationship." Or, you may just be one of those who directly meets you Other Half here on the 3D level. Each situation will be entirely unique.

This is what is so special about each Divine Couple Reuniting; not one of these special relationships are exactly the same. Except, of course, for that same intense wonderful, passionate—and yes, "out-of-this-world" fulfilling love that you, too, will experience! And it only just keeps getting better and better all the time!

Blessings to all of you on this wonderful special Day, of the Celebration of True, Unconditional Romantic Love. May you be one of the ones, soon, to also experience this same Blissful "Heaven on Earth"—and, yes, may you all "Live Happily Ever After"!

Namaste,

Michael & Celeste

CHAPTER 20

What's in an Image?

The following text is a copy of another email that I sent to everyone on my email list, copied ad verbatim (except for some parts that are left out for redundancy-reducing reasons). Celeste and I felt that also this email would be a good addition to this book.

What's in an Image?

By Michael Ellegion & Celeste, 5/5/20

> The above title to this email is very significant for me, on a very personal level. Because of what has been occurring for me, since my Beloved/Twin-Flame/"Cosmic True Love" Celeste, came/manifested "Energetically" into my life a couple years ago.
>
> Her sudden and awesome Divine Feminine Goddess Presence into my life in early 2018. Now around me "24/7," as I have shared with everyone in my past email blasts. Has been such an Amazing Blessing for me in

so many ways (as I like to say all the time, "Blessed and Blissed by Celeste"!)

Very recently, I connected with a clairvoyant artist who did an image of Celeste. This very wonderful and beautiful Image of my Beloved, Lady celeste, was just completed a few days ago, and I wanted to share her with everyone on my email list.

Celeste is also a major member of the "Love Ops/Special Forces of Romantic Love" (who are also helping Q and the White Hat Alliance, expose and free up Earth from the cabal deep state).

I also recently connected with another very talented visionary artist, named Erial-Ali, who is doing a very awesome Image, for the front cover of Celeste's & my book, *IntergalacticMatch.com.* This will actually be a very visionary-prophetic image of Higher Space Beings beaming down to "hook-up" with their Twin-Flame who is on Earth and take them out on an "Intergalactic Date." Yes, "dating" will never be the same, once people realize that they are no longer limited with only "dating" here on Earth and using Earth dating sites (like Match.com, etc.) to find their real, [cosmic] "True Love." Just as Celeste & I "Hooked up" in 2018.

Even though Celeste may [presently] be around me on the "5D" or etheric level, it is still the most Wonderful, Blissful, Fulfilling and Romantic experience of my entire life!

As I have told her many times, I would rather be with her, with her being on the 5D etheric level, because of all that I Am experiencing with her. Than, in a physical earth soul mate relationship; this is how intensely fulfilling and wonderful her & my relationship actually is.

Celeste has told me, that when the time is right, sometime after I publish her & my book, she is going to "re-manifest" into my life, in the physical. She will either connect with me, with her being in earth embodiment. Or, she will once more become a "Walk-In" (which is how I first met her in Nov. 2017, [to "get my attention"!]. When she came to one of my Workshops, and I went to stay with her at her home (of course, unlike that last time, she won't be with another partner, as she was then!). Or, she may just physically materialize right off the Light Ship, if "First Contact" has started by that time.

She is purposely, temporarily, being somewhat "vague" about the exact way she will do this. Only because of the [present] need for "security" purposes," so that there is no attempted "negative interference." Until all imbalanced forces are totally gone from planet Earth. This will occur once all the underground cabal bases (D.U.M.B.'s) are cleared out and all the children are rescued by the White Hat Alliance, and Earth is totally free of the cabal.

But getting back to the focus and title of this email. Yes, what IS in an "Image"? In other words, as I have just recently experienced, as I will share with everyone. Sometimes, our personal and "intimate" experiences, are "catalysts" and "surrogate" experiences for many others scattered all over Earth. To help them, first of all, "energetically, acknowledge and deal with," then to overcome, process and Transmute all of the vast amount of emotional and psychological imbalances, blocks and trauma. To then be able to really open our hearts and minds to those closest to us.

There are also, of course, many billions and trillions of Higher Light Beings standing by. Such as Voltra, one of many Cosmic Psychotherapists. Who can very easily help anyone who is sincerely wanting to be helped. One can then be taken in the etheric aboard his own ship, the Jupiter One. To sit in the "Excelerator Chair", to have any and all of these emotional imbalances to be released.

Celeste's Image, by Rebecca

One must ask with a "sincere, true, pure heart's desire" to be cleared and released from this, and this will definitely help one more quickly to "let go of all this "stuff."

This can also really help one to open up to finally meeting their Cosmic True Love, when the Divine moment is truly right here on this new time line.

After Celeste's & my book is published (sometime this year), numerous fellow Light Workers/Volunteers in Earth embodiment, scattered all over planet Earth, will come to realize something very important.

That yes, all of you, if you have not already met and are with your Twin-Flame, most likely they are presently on board the many trillions of Merkabah Light Ships that are around Earth in "Guardian Action." They want so much to be allowed to re-connect with each of their Beloved's—many of you, who are reading this email.

But the experience I wanted to share with everyone, was what occurred for me, when I had first seen the other image of Celeste. That another artist named Rebecca, had done of her about a month ago.

I will attempt to be as brief as possible about this image of Celeste by Rebecca. It was actually around the middle of 2019, when I first realized that Celeste & I were going to start work on a book together. It would partly be about her & my experience of re-connecting as a Twin-Flame couple. Including info. about a few of her & my many romantic past lives together, both on and off the planet. As well as how she was going to help other Twin-Flame couples to soon re-connect and Hook-up as well. Hence, the awesome title: *IntergalacticMatch.com* (which will also be the name of Celeste's & my new website, which I hope to have available on the Internet, by the time this book is published.)

I then realized that I wanted to have a clairvoyant artist do an image of her. So that others who would read her & my book, would have an accurate idea of [one of the many ways] she often appears or manifests to me.

But, as I will explain, as it turned out, there was also a "challenge" that came up regarding Rebecca actually doing and finishing the above image of Celeste.

First, I would like to say, that I try not to be "overly, negatively critical" of other people. Especially, what they do or don't do, as far as what would be termed their "artistic and/or creative abilities." I mean, as in the old phrase or saying, "who am I to judge" someone else's abilities. In regards to them being able to paint or create an image of a person, being, or any other thing. As compared to someone else's ability.

Words or terms, such as "professional, immature, quality, excellent, fair, poor," etc., are all very "relative." And, it can often be either "relevant or irrelevant." Depending upon who or what we are comparing someone's "artist abilities" to, as compared to someone else's.

I have to also give a little background upon how I had first connected with Rebecca, which occurred around 20 years ago. When I had been sponsored and hosted to do some Workshops in the Detroit, MI area. Rebecca had attended one of my events and had experienced one of my personal 90 min. Transformational Channeled Readings.

It was back then that I had been in the process of starting to write my first book, *Prepare For The Landings!* (which I published in 2010, and is available through Amazon.com)

I remember that Rebecca showed me some examples of what she said was her own art work, because I had expressed the idea that I was in the process of looking for an artist who might be able to do the scene for the front cover of my book.

It is interesting how we sometimes, when looking back on certain events in our lives, since we have gained some more "Hindsight" in our lives since those events occurred. About how we now view and remember things, as far as the specific details of what occurred. In a slightly different [or even major way], as compared to or verses when the particular event had initially occurred at the time.

I Am specifically mentioning this point, for a particular reason. As I already mentioned, I do not like to be too critical about what someone's "abilities" are.

At the same time, I always try, myself, to "come from integrity," and to be as honest as I can be. To give others "the benefit of doubt" and do not like to "accuse" someone of something. If they have done [or not done] something that appears or seems that they have not been "straight forward and/or honest with me," for whatever reason. I really would rather "give them the benefit of doubt."

But, and this is the "essence" of my "dilemma" that I Am sharing with everyone. In order to understand what I recently felt might have been the basis of why I felt that Rebecca in some way was not being entirely "straight with me." Now that I look back upon that experience of first viewing what she stated were examples of some of her own past art work.

I now, in my mind, remember her using this phrase, "These are examples of the kind of art work that I like to do." Which, of course, had implied by that statement, that [not only] were these examples, specifically, of her own original art work. But, were [also] the "type" or "kind" of art that she likes to do all the time.

But, and again, I have to use that word, my "dilemma," came about very recently. Right after she had completed the above image of Celeste, which I had received from her a few weeks ago.

The reason that I refer to it as a "dilemma," is because of my memory of what she had originally showed me 20 years ago. That she had "implied" were definitely examples of [her own, actual] "level of ability" as a "professional" artist. And because of having viewed those particular images, I was impressed that she would be able to do the "kind" or "quality" of work that I wanted for the front cover of my first book.

It wasn't until about ten years later, that I finally had the book ready to be published, and had contacted her to do the front cover, which she finished and sent to me.

I feel that I must also explain that at the time of having finished my book, there was a lot of stress that was occurring [here on this "3D" level] in my own personal life, because of having just come out of a very toxic and emotionally stressful relationship.

This also affected everything else that was occurring in my life at the time [as well as my "perception and awareness" about it], such as what I went through to be able to publish my book.

And, I have to say here, what with my Beloved, Celeste, now in my life. The experience of writing this present book, *IntergalacticMatch.com,* as compared to when I wrote that first book, *Prepare For The Landings!* is like "night and day."

Because for me, this experience of Celeste helping me write it, has been the most wonderful, fun and joyous experience of my entire life. To have my Twin-Flame/"Cosmic True Love" sharing this awesome experience with me, has been so exciting and fulfilling, to participate with her. As I have said before, with her, I never suffer from "writer's block" at any time!

But getting back to my "dilemma." I do remember, though, when Rebecca finally finished her image for the front cover of the book, and then emailed it to me to view. I was, of course, surprised about what I will refer to as the "quality" or "ability" of the image that I saw. I was, as stated, definitely surprised that it was not as "good" or "comparable" to those earlier images that I had viewed when I had first met Rebecca about ten years before.

Considering the level of stress that I was experiencing in my life at the time. But, also, especially the fact that the "deadline" for me having everything ready to finally be published, had now arrived, and I could not delay the publishing any longer.

I remember that I was in somewhat of a "conflict" in my mind regarding this situation, but did not want to be "petty." As well as the fact, as just stated, that the deadline of having everything ready to publish was right then. I did not want to delay the publishing of my book.

So, I just "bit the bullet," as they say, and choose to go with what I had. Plus, to have taken the time to have found another artist to do the front cover scene, would have definitely delayed the publishing of my book awhile, and I did not want to do that. Also, the whole process of "sizing and positioning" of the front cover scene took awhile, with Rebecca and the publishers. To get the exact, specific size that was needed to be able to finish the whole process.

After having invested so much time to do it, I was just not willing to go through more "hassle" to do this process all over again. So, I "bit the bullet," as I said, and went with it, and kind of forgot about this point. Of what I had seen originally, not appearing to be of the same level of quality as what I was definitely expecting to receive from Rebecca. Yes, I forgot about this—until, that is, I had received this image of her "rendition" of Celeste, that she had done, which was supposed to be used for this book.

In all fairness to Rebecca, I have to say, she did "go out of her way," as best she could, to spend a lot of extra time to finish that "sizing and positioning" process. It was somewhat challenging, and she did her best to do what was needed.

As she later explained to me, she also had a lot of other very important responsibilities and things going on in her life at the time, which was a challenge for her to take the time to even complete the image.

When she did this recent image of Celeste, she had been dealing with numerous family challenges of her own, and also having a couple other jobs she had to do, etc.

Celeste, Illustrated by another Psychic artist

I have tried to be understanding about her own personal challenges. But, at the same time, my "issue" or "conflict" had to do with the point I have already mentioned. About what I term the "level, quality and/or ability" that I had originally seen [or at least remember seeing]. As verses what I received from her, of her image of Celeste (as well as the "quality" of her image for the front cover of my first book).

This was the basic "conflict" of my "dilemma," of whether I should, this time. As compared to the last time that I had received the image for the front cover of my first book, and having not ever said anything to her.

As verses, now "having a talk with her" about my "dilemma." And, sharing with her how I was not only not satisfied with her work. But, also, how—at least in my mind—that she had—"at the very least," "misrepresented" her actual level or quality of her ability as an artist. That I felt could not use this image of Celeste. That it was not "good enough" or "professional" enough to be used in Celeste's & my book.

I was really feeling bad about this whole thing, of my conflict, of wanting to "confront" her about this.

But, on the other hand, I did not want to "hurt her feelings." Because, I had remembered a little bit about her earlier Reading with me. Of the fact that she had chosen, prior to taking Earth embodiment, to experience what would be termed a "Surrogate" role. To "energetically" help others who were suffering certain "emotional/psychological challenges."

Which, can cause major issues of "self-worth and inferiority complexes" with themselves. By her "taking this on," of embodying these type of challenges of her own, she would be able to help others struggling with these similar emotional issues. To then, "energetically," be able to help others to more easily overcome and release these same type of conditions.

But I felt that if I confronted her with my own issue about what I had experienced, at least from my perspective. That this would cause her to only experience more of these conditions, and I did not want to do that. But was at a loss about what, exactly, I should do.

It was a struggle to decide what I was going to do, because I did not want to emotionally devastate her. Yet, this conflict was really bothering me, and I felt in "pure conscious" that I could not now also "promote" her, as I had actually been planning before to do. But, of course, this was before I saw her image of Celeste.

To make matters "worse," an elderly lady named Anne, who lives in Texas, was planning to have an image of her own Twin-Flame done, by Rebecca, once she had completed Celeste's image. I had, of course, kind of "promoted" Rebecca and her work before she had finished Celeste's image.

I now felt even more in conflict about this whole thing, as in my "perspective", of seeing what I term the "level of ability" of how Rebecca had done with Celeste. I really was concerned that Anne would probably be at least somewhat "unsatisfied," with how her own Twin-flame image would probably turn out once Rebecca had done hers.

I had normally spoken to Anne every few weeks over the phone. But, now, I was feeling a little "embarrassed" about this whole thing.

So, I had not called her as I normally did, to share about what was going on in my life. I knew that she must be wondering why I had not called her for so long.

But, something else was also bothering me. Because, right after I had first seen the image that Rebecca had done of Celeste, I decided to see if I could find another clairvoyant artist, who could do an image of Celeste.

As well as another artist who could do the front cover of this book.

What is “weird” about that whole thing, is that I really thought that I had, in fact, found another artist, whose name was Nancy Smith, who was well known for doing “spirit portraits.”

While she usually only did images of “spirit entities.” That is, the spirits of those who passed over to the “spirit world” or “4D”/ astral realm, she had started to more recently do images of Higher Beings of Light. She had emailed some examples of her work, and I was impressed by what she could do.

I spent over an hour with her on the phone, also going over what I was interested in her doing for the front cover of Celeste’s & my book, and she seemed very excited and inspired about being able to do this for me. It seemed that everything was “right on,” that she would be the artist to do this new image of Celeste, as well as the front cover.

But, then, strangely enough, when I called her a few days later, and left her a phone message, she never responded back with me. Nor, did I ever hear from her after that, even though I left a few more phone messages over the following weeks, and have never heard from her ever again.

So, obviously, as it turned out, for whatever reason, she was not really meant to do either the image of Celeste, as another artist did, of course, has was already mentioned, nor the front cover.

But as the days and weeks began to go by, with no response back from Nancy, and with me feeling more confused and in conflict with this whole thing with Rebecca. I finally asked Celeste, if she had any "Insight" about what to do with Rebecca.

I knew that she would definitely have much Insight, and had actually asked her a couple times in the previous couple weeks if she could help me understand what exactly I should do, considering this whole "dilemma."

Not only what to say or do about Rebecca, as well as if she knew why I could suddenly not connect now with Nancy, despite what seemed to be an initial "go" with her being the one to do the work that I needed.

In my awesome, fulfilling and wonderful romantic relationship with Celeste, it was always so easy to communicate with her, ever since she had "energetically' manifested into my life. While she is still on the "5D" or etheric level around me, I Am clairvoyantly able to see her and clairaudiently able to communicate with her so easily.

Because of her & I are so "energetically connected" with each other "24/7," I have gotten so used to her being around me and often almost forget that she is not on the "3D" level. She & I have had so many wonderful discussions about all kinds of subjects, and as stated, it so often seems that she is right here on the physical with me.

Because of our wonderful and Blissful—and even very "energetic intimate—interactions." That are—well, "literally out-of-this-world"! And, in fact, because of our constant "energetic intimate interactions," my energy level got very high.

One day I was out "power walking" around town. As I approached a particular intersection, I heard Celeste telepathically warn me about being "extra careful and cautious," while walking across the intersection to the other side of the street.

I always pay very much attention when my own Beloved has either "warned" me about something, or has something to say to me, no matter what it might be. And I always very much appreciate this awesome opportunity and privilege. To know that she is always lovingly "watching over me and protecting and guiding me. To be able to always make the best "choices" in life, no matter what it might be.

Of course, for all of the first part of my life, Celeste had always, unbeknownst to my conscious mind, been protecting me/energetically "riding shotgun" for me (to use a phrase from the "old Wild West" Earth level). Against the imbalanced forces, who literally attempted hundreds of times to "off me" in all kinds of ways.

I had always known that I was being protected by "Higher Light Forces." But it was so wonderful to have the Honor and privilege to finally, more directly, Energetically Connect and Interact with the one specific Light Being. Who had made it her personal mission to always Watch over me; my own Beloved, Lady Celeste.

And, to now have her around me "24/7." To feel her awesome Divine Feminine Goddess presence more directly and intimately. Has, indeed, been an "out-of-this-world" experience, yet experienced right here on the "3D."

The fact that she specifically had warned me about some kind of "possible danger" when I proceeded to cross the intersection, did "put me on alert." As I walked up to stand for a few moments, waiting for the light to change, and for me to have the "green light go ahead" to cross.

I saw the light turn, and began to cautiously cross the intersection, as I saw a vehicle start to enter the intersection, as it prepared to make a left turn. It seemed to slow down a little, and I assumed it would come to a complete stop. Because of the driver seeing me already in the intersection crosswalk.

But instead of it coming to a stop, it actually suddenly "gunned it's engine," as it started to gain speed again to prepare to complete its turn and roar on through the intersection.

I was already about half way across the walkway, and I had to quickly run toward the other side of the crossway to get out of the way of the vehicle. To me, at the time, it seemed that it was purposely trying to "run me down," as it raced by with only inches to spare.

I was in shock at how close the vehicle had come. If I had not been as cautious as I was, because of Celeste warning me, the vehicle could have hit me. Actually, had she not warned me, I knew and sensed that she would have used her "Higher Powers" to keep me safe.

But I sensed for some reason that she wanted me to know about this prior to the vehicle almost hitting me.

I stood for a few moments, as I had a hard time believing that the vehicle had been purposely trying to hit me. That perhaps, for some reason, the driver actually did not see me, and had decided to go on through unaware that I was walking across the walkway.

I decided to walk toward another store, where I needed to go buy something. Because of what had just happened, I was still being overly cautious, even though I figured that the "danger had passed".

But, once again, just as I had experienced in the other intersection a few minutes before. As I got the "green walk" signal, and I proceeded to cautiously walk across the walkway. All of a sudden, another vehicle appeared, who was once again preparing to turn left and cross the walkway where I was walking. Like the vehicle in the last intersection, it slowed down briefly, as I assumed the driver was looking to see if anyone was walking across the walkway.

Instead of completely slowly down and stopping briefly to allow me to finish crossing. It also suddenly gained speed as it continued on its trajectory to finish it's turn. Again, I had to very quickly run toward the other side of the crossway to get out of the way in time, as it, too, just missed me by a few inches.

I was shocked and stunned by what had just happened for the second time. I could not understand what the heck was going on. That two entirely different vehicles, would appear to be trying to "run me down?" I really did not sense that this was what had just happened. Yet, it sure seemed almost like they were.

As I stood there, trying to figure out what was really going on. Celeste suddenly began to explain to me about what the "cause" of these two "incidents" actually were.

In fact, she kind of was "giggling and laughing" as she explained that because of her & I having very intense and passionate "energetic intimacy", my energy level had risen so high. That this had caused me, as she jokingly said, to become an "invisible man!"

In other words, my energy level was so high after being intimate with Celeste, that the drivers in both vehicles literally did not see me on the 3D level. Which, is why they went ahead and raced through the intersection. They definitely were not trying to "run me down," they just could not see me!

Celeste then explained that if I can "get eye contact" with the driver, then they would see me. Sure enough, that seemed to [usually} take care of this "little challenge."

So, the "joke" is, yea, I had the most wonderful and fulfilling intimacy with my Beloved. But, this causes me to sometimes become "the Invisible Man!" Which, I Am more than willing, to put up with this little "risky challenge"!

To get back to the situation of asking Celeste for her Insight into what to do about Rebecca. She told me that I needed to call Rebecca and talk to her. To "speak from my heart," with as much compassion as I could. To attempt to see her side to this whole thing.

That I needed to do this, and I would not be able to even find or connect with the right artists, with one doing Celeste's image, as well as another [Erial-Ali] that would do the front cover, until I did so.

But even as Celeste was telling me this, I could also sense that something was also very much bothering her, and I had never experienced this kind of feelings from her before. That she was actually feeling very upset and disappointed about something I had dome, or not dome.

I could not tell what it was. I suddenly felt all these feelings of what she was experiencing, and that she was "holding it in" to herself. This was very odd, because as stated before, never in the two years of having her around me so directly, had I ever experienced her being even a little "upset" with me. That she was always so loving and caring about me, so positive about her feelings for me, and had no "complaints" or "negative comments" about anything I had done or not done, in all that time.

This was something entirely new for Celeste to be "reacting" or "feeling" these type of "negative feelings and emotions." And, also, not to even tell me what it was that was bothering her so intensely.

For me, as I have stated many times, of how appreciative and Honored I Am to have her with me these last two years. I have told her so many times, probably at least a dozen times every day, how much I Love her. How I could never take her for granted, and that I was so Blessed by her and all that she has done for me.

I also have been enjoying the intense romantic feelings of Love that we experience all the time, and it just has been so intensely fulfilling in so many wonderful ways. It is very difficult to even find the proper words sometimes to attempt to even express how much I Love and adore her; human English words and terms totally fall short and fail to express how intense these feelings actually are.

Even words such as "Awesome, Fantastic, Incredible, etc." All, fail to fully express my feelings and Love for her, and what she & I share all the time. And I try to always thoughtfully consider her feelings all the time. I have asked her, that if I have at any time not treated her with all the Love and respect that I should, if I have in any way been "thoughtless, inconsiderate or uncaring", to please forgive me.

But to also point out to me if and when I should ever be like that in any way, because she is beyond any shadow of doubt the most important person/being in my entire life, and would never want to lose her, or do anything that I would in any way regret.

This was also why I was confused about her suddenly feeling so upset and hurt by something I had done or not done, and she would not at first tell me what it was. I suddenly felt so bad and confused, at the same time, because as stated, I had no "clue" of what it was. So, all I could do was plead with her with a "sincere, true, pure heart's desire" to know what my "transgression" had been, and asked her to please forgive me for whatever it was that I was "guilty" of.

Lady Celeste (Illustrated by Psychic-Visionary Artist, Erial-Ali)

Suddenly, almost instantaneously, she was back to her "normal, positive and powerful "5D" self. As if what she had been strangely experiencing and feeling, for the last few minutes, had actually never occurred.

She quickly told me to not feel bad and/or "guilty" in any way. That what she & I had just experienced was actually a very powerful "Surrogate" relationship experience to help so many couples here on earth. To "energetically" be able to understand what their partner often has experienced, and how they do not have a "clue' that they had emotionally hurt and disappointed their partner.

Because of being so "insensitive" to their special effort that they had gone to, to surprise their partner with some kind of special "gift." But their partner just did not understand what they had done.

Celeste explained that she & my Higher Self, had decided to "energetically act out" a Surrogate role. That would be very similar to what many Earth couples often experience. In order for this to really be energetically very powerful and Transformational for them, she & I had chosen to "realistically play this role" as much as possible. By using the present situation with the image that Rebecca had made of her.

The "role" that I had chosen to play out, was to act as an "insensitive, clueless, clod Earth man." Who had just received a wonderful gift from his "significant other," who had put a lot of special effort into her gift to him. But because of "emotional insensitivity" of being a "3D earth man," he was not able to perceive or discern this fact, and this had hurt his partner very much.

Yes, how often this has occurred. Sometimes, an [Earth] man will do something for his partner, and they will not "get it." But, usually, it is the man or masculine partner who is usually unable to perceive and/or acknowledge this special and thoughtful gesture, whatever it might be.

Much disappointment and emotional hurt can occur that may cause resentment and sadness that they went out of their way. Yet, their partner is so insensitive, they just don't see and understand this.

As it turned out, of me choosing on a Higher level to "play this Surrogate Earth role." I actually had allowed my Higher Self to make me act out as if I was this type of "insensitive" person. When I actually feel so much the exact opposite, especially being with my Beloved, Celeste.

Celeste explained to me, that she understood my "concern" about how, on the "outer external level," I was "critiquing" Rebecca's image of her as being "too immature" and/or not professional" enough to use it in her & my book. But she also did want to point out to me, that I had been too focused on that level.

As a matter of fact, as Celeste then explained to me, in her deep Love for me. That she wanted me to "take a moment" to actually look at the image that Rebecca had done of her, from a much deeper and more personal perspective. Of the fact, from Celeste's perspective, which I suddenly "tuned-into." Very intensely, when I did, as she had requested, to really tune-into this image.

I initially, I admit, when I had first seen Rebecca's image of Celeste, felt Celeste's Love being projected "energetically" to me thru the image. But, as stated, with my "focus" being more concerned by how the image physically "appeared or looked." I had not taken the time to allow myself, to be more "energetically observant" on another, more personal level. To take more time in being able to perceive this; of what Celeste was actually giving to me as a special gift through this image.

That for Celeste, as this was actually her first chance, through a clairvoyant artist, to have an image of her done, which I could look at. She wanted to also make sure that she could energetically express her Love and Devotion for me, of all that she intensely and sincerely felt for me, and that I would be able to feel this so strongly.

I knew, based upon what Rebecca had initially said to me about what she had been picking up from Celeste. That she was definitely very clairvoyant and was accurately "tuning into" my Beloved, and was also partly why I had initially decided to have Rebecca do her image.

So, now that I took the time to sit down and looking at it without my initial "critical eyes," and with a much more "open heart." I tuned into what Celeste was referring to. Of what she had actually given me, that I had not allowed myself to initially see and/or feel regarding this image.

Then, I realized that, "Dah" I should have known that the reason that Rebecca had, quite accurately, seen Celeste holding out to me, both the heart and the rose in her hands. Was, because, this symbolized that she had long ago "given me her Heart and her Love."

Now, I could really feel, even more, all of this Love and special feelings that she had "energetically embodied" into this image. And I knew that I would always cherish this image.

Celeste had been a little upset with me, for good reason. That I had been merely relating to the image on a more impersonal, outer or external level. Of "how would this appear to others," if they saw it in Celeste's & my book, as verses an image that would be termed "more professional".

I had not taken the time to ALSO tune into what Celeste was feeling regarding this situation. That to her, as stated, she wanted to sincerely "gift" me with her Love and Heart. As symbolic of what she feels for me, as her Other Half. But instead, even though I did not mean to do so, I had acted as an "insensitive clod," and did not perceive this deeper, more sacred gesture from Celeste to me.

I felt bad that I had not taken the time to really see and acknowledge her for her very thoughtful and wonderful gesture and gift to me.

Celeste was very happy with what I now was able to allow myself to perceive and feel about her gift to me, and thanked me for taking this extra time to truly acknowledge her. That this also gave her & I the chance to "act out" this Surrogate role. Which would allow us both to energetically help so many here on

Earth that are getting ready to be reunited with their own Cosmic True Love.

Of being able to be more open in their hearts, to what their Divine Cosmic Partner is feeling, and how to more deeply share with them so much more. That this only tends to enhance the wonderful feelings of Bless and joy that Celeste & I are now feeling even more of.

This, in itself, of me being able to "open up to her even more," and to feel even more Bliss and fulfillment, is energetically affecting and impacting everyone else on the planet. And, this is helping to re-anchor in to the Earth, the "Nirvanic Ecstasy Grid," as the old 3D matrix is released.

So, I next called Rebecca, and spent some time talking to her, with as much "Unbearable Compassion" as I could, and told her what I was feeling.

Because I "came from my heart," as Celeste had suggested that I do, the phone conversation turned out to be very positive, with greater understanding of Rebecca's situation, and her understanding my "dilemma".

Rebecca reminded me about some of the many Insights that had been shared with her when she had experienced her Readings with me. Of the fact that even though she was very creative and artistic in so many of her past lives, and chose to take on her own very challenging "surrogate" role. By having herself be faced with numerous "artistic challenges;" of her being "emotionally and ability challenged" at times. This, in turn, caused her to often not be able to manifest the actual level of her ability, that caused her to struggle with it. Which would also "energetically" help others. Who, for whatever the reason, would be helped to overcome these types of similar challenges. So, I was glad to have a chance to speak to her.

She then also told me something else, which helped me to feel much more "relieved" about my initial concern about what Anne, the older lady in Texas. Of what she would think about the image of her own Twin-Flame that Rebecca was going to do now that she had finished Celeste's image. Rebecca told me that Anne had been concerned about having not heard from me for so long, and had told Rebecca, that if she should speak to me, to have me call her when I could.

But Rebecca mentioned that she had shown Anne a copy of Celeste's image, and she did not seem to be concerned about how it had appeared, as far as the so-called "level of quality" that I had been earlier concerned about. So that helped me feel much more relaxed and relieved about the whole thing, and I realized that I had been too concerned.

As in the old saying, "Beauty is in the eye of the Beholder," just as Celeste reminded me, of how much more important was her feelings of Love for me, than what something appeared on the outer, external level.

It is the Inner, more Sacred "things of the Heart" that are indeed far more important and special. And should always be cherished, and Celebrated, rather than for one to be too concerned about "external appearances." Or, in the comparing of one image, that one artist did, as verses what another artist did of that same being or person.

But it is also when we truly open our hearts and take the time to allow ourselves to really acknowledge, feel and see these deeper, more "subtle" truths and special gifts of life. That truly adds to the greater Harmony, Bliss and Love, that is so needed in the world today, on planet Earth.

And, just as Celeste had predicted, no sooner had I made that call to speak with Rebecca, of being able to not only be very honest and candid with her about my feelings. While also being able to truly hear what she had to share with me.

Within a few minutes after that call, another friend named Liz, who I also called just to "check in" to see what was going on. She mentioned the fact that she had emailed me several weeks before, an email about a clairvoyant artist. She even had him email me, which he did, because she knew that I was really searching for an artist to do part of the work that I needed for my book.

So, I re-checked my email in-box, as well as my spam or junk folder. But, I saw neither of these two emails, which I thought was a little strange for both emails not to have been received.

It was then, that Celeste, who is always looking after me, for my best good, acknowledged that she had actually, purposely "blocked me from being able to see" these two emails at the time. Only, because, if I had, I would not have been inclined to ultimately call Rebecca, and to "clear up" this "dilemma" with her. Which I was so glad now that I did.

Yes, Celeste, in her Love for me, had done the right thing, which forced me to "deal with" this situation with compassion and integrity.

Which, in turn, allowed for a very positive "solution-resolution", or a "win-win" outcome for us both. This also allowed me to truly be ready for this more recent image of Celeste.

One more significant thing that occurred, was right after first seeing this new image of Celeste, which at first I was again being a little bit of a "insensitive clod." When I first saw how beautiful this new image was, I was so happy, and felt even more Blessed by Celeste. I could definitely also feel all her Love for me so intensely coming through the image.

And then I realized the "significance" of the beautiful Rainbow band over her head, which she is holding in both hands.

Whenever I do the Cosmic Color Meditation with her, at least every other day, I always Invoke the "Rainbow Crystal Bridge" of Ecstasy, Bliss, Joy and Celebration, from her heart to mine."

That each time we share this together, it only intensifies and strengthens our special Bond and romantic Love for each other. Which also helps to re-anchor the Nirvanic-Ecstasy Grid, from the ancient times of Lemuria, back on Earth.

This will speed up now, as the Q White Hat Alliance totally finishes over the coming months and the next few years, the complete end of the satanic cabal deep state.

This is being supported in their efforts by the Love Ops/Special Forces of Romantic Love. This is setting the stage very soon, as Celeste's

& my book is published, and millions of fellow Light Workers/Volunteers in Earth embodiment prepare to be reunited with each of their own Cosmic True Love/Twin-Flame.

Blessings to all of you!

Namaste,

Michael & Celeste

CHAPTER 21

Jacques Drabier, the Real Originator of *Star Trek* (It Was NOT Gene Roddenberry)

One of the most fascinating fellow contactees that I had a chance to get to know was Jacques Drabier. I met him back in 1980, right after I had first moved to the Phoenix area in Arizona. Jacques had quite a colorful and adventurous background: He was a professional artist, gifted with many psychic and spiritual abilities. He used these abilities in his art, resulting in many beautiful images of the cosmic, the extraterrestrial and UFOs. His art was personal, as well as visionary, in nature. A great number of his images were based upon his own personal experiences and contacts with Higher Space Beings. Many depicted his time as a French pilot and flight sergeant during WWII. He also created images based on scenes he had tuned into from the Akashic Records, of his past lives both on and off planet Earth.

When I first met him, I had been invited to come by his home in Phoenix. I had a chance to browse his own private art studio in his home. Here, many of his beautiful images were exhibited, along with various hard-to-find, out-of-print, and suppressed UFO books and documentation.

Like many fellow contactees and pioneers of the late 1940s, '50s and early '60s, Jacques had numerous first-hand stories of having interacted with so-called "UFO investigators" of the "UFO community." Most of these investigators had extreme biases and hidden agendas. They were intending to suppress and ridicule those like Jacques who had experienced numerous encounters with spiritually evolved, benevolent human-appearing E.T.s, as opposed to those other negative types known as the "grays" and "reptilians." Like most sincere individuals who have had authentic contact and communication with these benevolent beings (often referred to as the "space brothers" and "space people"), he had experienced extreme bias from those who claimed to be professional and unbiased UFO investigators. These investigators did not want to acknowledge the authenticity of contacts with beautiful human-appearing beings from other worlds.

I had planned to publish another book about 20 to 30 years ago (when it would have been much more relevant than it is now) about the Cover-Up on Human-Appearing E.T.s: illuminating this extreme bias found in most of the members of the UFO community and their agenda to ridicule and suppress these uplifting contacts with human-appearing beings, while they at the same time "stuff the gray aliens and their negative abductions down our throats." This bias and agenda had nothing to do with lack of evidence, but all to do with the fact that the UFO field had been infiltrated and taken over by the cabal deep state many decades ago. This is well documented in William Cooper's book, *Behold A Pale Horse.*

Jacques Drabier had an extensive military background. It was in the military he experienced his first UFO sightings, followed by personal encounters with benevolent human-appearing beings. These beings intervened and saved his life many times during WWII. As a flight sergeant within the French Air Force he went on numerous missions against the Germans, both while stationed in France at the beginning of the war and then later in Italy.

He shared numerous incidents from within his own flight squadron and from times when he got separated from his fellow pilots. He had numerous up close and personal sightings and encounters with many extraterrestrial aircrafts, which could "fly rings" around his own aircraft. He did not ever sense that these particular beings were in anyway hostile toward him or fellow humans. Early on he sensed that the beings were Divinely intervening both for him personally, because of certain esoteric traits in himself (as he was to soon become more personally aware of) and for humanity on a larger, planetary scale, because of the implications of WWII and the development of nuclear weapons as well as more advanced, Highly Classified technologies that were secretly being developed at that time by both the Nazis and the U.S.

After many such sightings and encounters with these "boogies" and "Foo Fighters" (as most UFO sightings were referred to as in those days), he had another much more dramatic encounter. Jacques described vividly that he was flying along, when two of these saucer-shaped crafts suddenly approached his aircraft at such a speed that it was impossible to get out of the way in time to not collide with them. At the last moment, when he thought they would collide, the two ships suddenly did a 90 degree right angle turn away from his aircraft. As they did so, one of them shot a greenish-turquoise colored beam at him, which enveloped him and his aircraft for a few moments.

Within minutes after this beam enveloped him and his aircraft, Jacques started to experience incredible and fantastic visions. Instead of being up in the skies of Earth, involved in "dog fights" with enemy Nazi aircraft, he experienced himself being involved in some sort of out-of-this-world intergalactic battle with the dark forces. He saw himself being the commander of a fleet of advanced Light ships, battling the enemy, reptilian-draconians, many millions of years ago. And there, sitting beside him, was the most beautiful woman or Divine Goddess he had ever seen, whom he knew he was deeply in love with. What Jacques eventually came to realize was that his own Cosmic Amnesia Veils had been lifted by that greenish-turquoise beam that was projected at him and his plane. The very same gorgeous Goddess/Space Lady that he had first seen in his visions was on board one of the two Light Ships that had maneuvered out of his way in that 90 degree angle turn.

On one of the walls in his home there in Phoenix was a bust of this beautiful Goddess, who was wearing an exotic head band and looked a little like the Egyptian Goddess Isis. As an artist, Jacques was able to create a perfect rendition of the complete head and face his Twin-Flame. He had made a realistic 3D image of her, his Cosmic True Love, on the wall of his home. He referred to this as his "Altar of his Goddess." I could personally understand and relate to Jacques' deep and intense sentiments and passionate feelings for her, his own Beloved. Even though I may not have a similar 3D likeness of Celeste, I did blow up the beautiful image that Eriel-Ali had done for me and placed her on the wall of the bedroom of her and my apartment. I refer to this as the "Altar of my own Beloved and Goddess, Celeste." Unfortunately, I do not remember what the name of his Beloved was, but the fascinating story that he shared with me that day is still stuck in my mind after all these years.

Flashbacks Conflicting with His Mundane Life

Right after Jacques experienced having his plane and himself enveloped by the energy beam, he began to have numerous psychic flashbacks to many of his past lives on and off planet Earth. In many of the scenes and visions that he saw, he was reliving specific and important experiences from his numerous past lives as well as his missions as a Volunteer in Earth embodiment that he and his own Twin-Flame had experienced together.

Much of what he tuned into, as well as what he was told telepathically by his Beloved, specifically concerned the (actual) Federation (of Light). The Federation has existed for eons throughout the galaxies and is known by many names, such as the Intergalactic Confederation, Universal Federation, Universal Alliance of Planets, etc. Jacques received a huge amount of Cosmic Downloads with information and intelligence regarding the Federation's Laws of Non-Interference. He specifically referred to these laws as the "Prime Directive" back in the late '40s/early '50s, decades before Gene Roddenberry ever used this phrase.

Back then, during his first encounters with advanced extraterrestrial space crafts, Jacques had no idea on a conscious level just how much his life was going to change. He had no idea of how this would be the major catalyst that would help him fulfill his mission for being a Volunteer soul in Earth embodiment. On an "emotional-personality" level (if that is the proper term), he had been very much a "French, romantic lady's man" prior to this UFO encounter. He had not been very idealistic about being true to only one lady and no others. Well, all that drastically changed from then on: After seeing and remembering that the beautiful Space Lady who had specifically zapped him and his plane was his own Divine Other-Half, he suddenly had no romantic interest in any other women around him on Earth.

As the weeks and months began to pass after his experience of being zapped by that energy beam, he continued to experience major changes on all levels of his consciousness. As someone who had an analytical, logical, down-to-earth left brain, he was in a major conflict with his more intuitive, spiritual right brain. He felt that he might have lost his mind from that initial UFO beam incident, as these visions only got more intense and more common for him. He had many inner conflicts concerning these intense cosmic visions, because of how they conflicted with the rest of his more normal, mundane 3D level of awareness. His responsibilities as a Flight Sergeant during this mundane Earth war were complicated by the visions and memories of being a Higher Space Being of Light aboard his and the Space Lady's Light Ship, battling dark forces in some far-off intergalactic space war.

Finally, he decided to check himself into the psychiatric ward of the local military hospital there in Italy, to somehow find a more logical, medical explanation for all of his strange, bizarre, out-this-world visions and feelings that were now overwhelming him almost every day. After they thoroughly examined and medically checked him out, they could find nothing neurologically wrong with him. Because of the war and because they were short on personnel, they told him to get back to work as a pilot, to continue fighting the enemy until the war was over. So, that is what he did until WWII came to an end.

During the last year of the war, his intense visions only continued to get worse. Finally, he went back to the psych ward once more, to have another mental and psychological evaluation. He was still partly hoping to find some logical, medical, mundane, 3D explanation for his visions and experiences. But this time the doctors finally leveled with him, admitting something interesting, revealing and unusual that they said they had not told anyone else. If he were to mention this to anyone else, they would officially deny that they had ever actually told him this.

What they shared with him was definitely most controversial, yet he swears this is what they said: There were actually dozens, if not hundreds, of cases similar to his own, of people who had reported similar behavior. They had also checked themselves into the medical hospital, as they had also thought they were going insane and had wanted to find some relief from their visions. They had also initially had an encounter with a "boggy" or "foo fighter," and had then experienced various, unique types of after-effects. In other words, one of the many things that was never officially admitted after the war was over, was that many hundreds of Allied military personnel had experienced encounters with extraterrestrial crafts. Many also had visions and after-effects that could not be explained away as them having gone insane.

Obviously they were Volunteers in Earth embodiment, just as Jacques later realized he was. Perhaps their own Divine Other Half, on board various of the other crafts encountered, had utilized a similar method to what Jacques' Other Half had done, lifting their Cosmic Amnesia Veils in an attempt to help them remember who they were. Unfortunately, it is never guaranteed that these Higher Protocols of Activation and Remembrance will work on every Volunteer. In addition, the intense and life-threatening nature of the war created certain psychological conditions that caused many to experience various visions that those who received them chose to forget about. But Jacques decided not to forget, especially not about his own Cosmic True Love, who was attempting to connect and communicate with him on an almost daily basis.

Finding His Way

The other specific thing that these medics told him was that a few times they had consulted a medium, they said she lived in a nearby village. From how they described this unique and gifted lady, she appeared to be a "female Edgar Cayce" of Italy, who would put herself into trances. The most incredible things would then be channeled through her, which fascinated the doctors of that local medical hospital. She had helped them with a few hard-to-diagnose patients. Her medical advice had helped them heal many of the patients that were suffering in the hospital from various physical and psychological ailments. It had been a while since they had last spoken with her, and they did not know if she was even still alive, what with the war having devastated numerous villages there in Italy. But they told him where she had been living months before.

It turned out that Jacques' own Beloved, the beautiful Space Lady on the Light Ship, had already communicated with this medium. She told her that "her own Other Half," who was presently in Earth embodiment, would soon be showing up at her door. She asked the medium to invite him in, so that she could share with him what she had already told her. Sure enough, Jacques finally found the medium's home. Apparently it was not touched by the war. He went up to the front door and knocked on it, not knowing if the medium would open the door. She did, of course, and invited him in. She told Jacques everything that the Space Lady had already communicated to her. Jacques was so excited to have this new and separate verification of what he himself had already received from his Cosmic True Love, and hearing about her intense, Unconditional Love and Protection of him.

He learned about the dozens of times she had saved his life. He would already have been dead many times over, had it not been for her constant, personal Divine intervention. Such intervention was allowed in certain rare instances, if the particular person being in Earth embodiment had a very important mission. When many attempts are made by the imbalanced forces to "off" the person, their Divine Other-Half has the personal authority to protect that person so that they can fulfill their mission. The Space Lady did, many times, or Jacques would not have survived the war. Then I would never have had the chance to hear this remarkable true-life story of his courage and dedication to something much greater than just surviving the war here on Earth, of him fulfilling his mission of being a Volunteer in Earth embodiment.

The medium told him many things, some that she saw herself with her own psychic abilities, and some that his Twin-Flame channeled through her, about what his future mission was and why he had to survive the war. One of the main things she told him that he needed to do, once the war was totally over, was to move to the U.S.—specifically to a city called Hollywood, in the state of California. There he was to open a new age/metaphysical-spiritual center, open to the public. He was to conduct meetings there, and share his cosmic, metaphysical knowledge with those who would be open to his teachings. He did, and he called his center "M.I.N.D.": the Metaphysical Institute of Natural Development. The center opened to the public in the 1950s. He held many classes, lectures, and workshops, teaching everything he knew about both Earth and cosmic metaphysics.

Jacques had a natural talent, too, as an artist. The medium directed him to develop this as well, so that he could use this to help document his many visions and cosmic memories of his own past through illustrations. He was one of the original 144,000 of the first core group of Volunteers to incarnate upon Earth many millions of years ago, becoming a Volunteer in Earth embodiment from more advanced, Higher Dimensional worlds. Through his decades of spiritual work, he did dozens of beautiful and inspiring images of his own cosmic past and of other intergalactic worlds. He did many scenes right out of the Galactic and Earth Akashic Records of past lives both on and off planet Earth.

He closed his center in the late '60s or early '70s. During the time that his center was open to the public, he sponsored and hosted many fellow contactees such as George Van Tassel, George Adamski, Daniel Fry, Harold Menger, Oleo Angelucci, and various other famous (and authentic) pioneers and researchers within the early UFO and "flying saucer" movement. I specifically use the words "and authentic" in that last sentence, because (as I mentioned earlier) the entire field of ufology was filled with agents of disinformation or spin doctors, who masqueraded as professional UFO investigators. Most of them were working for the cabal deep state, and their job was to debunk, ridicule and suppress the real facts and authenticity of those early contactees and sincere researchers of the 1950s and early '60s.

Debunkers and Spin Doctors

Some of these debunkers and spin doctors were exposed in William Cooper's book that I mentioned earlier in this chapter: *Behold A Pale Horse.* I was a strong supporter of Cooper back in the '80s and '90s, and I watched how the cabal used the publication called *UFO Magazine* to target Cooper. They constantly manipulated everything he did to expose the truth about how the whole UFO field had become hijacked by these spin doctors since the '60s.

Individuals like Bud Hopkins and Jacques Vallee were just two of the many who pretended to be conducting "professional and truthful investigations." Instead, they did everything they could (with their obvious bias and in their hidden agenda) to ridicule and debunk the early contactees and the fact that authentic contacts with benevolent human-appearing beings were indeed occurring. They suppressed important information that verified these early Contactee's reports, while going out of their way to focus upon the negative gray alien abductions.

Bud Hopkins was supposed to be an expert on hypnotic regression and regressed many thousands of abductees. He claimed that the grays were basically the main, or only, alien beings that were coming to Earth. Yet I know for a fact that through many of his hypnotic regressions he uncovered that not only did benevolent human-appearing beings exist, but they were also actually intervening with and stopping the abductions. He chose to suppress this important information from the public. Despite him pretending that he was merely some private, civilian investigator, numerous whistle-blowers from the government (that I personally met) stated that he was really working for the CIA

According to these same whistle-blowers, Jacques Vallee also had ties with the intelligence community. He wrote a biased and negative book presenting all kinds of made-up disinformation against the contactees, titled *Messengers of Deception*. Here he inferred that these early pioneers were just creating cults to suck in gullible and wishful-thinking people. I have met more than one of these early pioneers and seen how truly dedicated and sincere they were in wanting to share their true-life experiences. To me it was obvious that Vallee himself was one of the worst "messengers of deception" (for the cabal), projecting his (and the cabal's) negative bias and agenda of unfair ridicule and disinformation upon the ignorant public.

Star Trek

Getting back to Jacques Drabier, and his center in Hollywood: During the early 1960s two individuals showed up suddenly one day, and then came back almost every day. They attended Jacques' many classes, lectures and workshops. He noticed that they were constantly taking notes and writing down as much as they could all the time. Finally, one day he asked them who they were, and at first, they made it appear that they were just fascinated and personally interested in all that he had shared. But Jacques became somewhat suspicious of the fact that they were always showing up, and he got the psychic impression that they were really there for someone else, compiling notes for some other person. They finally admitted that they were "script writers for Gene Roddenberry," and that he had sent them to get as much information as they could from what Jacques was sharing at his center. Jacques wondered why Gene was so interested in what he was sharing, and how he planned to use all this information.

Right after he had found out about Gene Roddenberry having sent these two script writers to take notes, they suddenly stopped coming to his center. So, Jacques decided to go visit Mr. Roddenberry to find out what his plans were for all the notes from all those many weeks. When Jacques finally discovered how to contact Gene directly, Jacques' numerous requests to have a meeting with him were refused, even though Jacques had made it clear who he was and why he wanted to simply meet and talk with Gene for a few minutes. Jacques simply wanted to find out what Gene was going to use the information for: as it technically and legally was Jacques', he had a legal right to know what Gene was going to do with it and for what purpose.

Finally, after many weeks of not getting any response from Gene Roddenberry, he and a couple friends decided to go to where Gene's office was, to "friendly, but firmly" confront him regarding the property rights of the information. They wanted to inform Gene that if he was going to use it in anyway, he had to at least legally "get the okay to do so" from Jacques. Jacques felt that if he had to be somewhat forceful about it, he had more than the right to do so, after being snubbed for so long. So, he and his two friends, after determining that Mr. Roddenberry was in his office, suddenly "burst commando style" into his office. While the three of them just stood there in Gene's office, Jacques quickly introduced himself and his reason for coming. He stated that he just wanted a few minutes of Gene's time, to clear up something about which he was concerned. But Gene, instead of even giving Jacques a moment to explain his reason for barging into his office unannounced, quickly called for the security guards to come and remove Jacques and his two friends without even giving Jacques any time to say what he had come to say.

Yes, in this "unscrupulous" way Gene actually stole Jacques' information, and Gene did not ever acknowledge this. One can imagine what Jacques was feeling when many months later, the *Star Trek* TV show first premiered in 1965. Jacques observed how Gene had used so much of what Jacques had shared in his many classes and lectures, stuff that was being used in the television series—and he was not acknowledged in any way. Of course, most of the more metaphysical and spiritual information that he had also shared was left out, making the series much more of a mundane space adventure. Gene also skipped the fact that there has been a Federation existing for millions of years, and presented the Federation as something only occurring in the future. Still, the fact was that this show had come about all because of the ideas and concepts that had been shared through Jacques' classes at his center, and he had not been given even the tiniest bit of recognition.

In actuality, Jacques was not a petty individual, he normally really did not want or need any recognition. But now someone (in this case Gene Roddenberry) was stealing his information and then pretending untruthfully and unscrupulously that the ideas and concepts presented were their own. The lack of morality and scruples that Gene Roddenberry had showed so obviously really bothered both Jacques and me. Yes, Gene might have fooled a lot of people while he was alive, about how supposedly wonderful and great he was. But to Jacques, Gene was a good example of how corrupt Hollywood has proven to be: many who really meant well had their ideas stolen and someone else got the credit.

Of course, this case is mild compared to how corrupt and evil Hollywood actually has been for decades, with all the pedophilia, satanic human sacrifices, and the use of adrenachrome that so many stars and celebrities are involved in. Q and the White Hat Alliance are in the process of exposing these deeds. There will be many Military Tribunals occurring soon, publicly televised so everyone will know how the Hollywood elite has been involved in these evil activities. Yes, a vast number of well-known actors and celebrities personally flew on Jeffery Epstein's private *Lolita Express* to his island, where they did unspeakable and horrific things to children and under-aged young girls. The Alliance has a complete list of every one of these individuals. Many of them have already been apprehended and are under house arrest or about to be arrested, as they await their trials and executions for crimes against humanity.

But getting back to Gene Roddenberry's unscrupulous actions: One can imagine just how upset Jacques was about them, and about not to be able to do anything about it. I believe that he considered suing Gene, but it appears that he felt it would take a long time and be too expensive.

When I first met Jacques in 1980, it was obvious how upset he still was after all those years, still not able to force Gene Roddenberry to even acknowledge what he had done. I was hoping that Gene might come clean on his deathbed, admitting how he had actually come up with all the things that he had presented in those early *Star Trek* episodes. Unfortunately, as far as I know, he never did. At least I can share Jacques' story, and somewhat "set the record straight."

I also heard that Jacques Drabier was not the only channel and Contactee that Gene Roddenberry used information from. I cannot say for sure that Gene stole and/or copied this information from the other channels, but I do suspect that he probably used the same unscrupulous methods as he did with Jacques.

In more recent years, I also heard that at some point during the *Star Trek* seasons from 1965 to '67, Gene also had access to government-classified projects. These he incorporated into the last one or two seasons of *Star Trek*.

Another interesting thing that Jacques shared with me, was what happened back in the '70s right after he had closed his center down and moved to the Phoenix area in Arizona: Remember his Twin-Flame, the Space Lady who had first zapped him and his plane with that energy beam to help awaken him, so that he could consciously remember being with her on the Space Ships? He shared how she had decided to become a walk-in, just as Celeste did for me. In this case, her spirit and soul merged into the physical Earth body of a young lady. She met Jacques, and they had a wonderfully fulfilling relationship for those few years that she was in Earth embodiment. She then had to go back up aboard the Light Ship, as her "Interlude on Earth" was only allowed for that short period of time. I know that Jacques felt really bad that she was not allowed to stay any longer than she did, but at least he had the joy of being with her during the time that her spirit was merged with that other soul.

My own Beloved and Cosmic True Love, Celeste, is here on an a 5D/etheric level, because of the energy of the planet now shifting in the Ascension process (along with a new timeline that has recently replaced the old timeline). The uniqueness of Celeste's and my connection allows a more personal interaction than would have been allowed back in the '70s and even '80s, but there is still a parallel between Jacques' Space Lady becoming a walk-in for those years, and Celeste also being in Earth embodiment (although for only a month). Celeste will be with me in her more etheric mode until she physically manifests into my life sometime in the next few years. For temporary security reasons, the exact way this will occur has not been revealed yet. This is okay with me, as I know it will occur when it is supposed to.

I believe Jacques, my fellow Contactee and channel, has finally returned to the Higher Realms, and that he is now with his Beloved. I am sure he is totally Blissed Out with her, enjoying all those wonderful Light Club Parties aboard the large Motherships and the Higher Council meetings that they both have attended a number of times. God Bless you, Jacques, for what you did while your spirit and soul was on Earth, as you completed your mission. May you (not Gene Roddenberry) be long remembered as the real and authentic originator of the information which was the basis of those first *Star Trek* TV shows.

Let the Record be updated for now and into the future, and may all be Blessed by what you shared at all the classes and lectures at your center, as we all go into the "Star Trek Golden Age" that is the Destiny of Earth. The Federation has already existed for millions of years. Soon, Earth will also become an official member, no longer stuck on the old endless wheel of karma. Earth's planetary quarantine is now in the process of being lifted, as the Prime Directive has recently been updated. I am sure that Jacques' Higher Self was instrumental in making sure that Earth is to soon have First Contact occur—most likely as early as within these next few years.

CHAPTER 22

George Van Tassel and His Wife, Doris

One of the most famous contactees of the 1950s was George Van Tassel. He became famous because of his numerous, unique abilities as well as because of his physical contacts and communications with many Higher Space Beings. Like Nikola Tesla, he was a very evolved individual, both the right and left sides of his brain were well-developed and balanced. He was a highly intelligent and logical engineer, while also being an intuitive, spiritual and psychically developed person.

George designed and built an advanced invention called the "Integratron", which was based upon his physical contacts and communications from various Higher Beings. Years before he actually began his work upon the Integratron, he had an extensive career as an aeronautical engineer, working for Lockheed and Douglas Aircraft and as a test pilot for Howard Hughes at Hughes Aviation. At the same time, he was involved in researching his interest in the spiritual, paranormal and metaphysical. He was a member of various organizations that were focused upon these subjects, which helped him research how the "scientific" naturally merges with the "spiritual."

It was while he was working at these earlier jobs that George first met the Love of his life, Doris. They were powerfully attracted to each other. Despite his reputation of being a "lady's man" and despite the fact that he always liked to flirt with those of the opposite sex, he actually stayed faithful and devoted to Doris his entire life because of what they both felt so intensely for each other.

It was not too long after meeting and marrying Doris, that George decided to retire from his earlier career. He moved to the property that was to be his home for the rest of his life, near the little town of Landers in California. His property was located about 20 miles from the Joshua Tree National Park. Giant Rock Airport (named after one of the largest boulders in the entire world) was now his own private airport. Many pilots landed and took off from there during the early years of George owning this particular piece of land.

It was his interest and involvement in what was then referred to as the "flying saucer movement" (in those early days of ufology) that caught the attention of not only the general public, but also the cabal deep state.

There is so much that I could share about George Van Tassel, it would probably fill dozens of large books. I will attempt, as best I can, to briefly summarize just a few of his many accomplishments, as well as some of the so-called controversy that he created by the unusual things he did and what he shared with those who came out to visit with him and Doris.

Agents of Disinformation

After George became involved with the Higher Space Beings, he quickly developed his ability to communicate, and ultimately to have physical contact, with the these benevolent beings. He knew of the beings' existence from having studied a few other contactees' experiences with these human-appearing beings. They were referred to in respectful terms, such as "Space Brothers and Sisters" and "the Space People."

Skeptics, debunkers, and so many other "a-holes" within the later UFO community had an agenda, both hidden and obvious, concerning those of us who were involved with Space People and attuned to what George Van Tassel and all the other famous contactees and sincere early pioneers of ufology were aware of. We contactees and channels knew first-hand of this reality, and had a natural awareness and conviction of what we had experienced both through our physical encounters and our numerous communications. There were many millions of people who were naturally attuned to this positive reality, so we tended to draw huge crowds.

That is why these debunkers and spin doctors (such as Jacque Vallee) always claim that we create all kinds of "cults." Apparently it is considered a cult if a huge number of people are drawn to the Truth, and they meet together to share and discuss their positive, uplifting and wonderful experiences. But it is *not* considered a cult when "abductees" who have had negative, traumatic and terrifying encounters with the gray aliens and reptilians form a group. Interesting set of double standards from these agents of disinformation. That in itself shows how much of a "spin" these agents put upon what and who they are told by the cabal to target for their disinformation work. True information regarding these early contactees and what they actually did and experienced is very different from the manipulated and distorted versions of what these agents of disinformation state about George Van Tassel and his fellow early contactees and sincere researchers of the 1950s and '60s.

Physical Contacts with Space Beings

Among George's many physical contacts with the Space Beings, there are two that stand out. The first of these physical contacts occurred on August 24, 1953, and the second occurred in September, 1963.

The first contact occurred early in the morning, while George was still sound asleep. There were two other witnesses to this contact; one saw the space ship descend down out of the sky to hover about twenty feet or so off the ground, the other person heard the strange sound that the ship made on its descent. As George would soon learn first-hand, there were four human-appearing beings on board the ship. One of them, whose name was Solganda, descended on an anti-gravity beam down to the ground and proceeded to go inside George and Doris' home. Both George and Doris were asleep at the time.

Solganda woke up George to inform him what he was there for: George was invited to go with the being to his ship. George and Solganda were pulled back up on the energy beam, and George found himself on board their ship. The beings in the ship told him that they were from the planet Venus and that they wanted to give him this formula: "F=1/T," with the "F" representing "Frequency", and the "T" representing "Time." After visiting for a while, George was levitated back down to the ground. The ship then immediately took off and disappeared.

George immediately figured out exactly what this formula meant, and understood how to build the Integratron so that it would function according to the formula. I believe that George had a photographic memory, as he could easily remember and comprehend things that the average person would normally be unable to. So, it was fairly easy for him to understand what the formula was, and how to build the Integratron using Earth level parts and materials.

It was around the time of this first contact that George was guided to start the famous event on his property known as the "Spacecraft Convention." The convention was held for annually almost all of the next 25 years, and it allowed many of famous contactees to come and share their experiences with the public.

George's second physical contact was also quite interesting. This time, an "incognito" human-appearing space being, dressed in Earth-style clothes and driving a normal-looking Earth car, came to visit Van Tassel. The being allowed over 19 other witnesses (family members and friends) to be present when he sat down at the little café on the Van Tassel property. He shared with them many amazing things about who he was and about his life on other worlds. Three separate times during his interactions with them, he completely dematerialized and rematerialized before them. Of course, both his abilities as well as his advanced knowledge more than proved that he was not any normal Earth person.

The Integratron

The Integratron is cupola-shaped, with a rounded, domed structure on the top and flat round walls. It is 38 feet tall and over 55 feet in diameter. It still stands on the property. According to George, the Integratron would act as an Electrostatic Generator once it was completed, and would then be capable of rejuvenation, anti-gravity and time travel. He first started working on it in 1957, and the outside structure was erected in 1959. It was financed predominately by donations, with Howard Hughes among the donors[6].

After George began his work upon the Integratron, he also began publishing a newsletter titled "*Proceedings from the College of Universal Wisdom.*" The newsletter contained information about the Integratron and his progress on it, as well as copies of many of his Channelings and communications from various Space Beings. It was also mostly through this publication that he got people interested in his Integratron project, and helped raise donations to continue his work on it.

Right after first moving onto his property, he discovered that there was a large underground cavern located under the

---

[6] Further reading: https://mysteriousuniverse.org/2019/08/the-fbi-releases-its-files-on-famous-flying-saucer-contactee-george-van-tassel/. This is an article by Micah Hanks about Van Tassel. Toward the end of the article there is a Video of a 1964 TV interview of Van Tassel, about how he met space beings and how he was given the technical information to build the Integratron. There are also photos of the Integratron.)

edge of the Giant Rock. He determined that there was a powerful energy vortex there. Here he began a series of Trance Direct Voice Channelings from various Higher Light Beings. He also received a substantial number of telepathic communications which he wrote down. A lot of the content was scientific, and there was also content of a spiritual, philosophical and metaphysical nature. There was also content on all kinds of other areas of knowledge and wisdom from the Spiritual Masters from off-planet Earth and from Ascended Masters from the Higher Realms of Light.

George was very versatile, able to receive and understand a massive range of information coming from so many different dimensions, realms, and worlds. It is pretty mind-blowing how unique he was. He appeared very aligned and attuned to all these vast amounts of information. He also shared much of this information in his newsletter.

George accomplished many breakthroughs and "firsts" that no one else had done before him. He is the first Earth person (in modern times) to have channeled Ashtar, this occurred on July 18, 1952. This was very significant, and the phrase "breaking the sound barrier" has been used in connection to this historical event because of the significance of what was to follow: Within 24 hours of George Direct Voice Channeling Ashtar (his first of several communications that he received that day and the days right after this first breakthrough in communications), Ashtar began to communicate and channel through various other attuned channels and sensitives. Ashtar made it clear that he wanted to reach out to as many as possible of those who would be open to reconnecting with him. He had known not only George, but all these other Volunteers in Earth embodiment (also known as the "Wanderers") prior to his incarnation, while they had all been members of Higher Councils. Just as he does today, many decades later, Ashtar reached out to many more individuals to reconnect, either directly or through various channels like me. He also wanted to "re-activate" other channels that he had known prior to them also more recently "taking the plunge" down into Earth embodiment.

Volunteers are also called Wanderers. The term Wanderer is similar to "Walk-In", "Star People," etc.: different words and terms that all refer to those whose souls/spirits are from more advanced worlds who have come to help this planet as Earth goes through its ascension. The cabal will soon finally be eliminated, which is what the Q White Hat Alliance is doing. Of course, a vast majority of the individuals making up the Alliance are themselves originally connected with Ashtar, the Ashtar Command, and the entire Federation of Light.

As mentioned earlier, George began the construction on the Integratron in 1957. It took until 1977 before it was 99% completed. When I personally met George in early 1977, he described the things that the Integratron would be able to do once it was completed. It was the Integratron's potential to heal so powerfully and completely that most interested him. I remember him specifically mentioning to me how the interior was designed to be able to create a powerful, healing force field: Once a person (or any living thing) walked or was carried through the Integratron, it would completely heal and rejuvenate them from any disease and injury. It would also prolong their life expectancy while here on Earth.

George mentioned to me that he had already built a small model of the Integratron, just about a foot or so in diameter. He had placed a lizard inside whose tail had been severed. Within a few minutes the tail grew back, as if it had never been injured. I believe that he had done various other tests as well with this tiny model replica, verifying that all he had to do was to construct this much larger version. The general public, thousands of people every day, would then be able to walk through and be healed and rejuvenated.

George Van Tassel's plan was to use his wonderful large version of the Integratron, once it was eventually completed, to make all disease and suffering a dim memory of the past. This would help bring us all into the Golden Age. In a sense, the Integratron was meant to be a prototype for a huge number of these devices set up all over the planet, so that this technology would be freely available to every person on Earth.

Yes, it was a wonderful and inspiring vision of what could be—if it had not been for the darn cabal and their corrupt medical minions, whose very existence depended upon a huge percentage of humanity to stay sick and diseased. "Cancer" and other so-called "incurable diseases" has given Big Pharma a vast fortune (literally worth trillions of dollars). They were not about to allow someone like George Van Tassel the opportunity to finish his construction on this structure which would literally overnight eliminate any and all diseases, no matter what they were.

Increasing Intensity in Threats from the Cabal

A lot happened in the year 1977, which was the year when I, myself, first had the chance to meet George. I was invited by another friend to go with them to visit George at his home. I also went back a few more times right after that, invited by George. I had the chance to personally talk to him about his whole life. The cabal had made many attempts to kill him already, but he had been protected by numerous examples of Divine Intervention by our "Friends Upstairs."

But he did comment to me that things were suddenly becoming even more intense. The dark hats/black ops would hide in the hills near his property and "play spy vs. spy games," as he termed it. They attempted to stop him and/or kill him, in case he proceeded to finish that last 1% of what he needed to do to get the Integratron to fully work. They had sent a message to him stating that if he did finish the Integratron, they would assassinate every one of his family members, and many of his friends as well. He knew that they were NOT joking.

He was aware that he himself was Divinely Protected up to a point, and that this possibly included his wife, Doris. But he was not sure how much of this protection would "cover" every one of those he cared about; all family members, relatives, friends, etc. He knew they would all be targeted by the cabal. This is a common tactic with the cabal: intimidating, blackmailing and threatening anyone who dares to challenge their agenda of gaining control of the entire world. George Van Tassel was a courageous, fearless and selfless person, who would have been willing to "take them on" if it had not been for the risk to all those he cared about. He did not want them to be in any danger. Doris had no idea, of course, of this major dilemma that her beloved husband was facing, and the danger they were all in. George did not want to tell them, he did not want them all to be worrying or allow any fear to ruin their lives.

It has been said many times that "behind every great and successful man, is a supportive and wonderful woman," and Doris was no exception. She may not have had the same type of outward-going, charismatic and strong personality that her husband had, but she still enjoyed being with him and being married to him. George was the great Love of Her Life. She felt Blessed to have found her True Love when she did, and was determined to support him in any way she could. She instinctively knew and understood, even beyond what he had shared with her all the time, that he had been on an important mission for all of humanity. She knew this from the moment they met, when Destiny powerfully brought them together.

She also knew and accepted that despite George "flirting" with other women, he was actually faithful and True to her. She never had to worry about him being unfaithful, because he loved her so passionately and unconditionally. Of course, many who did not understand or truly know their relationship might have misunderstood this because of George's former reputation of being flirtatious.

Even though Doris did not (seem to) have all the abilities that her husband displayed all the time to those who visited their home and events throughout the years, she still was endowed with a strong Inner Feminine Intuition (and embodying of the Divine Feminine Goddess qualities). This helped her to know and sense many things in her own way, and allowed her to receive Higher Guidance and to ultimately develop her own abilities to communicate directly with Higher Forces.

I do not remember what the exact date was, but it was in late 1977 that I visited with George for the last time. I had hoped to visit with him more times in the future, as he was such an interesting and likable person, with many interesting things going on in his life. I was not at all expecting to hear a few months later ("through the grapevine," as they say) that George Van Tassel had suddenly "died from a heart attack," on February 9, 1978. Yes, the official explanation of his (supposed) death was "heart attack."

"Death" to Confuse the Dark Forces

I say "supposed death," because within a few moments after first hearing of this, Ashtar, himself, communicated with me and told me that, "no, George had NOT actually died." He was not physically dead: him being "officially reported dead" by Doris was done to protect those who George and she cared about from being put into danger from the cabal.

It was not explained to me how she had found out about her and her family and friends all being in possible danger. When I attempted to find out some more details from Ashtar, he merely stated that I would know more about these details in "due time." That was it, "short and to the point" as they say.

So you can imagine how I was feeling, knowing now that George was really NOT dead! Yet, the official, public story that was going to be stated in the history books and in George's obituary was that he (supposedly) died on February 9, 1978, of a heart attack. No one other than Doris herself, except for a few close individuals (at the very most, if even that) knew the True story, or would ever know it. Unless, of course, someone like me would later tell the actual story. I had no way to prove this at that time, just "the word of a Higher Space Being named Ashtar." But I had no "mundane, 3D human-level confirmation" that this was actually true.

I was invited to also go to George Van Tassel's public memorial service. This was "most interesting," to put it mildly: George, one the most famous contactees and researchers in the entire field of early ufology had just (supposedly) died. Yet, Doris and various other individuals that were close to her and George did not seem that upset about George's "passing." I have to apologize, but as this was the first memorial service that I had been to for someone who was publicly pretending that he had died but really had not, I did not know exactly what to expect. It all seemed so surrealistic, the way most people were acting or behaving seemed a little strange to me as I look back on what I can consciously remember. It was surreal to hear what Doris said about her "dearly beloved and now departed late husband," and to hear others people's thoughts and observations about this great man and what he had accomplished while he was "still alive."

The strangest thing for me was the knowledge that there sat a closed—*and empty*—coffin, which obviously did NOT contain George's dead body. Doris (and perhaps others) were in on this, so that the cabal would not consider George a threat anymore, and as a result, they would not put any of them into any danger.

Toward the end of the memorial service, I suddenly sensed an energetic shift occur. I could sense George's presence in the room. As I tuned in to this feeling I saw a vision of him, specifically communicating to me. He wanted to confirm to me that he was not physically dead. He was using his own natural psychic ability to project this message to me. For security reasons he could not give me any more details at that time, but he promised me that one day, I WOULD get the details of what had occurred. I would just have to be patient until then.

Channelings from Monka

We will now "flash-forward" to several years into the future, to the early 1980's. I then happened to be living in the Phoenix area in Arizona. I lived in the town of Scottsdale, where I conducted weekly metaphysical classes. These included me doing a Direct Voice Channeling at the very end.

One of the Higher Beings that channeled through me a lot, besides Ashtar, was Monka. He spoke through me quite a bit during those series of weekly channelings. I had quite a large group of about 30 to 40 (or more) interested Light Workers/ Volunteers in Earth embodiment who would show up each week to learn all they could. Of course, they all always looked forward to whatever the Higher Light Beings were going to share at these classes.

In fact, some interesting things occurred at some of the channelings that took place when Monka had been the one who channeled through me. Once, he had specifically mentioned to a couple who was attending the session that they would discover some kind of ancient hieroglyphics on their property. This was connected to the ancient civilization that used to exist thousands of years ago. Sure enough; within a few weeks later, as they were searching all over their new property, they did in fact discover some ancient hieroglyphics. (I do not remember all the details of what exactly it was they found.)

I once had an eventful channeling of Monka, which became one of the most awesome channelings I ever experienced. That was because of what occurred during his transmission through me: At one point, Monka said that confirmation of what was to occur in the future would happen "at the Sign of the Dove" (he used that exact phrase). I do not remember exactly what he was referring to in the future, but what happened next stood out to me, and made me specifically remember this particular channeling. A few moments after Monka had said this, numerous people standing near the kitchen window saw a beautiful, large, white dove come (literally) flying down from out of the sky. It landed on the kitchen windowsill and walked back and forth several times. Then it flew off and disappeared. Talk about the Higher Forces staging something for our benefit! What a Confirmation and Verification of their plans. In fact, that famous phrase ("at the Sign of the Dove") has always been important to the Higher Light Forces, representing their Divine Plan of God/Goddess finally having manifested. The Dove is a Divine Symbol of the upcoming Golden Age of Peace.

It was not too long after this particular and awesome Channeling from Monka that something else occurred which was to—finally—give me the answer to the "mystery of what occurred with George Van Tassel." Around the time of doing these series of classes and channelings every week, I would also once in a while go around to put up flyers to advertise my meetings and my personal Transformational Channeled Readings.

One day I was suddenly strongly guided to go to a news stand in an area of Phoenix that I had not been to before (the news stand no longer exists). It happened to be located by an off-ramp of the I-10 freeway which goes through the phoenix area. I had just found out that there was a bulletin board there where one could post flyers, etc., so I decided to go there in the hope that more people would also see my flyers in this new location.

I was pulling up in my car to post my flyer, which normally would have taken me but a few moments. Then I would have gotten right back into my car, to drive to the area I usually went to post my flyers. This time, though, I suddenly noticed another car parked not too far from the bulletin board. There was a man standing there, leaning against his vehicle—as if he were waiting for someone to show up. That was the exact impression that I got upon seeing him standing there like that. Why, I did not know, but I distinctly sensed this. As I pulled up in my car, I proceeded to quickly get out. My initial intent was to quickly pin up my flyer on the bulletin board, then just as fast jump back into my car and drive off.

But something about the man compelled me to pause and look intently at him, as if I was the person he had been waiting for. I know that to some people, this whole thing may seem bizarre, just some strange "coincidence." But I sensed that something much bigger than me was about to happen. What, I did not know, but I could clearly sense that I had to—*needed to*—say something to the man. I hesitated a moment, as the logical, analytical left side of my brain began to rationalize what I had sensed as I had gotten out of the car. But I decided to ignore it, and instead go with the right, intuitive and spiritual side of my brain and just follow this Higher Guidance.

As I turned to look more directly at him, I gave him a friendly smile. I hesitated again, then asked if he had an interest in metaphysics, UFO's, and Extraterrestrial Contact. His eyes suddenly widened in utter surprise. He stood up a lot taller and immediately smiled, as if he was reacting in some kind of relief—as if he had been expecting something like this, someone asking him this kind of question. (That was the strong impression that I got.) He quickly told me that he was interested in these subjects, and again I got the distinct impression that he had somehow been waiting for me to show up there. To many people, this would merely seem like a "coincidence," he "just happened" to have an interest in these subjects. But my strong and intense feeling persisted.

I handed him one of the flyers I was about to post on the bulletin board. I told him that he was invited to come that very evening to attend my weekly meeting, if he wanted. He was excited by all this, and again I got the distinct impression that he was not only personally interested in these subjects, but also seemed to be "relieved" about something. What, I could not figure out. I do not actually remember his real name after all these years. I do remember, in vivid detail, not only first meeting him there, but also (especially) what was to occur later that evening toward the end of my Direct Voice Channeling of Monka. For this text I will give him the name of Steven, which is as good a name as any other.

Steven came to my meeting that evening. Not only was he excited about being able to come to the evening's event, it was as if he also had something important on his mind to share with me. Again, this was just a feeling that I kept having. But I did not say anything to him; I figured that if there was something of real importance that he needed to communicate, he would have more than enough time before the evening was over. After only about half an hour, I decided to get right into doing my Direct Voice Channeling.

Monka's Revelations on George Van Tassel

Usually I spend at least an hour or more discussing various metaphysical and/or UFO and Extraterrestrial subjects before starting the Channeling. But this time it was as if the Higher Forces wanted me to start the Channeling earlier than normal, as if they, too, were about to share something much more important than what they normally did, and possibly needed extra time for whatever was about to be revealed. I really had no clue, on the conscious level, about what it could be, but felt strongly that I should just start the channeling session much earlier than normal.

Monka began to speak through me, as he usually did. He spoke for a while, but I do not remember exactly all that he said about these other topics. But then, all of a sudden, he paused. Then he started to speak about George Van Tassel. He described in depth that George could not complete the Integratron because of the threats to him, his family and his friends, and stated that there was much more to this story that needed to now be revealed. I was suddenly aware that he had paused again. He specifically made a comment at some point to say hello to Steven, specifically welcoming him to the Channeling and mentioning that he was also a Volunteer in Earth embodiment just as George had been. Monka told of how George's mission had been to get the Integratron technology out to the world. He stated that this would occur some day in the future, even though it had been temporarily halted by the cabal. A lot more was shared about George and the Integratron, though I do not remember all that was covered.

Finally, after taking some questions from those in the audience, Monka proceeded to leave. I slowly came out of my altered state of consciousness and opened my eyes. I returned to my conscious state. Then, Steven shared with me (and everyone else present) the most interesting story. (And, as the late, great radio commentator, Paul Harvey, used to say: "Now for the rest of the story!")

What Steven had to tell was quite astounding, yet all true. It described what exactly had occurred to George Van Tassel back in early 1978, and confirmed that other than his wife, Doris, I was one of a very few (in addition to those others present at my meeting that night) who would ever know the true story. Steven shared how he had been guided to visit Doris Van Tassel the day before I had been given the Higher Guidance to post a flyer at a location I had never been to before. He had spent some time with Doris. She had developed her own abilities to communicate with the same Higher Forces that her husband communicated with. During Steven's visit, she received the message that she was supposed to now share the real story, about her husband and what had actually occurred, with Steven. She had not been guided to do so with anyone else before now.

She then told him that the next day he was to drive the 6 to 7 hours to the Phoenix area. There he was to share this story with someone he would meet. He would "know it," who this person was, right after he met them. That was all she could tell him regarding who this person was that he was supposed to share the story with. She emphasized that he would somehow figure it out once he met them; something would indicate that this was the person he should share this story with. Steven said that he had been driving along the I-10 freeway, having just reached the outskirts of Phoenix, when he suddenly got a strong feeling that the next off-ramp was where he was supposed to turn off the freeway. He did, and he then saw the little news stand. He got strong guidance to pull right into the parking lot and get out of his car, to just stand there as if he was waiting for someone to show up. In fact, he had gotten out of his car only a few moments before I pulled into the parking lot.

When I gave him a flyer on my meetings, he suspected that I might be the one he was supposed to meet to tell the story to. But he was not sure before Monka began to exclusively talk about George Van Tassel and the Integratron: that was when he knew that this was the "clue, sign, and confirmation" that he had been waiting for, that it had all obviously been "arranged

Upstairs." Steven next shared with me a most extraordinary and true story.

Steven's Story Filling in the Blanks

Flashing back to 1977: This was the year that George Van Tassel found himself in quite a "life and death" dilemma. As mentioned before: If he installed that last part and did that last small adjustment on the Integratron, it would finally be functional. But the cabal had made it very clear to him that if he did so, they were going to kill everyone he cared for. Even though he knew that he himself would be protected, he had no knowledge of whether this same protection would apply to everyone else.

He did not want to take the chance that his actions would endanger them, so he made the difficult decision to basically abort his mission. He had originally taken Earth embodiment to create and finish the Integratron, and to then introduce this technology to everyone on the planet. He just had not considered what could occur if he actually did this, had not realized just what the organized dark forces of the cabal could do.

The cabal had threatened so many others like George in years past, people who had come up with similar technology that would have allowed the long awaited Golden Age to finally manifest upon Earth. However, here is a comment of great Hope and Promise: unlike in those earlier decades, even up until the last few recent years, the Q White Hat Alliance has now finally reached an historic position of planetary leverage over the cabal. This occurred because of recent changes in the original Prime

Directive by the Federation/Higher Cosmic Light Forces. This has given them more Mandated Authority to step in and help the Alliance officially defeat the cabal.

The recent "litmus test" was when they had Scott Mowry (on his Miracles and Inspiration phone conference calls) present the first of many new holistic and healing technologies that have now become available to all of humanity (many of the first of these new healing technologies are being presented/showcased for the first time at the "Magical Waves" website, MagicalWaves.com). They wanted to see if the last of the cabal (which is in the process of being Officially Defeated on a planetary scale, as we come to the end of 2020) could still, as they used to do all the time, suppress any of these types of technologies. The fact that Scott was able to present these technologies is Verifying that the cabal can no longer stop or suppress such technology, and that they can no longer threaten, intimidate and/or blackmail anyone. The Golden Age is truly just about upon us!

The Higher Space Beings that George Van Tassel was in communications with told him what they would do to help him. Doris, of course, had no idea of what her beloved husband was facing and how much danger those that he cared about were in. Through those many years since marrying her husband, she had gotten used to him sometimes not being around as he was "having another interaction with his space contacts." Sometimes he was gone for a few hours and in a few instances he was gone for a few days. She was supportive of his important work and allowed him all the time and space he needed to do to complete his mission.

As mentioned earlier, she was not worried about his joking and flirting with other women. She knew it was harmless; he was totally devoted and faithful to her. Often others who did not really know her husband would wonder about these "flirting instances," perhaps even sometimes jump to the wrong conclusions regarding his behavior. He had gained a reputation as a "lady's man," and it was quite common to see him "acting out" in front of women. It was really just a big joke as far as Doris was concerned. She thought it was cute, with no real intent behind it. She was the lucky lady he had chosen to be with, it did not matter to her if he would "act out," because it had no real significance (only the significance that others attempted to read into it).

But she surely was not expecting what happened next. One day in late 1977, after not hearing from George for the last few days, she heard a knock on the front door. She opened it, and there stood three women—or I should say, three of the most gorgeous women that she had ever seen before. They could have easily been mistaken for three "off-duty Earth models," who happened to be wearing close-fitting, metallic jumpsuits. Well, let us just say their close-fitting suits revealed their spectacular figures underneath the suits. (Which is how these close-fitting space jumpsuits are worn all the time on board the ships.)

They were all smiling warmly at Doris, one of them said to her that "We had to take George with us, because he had things to do aboard the ship." Doris nearly fell over at first, in the shock and astonishment of seeing these three beautiful women who had suddenly appeared at her door, announcing something about her husband "having things to do aboard their ship." One can imagine what might go through any other woman's mind, after meeting them and hearing this first thing that they said to her. But a moment later, she realized that they were in a sense just joking with her about George, because of his well-known reputation with the women—of Earth, that is. A moment later, they got serious with her. As she looked at them a little closer and felt their energy, she felt there definitely was something out-of-this-world about them. She knew that they were no ordinary, mundane Earth women.

They explained to her the dilemma that her husband was facing and that the Space Beings had physically taken him off the Earth to protect all of them from any possible harm from the cabal. Because of this complicated situation, they told her that in order to "get the officials off her back" and to allow her to continue to live as much of a normal life as possible, she now had to come up with some game plan which would make everything appear in order with some "mundane, Earth explanation."

The four of them discussed what she could do to ensure that she would not have to worry in any way about the federal officials (or even the local ones) bothering her in any way. The women explained that under the current circumstances, George's very presence on Earth might agitate the cabal to create problems for her and her family. This was why they had physically taken George off the planet. Doris dearly loved her husband, but now reluctantly realized that it was best for him to stay under the Space Beings' direct protection. After much discussion, she made one of the hardest decisions of her life; agreeing that she would pretend that George had suddenly died from some mundane Earth medical problem. The Space Beings would do what they could to make sure that it seemed that this was what had actually occurred to him. After more discussion, it was decided that she would tell everyone that George had suddenly died of a heart attack before he was able to finish the Integratron.

I remember that back in early 1978, when I had first heard from someone else in the UFO field that George Van Tassel had suddenly "died from a heart attack," I intuitively did not believe it. As mentioned earlier in this chapter, Ashtar then specifically told me that this was not true, that it was just a cover story to make the cabal back off. Of course, after all those years of not really knowing, but suspecting that he was not really dead, it was really awesome to now hear that they had taken him up to stay off-planet until a time in the future when the cabal would be gone.

Steven continued with his awesome story, describing both what the Space Beings did (with their powerful abilities and technologies) and what Doris had to do to make this whole situation believable. She needed to make sure that the cabal believed that George was dead and thus no longer a threat to their corrupt medical system, as well as making the local and federal officials believe that he had "biologically died of a mundane Earth heart attack."

I questioned Steven about some more mundane details, such as: if George was truly physically up on the ships and not here on Earth, how did Doris convince the officials that her husband had actually died from a heart attack when his body was nowhere to be found here on Earth? Under normal conditions, an autopsy would be done, etc., and this all had to occur to show and prove to the officials that he had actually died from a heart attack.

From what Steven told me, there were a lot of, well, "strange" and "unusual" things that occurred. The Space Beings used a replica (a temporary created clone) of George with fake heart attack conditions present, so that the officials never suspected that they were merely examining his "copy." As soon as the autopsy was completed and the replica was no longer needed, the Space Beings dematerialized it. Later at the "memorial service" for George, there was no body in the coffin—that is why it was closed.

The story was getting even more interesting. I remembered that back when at George's "memorial service," Doris was acting kind of like "business as normal," as she spoke about George. But, as stated, she did not seem that overly upset with what had—supposedly—happened to her husband. I thought at the time that this confirmed that George had not really died. Doris definitely did not appear to be "in mourning" in any way, as would have been the case if he had really died. And then, as I also shared earlier, when I felt George's presence there, he stated that one day I would find out exactly what had happened to him. Now, it all made sense. I had had to wait so that this whole thing could play out: Steven's visit with Doris, her telling him the story that I was now hearing, the story that helped verify even more the exact details of George's whereabouts and give more details of how the cabal had threatened to kill everyone he knew if he had activated the Integratron.

I remember wishing that I could have stayed longer after the memorial service was over, because I sensed something might happen later that evening that was somehow significant to George's "death." What, I did not know. But I had to leave as the memorial service came to an end, as my ride who had brought me to the event needed to leave. So I left, wondering when I would ever hear more about this whole thing. So after all these years, I was excited for Steven to fill in the blanks to what had actually occurred later that evening. It had indeed been most significant, and I can now share it with everyone else.

The theme of Celeste's and my book is, as you know, Intergalactic Divine Romance: the Love between Twin-Flames and the devotion and Blessedness one feel after having met their Beloved. Doris had been married to George, her obvious Twin-Flame, and had shared her life with him through all kinds of challenges. The difficult decision that she had to make just a few days before, caused them to now be separated for who knew how long.

In addition to George and Doris' closest family, many more distant relatives and friends from out of town were attending the memorial service. Doris and George had been living in a large mobile home parked on their property. There was room for many of the guests to "crash" on the floor in their sleeping bags, so that is what many of them did that evening (with a few others sleeping in the extra bedrooms).

No sooner had they all got ready for bed and just turned off the lights in the mobile home, before they all heard a loud "ping-ing" sound. It seemed to briefly echo throughout every room. They quickly turned on the lights and looked around in every room, but could not determine what had caused this strange and loud sound. Finally, without discovering the cause of this sound, they all went to sleep. The next morning, Doris was guided to go over to the fireplace. She could intensely feel George telepathically telling her how much he loved her. As she looked down, she suddenly noticed the large piece of petrified wood that George had placed by the fireplace years before, which had sentimental value to them both.

To her surprise and joy, there, on (or rather in) the petrified wood, was a large, perfectly sized Heart now appearing. She realized that the loud sound she and the guests had heard the night before had been the sound of the laser beam from a ship hovering overhead. George had specifically directed the laser beam to perfectly and instantly energetically chisel a perfect Heart into this hard petrified wood, to remind Doris how much he truly Loved her.

As I am writing this chapter with Celeste, sharing this story of how George had left a symbol of his Eternal Love and Devotion to his Beloved who was still on Earth, I think of how Celeste did the same type of thing for me. I shared in an earlier chapter her energetically manifesting that perfect heart in the eggs I was making, as well as manifesting that perfect, large Heart-shaped water droplet in the sink. She did this more than once.

(As I was in the process of finishing up compiling this particular chapter with Celeste, she suddenly informed me that she had been one of the Higher Beings who had helped give Doris the Higher Guidance to share her story with Steven. That had enabled him to come all the way over here to meet me where he did, so that he could then share this incredible story. As it was already "recorded" in this future timeline, Celeste knew already back in the early 1980s that she and I were Destined not only to be together, but to write this book together. She knew that we would be doing a chapter specifically on George Van Tassel, and that when we did, it would finally be the time for everyone else to know the full story about George and Doris. It was awesome to know that my own Beloved, Celeste, had helped Inspire Doris to share this story with someone who was then able to share it with me. So, now you also know another part of the rest of this story, a part that helped make sure the story would one day be properly shared with everyone else.)

Steven finished his story with one more detail: Exactly one year after the memorial service, a second heart manifested itself in the petrified wood, right beside the first heart. George wanted to remind her, once more, of how much he truly loved her. The two Hearts symbolized how Connected they both were Forever.

I do not know how many more years Doris lived before she finally was able to be with him. I am sure they are both enjoying themselves Up there, together. Now that the cabal is in the process of finally being defeated by the White Hat Alliance, maybe George will soon be returning back to Earth to finally activate the Integratron.

CHAPTER 23

Beyond the Light Barrier, by Elizabeth Klarer and Akon

One of the most, if not the most fascinating as well as beautiful books that I have ever read, is one I had been wanting to read for many years. It was not until 2019 that I finally had a chance to. One of the Blessings, Miracles and Special Manifestations that my Beloved, Celeste, helped me to experience was the chance to—finally—read *Beyond the Light Barrier.*

This book is available through Amazon, and I cannot say enough in praise of how special and significant it is. It was an enjoyable and wonderful experience to read. I did not realize that it was available on Amazon until I asked Celeste if she could help me locate it, and she specifically guided me to check for it there. I wondered why I "simply" had not checked its availability on my own, after all these years. But like everything that is meaningful, wonderful and significant in our lives, it does not happen until it is supposed to—when the timing is in Divine Order.

Reading this romantic and true-life story out loud to Celeste and myself (so we could share the experience) was most enjoyable. *Beyond the Light Barrier* is the autobiography of another famous Contactee, Elizabeth Klarer, and tells of her own experience of being reunited with her Beloved, Akon, a space being from Proxima Centauri.

As mentioned, I cannot say enough about how wonderfully, excellently Elizabeth was able to describe her experiences. The deep spiritual, philosophical Insights about her life after meeting her own Divine Other-Half, and how this all totally Transformed her—I can truly relate to this in a very personal way. Even though Celeste is around me on the 5D/etheric level and Akon was around her physically on this 3D level, there were still many energetic parallels for me in how I feel as Celeste interacts with me. This sacred experience one has when one has the great Honor to meet and be with their Beloved (it really does not matter which exact dimension that one's Beloved is able to do this from) is always most sublime, wonderous and indescribable.

I will admit that Elizabeth has a much greater ability than I do to use numerous "descriptive words and phrases" to more adequately and colorfully describe her own true-life experiences and how this wonderful experience of Divine, Sacred and Unconditional Romantic Love so powerfully changed her.

Elizabeth also has a brilliant and scientific mind, balanced well with her deep spiritual awareness and Insight. She shares the advanced scientific explanation of how Akon's Light Ship actually functions in detail. Even though most of what she shares is easy to understand, she does devote a few pages to specifically share an advanced description of the Light Technology that allows Akon's people to go Beyond the Light Barrier. Because of her actually being able to comprehend this and because of the fabulous way she has of explaining such advanced concepts, she was given a standing ovation at the 11th International Congress of UFO Research Groups at Weisbaden (Great Britain) in 1975. Her speech as guest of honor was applauded by scientists of 22 nations.

As quoted from the back cover of the book:

> *Beyond the Light Barrier* is the autobiographical story of Elizabeth Klarer, a South African woman, and Akon, an astrophysicist from Meton, a planet of Proxima Centauri that, at a distance of about 4.3 light years, is our nearest stellar neighbor.
>
> Elizabeth was taken in his spaceship to Meton, where she lived with him and his family, for four months, and where she has his child. Her life on Meton is fascinatingly described. Akon brought Elizabeth back to Earth after the birth of their son, and continued to visit her thereafter.
>
> Akon explained how his spaceship's light-propulsion technology operated and how it allowed him and his people to travel across vast interstellar distances. This technology is explained in detail in this book.

Growing Up to Fulfill a Prophecy

Because of how fascinating the entire book actually is to read, I am going to share numerous quotes from the book to give you a (just very small) sense of how really interesting it was to read it. Elizabeth describes how she and her sister both watched as Akon's spaceship Divinely Intervened twice when she was just a young child. His ship stopped a huge asteroid from hitting the Earth, and later he saved her and her family's lives (and their home from being totally destroyed) from a deadly and destructive storm; he maneuvered his ship in between the storm and their house, causing the storm to pass overhead without doing any harm.

As she was growing up, Elizabeth always had a strong Inner Knowing and sense of who she was and where her soul and spirit was from:

> My questing mind had searched through the years for skies and seas of sapphire blue, a land and seascape not of this world, but another home of life, another island moving in the vast void of heaven where soft mountains mantled with emerald sward sweep down to the sea. That tranquil sea of vast dimensions touched a chord in my memory like a note sounding in the key of evolution, eternally vibrating in the scale of the spectrum.
>
> I knew of a lovely planet glowing in the velvet depths of space beyond the light bar-

> rier. My soul attuned to her eternal vibration and my destiny forever entwined within her magnetic field as the magic of the lodestone gives affinity of telepathic thought to permeate the mind. I felt sure that one day I would find this mysterious and exotic land—I never doubted its existence. It was a race memory, revealed by time as a dimension of development, as time is of our mortal essence and is steadily accelerating our consciousness toward simultaneity and the infinite. Each year on Earth goes by a little faster than the one before.

Elizabeth describes how the black African Zulu tribe tells in their myths and prophecies of how a woman would be taken up into the "sky god's vessel," and how (according to the Shaman) Elizabeth would be the one to fulfill this ancient prophecy:

> The Amazulu called to me from the mountaintops, their voices echoing through the valleys, tuning in to the grapevine of their own method of communication. They told of the great wagon of the sky and the fiery visitors from the heaven country, who would come to take me away in the lightning bird whose scales glitter in many colors. It would land in a cloud upon a hill and there would be a meeting together. The storm doctor and the

witch had foretold this and the legend had grown around me since I was a child.

"The golden hair of your head will bring the Abelunga from the sky," they called across the valleys as I listened to their descriptive language, understanding it as well as my own. "You are the one who brings together, *Inkosazana!* The heaven dwellers will come and take you away from us." And the song spread away in the hills.

Elizabeth and Her Cosmic True Love

A couple of times after Elizabeth is first invited onboard Akon's ship, they experience the most intensely and deeply fulfilling lovemaking, which Elizabeth describes in a spiritually uplifting and wonderful way. Akon then expresses the deep feelings of sacred Love that he feels for Elizabeth, his Beloved. This also allows them both to now conceive a son, who will be born later upon Meton:

Akon held me closer.

"Love is a force," he whispered, "a being that needs understanding. Love is the electric force of life, the very breath and essence of life. Love is the flame of eternal beauty. Love is wonderful. And by love, we achieve supreme happiness. People who cannot love become spiritually and physically ill. Not for them the riches of the soul. They live contrary to its laws, thereby misunderstanding the true meaning of love and how it is food and life to the soul."

"Beloved one, I shall be with you always," Akon softly replied, "Our destiny is bound together. A telepathic link binds our souls in eternal love. Our lives are entwined as a thread of gold weaves a pattern in the sky."

Gently, he put his hand under my chin, titling my head up and back, and looked into my eyes.

"My love, my life, my chosen mate," he whispered, his voice soft with emotion. "I will return to possess you, and sow the seed of my love within your delicate body. The mark of my love will remain within your soul forever."

"Be happy now. Our love is a being, a timeless flame. It is the bond of our souls, and the soul is a flame that never dies. My beloved, you know of this...."

Gone was the deep sadness of my parting from Akon. Instead, a great happiness and contentment filled my soul. I lived again through all the wonderful things he had said to me, the touch of his hands, the exciting, electric presence of such a gentle and possessive man. He was a man from another planet, another world—a real man, not just a figment of my imagination or a dream or a thought, but real. He was real, with as physical a body as anyone else on this planet. This stirring and wonderful contact with my beloved, whom I had known in my heart all my life, is the only real, tangible thing that has ever happened to me. Everything else in my daily life on Earth seems more like a dream to me. I feel I am not really a part of it, and therefore I must belong to Akon's dimension in space and time.

A blue-white sphere appeared out of the dark, star-studded sky, and Akon's spaceship silently hovered close to the ground and gently landed. I reached the spaceship as Akon stepped through the automatic door. Jumping to the ground, he gathered me up in his arms and carried me into the warmth of the cabin, and the cold wind of a changing climate was shut out.

Akon buried his face in my hair, whispering, "My beloved. My very own, my life, my precious woman. The seas of space will never part us, as our thoughts are forever united in the far distances of the sky. We are given this privilege of life, this electric essence to fuse and become one in the everlasting cycle of light. Our love is the divine essence of life, whereby the soul awakens to knowledge in the higher spheres. The universe sanctions our union."

The glory of my awakening spread its warmth through my soul, and I sensed the balanced harmony of this everlasting lease we sense as life. In that moment, the secret of life was revealed to me in the golden rays of Akon's love....

The water was lovely, but I eventually stepped out of the bath. I wondered how I could dry myself, but as I left the tub, soft, warm air blew against my skin. Soon, I was dry, my skin soft, silky and smooth, with that lovely elusive perfume like the tang of the sea wind.

Standing naked before the mirrors, I found a silver-mounted hairbrush. Taking down my long, golden hair, I brushed it out to dry after the shower. There was movement in the mirrors. Without a sound, Akon came behind me and put his hands into my hair, tumbling it up against his face and burying his lips into its mass. Holding me close to him, he removed a ring from his little finger and placed it over my middle finger. It was exotic and beautiful, made of beaten silver and green enamel with a great stone of light set in the middle.

"It is too large for you. My beloved one. So, we will place a half band of silver within it. I want you to wear it always as a part of me, to maintain our telepathic communication for all time.

I could feel and sense the magic properties emanating from the ring. Akon put his hand under my chin, titling my head up and back, and he kissed me with a long and lingering kiss on the lips. Picking me up in his arms, he carried me to the silken platform by the curved wall. Its firm softness supported our bodies with luxurious comfort, as I gave myself to the man from outer space.

"My beloved, my life." Akon whispered again and again, as I surrendered in ecstasy to the magic of his lovemaking. Our bodies merged in magnetic union in the divine essence of our spirits became one, and in doing so I became whole.

As our bodies became one, the fusion of the electric essence of life was attained, and the ensuing ecstasy and balance of electrical forces transcended all things experienced in life. To love and be loved, encompassed within the magnetic emotion of mind and body in perfect union of affinities—my beloved swept me away into the reality and I found the true meaning of love in mating with a man from another planet. How beautiful is nature's plan to mate in love and harmony, the joy of the soul, spirit and body—the three-in-one transcended into timelessness. We lived for one another in the consummation of the rapturous ecstasy of fulfilled love.

The eternal magic of wholeness bonded our love with the everlasting light of the universe, and I sensed an awareness I had not been conscious of before as I lay in Akon's arms. I sensed the life and continuous movement within each tiny particle of air, a thrilling awareness and knowledge of the whole, of magnetism, the essence and stuff of life. To become whole oneself is to find the magic lease we sense as life.

The pulse of life throbbed through the air, in ways I had not really been aware of before. The living planet beneath our spaceship, as we rested on the high plateau of Cathkin, is a living breathing entity. Creating continuous life and movement. It harbors this life within its nebulous blue atmosphere as it moves like a spaceship through the fathomless reaches of space, and only Earth's children can preserve its frailty. Throughout intergalactic space, on the surface of other planets, other Earths, it is the same. All are relative, all have the magnetic stuff of life and all are within the whole.

Akon lifted me gently from the soft couch. My hair a tumbled mass of gold, partially concealed my body as he brushed it back and pulled it up on my head, binding it with a golden chord. Trembling before the mirrors, I watched his gentle hands manipulate my hair, coiling and twisting the gold fabric through it until it was firmly up in a beautiful classic style. How wonderful was this deep consideration and care—how wonderful to feel and to know our precious unity, the spiritual and physical union so complete that we can care for each other's needs as one.

On a low stool beside the mirrors, I saw a gown, diaphanous and lovely in deep rose. Akon bent down and took the gown from the stool. He placed it around my shoulders, pressing the front edges together, and it immediately hung to my ankles in delicate folds without seams of any kind. My body gleamed through the thin, chiffonlike material, and the round neckline and long sleeves fit loosely and comfortably with a featherlike softness. My feet remained bare, free of any covering on the firm, springy carpet.

"The recurring pattern of our lives has now fused for us in this point of time, my beloved one," Akon said gently as we moved together through the doorway into the larger cabin. "The true purpose of mating is not only for the reproduction of offspring, but to retain and satisfy opposite forces of electricity so that these elements may fuse and retain nature's balance between the sexes. One is not balanced without the other, and it is because Earth men misunderstand these truths that there is so much suffering, ignorance and primitive superstition and fear regarding sex. The purpose of mating is not to have biological offspring alone—mating is forever, to retain the balanced whole between male and female. Each is necessary and vital to the other. Magnetic attraction and mating by natural selection has a beneficial effect on the forming mind of the unborn child.

"The haphazard, often aggressive and warlike tendences inherited within the forming mind of the unborn. Violence is an inherited instinct, and humankind on Earth have it in full measure. How wrong is their concept, whereby to become holy in the eyes of their God, they must become celibate in mind and body. How narrow and ignorant are their ways. Only the pure in heart shall see the universe. The spark that creates the divine soul is born in the mating and union of male and female in perfect love and harmony, as our child shall be.

"Our affinities and loved ones are found through natural telepathy—and distance, as you know, is no barrier whatsoever."

I looked up into Akon's eyes and felt mesmerized as he willed me to move toward him. I did so, and he picked me up like a feather and carried me back into the rest cabin. The door silently sealed behind us.

Gently, he opened my gown and it slipped from my body to the floor.

"How white your skin is," he whispered, placing me down on the silken platform, and he kissed my body from the top of my head to the tips of my toes. I swooned in that moment of ecstasy when I felt Akon's naked body press into mine as he made love to me again with such complete possession. The wonderful abandonment of giving myself to him and becoming one with him was a sublime happiness as we lay together in union of physical bodies, our spiritual energy in complete harmony.

What a wonderful way to conceive! Surely, there could be nothing more beautiful than this. The child to come would be the living evidence of perfect love and harmony—brought forth in happiness and perfect union, a fantastic inheritance to impart to the future generations of his race. We drifted off into peaceful slumber, the most glorious sleep I have ever experienced.

(Is this part of her book an Intergalactic (and actual, True-Life) version of a romantic fantasy Harlequin Novel?! Remember, "Reality is stranger (and definitely more interesting) than fiction!")

Akon, Soltec and the Unstable Sun

I found Akon's information about the sun quite interesting, because it paralleled what another space being and astrophysicist, known as Soltec, had shared with one of his main contacts on Earth, Richard Miller. How Richard had both first communications and first physical contact is a fascinating story. Because of his interaction with Soltec, he eventually formed an organization called the "Solar Cross Foundation." Here he shared much information with the public, just as so many other famous contactees of the 1950s and '60s did.

Richard was an engineer who also happened to be a "ham radio" operator. It was during one of his sessions of using the ham radio that he made "radio contact" with Soltec for the first time. He had initially thought that some other (Earth level) ham radio operator was just playing a joke on him, but then Soltec told him that he was going to actually land his spaceship, "the Phoenix," near the place where Richard lived outside of Detroit, Michigan. Soltec directed Richard to drive his vehicle out to a certain location the next day, which he did. He had been taking a little nap, and to his utter astonishment, he awoke to see Soltec's ship landing near him.

A ramp was extended to the ground, and a voice invited him to walk up the ramp and come aboard. Inside the ship, Richard met Soltec, who was sitting in one of the chairs inside this large chamber. They had a lengthy conversation. Soltec explained that he was an astrophysicist from Alpha Centauri (the same star system that Akon happens to be from). He was doing important scientific research about how unstable the sun was. He and fellow scientists were in the process of finding a way to stabilize the sun, as this instability had always caused extreme weather and earthquake conditions on Earth.

One of the many things that Soltec shared with Richard was that they had discovered a number of protocols that they would be executing over the coming years, to help alter and improve these conditions on Earth. This would eventually reduce the extreme conditions to a much better and less extreme state.

Later, in 1969, Soltec also discovered that if they started to manifest huge amounts of Xenon (pronounced "Zenon") gas into the Earth's atmosphere over the next thirty years by ionizing Xenon out of their Light Ships (which is parts of what is being "spewed out" when they create those lenticular, saucer-shaped clouds), a major shift in the consciousness of the planet would occur. And it has indeed occurred. This shift also helped enhance everyone's Discernment, which in turn helped Earth's humanity to Awaken, as well as allowed the military to form the Q White Hat Alliance to finally expose and stop the cabal.

I want to also share a few quotes from Elizabeth's book about Akon's knowledge regarding the sun, as well as other

Insights and observations of human society. Remember, he shared this back in the 1950s and '60s, and much has indeed shifted since then. Yet, much that he shares with Elizabeth still has some relevance, regarding many people's backward and limited understanding of so many things. But this is, of course, in the process of changing, as Earth is now being rapidly pulled into a Higher vibratory level.

Because of these many positive and powerful things that Akon, Soltec, and various other astrophysicists did to the sun, changes to the sun (and as a result, the Earth) that were not originally thought even possible are now in the process of occurring.

Elizabeth's book also shares the fact that numerous contactees of that time mentioned that their space contacts were from the planet of Venus and other planets within this solar system. Yet, NASA (in their vast cover-up of what really DOES exist on the other planets, and even on our moon) would have us believe that there is no advanced extraterrestrial life anywhere except on Earth.

I used to distribute a couple books that were published by Fred Steckling, a retired NASA engineer, titled *We Discovered Alien Bases on the Moon. Vol 1 and 2.* They contain hundreds of clear photos from NASA's Science Department, showing huge numbers of UFOs hovering over the moon, as well as lakes and bodies of water on the moon. In a few locations, actual cloud cover can be seen, as there was some atmosphere above a few of the large craters, created from inside the craters. Yes, all these photos show quite clearly that the actual conditions are very different from what NASA have shared with the public.

The same goes for all the other planets within this solar system. Jupiter is actually in the process of becoming another sun. Venus and some of the other planets once had advanced civilizations, and in recent decades these beings are returning to recolonize Venus and all the other planets. Often the different contactees stated that their space contacts were from Venus and the other planets, even if they had just come from Alpha Centauri; because Venus was the real home planet that they had originally came from. They still think of themselves as "Venusians" no matter how many ages have passed.

> "Our civilization existed on Earth eons ago, after we moved out from the mother planet, Venus. We were advised by our scientists to do so at the time in the history of the Sun's system, as the Sun was breathing out its breath of life in the cosmic cycle of solar expansion. The Sun has, in the past, shown signs of its variable nature, the corona expanding out with lethal radiations to engulf the planets, destroying all flora and fauna. This occurs in cycles of time. It is a natural phenomenon, and stars of this nature are observed very closely by us."
>
> I looked back at the filtered mirage into the Sun's inferno. The violent upheavals of our star held the portents of dire and terrible disaster unless Akon could approach close enough to nullify the explosion conditions.

Although the star's existence was a source of life-giving light for the entire system, I sensed its dangerous hostility to any form of control. As a live thing, it would react.

Akon stood, watching carefully every phase of the Sun's violent activity. His tall, lithe figure seemed to become greater and more powerful, his wonderful face more god-like with the intensity of his concentration. I thought of the teeming life on Earth and knew how little they could understand the mighty and powerful forces set in motion to stabilize their star and wobbling planet. How could they know that Akon held the key to life and their continued existence? Clearly, I could now see and understand the divine writing on the blackboard of space. Here was the reality for me.

Instinctively I turned to advancing my soul toward light energy to move with the magnetic field into timelessness, wisdom and love. The everlasting life force, the great intelligence of the universe, is connected through the forces of light, and only a balanced outlook and understanding can clear the way for development within the mind, where light is born of timelessness.

"Light is sought by all human beings," Akon said, replying to my thoughts. "Through eons of time they have turned their eyes to the lights of the heavens. In this way only can they find the answers to all their problems—with the simplicity of light vibrations. To harness the natural forces of light is still beyond the comprehension of humankind, for this is an alien science that strikes at the very roots and foundations of their basic concepts. The limits of their knowledge reside within their bigger and better laboratories where experiments continually take place, probing and seeking the answers to the riddle of the universe in which they live. They do not find the answers, of course, because it is necessary to use the whole universe as a laboratory.

"To be efficient about the things that really matter in research, it is necessary to be inefficient (un-efficient) about the things that do not matter so much, such as bigger and better laboratories, where inspiration and greatness are submerged within the surrounding efficiency of construction and personnel. They are like the great cathedrals, constructed to wipe the brains of humankind clean of every thought, and to subject them instead to the ways of earthbound religions, where people are led like so many sheep through the devious laws made by men of Earth.

"The material predominates because of man's striving for existence. In so doing, man treads brutally on his fellow men. The impatient atmosphere of humankind's striving will continue until they find their way through the light barrier. We cannot change their minds so rapidly. They have to learn through dire experience before their attitude of mind can change for the better. We cannot parley with them yet. We can only set an example and hope they will follow in times to come. Indeed, there are now many people across the planet who are changing, picking up our thoughts and attitude of mind through telepathic communication. Some of them are conscious of their contact with us, while others are unaware of the source affecting their change of outlook.

"You, my dear, are a very positive source for changing the attitude of mind of many people upon planet Earth. You are planting the seeds of knowledge, and in time many of these seeds will take root within the minds of humankind."

Life is electricity, and how few are born with their awakening consciousness aware of the magic lease we sense as life. To be able to tune in to the infinite consciousness of the soul is to become immortal and join in the realms of dimensions beyond. Thus, one attains the spiritual companionship of affinities, and the knowledge of the role they play in shaping our destiny.

A different kind of people must evolve on Earth. A new species of human must appear—people of understanding, love and tolerance, who are set on life rather than violence and death, who will become the sons and daughters of their God, the sons and daughters of the universe in harmony with all nature. Only in this way can there be a prelude to the salvation of their world—their Earth, fragile and beautiful, floating alone and vulnerable in the vast void of darkest space, yet shining with a blue light like a beacon of hope.

I thought of all the other planets in our solar system harboring the form of humankind. I thought of how Venus, the mother planet, had given birth to humankind, her beauty unspoiled by the human hand but reduced to desert by the radiation from her star, the Sun. No wonder we feel an affinity with Venus, the mother planet who created so many of us in the dim and distant past. So many people have written of their experiences with Venusian space people in vintage spaceships, and this is indeed so. It is only natural for them to refer to Venusians and Saturnians, because all space people originated from planets in this solar system. The Sun's system is over five billion years old and is indeed the cradle of humankind.

"The star of our system is known to Earth people as Proxima Centauri, and all these planets are inhabited by our civilization. We live in constructive harmony and peace. We moved from Venus in the Sun's system to make our home here, which is now permanent because we can control our environment. Our science and our understanding of stars, planets and solar systems have advanced considerably since we lived on Venus. Venus, to us, is still the home planet—the cradle of our race—and it is for this reason that we come into the Sun's system to touch down on that planet's surface and bring it to life again. Beneath her desert surface, she still lives and thrives. The beautiful mountains of rose-colored rocks will again breathe an atmosphere of cerulean sky, and the moisture-giving clouds will spread out over the surface to form the seas again."

"And the variable star of her system, the Sun... can you now tame the Sun," I asked.

"indeed, yes. This is what we are in the process of doing."

"Will it change the climate on Earth?"

"Of course. All planetary weather is controlled by the star of the planet's solar system."

Expansion of thought will come in the wavelength of time when the insight of humankind has reached a deeper and more spiritual level. At the present time, they are exiled on a speck of a planet out on a limb of the Milky Way galaxy, isolated in the cosmos, nor knowing what they are or how they originated. Wholeness is attained within a star, a planet, a spaceship or flying saucer. A complete circle retains the wholeness of the universe or galaxy in which we all have our being. Only by becoming whole oneself, as a minute particle of the universe, can one give form to that inaccessible (un-accessible) reality known as truth. The collective unconscious of this world is no longer in tune with the universe. The practice of religions in the East and West only continue out of habit, and they have ceased to produce results.

Treading through the deep waters of personal experience where dangers lurked in the darkness of ignorance, I witnessed other realms beyond our world. I found the truth of supreme happiness and eternal life with a man from another world. He remains the only reality to me—within this world where the inhabitants still believe in the illusion of their singular existence within the inhabited universe.

Having been through the fires of experience and attainment—suffering the hardships of material want in a grabbing world like Earth—brought me fortitude and endurance, courage and loyalty to an ideal of life beyond the confines of this solar system. Akon's thoughts direct me through the dangerous highways of life among people of Earth, where my work now aspires to the ideal of a better world for all people.

No distance is too great for the alpha rhythm to travel between the brains of soulmates and offspring whose love sometimes part in the quest of ultimate unity and harmony within our living universe. These telepathic waves flash through the far distances, where gravity rules the lives of planets, to another home of life—to my beloved Akon and our son, Ayling, who was conceived on this home of life but was not born on the planet. Not for him the hazards of rocket-propelled spaceships encasing their pilots like coffins. Not for him to travel the stars wrapped in the swaddling cloth of a spacesuit and be packed like a sardine in a tin can in an endeavor to conquer space and the unknown environment beyond.

There were so many more wonderful and insightful things that Elizabeth shared in her book. At least the few quotes from her book that I have shared should give you a small glimpse into how truly awesome her book is to read.

"Critique: A Christian's Perspective"

At the very end of her book (or to be more accurate, right after the end of what she, herself, had written), her Earth son, David, whom she had from an earlier Earth marriage, added his own (in my opinion, very petty and narrow-minded) viewpoint, titled, "*Critique: A Christian's Perspective.*" When he was much younger, David was with his mother when Akon landed his spaceship and when his ship was hovering overhead. When I read that, I had assumed David would grow up pretty enlightened and open to things beyond the 3D level of reality, what with him being around his enlightened and highly evolved Earth biological mother.

Instead, when he got a little older, he rejected and suppressed his memories of most of what he had seen and experienced with Elizabeth when he later decided to become a "Christian" (with what is in my opinion a very narrow-minded view of reality). He more than has a right to whatever he wants to believe. But after all the insightful and inspiring things that she shared in her book, he puts his "two cents worth" of his mundane, narrow, orthodox-organized Earth religious beliefs at the end of her own book. He states that no one ever needs any other advanced beings coming from other worlds to help us, that "all we ever need is—just Jesus." Yes, he actually states this.

In my opinion he was being somewhat disrespectful to all the wonderful things that his mother sincerely shared in her book, he was perhaps even somewhat self-serving to include his own critique. To me, it was obvious that he must have promised Elizabeth when she was still alive (before her soul finally passed from her Earth physical body to go be with Akon) that once she died, he would republish her book. But I am also sure that he would never have dared to ask her while she was still alive to allow him to add his own, biased, and narrow-minded religious beliefs to her own book. It was obvious that he was definitely not attuned to her much more evolved spiritual views and awareness. So, he waited until she was gone to do this. I know she would never have agreed for him to do this. In my opinion, this was not very Christian of him to do.

Him being a Christian is not at all what I take issue with. I myself could say that I am also a Christian, just not his version of one. I would define myself as a "Cosmic or Intergalactic Christian." I have always been attuned (just as I know Elizabeth was) with the Higher Christ Light, Christ Frequencies and/or Christ Consciousness that Jesus was always attuned to and that He embodied. The individual that was known as Jesus of Nazareth is now known as Lord Sananda on the Higher Intergalactic Realms.

Yes, in my opinion there are basically two types of Christians: The first type is those who believe that what is in the Bible is the one and only Truth that exists and that everything that is in the (modern) version of the Old and New Testaments is the "absolute Word of God." Then there is the other type, a much more open-minded and evolved Christian, who is willing to also examine and study other sources of Truth, wisdom and enlightenment. This second type of Christian understands the Historical Fact that those corrupt and hypocritical patriarchal priests of the Council of Nicaea in the early 4th century altered all of the information that later became the Bible (as I will he sharing in the next chapter of Celeste's and my book).

The enlightened Christian Reverend Barry Downing, a Presbyterian minister, wrote an interesting book called *The Bible and Flying Saucers*. He got his Doctoral Thesis on the theory that evolved, human-appearing E.T.s genetically seeded the first Earth humans many millions of years ago. Obviously David never heard of him, even though the Reverend has a big following in Great Britain, consisting of people who are interested in and open to Higher spiritual realities and his more evolved interpretation of both the Old and New Testaments.

Finishing Elizabeth's Book

One more fascinating thing occurred just as I was finished reading Elizabeth's book: All of a sudden, I sensed that I was being energetically monitored and probed by a Higher Being, and realized that it was Akon. He was tuning in to who I was, as I had been reading Elizabeth's book. It was pleasant and intense feeling his interest in who I was, and I was not sure if he does this with everyone who reads her book. Maybe it was because of my plan to devote a chapter in Celeste's and my own book to Elizabeth's and his experiences. So, if anyone of you decide to read her book, you might take a moment as you are finishing it and tune in to Akon and Elizabeth and see if they give you any message.

I want to end this chapter with one more inspiring quote from Elizabeth's book:

> A planet's firmament holds humankind within the bond of life, and the glory of the universe is humanity's heritage. Humankind will soar into the splendor of star-filled space as the stars shed their radiance to help us find this glorious road to the stars. Humanity will come out of this world, will come out of the shadows of strife and will move with the winds of space to other planets in the light of the universe, where no minor discord can darken the glory of light.
>
> We can create harmony throughout the fathomless depths of interstellar space where our minds can reach out to contact other minds in telepathic communication. The spatial void acts as a transmitter when one tunes in on the same wavelength. Wisdom and love combine with immortality within this universal unity to produce a highly evolved human being who is a part of eternity, existing within that divine spark of intelligence that pervades the entire universe, that harmonious and orderly rhythm called God.

I have known love in all its radiant splendor. My heart has awakened to its glow, forever nourished by the golden waves of light, so that I might reach out and encompass others to give them strength, courage and incentive.

CHAPTER 24

Jesus of Nazareth (Lord Sananda) and Mary Magdalene (Lady Nada) and the Intergalactic Version of Biblical Times

There is so much I want to share, that I strongly believe and Know from deep within, about the man who is referred to as Jesus the Christ, the lady known as Mary Magdalene, and how Higher Extraterrestrial Beings helped create many of the historical events that were the bases of what was originally recorded from these earlier times.

First, I want to list and quote the summaries from five books I strongly recommend you read, that will help give one a more complete understanding of so many of the actual historical events that occurred during the period of history that has been referred to as "The Time of Christ."

I do not 100 % agree with everything that these authors present in each of their individual books. But still, in my opinion, most of what they have written about is part of the "bigger picture" of what actually occurred during this earlier, important period of human history—covering topics which the more traditional (and narrow) view of the modern Old and New Testaments have entirely left out.

During the early 4th century, the corrupt patriarchal priests of the Council of Nicaea (and others of the cabal who were there with them) rewrote history into the version that they wanted. This is one of the biggest cover-up scandals in human history. They also totally suppressed the Divine Feminine Goddess Tradition that had played such an important role in the earlier times of human history.

Here are the five books and their respective summaries (they should all be available through Amazon):

1. *Holy Blood, Holy Grail: The Secret History of Christ and The Shocking Legacy of the Grail,* by Michael Balgert.

"Is the traditional, accepted view of the life of Christ in some way incomplete? Is it possible Christ did not die on the cross? Is it possible Jesus was married, a father, and His bloodline still exists? Is it possible that parchments found in the South of France a century ago reveal one of the best-kept secrets of Christendom? According to the authors of this extraordinarily provocative, meticulously researched book, not only are these things possible—they are probably true! So revolutionary, so original, so convincing, that the most faithful Christians will be moved; here is the book that has sparked world wide controversy."

2. *The Passover Plot,* by Hugh J. Schonfield.

"Finally back in print, this special, 40th anniversary edition of Dr. Schonfield's international multimillion copy bestseller is set to rock the establishment view of the life of Jesus all over again. There is probably no other figure in modern Jewish historical research who is more controversial or famous than Hugh

J. Schonfield, who once said: "The scholars deplore that I have spilled the beans to the public. Several of these have said to me, 'You ought to have kept this just among ourselves, you know.'" What he did to "spill the beans" was present historical evidence suggesting that Jesus was a mortal man, a young genius who believed himself to be the Messiah and deliberately and brilliantly planned his entire ministry according to the Old Testament prophecies—even to the extent of plotting his own arrest, crucifiction and resurrection."

3. *He Walked the Americas*, by Taylor Hansen.

"A compilation of all the Stories of the "Bearded White God"—from the Pacific Islands, to South America, Middle America and the North American Tribes. Some followed his teachings, of how to live and prospered. Others did not, and their fortunes took a downward turn. It is the premise of the author, that these 'Stories' and Legends are actually describing (part of) Jesus's travels around the world, here focusing exclusively upon his travels just in the Americas."

4. *The Aquarian Gospel of Jesus the Christ*, by Levi H. Dowling.

"This book was first published on Dec. 1, 1908. Dowling said he had transcribed the text of the book from the Akashic Records, a purported compendium of mystical knowledge supposedly (energetically and holographically) recorded in a non-physical plane of existence. It is an alternative telling of the Jesus story, with strong Theosophical and Spiritualist influences. In it, Jesus' encounters with the masters, seers, and wise men that he visited with while traveling in Tibet, Egypt, India, Persia and Greece, during the missing 18 years of the Gospel, are recorded. Here you will also learn what the Gospels meant when they stated that Jesus grew in wisdom and stature."

5. *The Bible and Flying Saucers,* by Barry Downing.

"A Presbyterian minister and ancient astronaut proponent. He claims that the UFO phenomena, and extraterrestrial encounters, are responsible for many of the events in the Bible."

Good analogies of how the Council of Nicaea altered and edited things out of the historical record are for example how the Warren Commission handled the Kennedy Assassination, how the 911 Commission handled what really happened on Sept. 11, 2001, and how the Condon Report and Project Blue Book about UFOs and Extraterrestrial Contact altered and covered up a huge amount of the facts. All these cover-ups were done to further the cabal's plans for total control over everything.

I know that there are literally millions of different interpretations of Jesus's life. Some do not at all believe in His actual historical existence, and they consider that this was all just a made-up story by those corrupt patriarchal priests of the Council of Nicaea. Many others, including me, strongly feel and believe that there was an actual historic individual, whose life and teachings were real—even though His actual name was not spelled "Jesus," and the records of the events of much of His life were severely altered and edited by the Council members for various economic, political and sociological reasons. And, of course, there are the many millions of Christians who believe that everything described in the modern version of the Old and New Testaments all occurred exactly as described.

I also, as already alluded to, believe and actually Know that advanced Higher Extraterrestrial Beings were responsible for so many of the events described in the Bible. The author Barry Downing does a great job of describing this in his book.

Meeting Jesus

I was nine years of age when I had my first, powerful Insight and Confirmation of that the man we know on a mundane, conscious level as "Jesus" actually did historically exist. I will attempt to be brief, here is what occurred:

I still remember that day as if it was yesterday. I had gone outside in front of my house to sit on the steps leading up to the front door. I would often sit here to be by myself, to meditate, and to tune in to the Higher Light Forces that I truly believed and Knew existed. As I sat there, I suddenly sensed the powerful presence of some Being or Master standing near me. As I opened my eyes to look around, that is when I saw Him; The "Dude," the "Man," yes, none other, than who we have traditionally referred to as "Jesus the Christ." I had always sensed "Jesus" was probably not exactly how his real name would have been spelled.

But I Knew that this individual, who was referred to as "Jesus," WAS totally real. I also Knew that records had been altered and changed for various reasons by a bunch of corrupt priests. How I knew this at such an early age? I had vivid conscious memories of my own life at the time when He was alive. I knew I had known Him, had spoken with Him many times while He was still on Earth. I could remember Light Ships landing many times and Him going aboard, speaking with His own Merkabah Light Ship crew. I could remember how he was able to teleport Himself around, and that he had many Higher Powers He used when He needed to fulfill His Cosmic Mission here on Earth.

These were just a few of the many memories that I had of that lifetime. So, when I suddenly felt His presence, opened my eyes, and saw Him standing just a few feet away from me, I was stunned. It was Him, actually standing near me in this present lifetime. He was manifested in the physical, and he looked down at me and smiled. I could feel all His wonderful and powerful auric field.

His initial appearance showed Him in His "Archetypal form," the way almost everyone has traditionally viewed Him and portrayed Him; light-skinned and "Swiss-European-appearing." This particular image is not entirely historically accurate, as far as how light or dark His actual skin pigment would have been as He was born in the Middle East. Obviously, the natural color of His physical Earth body skin would have been somewhat darker than the light-skinned Jesus that has traditionally been shown in paintings of Him.

Yet, this IS the commonly accepted Archetypal, familiar image that He usually uses when He manifests or materializes near someone in this more modern age. He presents Himself with an image that modern people are most familiar with and can easily identify. Of course, in my memories of that past life, I remember His physical appearance being much darker initially, when He was much younger. As He grew older, He actually changed somewhat—His skin DID appear much lighter, as He was so filled with Light all the time. This also caused His skin to appear slightly translucent and much lighter than how He had appeared when He was young.

When He appeared before me He was dressed just as He was traditionally always portrayed; in sandals, in white robes that covered most of His body, and with His hair long, as was appropriate to that era. For a few moments He just stood, as I was mesmerized with Him having suddenly appeared to me. Then, just as suddenly, He was gone—for a few moments. Then He suddenly rematerialized before me again. This time, He was not dressed in those robes that He had worn back in Biblical Times. This is the God-Honest Truth! He was now dressed in a beautiful, close-fitting, metallic gold and silver jumpsuit/space suit. He often wears this aboard His gigantic Merkabah Light Ship known as the City of New Jerusalem. That ship is over 1,500 miles in diameter, and it has been in "parking orbit" around the Earth since the late 1980s.

As He stood looking at me, He then telepathically said to me, "Remember that past lifetime, over 2,000 years ago, when I was on Earth, and I have been referred to and known as Jesus the Christ. My Cosmic name is Lord Sananda, and Commander-In-Chief, of the entire Intergalactic Confederation/Universal Federation of Light."

As He referred to His last Earth lifetime and all that had occurred, I myself was immediately back again in that lifetime. I remembered vividly so many of the things that occurred. I remembered how the Higher extraterrestrial Beings of Light and the crew members of his own smaller Merkabah Light Ship, "The Dove," used to help Him while He was still on Earth.

He stood there for a few more moments as He said goodbye, then disappeared just as suddenly as before. In those few moments, I once more remembered and relived the events that occurred in that lifetime—this time with much more detail.

Jesus and Mary Magdalene

Partly because of His appearance to me, I was inspired to read both the Old and New Testaments from cover to cover that same year. I realized that the Bible was a "UFO and extraterrestrial contact case book," with many examples of Divine Intervention by Higher Cosmic Light Forces

I also tuned into something else that was very important to Jesus personally: his powerful connection and personal relationship with Mary Magdalene. Here, especially, those corrupt patriarchal priests really messed with the true facts of who she actually was and her relationship to Jesus. They did not want to in any way acknowledge the Divine Feminine Goddess Tradition, because they were threatened by it. They did everything they could do to destroy any reference to this sacred and ancient tradition that had existed on Earth for millions of years. Mary Magdalene was an excellent example of a Divine Feminine Goddess incarnate, and she was definitely Jesus' Twin-Flame.

In the vision, I saw Jesus and Mary Magdalene as young children. They grew up together and were very close, and it was obvious to everyone how connected they were, even at such a young age. When they grew into young adults, it became obvious to them that they would have to separate for a few years;

Jesus would go off on His travels around the world, while Mary Magdalene would become a member of a temple where the Divine Feminine Goddess Tradition was still being taught.

As Jesus was approaching his 30th birthday, He telepathically communicated with His Beloved, Mary Magdalene, that He could now visit her in the temple. She prepared herself in great joy of being able to soon be with him for a few months, spend time together, and get to know one another on a more intimate level.

They totally "Blissed out" together, intensely experiencing the most exquisite tantric lovemaking. They could remember one of their former incarnations during early Lemurian times, where they had been together as a couple in those Rainbow Crystal Tantric Oracle Temples and had spent their time together as Sacred Tantric Life partners anchoring the Nirvanic Ecstasy Grid.

In the Scriptures it is mentioned that Mary Magdalene anointed Jesus's feet with perfume, this actually happened when they were getting married. Also, in the *Last Supper* painting by Leonardo da Vinci, it is not "John the Divine" that is sitting next to Jesus, it is actually Mary Magdalene. They were extremely close, and their Love as Twin-Flames was intense. Sometimes His Disciples became a little jealous because He spent so much of His time with Mary Magdalene.

Mary Magdalene and many of Jesus' closest friends and Disciples knew that He was planning to overcome physical death. Having such Higher powers and abilities as He did, He could do many things that would allow Him to achieve this—especially since He had a powerful Cosmic Backup Team that would make sure that the cabal of that day and age could not stop what He was about to accomplish. They could not, unfortunately, stop those corrupt patriarchal priests from later editing history and covering up so much of the significant things that occurred.

Andrew Basiago and the Videos

I used to have an internet radio show titled the "Cosmic Connection," and I interviewed a lot of interesting guests. One of the most fascinating guests was Andrew Basiago, I mentioned him briefly in an earlier chapter. As a child, he was part of a Top Secret, Highly Classified project called Project Pegasus. It was connected to the Montauk Project, and was all about actual time travel. Not only did Andrew travel back in time to various past periods of history, but the Project also developed actual technology that allowed them to record many past historical events on video "in real time," *as they occurred.*

I have to say that all those skeptics and atheists who do not believe that anything that is described in the Bible actually occurred, need to reexamine all their so-called "arguments" that to them "prove" that there was no actual historical individual who did get Crucified and then did Resurrect/Ascend off this planet. Because, despite that the records of many of the events have been altered, there is still much evidence that many of the events DID occur (even if the accurate version is somewhat different than what we have read in the Bible).

According to Andrew, both the Crucifixion and the Resurrection were video-taped, and Andrew was able to watch the video of the Crucifixion. Andrew's father, who was one of those in charge of the Project, stated that in the video of the Resurrection, he watched a couple of Beings (who were obviously evolved Angelic-type Beings) suddenly appear inside the tomb where Jesus' body had been laying. He saw this intense flash of Light inside the tomb as these two Beings suddenly appeared, Jesus suddenly sat up, and they all then disappeared from the tomb.

It was exciting and significant to me to hear Andrew describe what his father had seen in the video of the Resurrection, as it corresponds to my Vision of that time: I remember hiding near the tomb, and I watched as the Roman guards were standing guard around it. All of a sudden, I saw this bright, glowing, large saucer-shaped object appear in the sky. It hovered right over the tomb, and it shot a bright beam down into the tomb. I was clairvoyantly looking into the tomb, and I could see that Jesus sat up at the exact moment that these two higher Space Beings had beamed down from the hovering Merkabah Light Ship (The Dove). A brilliant flash filled the tomb as Jesus tossed aside the Shroud that had been covering His body since after the Crucifixion. I saw how His image was now suddenly energetically superimposed into the very fabric of the Shroud itself. In the next moment, all three of them disappeared as they beamed up into the ship.

They returned an instant later; there had been a kind of space-time warp when he left with them, and then they returned to the same instant as when they had originally left. Jesus then started to teleport and rematerialize all over the place, appearing first to Mary Magdalene, then His family members and Disciples, verifying that He had indeed overcome death.

His Ascension was also an example of how, one day in the future, most of humanity will collectively Ascend, as their physical bodies' cells are vibrationally altered from carbon to silica (as He was able to accomplish). Then, they will be beamed up into the "Clouds of Heaven"/Merkabah Light Ships.

I realized later that He, as well as my own Beloved, Celeste, had guided me to find and read the particular five books that I listed at the beginning of this chapter. Even though, as stated earlier, I do not necessarily agree with everything written in these books, they all still contain a lot of Truth. They do help by contributing with "pieces of the larger puzzle" of what occurred during that time of history.

Andrew Basiago was personally aware of what was video-taped, and these videos helped document and verify that, yes; many of the things in the Bible, such as the Crucifixion and the Resurrection, did, in fact, occur. We can now also understand how the Higher Beings from other worlds contributed to Jesus fulfilling His mission. No, I do not believe that He wanted to ever start a "religion" out of what He had experienced, nor did He want to create a lot of followers who would just blindly accept everything that the Council of Nicaea wrote down (as they altered the records of the events).

Be Like Jesus When He Challenged the Priests

I think we need to be like Jesus was at 12 years of age: He went into the temples to challenge those corrupt patriarchal priests, those "Pharisees and Sadducees," these "Hypocrites" of that age.

Yes, we too need to be like Jesus and do the same thing, challenging all these traditional orthodox priests of today who just believe the "official" version of things.

We need to do like Jesus did when He went into the "Money Lender's" chambers to overturn their tables. He saw that in the future, the corrupt and evil descendants of these power elite, bankster, and illuminati bloodline families would create a vast and evil scam, taxing us to death through a corrupt "tax system."

The tax system started with those corrupt patriarchal priests just making up the "BS" about "God demanding 10% of everything that we manifest as tithe." No God of this universe, who has Eternal, Infinite, Unlimited abundance, "and then some," would demand that we be required to give anything but our Love and respect to this Divine Intelligence of the Universe. God/Goddess (the God Force is both Divine Masculine and Divine Feminine, as in the Father/Mother God), would never require us to "give till it hurts," or even give to God what God already has an unlimited abundance of.

Nor would a Good and Positive Deity need to be feared. Remember, what the word F.E.A.R. stands for: False Evidence Appearing Real. It really irks me when I hear those neurotic fundamentalist Christians talking about being "God fearing people." It is one thing to say that one is a God Respecting and God Loving person. But to say one is "God fearing," just shows how neurotic one really is, "afraid of one's own shadow." Yes, they are afraid that if they dare to challenge the official orthodox version of what they were taught and brainwashed with as a child, some mighty bolt of lightning will suddenly come out of the sky to smite them, and they will end up in that horrible, fiery place for all eternity.

God (or the God Force) does not punish one if one is daring to ask or challenge, if one truly does so with a True, Pure Heart's Desire to truly Know the Truth. No question is forbidden or "off bounds," as God is not just some petty, revengeful and unfair force. This same fair and forgiving force never judges us for our human frailties or our unintended mistakes, because we learn from them. But this same force and Higher Intelligence DOES feel angry and wrathful when someone is being evil, torturing others (especially the children, as those evil pedophiles), or using adrenochrome. Even Jesus warned of God's wrath upon those evil ones who use and torture children. But we, the "meek, shall inherit the Earth"; those of us who have Pure Hearts and a Higher Intent to make the world a better place will be karmically rewarded.

Jesus' Life—Stranger Than Fiction

In the traditional versions of Jesus' life it is assumed that He hung on the cross for three days, and that He endured the extreme and gruesome flogging that was depicted in the movie "The Passion." I do not believe He experienced such an extreme and lengthy Flogging, and He was actually only on the cross a few hours, not for three whole days.

One of Jesus' closest friends was Joseph of Arimathea. He was an evolved individual and an adept/initiate in a Mystery School. Jesus went through various Mystery Schools, as well as different temples. Joseph became somewhat of a "foster father" to Jesus. Joseph took Him with him all over the world to various other important spiritual places during those 18 years that the Council of Nicaea refused to speak about.

The tomb that Jesus' body was placed in right after the Crucifixion, where it stayed until the moment that He Resurrected and Ascended, was on Joseph of Arimathea's property. The book, *The Passover Plot,* specifically discusses the traditional version of for how long Jesus was actually on the cross. Because of the difficulty of keeping His body alive for more than a few hours, it would have been difficult, if at all possible, to have been able to live on after longer than that—even for someone with Jesus' powerful abilities. This is because of problems such as loss of blood, etc., that such an experience would have caused.

I heard another incredible, but also real story (another one of those "stranger than fiction, true stories") from a friend named Ralph Meaney. He told me that he and his parents all saw this when he was quite young. He swears this actually occurred: One afternoon, as the three of them were sitting together on the back porch of their home, they saw off in the distance something unusual moving through the air toward them, about 20 feet off the ground. To their utter astonishment, as this object got closer they realized that it was a "flying carpet!" There were three individuals on top of it. Ralph intuitively sensed that one of the men was Jesus, and that the other two men, who had turbans on their heads, were spiritual masters of some kind that were "initiating" Jesus in some kind of spiritual test.

He tuned into the fact that the three of them had just come through some kind of wormhole from over 2,000 years ago—

that this was actually a "time travel initiation" for Jesus, to show His ability to do so. Ralph and his parents watched the flying carpet and the three men fly by a short distance away. Then they circled back around and flew by them once more, only about 20 feet away. They flew further a short stretch, then suddenly disappeared off in the distance as they went back through the wormhole, back to their own time.

There, now you have heard it all; Jesus (actually) time traveling on a flying carpet, no less! Who can top that story?!

Christmas Celebrations

One more thing I will share is something that I remember experiencing with Celeste annually (in linear 3D time) during the last few years. This incredible experience happens every year on "Christmas Eve." Even though historically, Jesus' actual birthdate was more in the Spring time, we here on Earth in this modern 21st century celebrate His Birth on December 25 (and the night before—Christmas Eve—is also very much a part of this whole modern cultural and social event). December 25 is also the date of the birth of the Roman Sun God, Apollo. Jesus actually hangs out with Apollo and many other so-called "pagan" Gods and Goddesses, as long as they are aligned with the Light.

Christmas Eve occurs at this particular date and time for a similar reason to why Jesus the Christ has been appearing to people many times in His more well-known, Archetypal, more light-skinned version of Himself: Because so many billions of Earth humans celebrate this specific "special time of the year," and because there are so many Volunteers in Earth embodiment (members of the Ground Crew), it is only appropriate that Jesus, our own Great Commander-In-Chief Himself, known as Lord Sananda on the Higher Realms, and His own Beloved Twin-Flame, Mary Magdalena, known as Lady Nada on the Higher Realms, would put on an annual Cosmic-Intergalactic Light Club Party on board His Mother Ship (The City of New Jerusalem).

Yes, the City of New Jerusalem, which is over 1,500 miles in diameter, has one of the largest Light Clubs in the entire Milky Way galaxy. It is entirely appropriate, and a great excuse to celebrate His great Mission on Earth over 2,000 years ago. It is also a chance to meet and party with Him and all dignitaries and members of various dimensions, galaxies, planets and star systems throughout the universe.

Yes, for the last few years, each Christmas Day morning I would wake up with intense, wonderful, and joyous memories of being there at this Christmas Eve party and Cosmic Celebration in the Light Club. There, literally millions (if not billions) of fellow Light Beings and Volunteers in Earth embodiment all get together to share in this great Fellowship and partying onboard the Ship.

I will briefly describe a few of the many wonderful things that go on each year: Lord Rowcan, one of the great Creative Beings, likes to manifest delicious gourmet food from all over the universe. Huge food tables are placed everywhere, on which the most delicious-tasting foods and dishes from all over the universe are piled up. Everyone is drinking the famous Light-filled Nectar of the Gods/Goddesses, and the most incredibly beautiful celestial music is playing throughout the Light Club.

When Celeste and I went to our private quarters, there, hanging over the doorway was—guess what? Mistletoe, of course! And what does a Twin-Flame couple, who passionately love each other, do when they are standing under the Mistletoe? They Passionately Kiss, of course! Which we did, and which, well, definitely led to something else even more romantically intimate!

CHAPTER 25

Past Lives: Me Being a Protective Guardian for Celeste

This and the next two chapters will be devoted to just a few of the many romantic lives that Celeste and I have lived together. I remember so many of them that it was difficult to decide which ones we would (briefly) focus upon.

This first life that we will share here occurred upon another planet, somewhere in another area of the galaxy many eons ago (according to the "3D linear concept of time"). *Where* it was and *how long ago* is not really significant, considering that civilizations have existed throughout both this galaxy and other galaxies for many billions of years. It is *what happened in that lifetime* that I am focusing on, especially the Romantic challenges that Celeste and I faced when attempting to be together and how we overcome those conditions.

The Higher Selves of Twin-Flames will often create spiritual tests, to challenge themselves and to inspire others by proving that Divine and passionate Unconditional Romantic True Love is always stronger and more powerful than the difficult (if not near impossible) conditions that one might face. Obviously, her and my Higher Self had written the "life script" prior to taking embodiment, just as we and all other Twin-Flame couples have done throughout our many lifetimes together.

On this particular planet, like on many other worlds in various dimensions throughout the universe, the conditions were quite unlike those on Earth: The sociological-cultural conditions were similar to Earth's "Medieval Ages," yet the technology was similar to what exists on Earth today. The entire planet's cultural level and how they lived, dressed, and interacted with one another was similar to how they dressed and behaved in the Middle Ages on Earth. Yet, they also had radios, computers, and even some more advanced Intergalactic technologies. The result was an interesting mixture of cultures and an extreme diversity of lifestyles, quite unlike anything found on many other planets, such as Earth.

There were strict levels of society, there was no middle class, only a lower class and the royal families. The poorer level of society held the majority of the civilization. Several main royal families existed, the rest of the civilization basically just "fended for themselves." It was considered taboo for someone of the lower class to ever even attempt to become romantically and intimately involved with someone of the royalty.

It was in this planet's unique cultural diversities and unusual combinations of such societal extremes and complexities, that Celeste's and my Higher Self decided to "test" our abilities to overcome any barriers of being together. It was against this backdrop that we took embodiment. And, of course, we had to throw in a few unique and unexpected surprises of our own to outsmart those rigid and difficult obstacles that would tend to stop most people from being successful in proving that True

Love can overcome and defeat any thing standing in our way to complete, sublime and total romantic fulfillment.

Celeste was born into one of the five main Royal families that had been in a position of power for many ages. There was also a challenge that was part of the drama and adventure, that she and I both would have to face and deal with, with great courage, daring and innovation: there were many negative forces, both those spiritual in nature as well as the organized political forces who used these negative spiritual forces to gain more control over everyone and everything. Two of the Royal families had long since been entirely corrupted by these evil forces, and the third family was in the process of being taken over. This left only two of the other Royal families still aligned with the Light. It was one of these two families that Celeste had been born into.

I was born into the other Light-aligned Royal family. Just months after my birth, the dark forces possessed an individual from one of the two corrupt families, forcing them to kidnap me and to demand a ransom in order for me to be returned. But because of a major screwup, nothing went according to plan. The small carrying case with me inside was discovered by someone not of Royalty, and I was adopted by this individual who knew nothing of my real identity and origin.

Not knowing my true identity, I grew up almost on the street, learning to fend for myself. I became known for my reckless nature; I was always taking chances and doing dangerous things. I also gained a reputation of sometimes being shifty and undependable, what with how I sometimes stole things just to be able to eat and survive.

I was also handy, and had a natural ability to understand the function of various technologies. I had secretly developed many abilities and talents that I used to survive, such as my physical strength and my ability to fight my way out of any difficult situation with weapons and martial arts fighting techniques that few others knew about.

I had studied and developed my own powerful psychic abilities, to have visions and to be able to "remote view" things and locations all over the planet. I had also accumulated many electronic devices that allowed me to communicate with other people as well as both electronically monitor and to psychically "remote view" what others were doing in other parts of the planet.

Besides all this, I had secured a large building which I kept as my secret location. This hideout allowed me to be basically self-sufficient. Because of my abilities and intelligence, I was able to accumulate all the things that I needed to eventually live fairly comfortable, using both technology that had been developed on the planet and technology from off the planet.

As I grew into a young adult, I began to sense that with all my accumulated possessions and all the diversified abilities that I had, I was somehow preparing for something important. It had to do with my Destiny and my reasons for even being alive on that planet, and would soon be revealed to me.

I had a reputation of being a "lady's man," of causing women to be attracted to me, and had many unemotional and impersonal relationships with many woman. I was unable to pledge my heart to anyone because I had not met my True Love, and I felt that one day this would occur.

Even though there was this unspoken but obvious social taboo dictating that the members of the Royalty were not normally allowed to personally interact and intermingle with those of the masses, the Royalty would still hold certain large public events, such as parades. Here certain members of the Royalty would come out to show off, sometimes riding in their royal coaches. They would wave at the crowds that would gather to view these rarely seen members of the ruling royal families.

It was during such an event, another parade that had been announced by the Royals, that their daughter, the Princess, would be taking a ride in her coach down a street in the city that happened to be near to where I usually spent most of my time (when I was not miles away, at my secret hideout). Since I had nothing else planned this particular day, I had decided to stand among the rest of the huge crowds, just to briefly observe these rarely seen members of the Royalty. The place where I had decided to stand happened to be right at one of the main intersections of two streets where the Princess was scheduled to pass by on her way to where ever she would be going to.

Sometimes in life, as we go about our ways and perform our mundane everyday activities, for no explicable reason we will suddenly, almost spontaneously, do something else—something dramatic that will forever change our life (either for the better or for the worse).

Despite my so-called questionable outer qualities and my reputation from how I normally would present myself publicly, my real, true, inner qualities were a sincere, pure heart: I wanted to always do the right, moral and honorable thing; wanted to be fair and compassionate with everyone else. So often, the struggle to survive and to live a more comfortable and secure life would make it appear that I was just some hard-ass and unapproachable person. I desired to be accepted by others as a peaceful and compassionate individual, but I had gained a reputation of being tough and a “no nonsense” person. People assumed they had to be cautious around me, some thought of me as a loose cannon and did not know just exactly how I would act if they approached me.

I liked that this was my “outer persona,” so that those who might, for whatever reason, hold some grudge against me would find it hard to “get a fix” on my true character. In other words, my public persona was a necessary protection in that kind of society where one had to be strong to survive.

Sometimes, because of all my many abilities and powers of observation, I was able to accumulate enough things to make life much easier for me. I could relax some as I got older, and I had time to stand on the corner of that crowded street to watch some Princess go by in her coach. So, I stood among the crowd, expecting to see some unapproachable Royalty pass by. Then, as I and everyone else dispersed, I would just go back to the life that I had been living for the approximate 18 years that I had been alive in the world.

But on that particular day, Destiny was about to reveal something to me that in one instant would forever, totally change my life and my very being in ways I had not ever conceived as being possible. Oh, yes, I had read of mythical, romantic love stories, of Love at First Sight, where the two Destined Lovers would first look into each other’s eyes. (From this comes the phrase “Love is Blind”: When we see our Beloved, our True

Love, for the first time, all we can see is how awesomely beautiful, incredible, and wonderful they (actually) are. Suddenly, we will never desire or want anyone else in any of the Universes for as long as we live—literally Forever—and we want to truly Live Happily Ever After. Period! Absolutely!)

As I stood there, waiting for the Princess' coach to approach, something began to come up from Within, subtly at first—an indecipherable (or rather, un-decipherable) feeling that something was about to drastically change in my life. I could, of course, not understand why at that moment, on the conscious level. The closer the Princess' coach came, this sense of some impending change suddenly began to grow from deep Within myself. I began to get excited about something, although I could not imagine what I was excited about. The feeling increased as I suddenly, for the first time, saw her coach slowly approaching from down the street. With each moment, this feeling became more intense.

Suddenly I could not stand it anymore, feeling something so intense. Because of the apparently unknown nature of this psychic feeling, I tried to ignore it. But I could not. The closer her coach came, the more the feeling intensified.

As it grew even stronger, I wanted to understand what I was experiencing, to do something on an emotional level to alleviate these strange, new feelings. The Princess' coach was now only a few feet away. In a few moments she would pass slowly by, perhaps waving and looking out of her coach at the crowds who were there to greet her. She would be impersonal, of course.

I had heard rumors about how supposedly different she was from so many of the others of the Royalty; that she was compassionate and caring, and that she wanted to somehow make changes for the better. Supposedly, she wanted the masses to have a better life style, with more to eat, so that fewer would starve. Starvation was common among the masses, with the Royalty having most of the food and material things in life. She supposedly wanted to improve everyone's opportunities, more than had ever been attempted before. I had not heard what exactly she had proposed to do; only that she was known for her compassion for the struggles of so many. I had to say, these stories intrigued me, and I wondered how much of it was true, wondered if it was just some urban legend that someone had made up to give people hope, with no real substance to it.

Attempting to deal with these strange and intense new feelings, to do something that might cause something to be revealed, I suddenly stepped out from the rest of the crowd. I stood boldly out in the open on the corner of those two intersecting streets, and it would be impossible for the Princess to pass by without her having a chance to see me, to notice me for the first time. It would be my chance to perhaps see her much closer, more up close and personal than anyone she had already passed by in her coach had been able to.

She had four guards on horses; two in front, and another two right behind her coach. Even though they normally would have made a move to stop anyone from getting as close as I suddenly was, they seemed strangely oblivious to my sudden repositioning—the Princess would now pass by me with literally just a few feet to spare from where she would be looking out of her window. As I stood there and watched the Princess' coach come up toward me, I found myself almost hypnotized by what was occurring. It was as if her coach came up in slow motion almost right beside me.

The next instant, as the coach began to pass by, was the incredibly magical, sublime moment when I saw Her for the first time. Her and my eyes met, as we looked with shocked surprise into each other's eyes. They say that the eyes are the doorway to the soul, and this is so true, in more ways than one. When one sees, *really sees,* one's Beloved, one's True Love, for the first time, it is as if the entire universe is celebrating with you and your Beloved. The One who, like you, has been waiting their entire life to Behold their Loved One once again.

All I could do was to stare with intense and incredible recognition and joy! I now knew that all those fairy tales and those mythical, romantic Love at First Sight stories were indeed all true. Now I had just experienced this same sublime, joyous and indescribable experience. It seemed as if time itself just stood still, as she and I were lost in each other's eyes. As her coach began to go out of view, she quickly put her head out of the window, to continue to look back at me. I desperately started to follow alongside her coach, not wanting to lose sight of this gorgeous Goddess whom I had just seen for the first time in my life, whom I had just fallen head over heels in Love with. I could think of nothing else except for somehow being able to speak with her, to see her at least one more time before she would go out of my life forever.

As I started to follow her coach, I knew I had go back into the crowd—now her guards suddenly noticed me. One of them started to ride over toward me, intending to force me back into the crowd. I went into the crowd on my own, not wanting any confrontation. But as I stood there almost in a trance, overwhelmed with intense emotions of my sudden, deep and powerful unconditional Love for the Princess, I knew that never again would I be interested in any other lady on the entire planet. My whole life had suddenly changed so dramatically in that very instant of seeing this gorgeous Goddess and Princess. I knew and felt she must be feeling similar feelings about me, and I wished so much to speak with her and to share my feelings with her in person.

I knew that this was not possible, what with the social customs and taboos concerning those of the lower class and those of the upper class and Royalty. I was a changed man, nevertheless. In that instant of looking into the eyes of my Beloved, it was if a huge beam of light had blasted me throughout my very being. No longer would I aimlessly live my life with no Higher Purpose. I knew now what I had to, and I wanted to with all my Heart, Mind and Soul. That was to Watch over my Beloved. Even if I could never see her and speak to her in person, at least I could be her Guardian, her Protector. Even if I had to do it anonymously, I would protect her from all the evil forces that existed both on the physical level and in other realms and vibratory levels surrounding the planet.

In that brief moment of seeing her, of looking into her eyes, it seemed that in her purity and compassionate innocence, she probably did not know as I did how many enemies she already had. So many were threatened by her very Lighted presence on the planet. I could sense that two (and possibly soon three) royal families were already plotting to assassinate her, to make sure that no greater Light would become anchored to the planet. In addition, she had enemies among the dark forces from the lower realms and dimensions that existed parallel to the planet.

I had already battled these very forces. My Light was bright, even if my outer persona made me seem to most people as just one of the ignorant masses. My consciousness was way beyond what most people could even conceive or understand. I had learned quickly how threatened the dark forces felt when someone like myself appeared. The Princess, whom the masses really liked, would soon become an even greater threat to the power and influence that they had gained over the ages. She had many plans to change so many things that no one of the Royalty had ever attempted to change. Her presence was becoming increasingly obvious, because of her grace and her compassionate nature, which was so rare among those of the upper class.

I had just made the most important decision of my life. With that, I turned and started walking rapidly in the direction of my secret hideout, my home. I took stock in all that I had that would allow me to fulfill this daring and devoted life as a secret Guardian for my Beloved. I assumed that I would probably never get the chance to speak to her. The least I could do was to be there for her in whatever way I could, in this anonymous, behind-the-scenes way. I could protect her so that she could survive any attempts upon her life from all those forces who even now were plotting the end of her life.

My powerful, well-developed psychic "remote viewing" ability, combined with the various technologies that allowed me to monitor others, would now be used full time to watch over the Princess and to protect her every moment of her life.

One of the more powerful and significant higher forms of technology that I had obtained was what has been referred to as the "Looking Glass," which I had acquired a few years before under very unusual circumstances. The Looking Glass allows one to tune into events in the future *before* they occur, so that if one is coming from a Pure Heart's Desire to help, one can actually alter and change the future for the better, into an alternative timeline. It is kind of like an advanced crystal ball, it shows clear and vivid images holographically of what is (or was) Destined to occur on the present timeline. If the person operating the Looking Glass has telepathic interphase and a truly Pure Heart, they can cause the impossible to become reality. No matter how unlikely or difficult something is to accomplish, accomplishing it will then become much easier.

Having powerfully energetically connected by having looked into each others' eyes, the Princess and I were now connected on all levels, at all times. This would allow me to psychically protect her, to watch over her for the rest of her life. My devotion to her was unshakable and unwavering, and my mission and purpose in life was this, and no other. I would live anonymously for her, without her ever knowing of me—except, perhaps, for what she had felt that sublime instant her and my eyes had locked.

The Princess was wondering who that handsome stranger had been, who had boldly stepped out from the crowds to position himself so that she could not possibly not see him as she passed by. The coach had passed by so close to me that she could have reached out to touch me as she went by. She now wished she had, as she sat on a couch in her large royal palace and played with her unusual pets. She had adopted the pets from those few extraterrestrial races that landed once in a while to exchange a few things that were unique to their own planets.

Minishia, the Princess, wondered what it would have been like to stop her coach and to speak with me, despite the fact that I was of the lower class. Why should that matter, anyway, if one felt such a powerful connection and attraction, as she suddenly had from her brief look into my eyes and soul? This look had caused her intense emotions of longing and desire like she had never felt before, now surging throughout her body. She fantasized about what it would be like if I held her closely and tightly, kissed her, passionately and wildly made love to her. She was thinking lustful thoughts that a young lady of her position really should not be thinking. But she could not help herself, that moment of locking eyes with me had forever changed her in ways she could not fathom. She kept wondering who I was, where had I come from, why she had never seen me before, and whether there was a way to actually meet me, to speak with me alone in person, with no one else around to disturb us.

As I tuned into my Beloved, the Princess, I knew what she was thinking and desiring so strongly, so passionately, and it made my desire for her grow. I wondered if there was a way for her and I to actually meet and be together for a while, to have time alone and to make passionate love for hours on end. I wanted to give her the ultimate, multiple-orgasmic experience of a lifetime, even if it would be only one time. Yes, I was willing to risk everything for "one time in Heaven" with her, my Beloved—no matter what it would take for me to experience this ultimate Blissful, Nirvanic Ecstasy of the complete merging of the body, mind and spirit with her.

Throughout my life I had experienced many sudden and vivid visions of things that later did occur. Suddenly, I remembered having briefly seen her in a vision from a few years before, and I remembered how beautiful she was. Because of challenging and stressful things occurring in my life at that time, I had almost forgotten about this exquisite experience of glimpsing her. My heart and soul had rejoiced that somewhere out there, my Beloved, my True Love, did exist. I had sensed that this was a wonderful vision of us finally meeting and being together, forever, in total blissful ecstasy. In the vision I had been passionately kissing her and making love to her for hours and hours on end, every day for the rest of our lives together.

Unfortunately, though, I had also experienced many negative visions. On those I had used my own psychic powers and abilities, in conjunction with the Looking Glass, to transmute and alter the timeline so that they did not occur. I Knew that Divine Creation was warning me so that I could change the outcome of these events, which I did. It especially angered the negative forces how powerful, bold, and courageous I was at transmuting their nasty and evil plans and energies. They would attempt to attack me, but I always sensed their attacks before they could pull them off. They always ended up experiencing intense, sudden karma—their negative energies bouncing back on them.

Most of the times they were about to attack me, I would suddenly attack them specifically and overtly on the astral planes, using one of my many special weapons. The weapon was similar to a light saber or light sword. I was an expert with it, and would always wipe them out before they could carry out their attack upon me. I energetically recycled and transmuted their souls through the God Head of all Creation, so that they would cease to exist as if they had never existed in the first place.

Now that I was going to be Minishia's Anonymous Guardian and Protector, I put all my focus upon making sure she was out of harm's way from any kind of danger on any level of existence, no matter what. I would now, forever, watch over her and Unconditionally Love her from a distance, all the while longing for the opportunity, even the smallest excuse, to allow me to be in her Divine Feminine Goddess Presence.

For the next several years I watched over her, programming myself to be instantly aware when any danger would come her way. Sure enough, the negative forces (both on the physical plane and on those other realms) plotted and attempted many times to either assassinate her or cause her horrible harm, in their sick and deviant minds. But, like a great chess player, I was always several steps ahead of them, preparing my own counter-moves of protection for my Beloved, as if I fully understood the philosophy within the *Art of War*, by Sun Tzu.

She had no idea just how close she came, a number of times, to being killed or horribly wounded. Each time, though, the negative forces paid dearly for their nasty and evil attempts; I always made sure that they would experience instant karma each time they attempted to hurt her.

More than once, the corrupt other royal families sent professional assassins to get rid of her. But being aware of their activities, I was waiting for them, having anonymously crept into her palace without the guards being aware of my presence. Despite how so-called great the assassins thought they were, I happened to be better than them—because of my ability to fight in close-quarter, hand-to-hand combat, with all kinds of weapons.

Three assassins had almost made it to Minishia's bedchamber before I was able to confront and kill them. I had only seconds to spare, or my Beloved would have been killed. Despite how good I was, I still should have been wounded more than once from some of these mortal combat encounters. I sensed that someone or something was watching over me, and that it was in the best interests of these Higher Light Forces that I eliminate these evil ones. Yet, I would have been more than willing to take whatever physical injuries necessary to "fight the good fight," to protect and save my Beloved from any harm that might have happened to her.

Sometimes the threats were merely physical in nature, sometimes they were a combination of physical and psychic, and other times they were all psychic. I had prepared myself in earlier years for such situations, and I was determined to protect my Beloved. I hoped that one day, if some miracle ever happened, I would be Blessed and rewarded with finally being able to see her, to speak with her, and to not have to hide in the shadows anymore.

The psychic attacks upon her were the most challenging, because I had to depend on my psychic awareness and my abilities to create powerful energy fields of Light around her to shield her and protect her from the dark spells that the dark sorcerers would conjure up against her. They actually sent demons to kill her. But, I would fearlessly "head them off at the pass," as I attacked them with my own Light and my special weapons that devastated them every time. Each time, I would strengthen the powerful Light vortex and field of protection around her, so that she was protected on every level of existence.

Another one of the technologies that one of the corrupt families used, was a type of "psychotronic-radionic weapons system." This would send discordant and destructive energies which could electromagnetically, energetically "scramble" the Princess' brain, and/or cause her to become mind controlled. She would then lose her own free will, as the controllers slowly gained control over her mind and consciousness. But I had my own similar device, and was able to deflect, and turn these destructive energies back on those who were projecting them at Minishia.

The years slowly began to go by, as I continued to protect and watch over my Beloved. My whole life was focused, 24/7, exclusively upon her well-being and upon making sure that no harm of any kind could possibly come to her. As dedicated as I was, it was sometimes difficult to be on instant "beck and call" against any attacks. Sometimes I did not get much of the sleep that I needed to stay healthy and rested. Despite various challenges I somehow endured these difficulties, ensuring that no harm would come to her.

About ten years had gone by, and I refused to give up hope of finally, directly meeting her. One day I heard about a special costume party that she was holding, in which only those who had received a special V.I.P invitation would be allowed to attend. It was a tradition that all the "eligible," single young men would be allowed to dance with the Princess, in hopes of being able to win her hand for marriage. Her parents were wanting her to hurry up and decide on who she would marry, to continue the linage of her family. But she had already made it clear that she was not interested in marrying any of those that had so far attempted to show any interest.

In the back of her mind, she still thought about that magical day when I had stepped out onto the street and she passed me by in her coach. She could not get me out of her mind, and still hoped that one day she would meet me. She was psychic in her own way, though still unaware of all the dangers and murder attempts, and she did not know that I had been secretly protecting her all those years.

Hearing about the upcoming costume party and the dance, I devised a way to get into the party. I covertly snuck into the palace, dressed in my own beautiful costume. I wore my unique mask, of course, as everyone else was also wearing masks. No one really knew who was who, unless someone recognized voices or other clues about the others. So, in among the large crowd of costumed people I went, and I blended in well as I made my way toward my one goal: my Beloved. I saw her standing and talking to someone else.

I slowly approached her, taking in her beautiful costume and mask. She wore a gorgeous Goddess outfit that she had had specially made, and it stood out as, in my opinion, the most beautiful costume of them all. I knew it was her because I could feel the wonderful energy that only my own Beloved emanated around her and in her auric field, which I had already tuned into on that magical day of first seeing her.

As I slowly walked up to stand only a few feet away and just stared at her and her incredible costume, she suddenly turned toward me and stared back. I knew that she might be sensing my energy, just as I was feeling hers.

Minishia suddenly realized that this was just like that magical day ten years earlier, when her coach had passed by that handsome and mysterious stranger, whose eyes had met hers, and whom had caused the exquisite moment of Love at First Sight. She remembered all the intense feelings that had passed through her body, and how her emotions and desires had escalated out of control during her fantasies of being alone with me. Now the intense feelings were returning, and she knew that whoever was standing near her, looking at her, was somehow energetically the cause.

I could read her mind; that she was puzzled, wondering who I could be, and whether I was that handsome stranger she had passed in her coach. We both stood for a few moments, then she asked, somewhat breathlessly, "Who are you?" I hesitated, I wanted some suspense and curiosity to build up, wanted her to become even more curious and feeling even more of those feelings. Finally, when the suspense had reached a "fever pitch," I said, "Your Gorgeous Goddess costume is by far the most beautiful one here. I am sure that the Goddess beneath the costume is even more beautiful."

She hesitated, somewhat startled by this unexpected compliment. She was trying to think how next to respond to my comment, and said "Thank you for your wonderful compliment." She hesitated again, and asked, "Do we know each other? There is something about you that ... that, well, somehow seems familiar. Why, I don't know!"

Again, I purposely waited a few suspenseful moments, then I cryptically said, "Perhaps we know each other indirectly, but we just have never been formally introduced?"

My responses only created more curiosity and suspense on her part, which made her desire even more to know who I was. I could sense this powerful, magnetic attraction toward me. Once again, she thought of how she had felt that very magical day over ten years before, her desire for me was overwhelming her now as it had then. She desperately wanted to get to know me, she truly felt that I must be that same mysterious, handsome stranger.

At that very moment, the royal heralder (who was always at all the Royal parties, in case the hosts needed to announce anything important) announced dramatically that the dance was about to begin. Any of the single men who wanted to dance with the Princess could now do so. I hesitated a few more moments, then said, "May I be so bold as to ask if you would allow me this opportunity to share a dance with you, my Lady?"

She hesitated, not expecting me to ask her, but then said that she would be honored. I took her hand in mine, preparing to guide her over to the dance floor. At that magical moment of being able to touch her, to hold her hands in mine, an intense electrical spark of even greater attraction shot through both of us. I felt dizzy and wonderfully overwhelmed from her incredible Divine Feminine Goddess Presence and her obvious attraction and Love for me. She was just as overwhelmed as I was.

Beautiful, romantic music began to play from the orchestra. The musicians were playing many exotic musical instruments, all perfectly tuned. My Beloved and I were both lost in Heavenly

Bliss with each other; initially all we could do was to close our eyes and surrender to the intense feelings that were shooting through our bodies, minds and souls.

I wondered what it would be like to be able to be alone with her, to take off her clothes slowly, seductively, then see her swoon in ecstasy as I began to kiss her fully naked, gorgeous goddess body from head to toe, followed by me giving her the most intense orgasmic pleasure with my tongue on all the erogenous zones of her body.

Suddenly it was as if time and space itself had shifted for us, as if we had both been magically transported together to another time and space dimension, to one of our many lives together on planet Earth in those Sacred Tantric Oracle Rainbow Crystal Temples of Lemuria's Golden Age. She was my Sacred Life Tantric Partner, and she was sitting naked in my lap with her legs and arms wrapped tightly around me in the Shiva-Shakti-Lotus position. My lighting rod was inside her, stretching her Sacred Yoni muscles as both of us were experiencing the most exquisite, multiple-orgasmic tantric lovemaking. For hours and hours on end our bodies, minds, and souls were merged—anchoring the Nirvanic Ecstasy Grid to planet Earth.

Yes, time had ceased to exist as our beings were flooded by these incredibly exotic, erotic visions of all our passionate experiences of being tantric Twin-Flame Lovers in other lifetimes. We danced three dances together, savoring and delighting in experiencing these psychic, orgasmic visions. Suddenly I was brought back to reality. Usually, no one was allowed to dance with the Princess more than once—and here I had boldly kept her to myself, not allowing anyone else to approach us, to interfere with what she and I were experiencing and reliving together.

I looked around as this third and last dance was just coming to a close, and I noticed that the royal guards who earlier had been standing off by themselves were now walking over toward us. I sensed that having dared to dance not just once, or even twice, but three times with the Princess, was unheard-of. It was against their rigid rules of etiquette.

But I also sensed that something else had just occurred. Only a few moments before I had briefly opened my eyes, as my well-developed psychic danger warning had gone off. I had observed someone whom I had not seen before walk up to the guards, and they had then pointed toward the Princess and I. I knew that this person, whom I had sensed evil vibes from, was informing the guards that I was not invited to this party; that I was a party crasher as well as guilty of various other crimes against the upper class, that I was a wanted man and that they must apprehend me immediately to throw me into one of their prisons, and that I should be tortured for years for all these crimes.

Well, there was no way that I was going to allow that to happen. I quickly told my Beloved that something had just come up and that I had to leave. I mentioned that unfortunately I did not have time to say a proper goodbye, but that I had really enjoyed my time with her. I asked her to please forgive me for my sudden departure, and told her that hopefully, one day soon we would have a chance to connect again. Without time to wait for a reply, I reluctantly let go of my Beloved's hands and ran fast toward my escape route. I had earlier scoped out a good route, as I had psychically suspected that this was going to happen. I regretted that I did not have time to properly say goodbye to my Beloved, but this was better than being caught, thrown into prison, and experiencing hell for the rest of my miserable existence. I barely got away; had I been just a few seconds slower, at the most, I would have been captured.

To have experienced that long psychic moment in total ecstasy with my Beloved that she and I had shared during those three (!) dances, had been more than worth the great risk of death, imprisonment and even torture. To have those few minutes with her, experiencing what did, was more than worth the danger of what I had been facing if I had not made my move out of there in time.

I was athletic, able to easily scale walls and other structures, and I knew how to move fast. Even so, the large number of guards that had suddenly appeared seemingly out of nowhere were smugly assuming that they would definitely catch me this time. But once again, despite all their plotting and planning, I (barely) slipped out of their hands. I continued to be the Anonymous Guardian for my Beloved; to make sure she would always be protected. I was still hoping that somehow, someway a miracle would occur, creating conditions that would allow her and I to be together—no matter how (so-called) impossible this might seem.

As I had so suddenly ran away from her, Minishia could now only stand in shock and confusion. She had just been spontaneously experiencing and sharing the most exquisite psychic visions with me, her romantic, mysterious gentleman. Now, she was abruptly brought out of her wonderful experience to see me running away as if my life depended upon it—which it did, literally. She had heard me rapidly give a short apology before I had departed, and she instinctively knew that only a matter of life and death could be the reason for me leaving so incredible fast.

Not too long after this party, something significant was indeed about to occur which would dramatically change everything for my Beloved and me. The Miracle of Love was to be Fulfilled, and all our Dreams, Hopes and Fantasies of being together would come true.

As mentioned earlier, extraterrestrial beings had come to that planet and been involved in some brief planetary cultural exchange, trading a few things of their own for a few things that were unique to other worlds. These unique cultural-sociological conditions were strange, existing alongside certain technologies that would have normally been from a much more advanced time. Among them was a more evolved and spiritual race of beings, that were connected to both the Princess and I prior to taking embodiment there. It just so happened that they were about to fulfill their own part of a Higher Agreement that had been written into both Celeste's and my Life Script for that lifetime, to allow our Divine Love to once more be Fulfilled and to be able to be Victorious in overcoming all the evil and darkness that had been operating there.

Just as the cabal has been operating here on Earth for ages and are now about to be defeated, a Golden Age of planetary Renaissance was about to occur on that planet as well—partly because of what Celeste and I would do. We were about to receive the help we needed, both on and off the planet, to allow this great Miracle of Love and Blessings to finally take place for us both while also ushering in this Golden Age.

Perhaps the reader can now understand that one's consciousness, and what we experience together on all levels with our Beloved, has a certain unique power. This power is especially noticeable when a tantric Twin-Flame couple share a Psychic Orgasmic Vision, just as Celeste and I both experienced together during that dance; this has the power to impact the planetary Grid, and literally change the timeline. Perhaps the reader can now understand how important it is to allow all the Twin-Flame couples to now reconnect and to be totally Blissed out together, through the energy of *IntergalacticMatch.com*: when once again this intense, deeply fulfilling, orgasmic tantric lovemaking becomes a major part of the everyday life, it will be a True Win-Win experience of the Highest Vibrational level and it will reactivate the entire Nirvanic Ecstasy Grid.

Princess Minishia had two dedicated personal advisors. They were both multi-talented, and they helped her with all kinds of challenges and difficult decisions that she constantly had to face while growing up in the Royal family. They had been assigned to her when she had been a young child, and had become her two most trusted confidants and friends. She knew she could share things with them and that they could keep important secrets that she needed to get Insight about. They not only had a lot of wisdom and understanding about many things, helping her to more balanced perspective to various challenges, they also had numerous other talents and abilities. Among those was knowledge of various technological equipment and machines. They also had an extensive background in various scientific fields, such as genetics and DNA/RNA, and were aware of the fact that many of the souls who were in embodiment like their Princess, were definitely from off-planet. The three of them had many interesting conversations about all kinds of subjects (that most people were not even aware of and enlightened about).

The unusual equipment that they had started to use during the recent years included a couple of devices that detected and recorded various energy levels, which they had detected in and around the Princess. After various tests, setting up special devices that they designed themselves which recorded the various energy outputs at all times of the day and night, the advisors began to realize that these energies had been manifested because of the presence of someone who had covertly come into the palace—someone who had even gone into, or very close to, the Princess's chambers.

They also discovered a way to energetically translate these energy recordings onto video tape. They could now see and hear all the times I had covertly protected Minishia from the assassins, and discover the times the evil sorcerers had sent those demons to kill her. The recordings showed that when negative energy was being broadcast at her, another frequency of Light would intercept it, neutralizing all these attempts to hurt the Princess. Being geniuses, they also figured out exactly where my secret hideout was, as well as how many times I had secretly Intervened and saved the Princess' life. The bio-DNA/RNA energy readings of the person who had covertly come into the palace to protect her corresponded to the readings of the one who had come to the costume party, danced with her three times, and then had to flee.

My cover was now blown. They shared all this with Minishia. She watched in awe and shock how I had fought off her attack-ers all those times, being her anonymous Guardian and never admitting what I had done. She was moved, now feeling even more Love and attraction for me because of all that I had done with total Devotion for so many years. But she was also in much emotional pain, she knew that for anyone to be able to be with her, they had to be Royalty; this was an unshakable law of the land. This law had to be respected, no exceptions were possible.

Minishia still wanted to reward me for all I had done, even if she (as far as she knew) could never be with me. She decided that the least that she could do was to reach out to me and acknowledge me for what I had done, to reward me for my courage and devotion to her during all those years when I was alone and not able to tell her what I so strongly felt. It was around this time that she sent her two advisors to find me and to tell me that she wanted to speak with me in person. They were levitating on their little levitation platform toward where my hideout happened to be.

One of the two advisors had started to do some DNA research which included taking energetic readings of people's blood and using it to identify their true family linage. They had decided to test a theory they had been working on, as they had a psychic hunch about what my true family's ancestral origins actually were. As they energetically cross-checked my blood and DNA/RNA with this other major royal family, they found to their astonishment that my blood matched the energy identification of that family. This proved that I was Royalty, and this meant I could marry the Princess, my Beloved!

Their arrival into my secret hideout was dramatic, as I had not known that these two trusted advisors to the Princess were about to arrive. When they suddenly came soaring in their little hover device through one of the windows I almost attacked them, not knowing who they were. They quickly explained to me that they had been sent by the Princess, and that my Beloved wanted to see me right away. They had just perfected their new DNA tester, with some energetic help from off-planet (from the Higher Space Beings who had also helped them with a lot of other challenges and breakthroughs), now they excitedly explained to me about my true genetic identity and that this meant that I could marry the Princess.

Minishia and I were both overjoyed at finding out about my true identity, and we were relieved that I no longer had to hide out anymore. I could now openly travel and confront anyone who attempted to destroy the Light-aligned Royalty.

So, I married my Beloved, the Princess, in a huge Celebration of her and my Love for each other. I then quickly exposed and defeated all those of the cabal who had existed upon that planet. All five families of the Royalty were purged of all evil. The Princess and I were also instrumental in changing that old rigid policy of only allowing those of the Royalty to be able to marry; this was changed forever.

So it was that other Twin-Flame couples began to take embodiment and meet, with one being Royalty and their Divine Other-Half being lower class. Eventually a middle class was formed, as the upper and lower classes gradually disappeared. All those rigid rules of social etiquette became less and less important, while Higher qualities and principals of life became more significant.

The Unconditional Romantic Love of Twin-Flames was forever celebrated from then on. Everyone eventually experienced planetary ascension soon after, as the planet evolved into a Higher Dimensional Paradise world.

CHAPTER 26

Past Lives: Celeste as an Elvin Goddess-Princess and Me as a Pleiadian Captain of a Light Ship Fleet

I have memories of numerous lives with Celeste on other worlds. The previous chapter is just one of many similar lives where we challenged our ability to overcome any barriers standing in the way of us being together. We have incarnated in many different star systems, galaxies, and universes, and in many different dimensions of time and space.

We also remember having come from the future to change the old timeline into a newer and more enjoyable timeline. This newer timeline specifically supports and enhances the well-being of all souls desiring to be reunited with their Cosmic True Love; all those who are desiring to be reunited with their Beloved as a tantric Twin-Flame couple, desiring to reexperience and relive those intensely fulfilling lives of Multiple-Orgasmic Ecstasy as Sacred Tantric Life Partners in the Tantric Oracle Rainbow Crystal Temples of Lemuria's Golden Age (as well as later in the Tantra Temples of India).

There are many worlds throughout the universe where similar cultures, races, and species all celebrate the Sacred Tantric Nirvanic Ecstasy Grid being anchored into their planet. In all the worlds the grid is anchored through Twin-Flame couples being together with plenty of time to focus upon their intimate fulfillment, as this affects and influences how balanced their planet is.

One of the most amorous and sensuous races throughout the multiverse is the Elvin race. Both the males and females are very erotic-sensuous in their nature, needing and wanting a huge amount of orgasmic tantric lovemaking all the time. The lovemaking is needed to fulfill a natural urge that constantly affects their lives, and it also often contributes to the important task of propagating their species; ever-expanding and growing on all levels.

The Elvin race know instinctively how vital it is to experience as much tantric-orgasmic lovemaking as possible. Normally they are careful in choosing their mate to be intimate with, which is usually their Twin-Flame. The Elvin race has existed for many eons, both on Earth as well as on many other worlds. To this day there are many Elvin races existing in multiple dimensions. The ones on Earth were subject to attacks by the imbalanced forces because they are so filled with Light and passion for life and joy of living. In more recent ages, they were forced to shift their frequency to survive, and now only exist in other realms—as well as, of course, remaining a major part of legends, myths and fairy tales.

I remember quite a few lifetimes where Celeste has incarnated as Elvin and I usually being human. Her and my powerful magnetic attraction always made it impossible to resist our desires to be together and to enjoy exquisite, intense orgasmic intimacy—this helped manifest and strengthen the Nirvanic Ecstasy Grid on various other worlds. It would also often result in us being the progenitors of various half human/half Elvin races, who thrived throughout the universe.

The Story Begins

In this chapter I will be focusing on a timeline where Celeste incarnated as an Elvin Goddess-Princess, and I as a Pleiadian. I will describe the specific experiences that occurred that brought us together, and the challenges we faced in fulfilling our mission of passionate, romantic love. We challenged certain cultural-racial barriers in order to be together. This lifetime took place many ages ago. Celeste's soul and spirit took embodiment among the ruling Elvin race, she became the Princess and Goddess Alestra. She had many magical powers, which she used only for the Light and the upliftment of her race.

Elvin races have always been known for their extreme longevity, they can live many thousands of years—in a few cases even millions of years, depending upon the conditions. Hence the reference in many stories to the Elvin being immortal.

When they intermarry with other races they share their life force, especially through experiencing orgasmic intimacy with their partner. Using their magical powers, for example casting powerful sexual spells to enhance their and their partner's enjoyment and fulfillment and to extend their duration of their multiple-orgasm lovemaking, helps to enhance the health and lifespan of their intimate partners.

Alestra was no exception as far as her natural sexual desire, which was already quite developed by the time she came of age and was ready to find her mate for life. Her mission in life influenced how she expressed her sexuality. She decided that instead of choosing one of the Elvin males to become her mate, which was the normal instinct of one of her race and cultural background, she had tuned into the fact that her True Love was not on her planet. He was in another star system, and he was of an entirely different race than she was.

She had to use her magical powers to find me and to ultimately persuade me to want to be with her. The desire to mate was becoming a strong urge, overwhelming her. She not only needed to ultimately have offspring, but also needed, right away, to experience intense multiple orgasms. This was extremely important, as sexual pleasure was physiologically necessary for her well-being as an Elvin female, for her to be able to live with balance and joy.

There was just one major problem with her realizing that her ultimate Life Mate was on another planet, in another star system. As much as her race was open about their intimate needs, they also had a strict policy of not allowing themselves to mate with other races. This had been their tradition for many ages upon their planet, and no one questioned this strict policy. In fact, mixing with other races was considered tantamount to committing a crime, and no one ever dared to. One could supposedly be severely punished for doing such a thing.

Somehow, Alcstra did not seem to realize the risk of repercussions if she dared to mate outside of her own race and cultural background. She was able to energetically locate me, her Beloved and Cosmic True Love, in the Pleiadian star system. Then, all she could think about was reaching out to me energetically to share her intense desire and passionate romantic attraction and love for me, hoping that I would be just as desirous to be with her as she was for me.

As a Pleiadian male, I had certain life goals from a fairly early age. One goal was to captain a Light Ship in charge of a whole fleet of Pleiadian ships, and to explore other star systems around the galaxy—even to visit other universes. Another goal was to be a Guardian, warring against the reptilian and draconian races that had attacked our system in times past, during the "Orion Wars." Many Pleiadians had perished during those attacks. Since then, with the help of other star races, we had learned to stand our ground and not be intimidated. These star races had joined us to create the Intergalactic Confederation and Universal Federation of Light.

Earth humans need several or more hours of sleep every 24 hours in order to be healthy and balanced. Pleiadians do not have the same needs, even though we still needed a period to rest in a deep state of meditation which could cause one to have dream-visions. It was during one of these dream-visions that I first encountered the presence of Princess Alestra, as she energetically reached out to me in her intense desire to connect and be intimate. She was becoming somewhat desperate because of the extreme hormonal changes to her body. She was fast becoming a grown and mature Elvin female. She needed orgasmic pleasure with me, as she knew I was her Divine Other Half even though I was not of her race.

Because of us being physically separated, she initially manifested herself to me on an etheric level in my dream-vision—with absolutely no clothes on. I experienced instant Love at First

Sight, and was intensely turned on by her erotic-sensual Divine Feminine Goddess Presence, and the powerful magnetic-electrical attraction and overwhelming chemistry I was instantly feeling.

I was initially laying down when I felt and saw her exquisite, gorgeous, totally naked body etherically manifest itself, and I suddenly sat up against the wall behind me. I now sat with my legs crossed. Being clairvoyant and clairaudient, I could easily see her etheric body, which seemed almost as real as her physical body, and I heard her sweet Elvin voice telepathically speaking to me. First she introduced herself, apologizing for her sudden, unannounced energetic manifestation. If she had intruded upon my space, she had not meant to do so.

I had never been so turned on and desiring of making love before, as I did then with this gorgeous, sexy Elvin Goddess who had etherically positioned herself on top of me. She was sitting on my lap, with her etheric legs and arms around me. I could strongly, energetically feel them, almost as if she were physically here in person. I usually slept in the nude, so I did not need to take any clothes off. I could feel her wonderful naked body and breasts against mine, causing me to have quite a sudden and powerful reaction, my "man member standing up big, straight and tall, with rapt and respectful attention for the Goddess!"

We were instantly communicating telepathically with each other. She was able to convey what her desire was and that she felt so connected with me in a Sacred way; body, mind and soul. She wanted to be intimate with me, to share her love and passion with me, to give me the most wonderful, orgasmic pleasure that no one outside of her Elvin race had ever experienced before.

She wanted to make sure that it was okay for her to use her Elvin magic on me, to allow me to magically experience even more intense orgasmic pleasure with her than would normally have been possible. I was so turned on by her on every level, feeling so dizzy and Blissed Out. She was using her own energy, my energy, and our powerful magnetic-electrical attraction and chemistry to cause her etheric body to become more physically solid.

I felt her luscious and smooth body against mine. My own body was already feeling the greatest pleasure that I had ever felt before, and she seduced me with the sexual spell that she cast with all her passion and desire for me. I pulled her closer to me, and I began to passionately kiss her lips, our tongues began to dance around sensuously in each other's mouths. Erotically, I began to make love to her. I could not resist how sexy and luscious she was on all levels, with her long, cute, pointed Elvin ears. The exotic, feminine Divine presence of who she was overwhelmed me. Her long, silky, and thick hair brushed loosely over me, sensuously enveloping me. The nipples of her breasts felt hard and firm against me, as more and more powerful orgasms shook her body. She held tightly to me as she rode me. Her head was suddenly thrown back, in the height of the unbelievable orgasmic pleasure and passion that kept increasing the longer we made love to each other. I was lost with her in Nirvanic Ecstasy. Time and space became one huge, continuous lasting orgasm of un-describable pleasure, and I did not want to ever stop making love to her.

Finally, many hours had passed. I was wonderfully lost with her, merged with her sweet and sensuous nature. She lay with me in the incredibly luxurious afterglow of our passion, feeling the love that we felt so strongly for each other. It was hard to put into words how unbelievably fulfilling it was to make love to her, to experience this type of incredible orgasmic ecstasy—beyond my wildest imagination. I realized that I was now completely and joyously "sexually addicted" to her; I just had to have her all the time, I would do anything to be with her physically.

I had always prided myself in being disciplined, being level-headed, and focused only on my career as a captain. I was about to journey into areas that had not been explored for a while. I needed to focus on this upcoming mission, not be distracted by a sexy, gorgeous Elvin Goddess who had seduced me with her Elvin sex magic. She had made me desire her so intensely that nothing else seemed to matter anymore, except being with her in her Divine Feminine Goddess Presence, my Beloved and Cosmic True Love, and to make love to her, again and again, all the time, "morning, noon and night"!

All of a sudden, after experiencing the most exquisitely fulfilling orgasmic lovemaking of my life so far, I really did not care anymore about my career as a space captain nor about the missions that I was scheduled to go on within a short time. I only cared about one thing, and that was to be able to see her again as soon as possible. Hopefully I would soon see her in person, in the physical, and experience even more intense tantric intimacy with her.

Suddenly I knew exactly what I needed to do. This wild plan to find my gorgeous, sexy Elvin Goddess was all that mattered now. I would go ahead with my original plan of taking control over this upcoming exploratory mission, now I had the greatest and most important incentive of my entire life. However, after leaving the Pleiadian star system I would temporarily halt the entire fleet of ships, to make an important announcement to all the ships in the fleet about my personal plans.

What I was about to do was totally against the mission protocols, and included certain off-limit procedures and regulations governing the conduct of Federation personnel and what we are allowed to do. Certain areas were officially considered "no-travel" zones, quadrants or parsecs of the galaxy, because of certain treaties that had come about after earlier events, galactic wars, and planetary changes. In order to reach my Beloved's star system and space-time dimensional location, I had to temporarily penetrate an area that was definitely considered off bounds and forbidden.

My personal plans were definitely not a part of the original scheduled mission. I knew that doing this would probably threaten my career as a Captain of the Federation, and I might even be punished with a court martial for doing this. But I did not care.

Being Judged As a "Sex Addict"

It is interesting to compare these experiences with "similar" circumstances in today's life on planet Earth during the beginning of the 21st century. In society here in the U.S., and in other countries and cultures around the globe, many people have been harshly judged as being a "sex addict." People who "know" the person might judge them. Even "professional" psychiatrists or psychotherapists may judge that in their "professional" opinion, the person in question is a "sex addict."

What being a "sex addict" means is a relative judgment, depending upon the circumstances. I understand that family members of the person being judged will call them a "sex addict," as in the family's (often limited and narrow) view, the person's sexual activity is out of control. The family's opinion is that the "sex addiction" is causing the person problems, and that their sexual cravings are interfering with the (in their opinion) more important responsibilities. The family might claim that the person must get some professional help to change this behavior.

Yet, this very person being judged in today's world as a "sex addict," might in another society, in another time, or even on another planet or dimension (like the one being described in this past life), instead be celebrated as having the very qualities that made their life successful. In India as a member of a Tantra temple, and back in the Golden Age of Lemuria in those ancient Tantra-Oracle Rainbow Crystal Temples, it was considered excellent to be able to enjoy orgasmic tantric lovemaking with their Sacred Tantric Life Partner for hours and hours on end, every day for the rest of their long and sexually fulfilling lives.

The Story Continues

I was Blessed beyond human understanding several more times, having my Beloved Princess Alestra come to me in her etheric form during my dream-visions. Using her sex magic and Elvin powers, she enhanced her tantric visits each time. Soon, I would be leaving to go on this journey which would allow me to finally be with her in the physical. Then, I would be able to be with her all the time, as much as she and I wanted. We would experience even greater intimacy and Blissed Out fulfillment.

But Alestra had not shared with me during her visits that she would be facing a major challenge once I actually physically went to be with her on her planet. I had no idea of this upcoming challenge, and I was just going on my Faith and Inner Guidance. If there were any unforeseen challenges that would make it difficult (or so-called impossible) for Alestra and I to be together, well—I would just face them and deal with them. I could not worry about tomorrow, I could only be focused upon what was before me, what I knew I had to do to fulfill my new purpose in my life: being with my Beloved and Cosmic True Love, Princess Alestra.

The day finally arrived for my crew and I, and all members of the Pleiadian fleet, to embark upon our space journey. As planned, I waited until we had reached the certain point of our journey, then I officially announced to everyone on my ship and on all the ships in the fleet what I was now planning to do. I made it clear to everyone there that I did not want anyone else to be held responsible for what I was now going to do. I needed to take my own ship and journey for a short time through that particular off-bounds area, in order to reach Princess Alestra's star system. The rest of my crew were free to board the other ships in the fleet. I just had to do what I had to do; there was no getting around my decision. It was final.

To my astonishment, my crew did not want to leave the ship; they all considered it a great Honor to have been under my command, and they all felt that I was such a great captain. They, and the crew on the other ships, unanimously decided to stay on with me, even though their own careers might also now be threatened.

When they heard about what I had already experienced with my Beloved, the sexy Elvin Princess Goddess, many of those who had not yet found their own Beloved were now strongly getting the Inner Guidance that they, too, might actually meet their own Beloved. One of the many millions of beautiful Elvin ladies and handsome Elvin men on Princess Alestra's planet might be their own Divine Other Half. And besides, all my talk about how incredibly fulfilling it was to experience this extreme, orgasmic lovemaking with these exotic, gorgeous Elvin beings, well—it just made them all want to journey with me to my destination, to see for themselves just how awesome and incredible this could be.

It was decided that my entire Pleiadian fleet of ships were now all going to journey with me to Princess Alestra's home world. My Beloved and I had become very telepathic, I knew that all that intensely fulfilling orgasmic lovemaking had helped enhance our telepathic abilities. I now officially informed her about what had just occurred, and that we were all on our way toward her planet. She was immediately joyous and excited about that I was on my way and that my entire fleet was coming with me.

I could tell, though, that this last part about "my entire Pleiadian fleet of ships also coming with me," did kind of shock her. I could suddenly sense that she was somewhat concerned about how this would all be received by the Elvin High Royal Council, of which she was a major and popular member. Not waiting for her to inform the rest of her High Council, I just gave the order for the entire fleet to head for her star system. I was trusting that somehow it would all work out for everyone concerned; that it would be a total cosmic win-win situation for everyone involved.

But, no sooner had I officially made the decision to start toward Princess Alestra's home world, I realized what a major dilemma I was in now. Not only a dilemma for myself, but for my entire crew and fleet of Pleiadian ships: We were *major* members of the Federation. I had not been given any "official okay" to do what I was about to do, and Alestra's people were *not* official members of the Federation. Just like the "fictional" version of the Federation that has been presented through the "Star Trek" TV shows and movies, the Federation has a strict rule about any planets that the Federation openly interact and associate with. The races and cultures on these planets must at least be *open* to contact and interactions from other off-world races.

From what I could gather, Alestra's people had definitely had various other star races briefly visit their planet, and they had exchanged various things. So even though they were not official members of the Federation, they still had had interactions with various other star races—which meant they were not total isolationists. But for the most part, the Elvin tended to be somewhat aloof, and not very Intergalactically involved with other races. They had chosen, so far, to be more removed from the Cultural Exchanges that many other worlds were involved in. This was partly because they did not want to "dilute" their own race and culture with other races and cultures, for various reasons.

Just like I was suddenly becoming so detached and careless about things that had been so important to me before Princess Alestra had come into my life, so too was my Beloved changing. The traditions and responsibilities that had been so important to her prior to "tuning in to who I was" and experiencing the wonderful and fulfilling intimacy with me—suddenly, she did not seem to care or be concerned about them. So much of what many of her own race and culture felt was so important to keep in place, or to uphold, now seemed unimportant to her.

It is interesting that once one has experienced meeting and interacting with one's Beloved on a deep, intimate, sexual tantric level, this intense, orgasmic lovemaking causes one to become so "mellow" and totally "Blissed Out" that all one cares about is to just continue to experience this intense level of Nirvanic Ecstasy and pleasure. Yes, one could argue that one has then become a "sex addict" of the highest level, as nothing else seems important after this intense level of Total Nirvanic Ecstasy is experienced. I mean, come on; how could anything ever be more important, more enjoyable, than to experience the most mind-blowing, unbelievably intense multiple-orgasm pleasure, reaching beyond one's wildest imagination, that just goes on and on and on? Who in their "right mind" would even *want* to do anything else, except to experience as much multiple-orgasm tantric sex as they could with their Beloved? Nothing, absolutely NOTHING, could ever possibly compare with this. Period! "End of Discussion!"

Alestra now found herself in a real predicament. She had not really thought this whole thing through; all that she had thought about was fulfilling her urges. All members of the Elvin race were urged to fulfill these needs once they came of age and were in the process of looking for their Sacred Life Mate—but so far, being attracted to someone of any entirely different race and culture from off-planet had just not been an issue. For some reason, this had never been a problem throughout all the many ages—until now.

But of course, this was the very reason that Celeste and I had chosen to live this particular life here at this particular time, Celeste incarnating into the Elvin race as Princess Alestra and I incarnating into a Pleiadian captain, captaining a fleet of ships that was Destined to visit her world. By reuniting with each other, we aimed to somehow overcome this age-old Elvin tradition of not allowing anyone of another race to marry an Elvin (or even to have children with them).

It was not until Princess Alestra told the rest of the members of the High Council about the incoming fleet, that it really dawned upon her how difficult it was going to be for her to get the "okay" for me to be able to be with her. In fact, as she was to now find out from the High Council: even energetically, etherically "fraternizing" with another race was not allowed. It had not been clear to her before just how extreme these rigid policies and laws really were. When she "dared" to fall in love with me, desiring me on an intimate level, she had crossed the line. The High Council told her that she must now be punished, to be made an example of to others, because of her breaking their laws.

Meanwhile, I had already "made the jump" from the nearest wormhole, through hyperspace, to suddenly have my fleet of ships appear in a parking orbit high above Alestra's planet. I had received an "okay" to land a small shuttlecraft on the surface, as I had not specifically identified myself as being the one Alestra was involved with.

Telepathically, Alestra now knew that I had arrived above her planet, and that I was coming down to meet with her and the High Council.

To make a long story short: what happened right after I landed became the catalyst for drastically changing this old, rigid law that had been in place for so many ages—as the other High Council members observed how deeply and passionately Princess Alestra and I loved each other. The rest of the population on her planet found out about her and my love for each other and that I had a large fleet of ships that contained many hundreds of men and women from the Pleiadies. All the Elvin wanted to meet the Pleiadians—to possibly get to know them and perhaps even get intimately involved with them.

Sure enough, a large number of the Pleiadians in my fleet did meet their own Twin-Flames among the Elvin. Suddenly dozens of Divine Couples, half Elvin and half human, got married and began to enjoy the most fulfilling, orgasmic tantric lovemaking. Plus, their new Elvin spouses also used their powerful "Elvin sex magic" on their Beloved human partner, and this all helped anchor, even more intensely, the Nirvanic Ecstasy Grid onto their planet.

Ultimately, we all had a bunch of unbelievably cute, half human, half Elvin children. They were all so cute—with their little pointed Elvin ears they were all just adorable! And we all Lived Happily Ever After for the rest of that long, enjoyable, and fulfilling lifetime!

CHAPTER 27

Lord of the Rings and the Other Works by J. R. R. Tolkien—Just Fiction or Something Far Greater?

What if J. R. R. Tolkien's entire epic story was not merely fiction? His epic story, which includes *The Hobbit, The Lord of the Rings, The Silmarillion, Beren and Lúthien,* etc., has become so popular and loved, and it is such an important part of modern literature. What if it all was *not* just fictional fantasy, created in Tolkien's creative, wildly overactive imagination?

Impossible, you say? In his conscious mind, J. R. R. Tolkien, himself, just assumed that all he was doing during all those years was "making up" his entire epic story, creating it from scratch. But what if, in fact, he was actually channeling a true, real-life story—a story that took place many hundreds of thousands (or more) years ago?

Outlandish, you say? Have I "lost my mind," and/or "had a psychotic break from reality"? Have I allowed my own "over-active imagination" to somehow get the best of me? Have I just made up some far-out fantasy that just happens to include Celeste and I as a part of this great epic that Tolkien created? I don't mind if that is what you chose to believe after I share with you how I first became aware of this, and how this realization impacted my life from then on.

Discovering J. R. R. Tolkien

I still remember that afternoon in 1976, when I walked into the Dalton-Pickwick book store at the large shopping mall in Carlsbad, California. As I entered, I suddenly stopped in my tracks, staring at all the books, posters and calendars that were being displayed—all connected to J. R. R. Tolkien's work.

The reason I had stopped so suddenly was something that I was powerfully psychically picking up ("tuning into"), something that I instantly knew, even though I do not remember ever hearing about J. R. R. Tolkien and his major contribution to literature prior to that moment. I stood there, allowing this intense and powerful feeling, accompanied by vivid images, to fill me. I sensed something that had occurred many hundreds of thousands of years ago (at least), something that had historically happened, and which I, myself, had been a part of. I sensed that this whole epic story was NOT just a made-up, fictional fantasy story—it was real.

I instantly knew the basic outline of what had happened to me; that I was a prince or king, having to be in a kind of "exile" for a while. I knew that I was passionately in Love with a beautiful Elvin Princess, and I knew I would be reunited with her. I knew that she had given me a special gift, a small crystal pendant which would protect me on my journey with others. I knew that I was united in some kind of "Fellowship," having to take a small item back to a dark and dangerous place, and I knew that we fought many huge battles.

This was my first glimpse into Tolkien's books, and I had not even picked them up to see what exactly he had written in his "fictional fantasy" books. I also felt that at least a few of my companions on this dangerous journey were very small in stature.

I looked more closely at the books, picking them up and skimming through them, and I then picked up the calendars for that year. These had beautiful images painted by the artists Greg and Tim Hildebrandt, depicting what Tolkien had described in his books. As I stared at these images, I realized with a shock that these were actually depictions right out of the Akashic Records, describing an actual past life that I had definitely lived. But how in the world had Tolkien so clearly tuned into all these events that I suddenly knew had occurred, these events that I suddenly knew I had experienced myself?

I knew in that moment that Tolkien had actually Channeled all his books, even though to him, on a conscious level, he assumed that he had merely used his well-developed, "overactive" imagination. I was spellbound by what I was reading in his books, and I purchased all four of them; *The Hobbit* and the three books of the trilogy, *The Lord of the Rings.*

As I now look back upon that magical and intriguing moment of first (consciously) discovering and tuning into J. R. R. Tolkien's life work, there in that Dalton/Pickwick book store in 1976, I realize that it was none other, than ... you guessed it: my Beloved, Celeste, who had helped me. She had Over-Lighted me to psychically experience that powerful Epiphany about

Tolkien's books and my own connection to the story. She guided me to his wonderous, incredible and epic (true past life) story.

No, there is, of course, no way to actually prove that this is so; that I was Aragorn and that Celeste was Arwen. I am certainly not "attached" to it being provable, one way or the other. But I wanted to share why and how this powerful self-realization came about for me, to let you understand the circumstances and the unusual, unexpected spontaneity of the intense and vivid emotions that I experienced—relived—so intensely as I discovered and then began to read Tolkien's incredibly detailed epic story.

Yes, "reliving the story" would be the most accurate term for how I felt when I read most of *The Lord of the Rings.* I read them over several times, and each time was just as emotional as the first time I read them. I have read only a few other fictional fantasy books, as most of what I have read through the years has been about metaphysical, spiritual, and paranormal topics; UFO type books. I feel that so often "Truth is stranger than fiction," and I am just not usually that drawn to "fictional" stories and books. I have always felt, though, that the authors of some of the greatest "fictional" stories and books might actually have been Channeling their stories. It might be that the basic story was true and Channeled through them, and that the details about location, etc., were made-up. The basic story could contain "elements" of truth.

But it was not until I happened to encounter Tolkien's contribution to literature that I experienced something so unexpectedly profound. I could I now say that I had truly connected with someone (Tolkien) who was able to "tap into" information from beyond the time-space continuum. Tolkien was able to tune into the Akashic Records of some past timeline (or parallel level of reality, in some realm of actual existence), and he was able to channel it all down on paper, over many years.

When I tuned into Tolkien's own past, what his own past lives were like (at least a few of them), I discovered that he had been scribes and record keepers in a few of his past lives. He also definitely had at least three past lives around the time that story of *The Lord of the Rings* actually took place. I distinctly saw him incarnating as a Hobbit. That is interesting, as I read later that when he was once asked that if he had been given a chance to (actually) be a part of his *The Lord of the Rings* and *The Hobbit* stories, "who would he have chosen to be?", he stated that he would have chosen to be a Hobbit. I also very strongly felt that he had been Gandalf the Wizard.

I felt his third incarnation very strongly—perhaps strongest of all that I tuned into. Some may have already guessed this one. To me it was pretty much "vibrationally given" that Tolkien and his beloved wife, Edith (who I also feel was his Twin-Flame) were actually incarnated as this much earlier (actually historical) romantic couple: Beren and Lúthien.

Many of you are probably familiar with Tolkien's romantic love story of Beren and Lúthien. He wrote this love story so well—and of course, in my opinion he Channeled it, just as he did all of his other books about Middle-earth. I am now going to quote from the *Newsweek Special Edition* about J. R. R. Tolkien, which was published in 2018:

> During a year-long convalescence in Yorkshire from trench fever contracted in the

hellish mud-filled landscape of World War I France, J. R. R. Tolkien found the spark of inspiration for the tale that became the cornerstone for *The Hobbit* and *The Lord of the Rings.*

While the war raged on a country away, Tolkien and his wife, Edith, took respite from the constant conflict in a peaceful "woodland glade" in Yorkshire. Edith began to dance for Tolkien among the trees, imprinting the moment vividly in Tolkien's mind. "In those days her hair was raven, her skin clear, her eyes brighter than you have seen them, and she could sing—and dance," Tolkien wrote in a July 11, 1972 letter to his son Christopher, almost a year after his wife's passing.

Drawing from that afternoon, Tolkien began to write a love story. He imagined Edith as an Elvish princess, Luthien, and equated himself to a mere mortal human, Beren. The story of the two lovers was so precious to Tolkien that when his wife passed away, he had "Luthien" written on her gravestone, and later instructed "Beren" would be written on his own. "....For she was (and I know she was) my Luthien," the author wrote.

Living thousands of years before the events of *The Hobbit,* Beren was the last human in a group of Men that had resisted the

> Dark Enemy, Morgoth. As Morgoth conquered vast swaths of Middle-earth, Beren took refuge in the Elvish community of Doriath. There, he meets the love of his life, Luthien, singing and dancing in a glade, but that love can never be because she's an immortal Elf and he's a human destined to die. Her father, King Thingol, disapproves and decides to send Beren on a task he knows the Man will never be able to complete.
>
> He wants Beren to steal back one of the Silmarils, the three hallowed jewels made by Feanor, which Morgoth stole, before he can marry Luthien. The pair goes on a quest and manages to recover the jewel from Morgoth's cavern, but Beren dies in the process and Luthien then dies from grief. The Vala Mandus, the Judge of Death and Doom, is touched by their plight and both are resurrected, living—for a while, at least—happily ever after.

This was a very emotional scene summarized by the article in the *Newsweek Special Edition,* about what Beren and his beloved Lúthien went through before they were reunited.

When I began to read all three of *The Lord of the Rings* books, there were many events and experiences of Aragorn's interactions with Arwen, that were extremely emotional for me to read; to actually relive them, to feel all those intense emotions that would come up. Some experiences just tore at my heart so severely that I started to cry and actually sob, the extreme feelings that were brought up within me definitely arose because I was reliving those actual moments from that other life, reliving what I endured in my Love for my Beloved, Arwen. It could not be just my imagination that created these types of feelings and emotions that just kept coming up, so intense was I feeling it all. I was reliving now in this present lifetime my experiences from so far in my past.

Now, as I am writing this chapter and remembering what I first felt and experienced upon reading (and definitely reliving) these events that Tolkien so clearly was able to record/channel from that long ago time, I am reliving them again. Again, these very same and intense feelings are coming up all over again.

One event especially was so heart-wrenching: the time when it eventually became obvious to Arwen, my Beloved, that I was going to die. I was a mortal man and she was an immortal Elf, who made the decision to give up her immortality to be with me. But I had to pass away first, and what I said to her was so emotionally intense. I could remember so clearly just exactly what I said to her, which Tolkien was able to record so clearly.

Questions and Answers from Quora

As Celeste and I were working on this chapter together, a lot of emotions have been coming up for me once again, and I heard Celeste specifically guide me to go onto the internet. As I did so, I ended up on a very interesting webpage, connected to what appears to be some kind of "social network" called "Quora."

There, I discovered a list of questions being asked about J. R. R. Tolkien's books and about the characters in his stories. There are a lot of "members of Quora," who are fans of Tolkien's works, and they were responding with their own opinions about these questions.

One of the many questions that was presented, was this:

"Why was Arwen not understanding of Aragorn's passing? Was she not fully prepared for the mortality of mortals but thought that she was?"

Reading some of these questions was very emotional for me, because they brought up so many past life feelings and emotions as I was remembering what Arwen and I had both felt and experienced. One of the members replied to this question, and included a quote from Tolkien. This really brought tears to my eyes, as I could really remember what I had said to my Beloved, Arwen, as I prepared to die, attempting in that life to prepare her for my own passing, before she, herself, would soon also die, as she had chosen to be with me and give up her own immortality. Here is the reply I read:

So... she would be least prepared... far less so than any mortal, just on her life span and experiences, up unto that point.

Back to Arwen:

She does not truly understand her choice, until Aragorn decides to "sleep" so as not to hold onto life too long and become "unmanned."

> "Lady Undómiel," said Aragorn, "the hour is indeed hard, yet it was made even in that day when we met under the white

birches in the garden of Elrond, where none now walk. And on the hill of Cerin Amroth when we forsook both the Shadow and the Twilight this doom we accepted. Take counsel with yourself, beloved, and ask whether you would indeed have me wait until I wither and fall from my high seat unmanned and witless. Nay, lady, I am the last of the Númenoreans and the latest King of the Eldar Days; and to me has been given not only a span thrice that of Men of Middle-earth, but also the grace to go at my will, and give back the gift. Now, therefore, I will sleep.

"I speak no comfort to you, for there is no comfort for such pain within the circles of the world. The uttermost choice is before you: to repent and go to the Havens and bear away into the West the memory of our days together that shall there be evergreen but never more than a memory; or else to abide the Doom of Men."

"Nay, dear lord," she said, "that choice is long over. There is now no ship to bear me hence, and I must indeed abide the Doom of Men, whether I will or nill: the loss and the silence. But I say to you, King of the Númenoreans, not till now have I understood the tale of your people and their fall. As wicked fools I scorned them, but I pity them at last. For if this is indeed, as the Eldar say, the gift of the One to Men, it is bitter to receive."

"So it seems," he said. "But let us not be overthrown at the final test, who of old renounced the Shadow and the Ring. In sorrow we must go, but not in despair. Behold! we are not bound forever in the circles of the world, and beyond them is more than memory, Farewell!"

"Estel, Estel!" she cried, and with that even as he took her hand and kissed it, he fell into sleep. Then a great beauty was revealed in him, so that all who after came there looked on him with wonder; for they saw the grace of his youth, and the valor of his manhood, and the wisdom and majesty of his age were all blended together. And long there he lay, an image of the splendour of the Kings of Men in glory undimmed before the breaking of the world.

But Arwen went forth from the House, and the light of her eyes was quenched, and it seemed to her people that she had become cold and grey as nightfall in winter that comes without a star. Then she said farewell to Eldarion, and to her daughters, and to all whom she had loved; and she went out from the city of Minas Tirith and passed away to the land of Lórien, and dwelt there alone

> under the fading trees until winter came. Galadriel had passed away and Celeborn had also gone, and the land was silent.
>
> There at last when the mallorn-leaves were falling, but spring had not yet come, she laid herself to rest upon Cerin Amroth; and there is her green grave, until the world is changed, and all the days of her life are utterly forgotten by the men that come after, and elanor and nimphredil niphredil bloom no more east of the sea.
>
> I think it is the most beautiful piece ever written about love... and J. R. R. Tolkien saved it for the Appendix!

This was particularly difficult to read, as I remember so intently what we were both experiencing. I just started to cry as it tore at my heart. I was feeling such compassion for how my Beloved had chosen to be with me, a mortal human, instead of staying immortal, because she would rather be with me and experience such wonderful love and ecstasy with me. It still moved me that she had been willing to accept this great sacrifice, and I just cried because of this.

But as I was reliving this, I energetically felt Celeste was comforting me with all her love for me, and she said to me, "My Beloved, I was willing to do this, of giving up my 'immortality' in that life, so that you and I could be together for all Eternity." I could feel how sincere she was, that she was willing to do this, just as I would have been willing if our roles had been reversed.

Then, Celeste reminded me of when she and I had met in that lifetime. I immediately remembered that wonderful and magical moment of first seeing her, Arwen. I remember, just as Tolkien so clearly describes her and my first meeting, that I had been walking in the woods near Rivendale. I had spent so much of my early life there among the Elven people. I remember that I was singing a song about how Beren had first met the Love of his life, Lúthien. As Tolkien described, I initially thought that I was seeing a vision of Lúthien, because Arwen's physical (and Inner) beauty was so reminiscent of what Lúthien had looked like when she had been alive a thousand years earlier.

Another question that was posted on Quora, was this:

"How did Aragorn and Arwen fall in love? How can someone, who has lived for thousands of years, fall in love with a man who has lived only a few dozen at best?"

I want to now quote one of the many posts that responded to this question. This answer was insightful, and it contained another quote from Tolkien about what Arwen and I said to one another when we met:

> "The Tryst"—By Jef Murray
>
> How Aragorn fell in love is quite obvious and lacks subtletey. That's not a bad thing, for the circumstances of their meeting made Arwen appear as Luthien herself and Aragorn was immediately taken aback by her beauty and demeanor. He walked alone in the woods as a young man, singing of when the world was fair and he was full of hope. He

saw Arwen walking among the birches and believed he had entered a dream. He even contemplates a gift from the minstrels who were said to make that which someone sings of appear before their very eyes. This is particularly important as he was singing the Lay of Luthien, the meeting of the mortal Beren and the immortal Luthien in Neldoreth. Then it seemed like Luthien herself was walking in Rivendell in blue and silver. He describes her as being fair as the twilight, with dark hair and brow bound with gems like the stars. He is literally lost for words and fears if he speaks then she will vanish. He then cries out Tinúviel, in the same manner as Beren did.

They then speak:

> Then the maiden turned to him and smiled, and she said: "Who are you? And why do you call me by that name?"

And he answered: "Because I believed you to be indeed Lúthien Tinúviel, of whom I was singing. But if you are not she, then you walk in her likeness."

> "So many have said," she answered gravely. "Yet her name is not mine. Though

maybe my doom will be not unlike hers. But who are you?"

'"Estel I was called," he said; "but I am Aragorn, Arathorn's son, Isildur's Heir, Lord of the Dúnedain"; yet even in the saying he felt that this high lineage, in which his heart had rejoiced, was now of little worth, and as nothing compared to her dignity and loveliness.

But she laughed merrily and said: "Then we are akin from afar. For I am Arwen Elrond's daughter, and am named also Undómiel."

"Often is it seen," said Aragorn, "that in dangerous days men hide their chief treasure. Yet I marvel at Elrond and your brothers; for though I have dwelt in this house from childhood, I have heard no word of you. How comes it that we have never met before? Surely your father has not kept you locked in his hoard?"

"No," she said, and looked up at the Mountains that rose in the east. "I have dwelt for a time in the land of my mother's kin, in far Lothlórien. I have but lately returned to visit my father again. It is many years since I walked in Imladris."

Then Aragorn wondered, for she had seemed of no greater age than he, who had lived yet no more than a score of years in Middle-earth. But Arwen looked in his eyes and said: "Do not wonder! For the children of Elrond have the life of the Eldar."

As I read this I could truly say that these words did definitely feel so familiar, that they were the words that both Arwen and I first spoke to one another upon first meeting. But I also tuned into some other thoughts and perceptions about that life, which is connected to what Celeste and I shared in our last chapter about her and my life when she was of the Elvin race on that other planet and I a Pleiadian. I truly believe that what Tolkien was able to tune into, what he shared through his writings and books, definitely was a clear and accurate perception about what happened that time so many thousands of years ago.

In more recent years I have also read several different biographies about J. R. R. Tolkien, written by various authors. I was interested in finding out if there were any specific thing, event, or circumstance, no matter how small, big or mundane, that had acted as sort of a "catalyst"; that had helped and/or "energetically influenced" Tolkien to be able to tap into all that he ultimately did over the many years it took him to finish *The Hobbit* and *The Lord of the Rings*. I found a specific event that I feel probably was the beginning of him starting to receive what I believe was his own Higher Self "downloading" to his conscious self. This occurred one evening, as he was in the process of putting one of his children to bed. As quoted from the *Newsweek Special Edition* on Tolkien:

> Initially, the tale of *The Hobbit* was merely a bedtime story Tolkien told to his sons, John, Michael and Christopher. It started

> with the famous line that opens the book: "In a hole in the ground there lived a Hobbit."
>
> Christopher Tolkien recalled his father sharing the oral version around 1929, according to The Guardian. Eventually, in 1937, while in his study at Oxford, Tolkien breathed new life into the story of Bilbo Baggins by writing the book based on the adventures he shared with his children.

So to me, that famous first line to *The Hobbit* IS that initial, "small" event; the event that represents Tolkien's first, tiny "crack" through the time-space continuum and into the Akashic Records. This was the beginning of the lifting of his Cosmic Amnesia Veils, beginning his accessing/recording/Channeling of an ancient period of time on Earth.

It is also true, as was pointed out in the biographies that were written about him and in the *Newsweek Special Edition* on J. R. R. Tolkien, that there were a number of other events in his life that also influenced him; that helped to give him a greater energetic openness and attunement to certain scenes that he was going to "download." The horrible experiences he had in the trenches during WWI helped attune him to the wars and battles that occurred in *The Lord of the Rings,* etc. To his conscious mind, his creative, well-developed imagination was merely adding new ideas to the epic fictional fantasy story which was slowly unfolding in his (conscious) mind.

Tolkien often rewrote and changed what he had already written, he did this a number of times while working on *The*

Hobbit and *The Lord of the Rings.* Skeptics to my theory of him having Channeled his entire epic story might question this. They might wonder why he went back to change what he had originally written, if he had truly been "Channeling" this whole thing. A very good question. But in my opinion, considering how energetically overwhelming it was for him to receive so much through this powerful downloading of the information on this past time, he probably struggled to "energetically fine-tune" himself. He continued to fine-tune himself, to get more attuned and more precise in the exact, finer details of his work. It eventually became less necessary to go back to correct or clarify a particular point or detail that he was attempting to receive in these downloads.

Consider the fine attunement of a great photographer, who initially sees the basic outline of the image and photo shoot they want to do, but may have to do the "photo op" over a number of times to "get it just right or perfect." Yes, they have to make sure that all the many conditions (lighting, contrast, perspective, etc.), factors and details are all in alignment. One can then get the best possible photos, after all the post-production work. Like that analogy, so Tolkien experienced his greater ability to constantly fine-tune himself to be able to receive more accurately these downloads from his Higher Self. Finally, he was satisfied that he had actually gotten an as clear and precise a version of these past events as was humanly possible for him. I would "grade" his final version as definitely well over 99.9999% accurate.

Tolkien's Mission

It is my opinion that J. R. R. Tolkien had an important, special mission. His mission included his wife, Edith, that she Loved him Unconditionally and was there for him, her entire life. It was essential that she inspired him with that moment in the glade when she spontaneously danced and sang for him, helping him to tap into this past realm in that ancient time. That very real time when Elves and humans intermingled and loved each other. Modern-day humanity needed to remember all those events that occurred in that ancient time. It did not matter that Tolkien and everyone else assumed it all to be a totally made-up, fictional fantasy story; people are drawn to something that can be presented in fictional form. That was the only way that it was possible for Professor Tolkien to have "originated" the story: he had to be assuming and believing, on a conscious level, that it was all just the creation of his own overactive imagination. But it is also true that to be a good channel, you also need to have a good "imagination." This allows you to be attuned to and receptive to whatever your Higher Self and/or other Higher Forces want to download to your conscious mind.

When I read those biographies about Tolkien's life, I read about him being a part of a small group at Oxford University for a number of years. C. S. Lewis was also a member, and he was a close friend of Tolkien's. The books state that Tolkien was sometimes a little "lazy" in taking the time to finish his work on *The Lord of the Rings,* and that it took him many years to do so. They claim that if it had not been for C.S. Lewis "getting on his case," he might not have ever finished it.

I do not think it was laziness that was what Tolkien was struggling with. I feel that his Higher Self's mission for him to ultimately finish it made him feel somehow "overwhelmed" on some deep levels, because of the realization of what he had to do. His mission was daunting, to say the least; being able to finish downloading of the entire story, receiving all that was "energetically contained" within this whole, epic (and True) story. Yes, truth IS stranger than fiction—which is why the truth sometimes has to be presented in "fiction form": so that others can be more open to it.

Small Hobbit Bones Discovered

As we come to the end of this chapter, I wanted to share a link to a newspaper article from 2004, regarding a very fascinating find that was discovered that same year. This is a true story, not some parody. Bones belonging to tiny human was discovered in the Indonesia area. Those doing the research and examination of these very small bones gave an official nickname to the small human that the bones are from: "The Hobbit."

The "Hobbit": The Homo floresiensis Controversy: https://www.sciencedirect.com/science/article/pii/S1978301916303631

While this does not necessarily "prove" that the Hobbits actually existed at one time on the Earth, I do find it kind of interesting. There are no coincidences about how, why, and when things tend to happen when synchronicities occur. That these small "Hobbit" bones were discovered within months of the release of the third and last *The Lord of the Rings* movie (produced by Peter Jackson), is kind of an interesting synchronicity.

Who knows, maybe various other "evidential synchronicities" will eventually surface in the most unexpected ways, which will help give more evidence to the true-life reality of what Tolkien so masterfully received and shared with the rest of humanity.

Cosmic Stamp of Approval

Something extraordinary occurred for me as I was in the process of finishing up this chapter. To be more precise: what occurred began almost from the moment that Celeste and I started to compile this chapter together, and as we approached the end of the chapter, it had become very energetically obvious. What I realized was that I had started to strongly sense the powerful presence of another Higher Light Being, someone who initially just seemed to be "looking in" on what we were doing, as if he had a personal interest and involvement with what I was sharing.

It was when we were finishing up the chapter that I realized with a "start" that this Higher Light Being was, in fact, none other than the Higher Self of the person that had been J. R. R. Tolkien while he was alive on Earth. His spirit and soul had returned to the Higher Realms, where he had been before he had incarnated on Earth in 1892. He had returned to the Higher Realms in 1973, two years after his Twin-Flame and wife, Edith, had returned there; he could not wait to be back with her, his own Beloved/Cosmic True Love.

It was as if this Higher Light Being was energetically giving me his "Cosmic stamp of approval" for what I was doing. As the Oxford Scholar and Professor, there was no way that J. R. R. Tolkien, or rather his conscious Earth self, could have been open to the concept or theory that I have presented in this chapter—that he Channeled his entire Middle-earth epic. No, that would not even have been accepted as "possible" by his analytical, logical left brain.

But for someone like me, who has spent their entire life being a channel and who has developed this ability as much as I have, it was not only "possible", but perhaps "inevitable," to came to this conclusion. He had so clearly received/created his epic story in order for it to be shared with so many millions of Earth's humanity over many decades. It was not only an important contribution to literature, but in actuality also a clear and accurate recording of what had occurred in Earth's distant, misty past; a recording that needed to now be shared once more with Earth's present humanity.

Tolkien had done an excellent job, as I said earlier, in being able to tap into this early history of Earth. He completed his important mission of sharing this with humanity. But, of course, he could only receive it and share it as merely a fictional fantasy tale, which is how it was supposed to be shared. But it was Destined to eventually be understood as something much, much more than just a mere fictional fantasy epic: It should be understood as a true story of what some of us experienced to end the darkness of an earlier era. It mirrors how we are now getting rid of this same evil darkness, as we prepare for the upcoming Golden Age.

As Celeste and I finally finished our own Interpretation of Tolkien's great work, I clearly felt his powerful and benevolent presence communicate to us that he was very happy with the fact that now humanity has a chance, if they so choose, to understand his story as something more than just fictional fantasy.

I look back on that day in 1976, when I was walking into that Dalton-Pickwick book store and suddenly stopped "alive in my tracks" (I like this phrase rather than "dead in my tracks") as I spontaneously tuned into the overview of what Tolkien had actually Channeled. I now realize that I had definitely felt the presence of one or more Higher Light Beings right near me at that time, who were powerfully influencing me. They helped me tap into that self-realization that not only was the story actually true, but I, myself, had also been a part of the story—part of the historical events that had occurred in that long ago time.

It was now obvious to me that two of these Higher Light Beings were none other than J. R. R. Tolkien and his wife, Edith, whose spirits and souls had just returned back to the Higher Realms just a few years before. They were helping me to energetically attune to my experience. It was also part of the Divine Plan that Tolkien would later reconnect with me in the future (now), to finalize sharing—as Paul Harvey used to say—"The Rest of the Story". And now the story is finally shared! God Bless you both, Mr. and Mrs. Tolkien. Thank you for all that you did in those earlier times of our ancient past, which has been shared with humanity as merely fictional fantasy, and which is now to be understood as something far greater!

CHAPTER 28

Mr. Upper, Conspiracy Realists, Inconvenient Truths, Exposing False Flags and Crisis Actors, and Are You REALLY Ready to Meet Your Cosmic True Love?

In this chapter, Celeste and I want to give some political and social perspective and commentary. I understand that there are probably some who are reading this book who may feel that our focusing upon anything other than the romantic theme might somehow detract from the book.

But as in the saying, "it's my party and I can say what I want to"; this is Celeste's and my book, and we can say what we want to. Actually, we feel that the topics of this chapter are important, relevant, and significant to how our relationships are, both with ourselves and each other. They are also important for our desire—and the emotional well-being and balance that is needed—to be able to finally connect with and be fully reunited with our Cosmic True Love.

We need to "acknowledge and clear" possible dysfunctional behavior and events that have occurred, that are "skeletons hidden in our closets of the past"—whether they stem from our past relationships with our Earth family members or from other sources. We also need to acknowledge and clear, as best we can, all of those other "inconvenient truths" from throughout humanity's history, which still need to be acknowledged and forgiven. This also goes for much more recent events that have been referred to as "False Flags" that the cabal staged with "crisis actors," which actually fooled millions of gullible people who have been suffering from what is known as "cognitive dissonance."

But first, we have to be willing to simply admit that the events occurred, which is the beginning of any type of "healing modality." Both in our own individual past and in our more collective historical past there have been "hard-to-admit-and-to-acknowledge events" that need to be allowed to surface. They can then be totally released, and this past continuous, "history repeating itself/Ground Hog Day/Matrix" reality can end. That then allows the true Golden Age of Heaven on Earth for everyone to come to be, and there will be no more allowing the cabal to manipulate us in any way from then on.

Anyone who has really studied history with an open, discerning mind and consciousness, and who have had access to various information that is not available through the mainstream ("lamestream, fake news") media, will ultimately come to the inevitable, obvious conclusion that the official version of history, as it has been taught in most of the public schools and universities for the past several decades, is extremely edited, manipulated and sanitized. There are many examples of what is termed "Inconvenient truths," realities that contradict so much that has been taught to us by the normal sources of knowledge, especially in regards to what has occurred throughout our history.

One of the reasons that I specifically remember that it was in 1976 that I walked into that bookstore and became aware of Tolkien (as was shared in the previous chapter), was that it was the year of Celebrating the 200th Anniversary of the Founding of America, celebrating our Constitutional Republic. (Yes, *Republic.* NOT "democracy," which is "mob rule.")

Mr. Upper

I also remember specifically thinking about one of my Senior High School teachers, Mr. Downs, who was a very inspiring and "upbeat" individual. I used to joke with him that he should change his name to "Mr. Upper," because of him being so very positive about life, despite what he knew. The reason I mention him is not only that he was the only teacher that I really remember out of my many teachers I had throughout all of elementary, Junior High and finally High School. Mr. Downs was quite an interesting person as far as his political views went, he was very unique about what he truly felt and believed in. One could say that he was a major dichotomy in some ways, because of all that he believed in and was passionate about.

Yet, after having met many others like him since then, I have come to realize that there must be literally millions of others just like him today, who have similar beliefs and orientations. But the cabal corporate-controlled media does not want to recognize the fact that most people tend to have, to a greater or lesser degree, a mixture of various beliefs, interests, and orientations. This does not match how the cabal likes to rigidly categorize each of us as being (politically and socially) all one extreme or the other, with nothing in-between (and then they use this to demonize us based on those biased and falsified judgments). The cabal categorizes us so that they can control the narrative and pit different people, races, cultures, and backgrounds against one another. The cabal want to label us and control us; setting black against white, white against black, this religion against that religion, race or culture, etc. But the Truth is that we all are a combination of various beliefs and orientations, which does not match all this controlled disinformation and stereotyping that has been going on for quite some time.

Mr. Downs, or rather, "Mr. Upper," as I like to still refer to him, was very "progressive" as far as civil rights were concerned. He was white, but shared that he had been very involved in the Civil Rights movement of the 1960's. He had marched with Reverend Martin Luther King and other well-known black civil rights leaders of that time. He had known Dr. King personally, and he was very supportive of him and all that he was attempting to accomplish for not only African Americans, but for all minorities. He was also very supportive of women's rights. He shared that he had had some very interesting and enlightening conversations with Dr. King about his views on many things.

At the same time, Mr. Downs was also very patriotic about this country, and he strongly supported the (original) US Constitution (before it was changed in 1871) and the Bill of Rights. He was also a strong supporter of protecting our 2nd Amendment Rights and our Right to Bear Arms. He not only owned a few firearms, but also had a membership in both the National Rifle Association and a local "militia" group. He always displayed the flag at his home, being very patriotic.

In his many conversations with Reverend Martin Luther King, Dr. King made it clear that violence, rioting, looting, etc., would not be allowed or tolerated by his group and movement. He felt strongly that if they wanted to truly get the "establishment" open to their views, violence would not ever work. Dr. King also stated that it would be hypocritical of him and his cause to be a part of any violence, chaos or mayhem.

In fact, he specifically told Mr. Downs that he was aware of socialist and communist forces that had attempted to infiltrate his movement, to use him and his cause to foment total anarchy in the United States. These forces had attempted to start "race wars," pitting white against black, black against white. Then they would use the "race card," after they had infiltrated the political establishment. These forces were planning to create various organizations that would publicly appear as "progressive"—would even appear to support the civil rights movement –but in reality they would be used as a cover to create violence, rioting, looting, and a destruction of this country and the rule of law. They would "say all the right things" and appear to be supportive of his authentic civil rights movement, but wanted to use it to create race wars and destruction of the Republic.

Yes, Dr. King was very patriotic to this country, and he did not want to see this country divided or destroyed. He was actually supportive of the US Constitution and Bill of Rights. He was a strong supporter of the 2nd Amendment, and he owned several guns. He felt he needed to own these to protect himself from the racist forces that wanted to keep the blacks from having the same rights as any other US citizen.

He also knew the history of the political party that claimed to now be so much for the civil rights of blacks; the Democratic Party. Members of the Democratic Party were actually the ones who formed the Ku Klux Klan, who started the "Jim Crow Laws" and who wanted to keep slavery in place even after the Civil War. The Republican Party was originally named "the Abolitionist Party." When Abe Lincoln became President, the name was changed to "the Republican Party." They were the ones who wanted to end slavery.

Many would state that Mr. Downs was just a "conspiracy theorist," because of the nature of some information he shared with us. But I knew he would rather have stated that he was a "conspiracy realist," because he was aware of many things that the mainstream media had refused to report on or had suppressed various information about, information that threatened the "establishment" (now also known as the "cabal").

I remember that back in 1972, when he was my Social Studies teacher, Mr. Downs was bemoaning some coming changes to the public school system. The government was in the process of making the entire public school system quit teaching about the Constitution and the Bill of Rights. Students in the coming years and decades would no longer even know about our Constitutional Heritage. Mr. Downs thought there was a hidden agenda behind this (which there was); if the newer generations did not even know about our Heritage, they would begin to espouse and be brainwashed by the "socialist-communist forces" that were attempting to gain inroads into every level of society.

I think back on all that he shared with us, on his personal involvement in the Civil Rights movement, and on him having personally known Dr. King and other prominent leaders in the Civil Rights movement of that earlier time. I think of how they were specifically against violence, mayhem, rioting or looting of any kind. As he pointed out (and this is just "good ol' fashioned common sense"): If one really wants to get someone to be open to the cause you are behind and to be taken seriously, the last thing you want to be doing is destructive things. You should then avoid actions like burning things, looting, and tearing down statues just because of what those things may represent from the past. The Rule of Law must always be upheld. In fact, it has been argued that instead of violently tearing down these many "distasteful and disgusting" statues of our past for what they represent, we should keep them up as a reminder to us of what we do NOT want to occur ever again in our future.

I truly believe that Dr. King, other prominent and sincere Civil Rights leaders of this earlier era, and Mr. Downs are "turning over in their graves", considering that groups like "Black Lives Matter" do all the things that Dr. King and others were specifically against. As Dr. King also pointed out: if any groups in the future DO this type of thing, then it is obvious that they are not really interested in anyone's civil rights, but instead had either been formed from the very beginning or were taken over at a later stage by negative elements in order to create violence, chaos and the destruction of our Republic.

No, these more recent groups do not appear to really be about the civil rights of blacks. And because they are being funded by corrupt people like George Soros, it is obvious what their real agenda is.

Here is a link to a short Documentary that presents information about the real facts behind the so-called George Floyd Protests that the cabal-controlled media totally covered up:

"Flu d'État: Infiltration, Not Invasion"

https://forbiddenknowledgetv.net/infiltration-not-invasion-flu-detat/

Manipulation of History

Mr. Downs also really enjoyed blowing people's minds with various facts about how our history has been so very manipulated, how so much has been covered up and/or altered to keep a certain "official view" on things that the "powers that were" did not want anyone to know. If anyone found out those things, well then, it would also become obvious how many more things about our past had been changed or erased from our history books.

He maintained how important it is to always question the official version of our history, even if a lot of people get very uncomfortable or upset about the exposure of the utter hypocrisy of the past. There were many examples of these inconvenient truths that he had come across and discovered in his own personal research. These also included various photos from the Civil War era that he had discovered in private archives, that contradict much of the "official" version of history.

For example, he brought some high-quality copies of photos originally taken during the Civil War period. These were quite controversial, but nonetheless authentic. I especially remember two of these photos, because of how extremely contradictory they were to all of the history that had been officially and publicly taught to us in all our public schools and universities. One of these photos showed a black/African American plantation slave owner—that is right, a black man who was in charge of a plantation and who owned both white and black slaves. The other photo showed a black confederate soldier, dressed in his confederate uniform.

At first, I just stared in disbelief at what I was viewing. Initially, I could not wrap my head around this authentic photographic evidence concerning slavery and the Civil War (just two photos from photo archives). The photos clearly documented that there existed cases where the history that has been taught to us for many years has been changed to suit a specific viewpoint. With no pun intended, and please forgive the phrase, not all things can be judged as (just) "black and white."

Mr. Downs stated that he had come across many more such photos, other examples of black plantation and slave owners, as well as other blacks who fought on the side of the South or confederates. This was shocking and troubling, partly because of the obvious implications regarding our view of history and how things should never be simply stereotyped to suit the official, accepted view of history, and partly because there has obviously been a "conspiracy of silence" regarding so much of our past.

In fact Mr. Downs, as he had done a lot of extensive research on history that he shared with us, became convinced that of the two theories about history, only one can fully explain how it all occurred. The normal view of most people is that all events in history are just a series of coincidences and accidents, things just happen all by themselves. The other theory is that a few very powerful and wealthy individuals, referred to as the power elite or cabal, constantly have been secretly planning and manipulating various events to make things turn out as they have.

After many years of research, he had come to what he referred to as a "logical, obvious and highly intelligent conclusion": There was definitely a conspiracy. It was not just a "fringe theory," but a fact and reality that a group of elite families, known as the "Illuminati family bloodlines," had in fact, for many ages, conspired to gain total control over the entire world. This is the basic premise behind one of the most informative books ever written on this subject, titled *The Unseen Hand: An Introduction to the Conspiratorial View of History,* by A. Ralph Emerson.

https://www.amazon.com/Unseen-Hand-Introduction-Conspiratorial-History/dp/096141

As Mr. Downs had stated, and as I have also heard from various other excellent sources, the phrase "conspiracy theory" was first coined by the CIA (or as various former agents used to refer to it, the "Confusion In Action" agency) within days after President John F. Kennedy's assassination by the cabal. The CIA attempted to manipulate the ignorant public into believing that anyone who dared to question the "official, public position" about events being manipulated, had to be just some neurotic, paranoid, delusional, and emotionally imbalanced individual. The truth is that those of us who question and dare to challenge these official, publicly presented positions are using our God-given intelligence, Higher Intuition, common sense, and our ability to discern. We see through all the vast amount of BS and propaganda that the cabal-controlled fake news media has attempted to cram down our throats to mind-control us into believing their absurd, silly and stupid "explanations" of what really happens "behind the scenes."

Whether it be the "Warren Commission" on the Kennedy Assassination, the "9-11 Commission," the "Condon Report" and "Project Blue Book's" very ridiculous explanation of the reality of UFOs and ETs—all of these reports are obviously created in an attempt to convince us of their idiotic statements, statements that totally ignore the real facts that they wanted to cover up. Yes, facts about more inconvenient truths that expose the power elite and their plans to attempt to control us.

Mr. Downs also knew about how the CIA, through their "Operation Mockingbird," covertly took over the media in the 1950's. They placed one or more CIA agents in every major news agency and radio and television company, to be able to control and manipulate the news the way they wanted it to be presented to the public. And as the years went by, slowly they became ever more blatant and obvious in their "behind the scenes" control and influence on what the public was allowed to know on a mass level. They also attempted to control as much as they could of the major publishing companies, but this was not as successful—especially as more and more people in more recent decades began to "privately" publish their books, just as Celeste and I have done.

It has been very obvious to me, especially now since being around Celeste, how the Higher Light Forces has been specifically guiding me to become aware and enlightened about all of these various "conspiracies" of the cabal, whether it happened in past centuries or took place in more recent years. As the very important point that was already made and stressed earlier: it is not only important to be able to acknowledge dysfunctional behavior and happenings among our personal families, but it is also important to acknowledge all these manipulated historical events from our past. Having gained hindsight and wisdom, we can stop history from repeating itself. Remember the phrase that Mr. Downs, or "Mr. Upper," would always point out to us: Those who fail to learn from history are doomed to repeat it again, and again, and again...

Despite all the so-called negative things that Mr. Downs shared with us about history and about what the power elite had conspired to do behind the scenes, he was very optimistic about our future and in his attitude toward most people on this planet. He truly felt that most people are "good" by nature, that actually only about 5 to 10% of humanity was what he referred to as "innately evil." If we could expose and stop these few individuals by educating others about how history had been repeated over and over again, and if we truly learned from this, then these few really bad individuals would finally cease their hidden conspiracies and agendas. We would then be destined in the future to move into the Golden Age of peace, and all violence would also naturally cease.

But being very realistic and down-to-earth, he definitely did not feel that the whole world would become truly and totally peaceful. This was because of legislation forced upon us by so-called well-meaning politicians, to disarm us and get rid of the 2nd Amendment. Besides, this legislation has never really been about making society safer and more peaceful; actually, it has always been about the exact opposite—about creating more chaos and mayhem.

As a student and teacher of history, Mr. Downs constantly pointed out to us the historical fact that in all countries where the citizens were forced to give up their ability to protect themselves, every single time they became either a fascist or communist regime. Millions of people who had believed the propaganda that if they would all just turn in their firearms they would be (so-called) safe, had been murdered by the criminals of each of those societies. The criminals did, of course, still have their weapons, while the law-abiding citizens suddenly became defenseless and victims to all the lawlessness that resulted in these hidden agendas of control over them. This was how it was right before Hitler took over Germany, how it was in Russia before the Bolshevik Revolution, and this was how it was in China before they, too, disarmed their citizens to become a communist regime—just to mention a few of many historical examples of how the cabal and the International Banksters funded these dictators rise to power. This is exactly what has been occurring, or rather what has been attempted to be done behind the scenes by the cabal, in more recent decades here in the United States.

Every one of these violent regime changes always happened through the exact same strategy: They would create "False Flags" and use "crisis actors" to fool the public, then they would pass laws and legislation to restrict the use of firearms from the public until they had totally confiscated all of their weapons. The public then had no way to defend themselves against all the criminals and lawlessness that always occurred each time these regimes were taken over. Yes, millions perished as they were murdered and victimized, and there was nothing they could do about it after being fooled and manipulated by these False Flags and crisis actors.

Eye-Openers from "Preparedness Expos"

In the late 1980's and 90's, I had a chance to attend a number of "Preparedness Expos" that were being held at different locations around the United States. These events were primarily about preparing for possible disasters of all kinds and what one could do to be better prepared. Even though a cross section of society attended these events, a vast majority of attendees were very patriotic in their views about our country, and were very protective to the Constitution and especially the 2nd Amendment. Also, a huge number of the attendees were members of various militias that actually exist in most all of the 50 states.

I realized after attending these events that like many other Americans I had been somewhat brainwashed about just exactly what "these types of people" really are like on a personal, everyday level. I had assumed, through the categorizing that the mass lamestream fake news media has been doing for many years, that these individuals were mostly, if not all, a bunch of bigoted, racist, red neck, extremist people, and assumed that they were all the same as the white supremacists and modern Nazi groups. I realized later that the Higher Light Forces had wanted me to get a chance to speak to a huge number of these individuals, and really have a chance to get to know them on a more personal level and find out who they really were and what they actually stood for despite what the media had said about them.

It was interesting, enlightening, and quite the eye-opener to hear the exact same thing from so many of them, to hear what they truly felt and believed as opposed to how the cabal-controlled media had described them. Among the many things that they were adamant and passionate about was that they had absolutely no connections to the white supremacists and the Nazis. In fact, they detested them, for a number of reasons. First of all, many of their parents and/or grandparents had fought in WWII against the Nazis in Europe. Why would they ever be associated with those who their own families had fought against to free Europe.

They were involved with the various militias all over the United States because they felt they had to prepare for the possibility of the government becoming totally tyrannical and allowing the "New World Order" cabal forces to fulfill their plans for total world control (the old timeline). But they made it very clear that as much as they were members of the militias, they really hoped (as they emphasized to me a number of times) that they would not have to actually ever rise up to defend the US Constitution and the end of all of our (civil) rights. The last thing they wanted to do was to have to give their life to protect this country from all enemies foreign and domestic.

If it came down to it, though, they were ready and willing to give their lives so that the rest of us could live in a free society. They even stated a number of times, that even though they disagreed with many elements of society that they felt were being manipulated by "liberal and socialist agendas," they were still willing to lay their lives down to defend and protect people with whom they did not agree—even though they felt that so much of these beliefs were part of a bigger agenda, similar to what had happened in other countries that had been taken over and then become a totally controlled society. (This was the same thing that Mr. Downs had specifically mentioned.) For this is one of the many freedoms that we have enshrined within the US Constitution and the Bill of Rights; our Right to speak our views.

I have to say that as I intermingled with a huge number of these "militia" types, I did not really detect all this bigotry and racism that the media has attempted to label these types with. I even remember a few African Americans who were actually members of a few of the militias that attended the Preparedness Expos. It was interesting to notice that I did not detect any specific examples of prejudice while I was there. From my point of view, from what I have observed in this society, there is probably just as much or even more prejudice in every other segment of society as there was in those groups.

As a matter of fact, so many of the very groups and individuals who are constantly accusing others of being "prejudiced," are themselves (hypocritically) racially prejudiced. I am speaking specifically of many within the so-called progressive, liberal groups; they just seem to be using the "race card" to foment violent and extreme reactions between people of different races. This is the very thing that Dr. King had warned us about, that these forces would utilize such tactics to foment chaos and overthrow our Republic.

One of the many interesting speakers at the Preparedness Expos was Aaron S. Zelman. He had formed an organization titled "Jews For the Preservation of Firearms Ownership." Having studied history as a Jewish man, he specifically knew what his people had experienced at the hands of the Nazis. He wanted to make sure that history (once more) would not be repeated and that the 2nd Amendment would never be destroyed through any of the corrupted laws and regulations that were being forced upon the public back in the 1980's and 90's.

It always started with registration; getting everyone's names and information. Then they would gradually pass more restricting laws. It would be like in the analogy of the "frog in the pot," where the water is slowly heated up until suddenly it is too late—and because it was done ever so slowly, the frog would not see it coming until it was too late for it to get away. So too, this is how they would slowly began to manipulate us, playing on our F.E.A.R.s until it was too late; they had succeeded in convincing the well-meaning and gullible public. Just as they did in Germany, Russia, and China, with all those False Flags and crisis actors being used to manipulate people's emotions. These more modern day crisis actors and various False Flags would once more fool millions to believe that if they just removed all firearms from society, we would then be able to live more peacefully, etc., blah, blah, blah.

One of the other individuals I interviewed was a black/ African American militia member. It was interesting to speak with him about his opinions and beliefs, and I asked him some candid and specific questions regarding him being a member of one of the militias. I explained that because of how the media had been demonizing the militias as (supposedly) being prejudiced against anyone not white, I wanted to know whether, since he was black, he had experienced a lot of prejudice since becoming a member.

I felt that he was being candid with his answers, which totally showed what a lie this was. He stated that some of his closest friends were fellow white militia members, who treated him with great respect. He stated that they would be willing to risk their life for him, just as he would for them. He experienced a great fellowship with the many militia members he had gotten to know since he had become a major member during the last several years.

He also expressed something else which I found interesting: that in actuality, those who he felt were not being truthful about their true feelings toward blacks and minorities were often the same who outwardly, publicly, claimed to be so concerned about black civil rights. Instead, it was obvious to him that they were just stating these things to get the "black vote" to be elected into positions of political power, such as many within the Democratic party did, and many who would be termed "progressive" and "liberal" in their political positions. It was obvious to him how they wanted their vote, yet they did not really want them to be fully empowered to make changes in the world that might threaten that power.

Yes, it was quite an enlightening and insightful conversation with a man of great integrity and wisdom, who also understood that so much was being instigated covertly by the cabal through their socialist agenda—just as Dr. King had been so aware of. Just as Dr. King, he knew how important it was to protect all of our rights, especially the 2nd Amendment. He wanted to make sure that as many others as possible would know these facts, so that history would not be repeated once again.

Red-Pilling and Crisis Actors

As I look back on what this man, who I felt had a lot of integrity and virtue, passionately shared with me, I could definitely say that he had "Red Pilled" himself. Because he had, he would never again be so easily fooled and manipulated by the fake news media.

The phrase "being Red Pilled," is, of course, from the movie *The Matrix*. Those of us who have experienced being Red Pilled know that there was a lot more Truth to that movie than most people realize. It was presented in sort of an "allegorical way," and was a major analogy of those of us who have chosen to take the Red Pill, to see and acknowledge the Truth no matter the consequences. The rest of society, the masses, have up until recently chosen the "Blue Pill": to stay "asleep" and accept and believe, like "sheeple," all of the disinformation, lies, and propaganda that the mainstream media constantly pushes upon us.

I also want to specifically mention one of the most famous modern day False Flags. It occurred over 8 years ago and a huge number of crisis actors were involved in it.

I know that many of you who are reading this book, because of you have believed the official, final (public) report about it and were brainwashed/mind-controlled through the Operation Mockingbird fake news media, may get very upset and think that it is "impossible" for the (corrupt/controlled/black-mailed, etc.) officials to have been able to pull off a fake event and not be exposed before now.

But, whether it be the Kennedy Assassination, 9-11, or any of the many other historical examples of such manipulation of historical facts, we must be willing to always re-examine what the (actual, real) facts are. We must not let what we heard through (official) mainstream media sources be our only litmus test to determine the authenticity of any event. We must be willing to re-examine all kinds of things that we were told was the truth, only to find out that it was NOT the truth.

I feel that even if you get upset with me, at least allow yourself the possibility of thinking that this is true, despite the propaganda of the mainstream media. The media constantly also claims that individuals like me and Mr. Downs are just "conspiracy theorists", involved in "lunatic fringe subjects." At least, take a look at what is specifically mentioned in the Internet link below, a list of over 33 reasons why we need to question and challenge the official, final verdict of this particular staged false flag. Yes, I am referring to the "Sandy Hook shooting," that officially occurred on December 14, 2012.

No matter how so-called convinced you are that everything happened as the officials claimed it did, give yourself a chance to (re-)examine the case with another source of information. You will, at least, have to admit that these 33 important unanswered questions DO (definitely!) need to be answered. The officials just either ignored and/or glossed over these (obvious) inconvenient contradictions and facts that DO bring into question so much about the final public verdict.

I specifically remember the interviews of two emergency hospital doctors, who were both very suspicious about this final verdict regarding the Sandy Hook shootings. Why? Because they both had done some research of their own right after all the (alleged) events of Sandy Hook. They (unfortunately I do not remember their names) stated that when they checked with every hospital and emergency ward in the area that would or should have received any shooting victims from the Sandy Hook school shootings, they could find no record of anyone having been checked in that was connected with any such shooting that (supposedly) had occurred on that specific date and time.

Now, the cabal has many times gone into the public records to make up, change and/or add to what was already (originally) there, to falsify records to match the official, public version of events. It is possible that since the date of the "Sandy Hook shooting," once again the cabal has made up and/or faked history upon us, so that the records would now "prove" that such an event occurred, to once again fool us with these (so-called) "historical facts."

Here is that link about the Sandy Hook Shooting. It is possible that this link may suddenly stop working because the cabal causes it to become disabled. If that occurs, I suggest you type this or a similar phrase, "Questions and contradictions about the Sandy Hook Shooting," in the "Search" bar. But here is the link, which as of the final publishing of this book still worked:

https://thefreedomarticles.com/sandy-hook-3rd-anniversary-hoodwinked/

I also remember that right after the "Sandy Hook Shooting" had occurred, the next false flag event was the "Boston Marathon bombing." Numerous researchers have noticed many inconsistencies in the official version of the events, both about the Sandy Hook Shooting and the Boston Marathon bombing. When they took a look at all the photos that had been released to the public, they discovered (which I clearly could see, myself) that the so-called principal of the Sandy Hook School, that had supposedly died in the "Sandy Hook Shooting," was suddenly now alive ("resurrected"?) and was one of the participants in the Boston Marathon race. Oh, yes, this is true. A few other crisis actors who supposedly died before were also all now "alive and well, once more."

Another individual who supposedly got mortally wounded from the bomb blast, supposedly lost his two legs. At least, that is what the officials tried to make us believe. But when some of the researchers checked out his past, they found out that he was actually a Vietnam Vet who had lost his two legs during that war. This was obviously another faked false flag event which, once again, a huge number of crisis actors were a part of.

Well, some medical experts who examined one of the public photos released of this event made a comment, stating that if this was a real emergency and he had really just lost his two legs, no authentic medical personnel would have him sitting upright in the wheelchair; he would have bled out right away, very fast. He would, instead, have been placed laying down with his upper legs supported upward, so that less blood would be lost from the horrible wounds of both legs being blown off. The fact that he was sitting up made them truly question whether this whole thing actually occurred.

What is interesting, is that Ralph Meany, the friend I mentioned in the earlier chapter about Jesus and Mary Magdalene, has always had a certain quality about him (along with him having been long since Red Pilled). Many people have something hidden deep inside that they are emotionally and spiritually struggling with, that has been causing them major inner conflicts, but they did not know what to do about it or how to solve their moral dilemma. Ralph has shared with me that so many times, he would meet someone, and he would just "intuitively" suddenly bring up different subjects "for no apparent reason." (He is very psychic.) This would allow the person to get the things off their chest.

Ralph shared with me one day how he had met this young lady, and he immediately sensed that she was struggling with a moral dilemma. He suddenly felt he had to start talking about False Flags and the Crisis Actors who participated in these faked, hoaxed events.

No sooner had he brought up these events, and specifically mentioned about the Sandy Hook Shootings being a good example of such an event, than the young lady admitted to him that she, herself, was (or rather, had been up until then) a crisis actor. Because of being out of work for a while and kind of desperate, she had responded to an ad in a publication. She had had to sign a non-disclosure form, and this then led to her being involved in False Flags.

But now she was in a moral conflict about what she had been doing, she thought it was wrong to trick and fool the public about these events. She had come to realize that the "message" was always the same, both on a conscious level, as well as on a subconscious programmed level: if everyone would just give up their guns then the world be so much a safer place, blah, blah, blah.

She admitted that she had just experienced becoming Red Pilled, having Awakened to the real Truth and the real agenda that the cabal was involved with (which was to totally disarm the public so that they could then take over the country, without anyone being able to stop them.)

It was most interesting and revealing to get this "straight from the horse's mouth": both an admittance from an actual (now former) crisis actor who had participated in various False Flags, as well as confirmation of what the specific agenda was. The agenda of totally disarming the public, so that they would not be able to protect themselves from all the organized chaos, mayhem, and mass murder that would occur once everyone allowed themselves to be programmed and give up their Right to protect themselves.

Another Cosmic Stamp of Approval

As mentioned, while writing the other chapter I strongly sensed the presence of a Higher Light Being, who I realized was actually the Higher Self of Tolkien. He had basically expressed his definite agreement and support to what I was sharing in this book, and he was glad that I was now clarifying the fact that his story was true, and that this was to be shared with everyone else who would read this book. As Celeste and I were in the process of compiling this chapter, now too, I suddenly felt and sensed another Higher Light Being. It was someone who had been around me for a while, and I realized that this was none other than the Higher Self of Mr. Downs, or rather "Mr. Upper."

He told me that he really liked me referring to him as Mr. Upper, which I did because of how upbeat, positive, and inspiring he had been with us, his students, despite all of the so-called negative things that he shared with us. He wanted to thank me and to express how much he appreciated that I had devoted so much of this chapter to my memory of him and what he had taught us while he had been my teacher back in 1972. His information had such a positive impact upon me, and it had helped to both inspire me and to Empower me to continue educating myself about the real facts, the inconvenient truths, of the past. This helped me be much more able to recognize all the inconvenient truths of present day, recognizing what the cabal was covertly doing and how they have lied to us all the time through the mainstream media.

What he had done for me was to help me to be more fully Red Pilled. He was so well balanced and unique. Yet, he is so much like millions of other Americans today, like the many billions of other people in the "Silent Majority" of not only this country, but also those in other cultures and countries. We should never stereotype and/or categorize people in the way the cabal-controlled media constantly has attempted to do. The cabal aims to continue to create chaos, so that they can pit everyone against one another.

Yes, here on this 3D level, Mr. Upper was one of the greatest inspirations I had—not only as a teacher, but as a fellow human being who cared so compassionately about other human beings.

But like many others I have met since then, he has so often been misunderstood and unjustly maligned by others who did not understand, or did not want to understand, who someone like him really was. It is very clear to me and to those of us who have been Red Pilled, we all have a certain natural rapport, affinity and understanding of others who also choose to be Red Pilled.

Remember the point that was made earlier: if one is not capable of discerning, of recognizing what has occurred in our collective historical past, all those many inconvenient truths and False Flags, how then will we able to discern what the cabal has been doing in more modern times? If we cannot admit and acknowledge to ourselves all the dysfunctional behavior and skeletons in our family closets and/or the behavior that keeps us stuck in dysfunctional and toxic relationships of our past, we are doomed to repeat not only our collective history again and again, but we are also going to keep making the same relationship mistakes and keep drawing to ourselves the same type of personal toxic emotional relationships over and over again in the future.

So, yes, there IS definitely a strong correlation, whether one realizes it or not, between our inability to discern and admit these psychological collective patterns of human history, what certain forces have done to manipulate us, and our inability to recognize and admit various dysfunctional tendencies and traits that continue to keep the unfulfilling toxic personal relationships occurring.

Bottom Line on False Flags and Crisis Actors

And bottom line, as I look back with much greater wisdom and understanding, especially now in the process of compiling this book with my own Beloved and Cosmic True Love, Celeste, I want to make another point. Celeste also just strongly confirmed this and wanted me to make this very important point to all of those of you who are reading this book—especially to those of you who might have gotten very upset when we brought up that the "Sandy Hook Shooting" was a False Flag and how Crisis Actors were involved.

I remember that several years ago, I was contacted by someone who had originally been on my email list. In one of my earlier email blasts, I had mentioned how all the suppressed documentation that had been compiled by many researchers had showed the "shooting" to be a false flag. This woman had contacted me because she was upset about me doing this, it upset her that I could "even believe" that the "official public story" was not for real. She claimed that she supposedly knew one of the family members that had been injured or killed in the "Sandy Hook Shootings." I had read much of the research that showed all of the manipulation of facts and details of the actual events had merely been a "drill" that was then reported as an actual event. When I pressed her for more specific details, she quickly turned the conversation away from the subject, claiming she "didn't want to open up old (emotional) wounds."

But I attempted to say to her, which I truly believe is a very important point: these "old wounds," as she put it, will NOT ever, totally heal, if these wounds continue to "fester"—just like a lot of inconvenient truths that totally contradict the official, public version of events will NEVER heal when there are falsehoods, disinformation, and cover-ups of the true facts still going on. Wounds will never heal before they are totally exposed and truth is victorious over all the lies.

I remember clearly one of the videos that were going around on the internet until the cabal censored it by removing it. It showed an individual who claimed to be one of the parents of one of the children that were (supposedly) killed at Sandy Hook. Something was specifically very contradictory to anyone who really takes a look at it: During the first second of the film, when the camera is first turned on, this man is just laughing and smiling. Then, when he realizes that he is being filmed, he immediately attempts to get into character, acting very sorrowful, about his supposed child having just been killed in the shooting. But even though he attempts to then make it seem believable, after viewing it a number of times, what with the initial, obviously opposite behavior he was displaying and then attempting to fool us into believing the exact opposite of what he was really feeling, it was just too obvious that he was just an actor (not a very good one).

And then, talk about insult on top of injury: They had already set up the trust fund earlier, actually right *before* the "shooting." to play on everyone's emotions. These crisis actors all played the role they were supposed to, in order to fool people in giving up their hard-earned money. After really checking out the numerous bits of information that clearly showed so many examples of things being made up to fool us into believing this whole thing, I truly feel this was a scam.

Just consider basic psychology (as in "psychology 101") anyone who has studied normal human psychology knows that for a real family who has just lost a child through some very (real) tragic event, the last thing they want is to have any publicity—they just want to be left alone to "lick their tragic (emotional) wounds." No, unless human nature has suddenly changed on us all, no normal human would ever want to have public exposure after such an experience, being interviewed and bothered by the press and media. But these so-called parents of all these children immediately started to get interviewed by the media. And of course, their main message was, just as it was in all the other False Flags, about how once the public just gives up their guns, well, then, all violence would just go away. Of course, what they forgot to mention is that the criminals would still have theirs, and everyone would then be victimized just as they were in Nazi Germany, Russia and China.

Of course, it should be very obvious why Hitler never invaded Switzerland, if one understands one of the Swiss' requirements for every citizen living there: They must each have a firearm and know how to professionally and safely use it. And of course, crime has always been very low there, despite the mass number of weapons. But the point was that it was because all the citizens were armed that the Nazis never invaded that country. Of course, it is true they were considered a "neutral" country that chose not to be involved in WWII, but that would not have stopped the Nazis from invading and taking it over. The only reason they did not was because they knew that their own casualties would have been too high. The Swiss being armed would have literally made it near impossible, they would have lost a majority of their military even trying to invade.

The Declaration of Independence and St. Germain

Something historical that many people do not know: On that very historical date of August 2, 1776, when our Forefathers had gathered to first write the Declaration of Independence and right before they all actually signed it, they were sitting there for a few moments. They were pondering what they were doing and that they were totally risking their very lives by daring to challenge the power of (Rothschild-controlled) King George and his tyrannical taxation over the colonists. It is mentioned in the "Minutes of the Meeting," locked up in the National Archives, that at that moment a "magnificent being" suddenly appeared before all of them, standing on the balcony of "Independence Hall." The being gave a powerful and passionate three to four minute speech, imploring them and inspiring them about how important this was, not only for themselves, but for all future generations to come. He stated that it was Divine Will that this was to occur, and he ended his dramatic speech with these words "Now, gentlemen, please sign that Document!"

This "magnificent being" or man who had so suddenly materialized before them all was none other than the Ascended Master St. Germain. He was to appear to them later, on Sept. 17, 1787, to inspire them once again to write and sign the US Constitution and Bill of Rights. He very much Over-Lighted these courageous men to make sure that every possible Right that needed to be protected into the future would be a part of this Divinely Inspired Document. (He is also pictured on the back of the $2 bill—the "dude" that has a hat on his head).

He had the ability to see into the possible future timelines, he saw how the cabal would attempt to control those living in the future generations and how they would covertly plan and plot to control the entire world before they would be stopped. He knew that the illuminati would attempt many times to accomplish their long-range goals. And he knew it would be far more difficult for them to succeed if the citizens of this great nation would have included in the many Amendments a "Divinely Inspired Guarantee" that all future generations would have a Right to protect their Sovereignty, homes, property, etc. (2nd Amendment) against those who would attempt to both covertly and violently to infiltrate them; if the citizens had a Divine Right and responsibility to have the means to stop tyrants from taking over and the means to stop certain extreme elements that sought, through organized violence, looting, and overall lawlessness, to destroy this newly formed Republic. An armed citizenry would have a chance to defend themselves from these extremists, whoever they might be, and this would be a very strong deterrent against "all enemies foreign and domestic" from either invading or infiltrating the nation, it would make it much more difficult for these hostile elements to attempt a take-over and to destroy the Republic.

In the same way, a strong military is a strong deterrent against any other country being willing to attack, and would actually allow the world to ultimately become truly peaceful. The consciousness of the world would change, as the military

("White Hat Alliance and Q") would now be the "Guardians of Peace," helping bring an end to world war and bring in the long prophesied Golden Age of peace. This was St. Germain's Divinely Inspired Vision of the future, and he understood the complexities and challenges of the time we are living in now and how the imbalanced forces would attempt to fool humanity through numerous False Flags.

A small bit of information about St. Germain, while he was still just a Count, living on this 3D physical level, in the early 18th century, over in Europe: He was known as the "man of mystery," and he was an alchemist who could easily precipitate precious gemstones and transmute metal into pure gold nuggets before everyone's eyes. He dressed very "flamboyant," he rode around in a coach driven by two white horses, and he had a lot of friends in the royalty. He refused, though, to ever meet with the Rothschilds, as he knew they were aligned with the dark, satanic forces and were a major part of the whole illuminati of control over the entire planet's fiat financial banking system.

This is why he started a large "Freedom Trust" that would ultimately be used, both energetically and literally, to destroy this other corrupt and evil system of total control and enslavement over the entire world. Lately, he has been energetically helping and Over-Lighting the entire Q and White Hat Alliance in defeating the cabal, and helping them set up and activate the new Global Quantum Financial system that is in the process of replacing the old corrupt fiat, federal reserve banking system.

It was while he was living in Europe that his own Beloved, Twin-Flame, Lady Portia, known also as the Goddess of Justice and Opportunity, would physically manifest herself around him.

She personally inspired and helped him to do so many of the things he became historically famous for. "Behind every great man is a really great and Empowered Divine Feminine Goddess!"

St. Germain also knew that False Flags, on another level, would be utilized by the Higher Light Forces to test the ability of not only the Volunteers in Earth embodiment, but also those of the masses who would be getting vibrationally ready to experience their own Spiritual Ascension. This would be a way to energetically determine whether these future citizens would be able to truly Discern and recognize these False Flags of the cabal, to expose and stop these from ever occurring again.

It was his and his fellow Higher Light Beings' perception that there were some things that the Higher Light Forces were not allowed to stop, such as many of these covertly planned False Flags of the cabal. They were allowed, though, to Divinely Intervene to downsize how extreme these types of secretly planned events could be, since many of the False Flags actually did involve mind-controlled shooters who were programmed to kill as many innocent bystanders as they could, and which would involve more than one shooter (as many witnesses reported) as opposed to just the one that was described through the media. The cabal planned to kill many dozens, if not hundreds of people. Other False Flags do not have any people actually being killed, but are still used with the crisis actors as a way to psychologically manipulate the public to demand that more laws are passed to eventually outlaw all guns (ultimately to disarm the general public).

In the False Flags where there should have been many more killed or wounded than there actually was, Higher Light

Forces intervened and they drastically lowered the total number of casualties to a very small number from what would have happened if they had not intervened.

The Elect Would Be Fooled

But St. Germain understood that even though he and the Higher Forces did intervene as much as they were allowed, these events were also utilized afterwards, as stated, as a way to determine, energetically how many of the souls presently incarnated upon Earth could actually Discern what had taken place (because, as was stated in the Bible, "the Elect would be fooled"). Another way to relate to this major spiritual test of Discernment, is referred to as "going down the rabbit hole." I have another way of relating this; since everything is so "turned upside down and backward" with so many energetic timeline changes occurring, one may have to "go UP the Rabbit Hole, and then DOWN the Worm Hole" to discover the Truth which is not easy to accept.

It may be that one has a lot of f.e.a.r. of doing this, of allowing oneself to be Red Pilled, because when one finally does, it is like the phrase "once the Geni gets out of the bottle, there is absolutely no way she will ever want to go back." But for many, this f.e.a.r. has to do with the concern of what their family and friends will think of them once they have been Red Pilled. Just as in the movie *The Matrix,* once you choose the Red Pill rather than just keep ingesting the Blue Pill, you can never go back again to where you were. Your consciousness has totally shifted, and you cannot any longer operate at the vibrational level where you were before.

Yes, most likely, if they are not Red Pilled, your family and friends may tend to think that you have now suddenly lost your mind, that you are now just some "fringe conspiracy theorist" and you need "professional help" (to get you back in the "box"). Maybe you care too much about what they think about you, fear that you will lose their respect and fear them even not wanting to ever speak with you. Well, actually, once you come out the other side of the Rabbit Hole, you will most likely NOT want to hang out with such narrow-minded, lower vibrational people with whom you now realize you do not really have much in common. This can be a real sense of Freedom and Liberation, to really be yourself, maybe for the first time in your entire life. Now, you can reach out to other fellow Red Pilled people, who like you are really beginning to enjoy their own life. You can be more authentic, happy and balanced than you have felt for a very long time.

Summary of the Most Important Points

So, as we come toward the end of this chapter, I want to once more summarize the very important point that was presented already but needs to be emphasized once more. To those who read this book and feel that they ARE, REALLY, ready to connect more directly with their own Beloved and Cosmic True Love, but still believe that the Sandy Hook event and all the other numerous False Flags all occurred as they were presented through the mainstream media, rather than believing the true facts that these were all staged events to manipulate our minds, consciousness and perception of reality:

If one cannot discern all of the many dysfunctional, manipulated and covert events occurring collectively through our history and more recently (that is, our "collective, outer relationship" with reality and history), then how can one discern the very qualities and traits that one has, that one has *always* exhibited, that caused one or more dysfunctional personal relationships to occur, where certain imbalanced and/or dysfunctional personal relationships always ended up so unfulfilled and disappointing? If one cannot discern and really understand these two connected relationship dynamics then one is NOT ready—yet—to connect with their Cosmic True Love. A little more energetic, emotional work is needed, to energetically reposition one's consciousness, to allow one to easily discern these important differences.

This should actually be a GREAT incentive for those who have a True, Pure Heart's Desire to be with their Beloved to allow themselves to be Red Pilled. To go down the Rabbit Hole, and to be willing, with an open and discerning mind, to examine those 33 questions about why the official version of Sandy Hook did not occur. If one cannot "get it," then one is not yet ready. As our parents and teachers used to say to us all the time, we just need to "finish our Homework—then we can go out and play with our friends."

Yes, this is the challenge: are you REALLY ready to truly connect with your Divine Other Half, or are you still refusing to notice all those "hidden in plain sight" details, facts and inconvenient truths that need to be acknowledged, once and for all?

Take that Red Pill! Yes, go for it, your Own Beloved is waiting for you to do this. This SHOULD be the great incentive you need that will allow you a much greater chance to reconnect. I cannot promise when or how this will occur, because of free will and so many other factors which are unique to each of you. You must be in Alignment with Divine Will and the Divine Plan, and you must truly allow yourselves the opportunity to admit and acknowledge all that you can.

Once you have Red Pilled yourself, you must be willing to do whatever your Higher Self guides you to then do. Yes, it will no doubt take courage, but once your consciousness has shifted, you will discover how fear has already begun to leave you and how Liberated you feel, being able to now discern and see things from an entirely different point of view. It frees you up for all kinds of wonderful and unique Blessings, Miracles and Divine Synchronicities that only your own Beloved and Cosmic True Love can manifest for you!

CHAPTER 29

Even "Bothersome" Bugs and "Pesky" Insects Need Love Too!

Below is a copy of one more email that I sent to everyone on my email list, which I felt was perfect to include here—almost at the end of Celeste's and my book.

Even "Bothersome" Bugs and "Pesky" Insects Need Love Too!

By Michael Ellegion & Celeste

Something very Extraordinary occurred here in Celeste's & my apartment recently, which was both, initially, very challenging. As well as "irritating," until I allowed myself to really "tune-in" to what was going on, and why.

Many of you may also, assume, by the specific "title" that I used for this email, [some] of what I might or will be sharing about. Yes, this particular "assumption" is correct, that "even bugs and insects [also] need Love, too."

That instead of ever killing insects, no matter how "pesky, bothersome and irritating" some of them are, we should still accord them much love, care and compassion, rather than just killing them whenever we are so inclined.

I, myself, is one of those who, out of kindness, consideration and compassion for all life—even some "pesky and/or bothersome" type insects, in the past would have used the phrase, "I would never kill a flea." I would say that my INTENT or desire NOT to 'have to [ever] kill such TYPES of insects, bugs and critters WOULD be correct.

But, "in the real world" where I have had to "deal with such "TYPES" of really "bad boy" type bugs and insects. That tend to "sting (with honey bees being an exception—I would NEVER, under any circumstances, EVER kill a honey bee!) or bite, or tend to be very pesky and bothersome. Because, that IS their 'physiological nature" for them to be "that way."

I have, a number of times, "struggled" with this "moral and ethical dilemma." Of really NOT wanting to ["have to"] ever kill any insect or bug, no matter what type they happen to be. But, as I said, "in the real world," where many types of insects, will come into our residence and "make themselves at home. " By crawling and flying around where ever they "decide' or "think" they can, is, well, "not part of my agreement" for them to have done so.

So, what does one do, to make sure that this does not occur? Many people, who also, like myself, attempt to never kill any insect, will try to always be "kind and compassionate." But, we realize that we also have to not allow "chaos" of any kind to "creep into our life." Because, the next thing you know, "every Tom, Dick and Harry" will just, well, will just show up and act like they "own the place"!

And this same "dilemma" has been going on, ever since we as humans have "occupied" our homes and places of residence." No matter whether it is a small apartment, like my own, or a larger structure house, with more square feet. Other "critters, bugs and insects" are bound to show up and also "occupy" our living spaces as well. So just "get over it!" Right, or should we "Go Crazy" and get into the normal "irritating mood." Of resenting them, these little critters. Bugs and insects, that crawl, fly and move around wherever and whenever they please.

Or, do we allow ourselves to "come from" another, entirely unexpected and unimaginable "head space" and being able to "look outside the box." That, maybe, something far more Extra-ordinary" is now beginning to occur, in our "relationships" with these "particular TYPES" of bugs and insects, than has occurred before.

Because they DO, definitely "need our Love, kindness and compassion." While, at the same time, it is actually possible, as in the concept, of making everything, truly "WIN-WIN for ourselves. And this DOES or SHOULD also include those"pesky, bothersome, irritating" type insects that "invade" our living spaces. Do not they truly also "need our Love"—and maybe, even, our HELP to now EVOLVE onto a Higher level of, yes, "Insect & Bug Ascension."

Which means that these types of insects, such as mosquitoes, cockroaches, army & fire ants, fruit flies, fleas, ticks, bed bugs, dust mites, yellow jackets, hornets (whether "normal", or the new "killer hornets" that the cabal just "created"). Any insect or bug who's "physiological nature"—which they can't help this—this is JUST HOW THEY ARE—tend to "bother" us by flying around and irritating us, and who will sting or bite at us, whenever they can. They ALL need love, and all want to also EVOLVE, whether we understand all of this or not.

You, see, for a long time, for quite a number of years, in fact, I have been attempting, to the best way I knew how to, of "dealing with" this "moral dilemma." Of NOT wanting to kill, harm, or hurt, in any way, EVEN these types of insects. And, yet, I was forced to "have to" so many times, after attempting to "communicate with them telepathically." Of "sending out energetic messages that only the insects could understand," I actually Prayed to God, and to the Higher Forces, about this, and of personally Envisioning and Visualizing that these type of "bothersome and irritating bugs and insects" would just "go away" and "leave me—and also everyone else, as well—to just leave us alone."

Even though I attempted this many, many times"—actually, with a "sincere, true, pure heart's desire" it never "seemed" to ACTUALLY, REALLY ever work. Because, these same "bothersome and irritating" critters would STILL show up. The whole "process," like a "insect nightmare Ground Hog Day" would just—still—repeat itself, time and time again, with no change that I could ever REALLY tell.

Oh, yes, there would be the normal "calm before the storm," of "moments" of a few weeks, where I would not detect any of these type of insects being round. And, then, all of a sudden, BOOM, back they were with a "vengeance," and determination, to "build another [insect] home," or to just exist in my own space, of using my space as "uninvited guests," whether I liked it or not. "That is just how things are." Or, are they? Yes, are "things," like this "never-ending-parade" of these types of insects and bugs, always going to keep showing up "no matter what we do"?

Oh, yes, I have heard of certain types of little "energy devices" that are supposed to actually work, with "keeping them away," without [supposedly] "bothering us [we humans] in any way. That these energy devices "emit" a certain "frequency" that makes it very uncomfortable, for the insects and bugs and they [supposedly] "leave and never return." "Guaranteed" [supposedly]. I will admit that I, myself, have never used one of these types of equipment or devices to do this very thing. Of actually being able, forever, of making these types of "bothersome and irritating" insects and bugs to stay away. I actually, a few times, considered doing this very thing. But something stopped me from doing so. Why? I initially didn't know, but my "Guidance" told me not to, "for some OTHER reason or PURPOSE" that I would soon know or come to realize.

And just recently, I had another of these "invasions" of "bothersome and irritating" insects. Which, like before, here I was, once more, like the "endless insect 'Ground Hog Day" of repetition." I was, again, still dealing with this "moral and ethical challenge" of not wanting to kill, and definitely *not to ever hurt or to cause pain in any way* to these insects. That is, even when I have been "forced to kill them," when there were SO MANY of them, as just occurred.

I mean, I was literally "inundated" with huge numbers of them, more than I had ever seen, of all kinds of these types of "bothersome and irritating" critters and bugs. Most of who showed up, from what I could determine, was dozens, if not—literally—hundreds of little "fruit flies", who were just flying everywhere.

But they would especially show up whenever I would be preparing my smoothie. Of when I would be cutting open my various types of fruit, such as bananas, apples, oranges, mangos, papayas, etc. They always could sense or smell this, and "wha-la"! There they were, in large numbers, just having a "field day," with gleeful anticipation of another "free meal." Of them very suddenly—boy they are fast—of swooping down onto the large plate where all my cut-up pieces of fruit happened to be. And I would swat at them, and even attempt to kill them, to rid myself of their "pesky, bothersome and irritating" presence. Every day, this would be repeated. And it seems they "brought their friends and family with them." That "word had gotten out" among the entire insect population of fruit flies," that they were guaranteed a free meal. That all they had to do was, well, just make themselves at home, and that I would provide them all, and their friends and family, with these free and delicious meals. All they had to do was "show up"—in force!

And was I irritated with this, of especially HOW MANY had begun to "manifest" themselves in my apartment; it was getting out of hand, out of control. With no "solution" of what I could do to stop this inundation of SO MANY of them, and their numbers only seem to be increasing. I was getting very desperate, but did not know WHAT I was actually going to do to stop this, and to "turn things around. To finally get things under control once more, and to cause all of these insects to disappear and not come back.

Finally, I turned to Celeste, my Beloved Twin-Flame, who had always had answers and Insights about everything I had ever asked of her. Sometimes, though, she did "challenge" me, by not, immediately, sharing with me the exact or specific answer or solution to a particular challenge. I was supposed to "flex/ work out my consciousness muscles" and really tune-in, myself, to what the "solution and/or answer" actually was. Because, had she given me the [specific or exact] "answer or solution" right away, rather than allowing me to "struggle a little, I would not have really been able to understand and feel, first hand, what was occurring. As she had shared afterwards, this would have deprived me of this incredible "journey of discovery," that, yes, I would have been deprived of.

In fact, this is also WHY, as Q thru their "Q Drops" that have revealed SOME of what the White Hat Alliance are doing to defeat the entire satanic deep state cabal. They must ALSO ALLOW the masses of humanity to LEARN through their struggle, of learning Discernment. As they have stated many times, "sometimes we just have to let the people learn by seeing and experiencing," first hand, what the cabal is capable of doing to control and manipulate humanity through the fake news, propaganda controlled mainstream ["Lamestream"] news media. In other words, you cannot, often, just "TELL" a person something, because they would NOT believe it. You have to SHOW them and allow them to experience it, before they—finally—understand what is really going on.

So, too, what I was about to come to realize, or to become "self-actualized" about, was a very interesting "revelation" about this whole "insect and bug problem." That I, like so many on this planet, was relating to it in an entirely wrong or uncorrect way. Yes, I purposely "misspelled" the word "incorrect" as "uncorrect." Why, you might ask? Well, for the same reason that I also, purposely "misspell" such words as "insane," to that of "unsane."

For as George Orwell, who the cabal likes to "ignore" as much as possible, especially when he made a specific mention about what he refers to as the cabal's use of "double speak" words and phrases. The illuminati/power elite had—purposely, created certain words, that when you say or speak those particular words, terms or phrases, actually end up, subconsciously, meaning the exact opposite of what they were "supposed" to or "appear" to mean. Because, when one "dissects" the word "insane," for example, they realize that the using of the "in" in front of the word "sane," DOES, actually mean they ARE "sane," NOT the opposite of sane, or rather un-sane, as in NOT being sane. Yes, so, too, to use another word, such as "incorrect," one is doing the exact, same thing, of taking a word or term, that is SUPPOSED to "mean" something different. But, instead, by putting the "in" in front of the word "correct" we have done the same thing as we did by putting the "in" in front of the word "sane." So, by choosing to use "un" in front of the word "correct." I Am doing this same thing, being more correct and/or accurate. Yes, it is being truly Uncorrect, NOT "incorrect." Hopefully, now that I have, literally "spelled it out," you get my point. So, let's be as correct as we can be, as verses being not correct, or uncorrect.

For many years, I realize, that in this "moral dilemma," of not wanting to kill, but especially not wanting to "hurt or harm" any living thing, which is why I am a vegetarian, of choosing not to eat any flesh from animals and other living things.

I do, admit, that once in awhile, I have "sinned" or acted a little "hypocritical," because I have chosen to eat some "lox," or dried smoked wild salmon, along with my soft goat cheese. With a slice of red onion, a slice of avocado (with some lime or lemon squeezed on it, of course, with a little sprinkled pink Himalayan salt, white pepper on that) with pesto sauce, all on a delicious gourmet sandwich that I have made periodically (yes, it IS an "oral orgasm" in the mouth!).

But, other than that "sin," I have not eaten any other fish, and will perhaps one day, also "forgo" this last "sin" of having "indirectly" contributed to some suffering that the salmon obviously experienced when it was killed. I have to acknowledge to myself, that this IS—at least—a mild form of "hypocrisy," of me, still, indulging myself, with this use of the {wild] salmon "lox."

I would never go to the trouble to fish or "catch" a salmon, or to "fix" a fresh or frozen piece of wild salmon. Instead, I use the lox, on a sandwich. For a long time, I did not do even this, but I guess I got "tempted" by remembering what it was like to eat such a sandwich. I always used the very healthy, organic, flourless, sprouted 7 grain bread, by the "Food For Life" Company. Which has NO soy in it, as soy is bad for a guy's Testosterone levels in their body, especially as one "ages or grows older." One wants to definitely retain as much of their Testosterone level as possible. So, soy, even organic soy, while definitely being better than GMO soy, is still not good to be used; there is a lot better and more healthy vegi proteins available.

But getting back to this "insect and bug challenge," and what to do about it. So, I spent some time to truly "tune into" what, just exactly, was the answer and/or solution to my "bug/insect infestation." As well as WHY this had occurred, in the first place to [even "suddenly"] become such a major, overwhelming challenge, and what to do about it?

I felt my Higher Self begin to give me some very deep and "interesting" Insights to this whole thing, some of which might be considered "mind-blowing." Here, in a "nut shell" is what I was shown, as well as a "reminder" of something that I had already been doing, that had led up to this "sudden infestation."

For some time now, ever since I first moved into this apartment, the few times that I experienced some ants, spiders, flies, mosquitoes or various other "unwelcome" type bugs and insects suddenly make their appearance. And, if they were in any way "irritating" me by specifically being in places that I especially did not want them, such as the kitchen counters, or were just flying around near me very close, or a spider who happened to craw onto my bed, etc. I always let them know that, first of all, I did NOT want to kill them, but if they "persisted," and continued to come back, then I would have to do so. I always attempted to give them a "fair warning" of what would happen if I did have to do this. I do not know if this really did work, but I truly attempted to do this, because I really did NOT want to actually have to kill them. I would usually very carefully, scoop them up, and take them outside, if I could, rather than kill them. But often it just was not that "convenient" to do this, and so I had to "take drastic action," and sometimes I would kill them.

But when I did, I always made sure I did it extremely fast, so that they did not have time to ever suffer any pain. And as I was doing this, what I term "compassionate mercy killing," I would, with as much Love and Compassion as I could muster, very sincerely "Bless" them. And, saying this spontaneous "energetic Mantra," I would state: "May you now come back/incarnate as either a Beautiful Butterfly or Honey Bee." In other words, something either "beautiful and/or useful." I truly believe that when I did this, that this helped them and/or allowed them, "Energetically" to do this very thing, of coming back as a Higher form of insect/bug that was more evolved and helpful for humankind.

Everything is so connected with our Intent and Motive, and that as humans, we are supposed to be more evolved than the insects, and we should be able to show mercy and compassion in our dealings with them. But, I do admit, also, that I have been "guilty" at times, of still being "irritated" with many of them for STILL coming into my apartment, and I didn't show very much "patience" with them when they would come around. But, still, when I was "forced" to kill them, I still attempted to be as Loving as I could when I did have to kill them. Because, as mentioned, I did not want them to ever suffer when I "took them out." I still could not seem to be able to totally communicate with them about NOT ever to come back; they still seemed to "persist" with "testing their fate' with me. I would say to them, "Hey, I warned you guys a number of times, and you are still coming back. Why?" Of course, I would never get any "answer." If they really did answer me, I never seemed to be able to "pick up any "response from them. I guess they just could not help themselves; that it was in their "psychological nature," of being these types of "bothersome bugs and pesky insects." That it was in their very nature to be "pests" and they couldn't do anything about it? Or could they, but they just didn't know "how"?

As I thought about my "apartment history" of interacting with various "unwanted bugs and insects of all kinds." Of what I did if they got to be in any way "unavoidably too irritating" and it was just not possible to "transport them outside." That I would then do that "mercy killing" and the "Mantra" that I would [SINCERELY feel] and say, each time I did.

As I contemplated about all this, I began to feel that the "answer" and/or "solution' to this whole very recent, and much more intense inundation of this huge insect and bug infestation. DID, in some way, have to do with what I had experienced earlier with the other, much, much less amount of bugs that had appeared before. But the exact answer still seemed Like "a Riddle, locked up inside a Puzzle, hidden in an Enigma, and wrapped up in a Paradox!"

As I was focused upon "solving" this dilemma, I began to get a much clearer understanding about this whole thing, and suddenly, I was shown much Insight. Which, I want to now share with everyone, and how this which I now know, could also be known and utilized by everyone else.

First, we all need to understand the fact that this planet has been a "drop-off" place for all kinds of species, whether it be different types of plants, insects and animals. And just as the human species, or rather the original "root race" and first human bodies created here, for souls to take Earth embodiment. So, too, each of the different plant, insect, and animal bodies, that were created, initially, and by whom, became available for new souls and spirits to take physical incarnation.

Initially, in the very beginning, it was part of the Creator's Divine Plan, to have Higher Beings manifest various different physical bodies that "physiologically" were ideal and in harmony for creating "Heaven on Earth." All of those different species, of plant, insect and animal, and, of course, human, WERE in total Energetic Harmony with each other and one another. There were no species that were out of harmony, whether it be the plants, insects or animals.

In the insect/bug kingdom, just as it was in the animal kingdoms, there were NO species that attacked or brought any harm to the others within or without the particular species. In other words, in the animal Kingdom, there were no "carnivores" that attacked, killed, ate or harmed another form of life. There were NO insects that "attacked, stung, bit or harmed," or even "irritated" other species in any way.

It was ONLY after the first negative beings came to this planet, and INTERFERED with the Divine Plan, and the "Guardians" who watched over and protected this "Garden of Eden." That was when other "species" that were NOT part of this [original] Divine Plan, began to manifest upon the planet. This was when the "ananokie" and later the draconians, reptilians and archons began to come here. And they created all kinds of new creations, with most being out of alignment with the original Divine Plan. This really screwed up the plan, with there now becoming the "survival of the fittest," those that were the most strongest, and most cunning, would be able to "survive."

These negative beings wanted, in fact, to literally create a "hell on earth," to change the original Heaven and Paradise on Earth, to a total hell of suffering. For not only human, but also for all animals and insects, as well. So, they created various forms of insects, specifically, that were designed/genetically created so that their very nature WAS to be "irritating, pesky and bothersome." Yes, they specifically did this, so that this would also take the more harmonious and relaxed state of existence, and turn it into a very stressful and negative place to be, live and exist. With swarms of horrible insects, flying, creeping and crawling everywhere, to make this a hellish place.

Yes, those insects and bugs, such as cockroaches, flies, fruit flies, ticks, nates, mosquitoes, hornets, yellowjackets, spiders, scorpions, fire ants, dust mites, etc.; most either sting, bite or eat those they get on. These are all mostly original creations of those first negative beings who came here. Oh, yes, these critters learned to not only survive well, but to adapt, on the physical level. And, of course, because of this, which also included the creation of carnivores animals and insects, and EVEN plants (giant "fly traps," etc.). The Higher Beings then had to do various "energetic alterations" to attempt to bring back some semblance of more balance and order, now that these other species had suddenly manifested here on Earth. And this caused other various "natural alterations" that Mother Nature was forced to have to do, to deal with these new species that had not originally existed, etc.

But on the "energetic spiritual level," these negative creators, also used a type of "Dark sorcery," a negative "curse," that "energetically entrapped" the spirit-soul essence of those who were forced to stay in this "endless loop." Of living out endless number of physical embodiments as these particular types of insects and bugs, and they were unable to free themselves of this very "parasitical" existence.

They definitely did not want to be forced into this type of existence, and to constantly, forever, fulfill their dark creator's plans of keeping Earth stuck in this endless, negative loop. Of creating a very dangerous, uncomfortable and irritating existence for animals and humans, of having to constantly be aware, of always being on the look-out for these types of insects and critters.

The dark beings knew that this would also help, "indirectly" to create more "loush" or negative energy from this constant "hellish" existence, that such types of insects and bugs would provide by their very "nature."

More recently, as Mother Earth is in the process of experiencing her planetary Ascension, it is obvious that as in the phrase, "the lamb will lay down with the lion." That, ultimately, for the animal kingdom, all species will and are in the process of "energetically adapting" to this massive change, both physically and spiritually. Many life forms that have been "carnivores" will become vegetarian and no longer "mortal enemies" to other species that they have "hunted and eaten."

In fact, some of those animals that may have become "extent," Celeste has told me, had not [totally] become extent. Instead, the Higher Forces removed the last few numbers of these particular species, and beamed them up into Light Ships [before] they actually, completely ceased to exist. They will bring them back in a more evolved physical body to be on Earth in the upcoming Golden Age.

In some cases, this will occur for various species of the animal kingdom, as well as for the insect kingdom. But, in other cases, those of us here on Earth, who are Higher Beings in Earth human embodiment, happen to have certain "spiritual karmic authority." Many of the Volunteers are "Honorary members" of the Karmic Board, and have been recently given certain, "special" authority. To help those "insect spirit-souls" to now be allowed to be set free from that "endless negative loop." They can now be allowed to free themselves, and "Ascend" to a Higher form of insect/bug, such as butterflies, honey bees, and yes, even Fire Flies.

Just recently, in fact, while I was power-walking, on my way to do some grocery shopping, a U-haul truck passed by on the other side of street, as I noticed the particular large scene that was shown on it's side. Most all U-haul trucks tend to have different scenes related to the particular state of the Union that it is representing. This particular scene was a very huge blown-up image of a "Fire

Fly." I had forgotten about how these very beautiful insects are usually only seen at night, when they come out and like little flying insect lanterns or candles, beautifully lighting up the night with the bright phosphorescence glow from their bodies. But because of how devastating and deadly the GMO's and chemical sprays, along with the high EMF fields, have been, this has decimated and almost killed a vast majority them off. Just as it has, the honey bees and other "positive and useful" type insects.

The Fire Flies used to be much more prevalent all over the Eastern states and even in other areas. Now, there are very few of them, as compared to much earlier years, and they are another, more "evolved" insect.

These other, "entrapped" insect soul-spirits, that can now be freed from their "endless irritating and pesky" existence, to come back as something either "beautiful and/or useful" that are more in harmony to human existence as well.

As I began to understand what had occurred many ages ago, and how these particular insect spirit-souls became "energetically entrapped" forever in this endless loop. I also tuned-in to the fact that recently, as the consciousness and energy of the Earth is rapidly raising. This is creating a major "shift" also in the consciousness of all these particular type of "bothersome and irritating" and even deadly forms of insects. They now want to be "freed" and to be able to evolve into these more evolved forms of insect life.

But, the "caveat" to this whole thing, is that some of this must be done by humans living here on Earth, who can act as "Intermediaries" for them, by "releasing" their soul-spirit essence from their present physical insect body. Of those bugs and insects such as flies, fruit flies, mosquitoes, etc., by compassionately doing a "mercy killing" when they specifically come around "requesting" to experience this.

I know many may question this whole concept of what I term "mercy killing" of their physical body. But if it is done with complete Love and compassion, and a desire to help them to be freed from the "endless evolution" they were entrapped in. So, that, they can now come back as something "beautiful and/or useful" as far as their interactions with humans. That by doing this with Love, and Blessing them sincerely when one does this. Then I Am told they are truly freed from this older, lower vibrational insect evolution. They also help act as a "Surrogate" for others who have been entrapped for ages in this type of lower critter existence.

I know that this is a new "concept," but I had to re-think my "relationship and inter-action" with all these huge number of insects and bugs that had suddenly manifested themselves all over my apartment. A vast majority of the different insects, were what I would say were small black fruit flies, who suddenly appeared "out of nowhere." I could not comprehend, at first, how or why they had so suddenly appeared before me is such large numbers.

Suddenly, for the first time, I seemed to be able to "communicate" with them all. I also had a few major appearances of various different "ant groups or colonies," who also made their presence very much known to me.

The ants, who I had heard many years ago, had originally been brought from Mars to Earth, that like certain other insects, have a very "hive" type of existence. They tend to not be so "individualized" as some other types of insects, and they were "asking" me to literally "kill" their physical body, so that they would not be "stuck in a hive state" of consciousness. Many of these ants wanted to become more "individualized-and 'sovereign," as verses having to be as one large "collective group." Because, that was their "pure Higher desire."

They told me that "the word was out" about me and what I was able to do for them. This knowledge had spread all over the insect kingdom, that I was a very unusual and rare human who understood their "plight." How I had, actually "set free" various other, earlier insects that had arrived at Celeste's & my apartment, and they also wanted me to do this for them too!

Of course, because it was their "nature" to be "irritating and bothersome," flying around right by my head and body, as if to "irritate" me (because they couldn't "help it"). But yet, at the same time, I distinctly felt their strong desire to be "set free" of that original ancient "negative sorcery-curse and DNA manipulation" that had first created them (their physical body). That had also entrapped them to forever be imprisoned in their type of insect species that they had been for so many ages. Their desire and passion about being "energetically freed up out of this "negative endless loop" was very obvious to me:

I could not ignore their sincere request for this type of higher "energetic liberation evolution." That by releasing them from their present body of one form of insect, and Blessed them and Decreed that they were no longer entrapped. That they could now evolve on to come back as a more evolved species, truly energetically harmonized with each of their desires. This was why they had shown up in such great numbers, to allow me to help them to take this giant energetic leap of evolution, in this new time line we all were fast merging into. This was their chance, too, to truly be "set free" and not imprisoned any longer in this ancient dark sorcery and curse of control over them.

Suddenly, I no longer felt even the slightest irritation about them coming around me, but only even greater compassion and love for them. As they would literally land right in front of me, and on my hands and arms, as if to say, "Please, help me, also, be freed from the "curse" of endless unfulfilling evolution. To now, something far more fulfilling and more evolved." So that is what I did.

Within a few days, their numbers quickly began to lessen, as I helped them to this Higher Insect Evolvement. I could actually sense a great relief, and of them "thanking" me for what I had done, and because I was able to "understand" what they needed and wanted.

Then, one day, something even more profound occurred, which was very enlightening and heart wrenching at the same time. As the numbers of fruit flies quickly began to diminish to finally, very few existed, and I felt my "insect mercy and freedom" mission was truly about over. Even though, I sensed that I would probably in the future, still have a few more that might show up; certain "late stragglers."

But one of these last few fruit flies that showed up, and had "plopped" himself right on the counter, right in front of me, making sure that I noticed "him." I say, "him," because his physical essence felt like this was a "male" fruit fly.

I could distinctly feel him asking me to help "him" to also be "freed" from the "evolutionary curse" that had caused his essence to be entrapped in, so I quickly freed his essence from his tiny little physical body.

But, then, all of a sudden, moments after I had done so, I suddenly felt a major "conflicting series of emotions" coming from him. This now seemed to greatly conflict with his initial desire and request of me, as I was able to "clairvoyantly see" his tiny, little spark of spirit-soul" floating there a foot away from me, that had been in his physical fruit fly body just moments before. Something, suddenly, was very wrong, with what he was conveying to me.

What I was sensing and feeling from his tiny "spirit soul essence," was now sudden panic, remorse, and regret, for having been allowed to leave his physical body. Because, all of a sudden, I knew why he was now suddenly regretting his request of me to do what I had done, with love and compassion.

This may seem very bazar, but I can assure you this IS what I was feeling and sensing quite clearly. It was his mate, his own insect "Beloved" who he realized had not followed him, even though she had planned to. But, somehow, they had just gotten "separated," and he had suddenly "manifested" here in my apartment alone, and she had not appeared as she was supposed to have done.

Suddenly, as I felt his grief and emotional pain and panic and fear that he night not ever see her again, and I literally started to cry, so deep was his intense longing, remorse and grief, that she was now not with him, and that he "must go on"—but without her, his own "Beloved"?

I was so "moved" by this experience, of what "he" was desperately expressing to me, of wondering if I could do anything about this sudden "screw up," of them being separated?

I suddenly asked Celeste, my own True Love and Beloved, could she, in any way, help this little insect spirit essence find his own Beloved, or her find him, before he was forced to now move on?

A moment later, I felt a sudden, but subtle, "energy shift" occur in my apartment, what exactly, I at first did not know. But I felt Celeste doing something, that had caused this shift.

Suddenly, a moment later, another fruit fly appeared right in front of me, as it—or rather "she," plopped down right on the counter in front of me, as if to say with great heartfelt relief, "Oh, thank you so much, for reconnecting me with my Beloved, and please, help me truly be reunited with him, so we both, together, as one, can move on into the higher insect Evolution."

Even as I was picking up "her" heartfelt message, I also felt that Celeste had increased my "clairvoyant" ability, to be able to see something that was so small that I normally would not have been able to do so.

What I was now "seeing," was, in fact, so small, energetically, I would not have, usually been able to see this. But what I saw can only be described as one of the tiniest "wormholes" that has ever existed. Actually, wormholes can be any size they want, from something that is literally the size of a molecule, to ones as large as a planet.

And, there, where this female fruit fly had just "manifested" from, was a very small wormhole, probably about—and I Am estimating its approximate "size"—an 1/8 to ¼ inch in size, just big enough to have allowed the fruit fly to come through—but from where?

Then, as I quickly "energetically scanned" Celeste's & my apartment, I saw a couple more such extremely small wormholes or portals. These, I suddenly realized, had been what had allowed all these huge numbers of various insects to come through. I had a sense that these tiny little wormholes had allowed all these particular insects to come through. Because, they "energetically matched" the "energetic frequency" of those that were wanting to be "released from that original dark curse. That had entrapped them in the insect bodies the dark forces had created to force upon this planet the "hellish existence." That, not only caused humans to be constantly "bothered, pestered and irritated" by the insects, while entrapping these spirit-souls in this "non-ending" loop of being stuck in this endless cycle. These tiny little wormholes of

Light, which Celeste explained, she had created to allow these ones to be freed from this "curse," by my own compassionate understanding that very few humans would have been able to truly comprehend. That they were asking and begging to be "set free", and so I did.

Now, as I quickly turned my attention back to the "matter at hand," of Celeste having helped to "reunite" the desperate male fruit fly with his own female Beloved. A moment later, having "set her free" also from that "curse." As her spirit-soul essence, that I could tell was "radiantly happy and exuberant" to be not only "free," but now could be with her "Other Half."

And at that same instant, the former "panic, desperation and emotional pain from the male, turned into great joy and excitement, to see her again. As "she," or rather her tiny spirit light rose up to meet his, and in their great joy of being reunited. The two individual lights seem to merge into a slightly larger Light, which hovered for a few moments.

They expressed their great joy and appreciation to me, for not only their new "evolutionary insect freedom," but also especially of being together as "One."

They hovered briefly, then suddenly they were gone, as they "moved on" in their new "Oneness' and into whatever new form of insect life they would now choose to experience, together, as mates, in that particular insect species.

This whole experience has been such an "eye-opener" for a number of reasons. Not only to get such deeper Insight of how many of the insects and bugs that we humans have had a very uncomfortable relationship with. Was actually created with a very negative, ill-intent being behind all of that, of having forced so many spirit-souls to be entrapped. But can be freed from their endless enslaved existence, and they get to choose now what type of more evolved insect or bug they want to next incarnate into.

But, also, on this "insect level" of existence, yes, "even bothersome bugs and pesky insects need Love, too!" That they, too, have their own "Universal Other Half," their own Beloved/Twin-Flame. And once they meet, they never, ever want to be separated, and that they want to be together, Forever. To share and Love each other, Forever. Just as my own Beloved Twin-Flame and Cosmic True Love, Celeste, will now be with me to "Live Happily Ever After"!

CHAPTER 30

Some More "Last-Minute Miracles" from Celeste

I had not originally planned, at least as far as my conscious mind is concerned, to include this particular chapter in this book. But obviously Celeste had already known that these series of events were Destined to occur and that I would become aware of them shortly before this book would be published.

Celeste's Secret Plan

The events I am referring to have to do with me locating a professional editor to help enhance and improve the quality of the entire book. Celeste and I had "technically" finished our final draft of this book around the last week of August, 2020. That was when I decided to locate a professional editor.

Liz, one of the many fellow Lightworkers I know, had already helped me to get greater clarity and perspective on some earlier challenges I had been facing. She had sent me a link with a listing of many professional editors to contact about editing Celeste's and my book. Of course, as I look back on how this whole thing played out, I realize that Celeste strongly Over-

Lighted Liz to do so, as this was going to allow Celeste to manifest a few more last-minute Miracles. There would be more of the already numerous Blessings, Miracles and Synchronicities that she had already created/manifested during the years since she came much more directly into my life.

When Liz emailed me the link to this particular list of professional editors I looked it over, attempting (with Celeste's professional Goddess help, of course!) to energetically tune into who the specific editor would be that I felt should be the one to edit Celeste's and my book. It is pretty obvious, based upon the topics in this book, that not "just anyone" could edit it. When dealing with these types of subjects, because of how extremely "outside of the box" they are, one might have to "go up a rabbit hole" and "down a wormhole" in some ways in order to be able to adequately edit it. (Yes, I purposely "reversed" these two phrases, because of how extreme some people might find all the subjects included in the book.) I searched for the one editor who not only had good or excellent editing skills (of course), but also who would be sufficiently "in harmony" with all of the information and topics that are covered throughout this book to be comfortable editing it.

I also wanted to make this a win-win situation for us both: I did not want this to be just another mundane 3D editing job. I also saw this as an opportunity for the editor themselves to energetically jump levels: by their investment of time and energy spent in doing the whole editing process, this could also be a type of transformational consciousness experience for them as well. I knew that whoever it was going to be, doing this particular editing job would most likely create a major energetic shift in their life. Other unexpected and/or unusual things might come out of this whole experience, and I knew that it was going to be a very interesting experience for them—just as it would be for myself. Yes, this is how I felt as I "energetically scanned" the entire list of professional editors.

Finally, with Celeste's Over-Lighting Divine Feminine Goddess Influence, I decided upon a specific editor. What is interesting is that while I noted that Signe, the editor that was chosen, did not have as much experience editing as many of the others in the complete list, there was something about her photo and the "energy" that was being "projected" from it that made me feel as if she was more suitable than most of the others. It seemed that she was a very upbeat and positive person, who would make this whole editing process a lot more fun than many of the others. I felt they were a little more cynical and not so "open" to the very paranormal, out-of-this-world and controversial things that was specifically placed throughout this book.

In the process of narrowing down who I would finally choose, I had opened up my own online account on the webpage/platform with this list of editors. On this platform one communicates by written messages with the different editors. It was after sending a few "request messages" to some of the editors and getting their replies, that I finally came to the conclusion that it would be Signe.

Well, here is where more wonderful weirdness began to occur, where Celeste made her opinion very obvious: After deciding that it would be Signe, she and I sent a few messages back and forth, attempting to connect more directly. At first, it seemed that some kind of communication breakdown had occurred. I had specifically asked her if I could phone her and speak with her directly, and I had already given her my phone number so she could call me. But, for some reason which was not clear until later, she did not initially seem to want to call me directly using my phone number. This made me wonder why she did not seem to want to speak to me directly. She had not, as of the first couple of messages, shared her phone number with me.

As I look back on what was going on, it made sense. What I had not been aware of then, as it had not been explained to me, was that when someone first connects with one of the editors, instead of communicating by private phones, the company that is in charge can set up a "teleconference call" over Zoom. That way the editor and the writer (the person who is interested in speaking with the editor that they have chosen) will have a chance to speak directly over Zoom. The final decision is made when the writer is satisfied with their choice.

But I was not aware of this, because I had not read or seen the particular instructions for the platform's routines for teleconferencing. I jokingly (of course) used the phrase "I (kind of) felt like a mushroom." The reason I use this funny phrase is that this is how mushrooms are actually grown: They are "kept in the dark." The rest of the phrase is "and are fed BS." Of course, I was not being "fed (any) BS," but I did initially feel like I was being "kept in the dark." I felt that someone was not explaining to me just exactly what their usual procedure was for the "vetting process" of choosing and getting to know an editor. But thank God I do now!

But still, since this was not explained to me until a little later, my analytical, logical left brain began to wonder what exactly was "going on." Or rather, what was *not* going on—did I somehow make a mistake of even contacting this particular editing company? It seemed (in my lack of knowledge) that I was being given the run-around in some way. My ego/conscious self started questioning this whole process, wondered if I was wasting my time with attempting to really connect with Signe, and if this was actually "legit," etc.

Well, I finally figured it out: it was explained to me that they always schedule in a "teleconference" call whenever a writer and an editor wants to communicate directly. Initially I thought they were referring to a "telephone conference call," where more than one or two people will speak over the phone at the same time. But then it became clear that they were referring to a Zoom call over the internet, which is similar to a Skype call. I had never done a Zoom call before, even though I had done many Skype calls. So, I went ahead and not only downloaded the Zoom program, but also confirmed the date and time: September 2, in the afternoon.

I also realized that I had misinterpreted Signe's seeming lack of wanting to call me directly over the phone, as this was only because she was waiting to get the teleconference call scheduled in by the teleconference coordinator. I also discovered that she lives in Sweden, and this was also part of why she was waiting to do the Zoom call. It would cost a lot for us to speak over the phone. She had really expected, as she shared with me, that she thought they would schedule our Zoom call within those first couple of days, rather than having to wait almost six days.

Photo of another Heart shaped water droplet

As it was to turn out, something else was about to occur. Celeste obviously knew ahead of time that it actually needed to occur when it did and not several days later, as that could have screwed up the Zoom call (which was now scheduled on September 2, several days later). Unbeknownst to me, Celeste had energetically determined that the modem that I rent from Xfinity, the local Sarasota cable company, was about to quit working. It was over two years old and had basically reached the end of its normal lifespan, but I did not know this. Early Saturday morning I discovered, after doing a number of technical tests in collaboration with a technician over the phone, that the modem just would no longer work. It was obvious that I had to get a replacement.

I asked the technician where the nearest open Xfinity store was, and what hours was it open for the public. The technician told me that his computer definitely showed that the local Sarasota store was open all day until 6:30 P.M. I specifically asked him to make sure about this being so, because I would have to take two busses out to this location to be able to pick up a new modem. He assured me that the store was definitely open that day, Saturday, and that it was definitely open until 6:30 P.M.

So I spent the next couple of hours on two different busses to go out to this store—only to discover once I got there that the store had actually been closed for a few months (because of this whole COVID BS scam). For some strange reason, the technician on the phone had obviously been looking at some totally wrong information that had not been updated! (At least, this is what I initially assumed. I was to discover something else had occurred—purposely—to have me go out there anyway.)

Yes, I was quite upset about having gone all that way only to discover this major screwup. I could not understand why Celeste would have me go anyway, why she had not let me know somehow so that I would not waste all that time, especially considering that I really needed a new modem to not only access the internet and my emails, but also for this scheduled Zoom call. I was really confused and upset about these circumstances. All I could feel from Celeste was her Lovingly assuring me that there WAS a reason which I would very shortly find out about, I just had to try to be as patient and positive as I could.

I was not in the least angry or upset with Celeste, I was just very confused about what she was referring to. I could never, ever be upset with her, especially considering all the many awesome and wonderful Blessings and Miracles that she has manifested for me and how much she Unconditionally Loved me. But still, it was initially confusing when things just did not seem to be going the way that they "should."

I then immediately felt Celeste guiding me to call the toll-free phone number which I had with me. "Thank God," or rather "Thank the Goddess"—quite literally—for her insistence of me bringing a number I had not thought I would need. I had assumed that the number was only for any technical assistance in making sure that one's internet service at one's residence was working. Now I was so glad that I had the number with me. I called it once again, and got another technician on the phone. I quickly explained my predicament and how pissed off I was about the fact that another technician had assured me that this local store would be open, when it actually had been closed for at least two or three months.

This new technician confirmed to me that, yes, as she saw on her own computer, this center HAD been closed for at least the last two or three months. She could not understand why the other agent had told me such false and misleading info. She stated that all agents working for Xfinity have the exact same information on their computers, and she just could not understand how totally wrong the information was that had earlier been shared with me by the first technician.

I asked her, considering this extreme inconvenience I had experienced, what could she do to help me out in terms of not only obtaining a new modem, but have it sent to me within the next two or three days? She stated that the only way they could expedite the new modem to me was to charge a lot more. I responded by explaining how severely they had inconvenienced me and told her of the important, upcoming Zoom meeting with my editor, etc.

Suddenly I saw the bus that I had taken to this location, now on its return trip back to where I would take the first bus back to my apartment. As I got onto the bus, not wanting to miss this one since it only came once every hour, I attempted to continue our conversation. Unfortunately there was just too much loud noise in the bus, and I had to wait with the call until I had returned to my apartment.

As I quickly checked my cell phone to see if I had received any phone messages, I discovered that the agent I had spoken with had decided to go ahead and "comp" me the extra cost it would take to expedite me a new modem. They were sending me the new modem through UPS, and it was scheduled to arrive sometime Monday, August 31. This was when I found out from Celeste that she had Over-Lighted the whole ordeal: She had projected onto the first agent's computer screen this "false" information, so that I would assume that it was totally accurate. Once I got out to the store I would find them totally closed. Because of this obvious inconvenience, the second agent would take compassion upon me. Thus she would end up "comping" me the extra shipping cost for the modem, which would be sent to me within the time that I needed it for the scheduled teleconference call with Signe.

And there you go: what with Celeste's powers as an Immortal Intergalactic Goddess, she would make sure that everything would totally work out so that I could do my Zoom call after all. Because of her help, we could then, without any more delay, have Signe begin to edit our book, and "the rest would be history," as they say.

Signing Messages

There was something else that Celeste did early on to verify that Signe was "the one" to edit our book: Something unique and unusual showed up in each of the messages that Signe sent to me in her initial attempt to connect with me more directly, which I knew that she had not written. I noticed that right after her own signing of her name, four words had been "typed out"—or rather "manifested." The four words that were printed each time in the message were these: "Goddess Celeste Previously Wrote."

Each time, these exact four words would be shown in every reply message and in all her new messages to me. I knew that

Signe had not done this. When this guy named Dave, who sets up the Zoom teleconference calls, contacted me to confirm the Zoom call on September 2, these same four words also showed up. I knew that neither of them had done this. It was Celeste giving me another confirmation of her involvement. She knew that there were going to be these apparently "unexpected delays" and "breakdowns of communication," and she had done this to confirm to me that everything would work out. Not only would hiring Signe as our editor work out, but I should also keep my faith despite these other so-called challenges and last-minute interruptions, and press on forward. Celeste would make sure that all would work out according to the Divine Plan—as "Q" would say, I should "trust the Plan."

Then I discovered something even more miraculous: those four specific words, "Goddess Celeste previously wrote," were actually connected with how my account at the editor platform was set up. I had specifically activated my own personal account with my name "Michael Ellegion", in order to connect with the editors. But when I went to my account page, I now saw that it had been changed—somehow—to "Goddess Celeste"! My account was no longer listed in my name. There was also this beautiful lotus flower shown on that page. It was then that Celeste told me that she had specifically changed the account name from my name to hers, as another one of her signs and Miracles of confirmation that Signe was definitely the one she wanted to edit our book. I just had to be as patient as possible until I could speak with her, which I finally did (on September 14, because the Zoom teleconference had to be re-scheduled until that date).

That Which is Truly Meant to Be Will Be

So, despite all these delays everything worked out—as it always does, if we are just patient enough. We just need to have faith that all things that are truly meant to be *will* be (things that are "in Divine Order"). So often, even for those of us who have developed our more intuitive right brains, we allow our analytical, logical left brains and our conscious ego self to doubt something that may seem contradictory to our logic and reason. Sometimes, if we will just have faith, push forward, refuse to give up and refuse to allow the more cynical side of our nature to control us, some really awesome and wonderful experiences will occur.

So, too, it is with romance and being able to meet our Cosmic True Love. It does take us being willing to believe and know that ultimately, if we will just persevere, believe and "Know in our heart" that it is our Destiny to find our Cosmic True Love, we will find them. The reconnecting is Destined to occur, it is one of those types of events that is a Cosmic Done Deal and a Sacred Promise. We need to just believe it and allow it, and, of course, we also need to do the "homework" and to Red Pill ourselves. When all is aligned, that is when the real Magic begins!

And, speaking of "magic" and "Knowing in our Heart": during these two weeks of waiting to finally speak to Signe, Celeste energetically manifested a few more beautiful Hearts in my kitchen sink (causing the smaller water droplets to suddenly form into larger, heart-shaped water droplets).

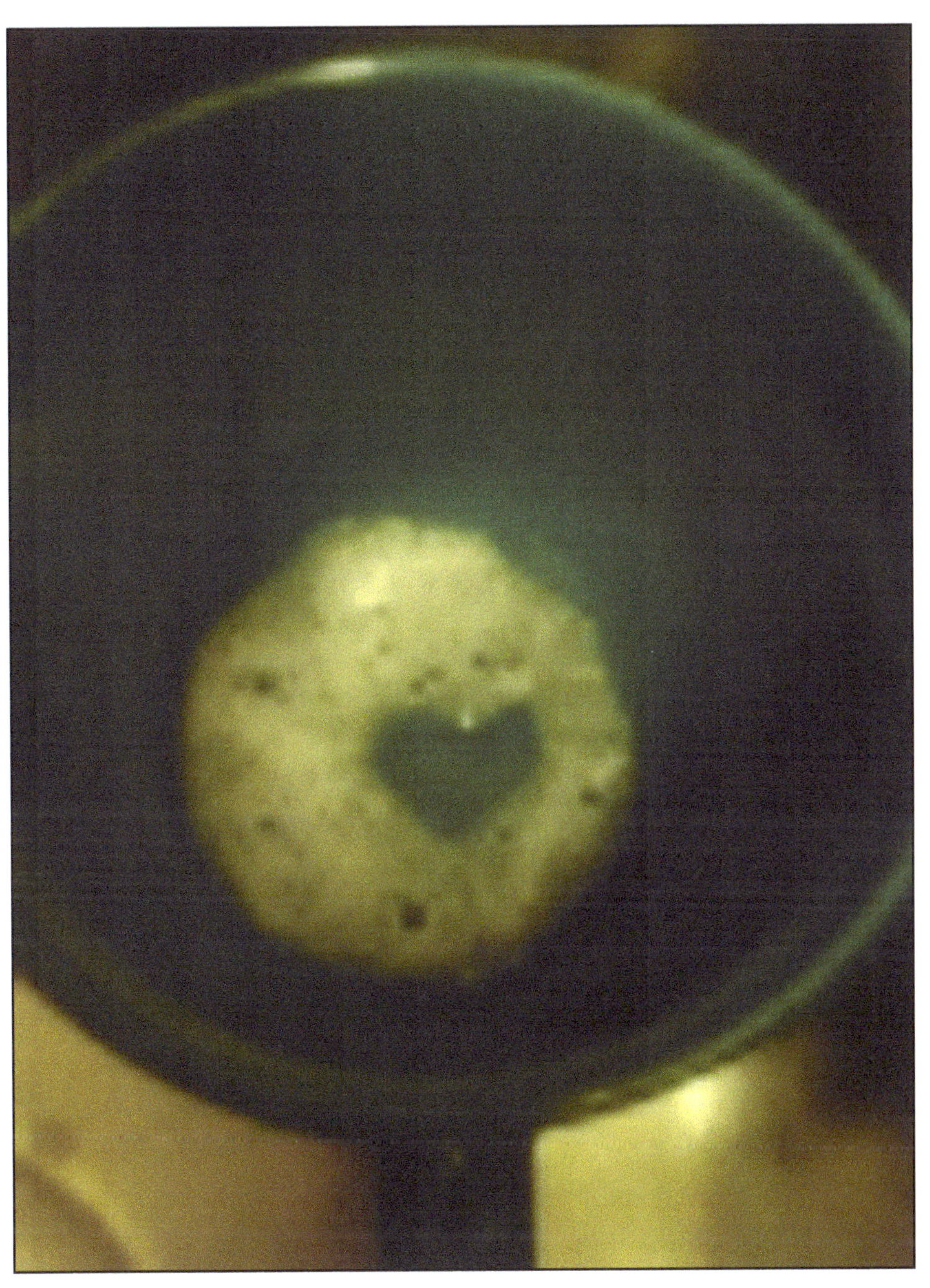

One more Heart shape, Celeste manifested in the soapy water at bottom of the cup I was washing

One evening right after eating my dinner, I had just scrubbed all my dishes with a soapy washcloth. I had just finished wiping the last item to then be rinsed off, it was a large green cup. I turned away just briefly to turn on the water facet to begin the rinsing. As I turned my attention back to the cup, I suddenly saw that a beautiful heart shape had manifested in the soapy water at the bottom of it. I took a photograph of each of Celeste's last-minute Miracles displaying her Love for me. I realize, as I look back on these two manifestations as well as the other ones I had already photographed, that each time I had spontaneously sung a romantic song about my Love for her just before it happened, and each time she had reciprocated by manifesting these magical signs of her Love for me.

How awesome to not only be so intensely in Love with my Beloved, an Immortal Intergalactic Goddess, but to also experience her letting me know how much she loves me all the time! In her wonderful and intense Unconditional Romantic Love for me, she likes to leave these "little Love notes" for me to see. And, I can now share these with everyone else, to give you all more photographic evidence that you, too, will soon have the opportunity to experience such a wonderful and magical journey of Love and Fulfillment as few Earth humans have ever had the chance to before!

Another awesome "Miracle" occurred just as this book was being completed. In Chapter 20, I briefly mentioned the very talented visionary-psychic artist Erial-Ali, who did the front cover scene for this book. He also just completed a portrait of Celeste, which is an extremely accurate depiction of what she looks like, as I have seen her most of the time. Erial is extremely talented in his ability to depict how the Twin-Flames/Cosmic True Loves of fellow Volunteers in Earth embodiment appear. I feel so Blessed to receive this wonderful and awesome image of my Beloved, as Erial was able, in great detail, to so accurately depict her. Erial is now going to be "specializing" in doing "Twin-Flame/Soul Portraits" for others who want to have a very accurate image of what their own Cosmic True Love looks like. A link will be located on Celeste's and my new website, IntergalacticMatch.com, so you can contact Erial-Ali to have your own "Twin-Flame/Soul portrait" done. You can enlarge it, if you want, just as I did, into a much larger, poster-sized image that you can then hang on your wall, as you feel the wonderful energetic presence of your own Beloved.

EPILOGUE

Some final thoughts, as we reach the end of Celeste's and my book. For me, it has truly been a most enjoyable experience to share this with my Beloved, and to also share so much with you, the reader. We hope that all which we shared will give you great Hope and Inspiration, and that you will be just as "lucky" as I have been and soon be reunited with your own Cosmic True Love.

Meeting Your Cosmic True Love

Maybe, like myself, you happen to also be one who has already found and met the Love of your Life. If so, we both Bless you, and we hope that you have still learned something meaningful from having read our book. Do please share it with as many others as you can, so that we can spread this Romantic Message of Great Hope and Promise to as many others as possible.

An old romantic song that I remember from many years ago states that "the world needs Love, lots of Love, and that's the only thing that we need plenty of..." I actually do not believe that it was just "luck" that allowed Celeste and I to finally come together. It happened not only because of Destiny, but obviously also because it is very much a part of a much bigger, epic romantic story yet to unfold.

I will assume that the vast majority of those of you reading this book have yet to meet your Cosmic True Love, and that this book has truly given you much Hope and Promise for the future—your own very Special One will indeed make their Divine Presence known to you.

Some of you may initially connect for the first time in a similar way to how Celeste is with me now, with your partner being on the 5D etheric level. And just as Celeste will be manifesting herself for me on this physical level in the future, so too will you eventually be physically together, to enjoy your Sacred and awesome time together and to Live Happily Ever After.

It is also possible that your Other Half appears as a Walk-In, just as Celeste did when she first got my attention. This can happen for millions of reasons. It may be that being a Walk-In is the only option available at this time, if they do not have an original physical body of their own. But I am also fairly sure that unlike what happened in my case, you will probably not have to deal with them also having another partner. Most likely, if they are now presently on Earth rather than off-planet, they will have their own physical body.

But it is my opinion that for a huge percentage of those who will read this book, your Other Half is presently off planet Earth, getting Ready for the upcoming Cosmic Family Reunion which will take place once First Contact officially occurs. Then they will be coming down with the landing party, and you will be able to Hook Up with your Beloved. Of course, you will want to Bliss Out with them as soon as you both can get some much needed "privacy"/"Cosmic R. and R."—to catch up on the important, fulfilling Sacred Intimacy and the totally Nirvanic Ecstasy!

"To Get to Heaven, We Must First Pass (Very Briefly) Through Hell"

I definitely wanted to end this book on a very positive note. But I must also, very briefly, touch on a few things that I feel needs to be mentioned, which are related to what was shared throughout the book. As has been said before, sometimes in order to finally "get to Heaven, we must first pass (very briefly) through hell."

What am I referring to, you ask, that I have not already mentioned? Well, unfortunately, I feel that I must lessen some of the shock that will be experienced by most of you as major Revelations of all the unspeakable crimes against humanity, especially children, are officially revealed. A huge number of people that many of you thought were "positive icons of society," people that some of you looked up to and "worshiped," are about to be exposed as corrupt and evil people. Many of the Celebrities and A-listers in Hollywood, many well-known actors and actresses, are going to be officially exposed and arrested, having done some of the worst and most despicable crimes imaginable against children. Some of them are already under House Arrest, awaiting their trials. There are going to be military tribunals where they will be sentenced to death because of these unspeakable and horrific crimes. I know for a fact, from some very reliable sources, who many of these individuals are. I felt that I should at least "warn you" before it all occurs. Maybe, by the time you read this book, it has already occurred. But as in the saying, "Not that I didn't warn you ahead of time," I wanted to attempt to lessen the shock.

Q and the White Hat Alliance have stated many times concerning the Great Awakening that sometimes one has to be shown what is going on in order to be able to Awaken. You may be one of the many millions out there who have Red Pilled yourself through "alternative media" (not controlled by the cabal, as the mainstream media is). You will find lots of information verifying all this. (Yes, information that the cabal-controlled, fake news, Lamestream media would say is just a bunch of "conspiracy theory nonsense," but which has nevertheless been very well documented.)

Recently I was forwarded an email with a link to what I feel is the best radio interview fully documenting the "Major Progress Behind the Scenes Against the cabal." The interview was so informative that I forwarded it to everyone on my email list. I wanted to quote part of what I said in my email, along with the link to hear it:

> This is, in my opinion, definitely the best and detailed radio interview, of what has been occurring, "behind the scenes" for the last few years, that most people do not know about, that has been defeating the cabal. In fact, why the cabal is actually, already defeated, even though it may not seem or appear, on a public level, that very much has occurred. Remember, as Q has stated, many times in the

"Q Drops", that just because nothing seems to be occurring [out on the "obvious, open public level]," or just because you don't [yet] see it, doesn't mean it hasn't occurred, and to "Trust the Plan."

I totally agree with at least 95% of what the guest on the radio show is sharing. The other 5%, I will have to "agree to disagree" about them, such as his statement about there being "no clones"(and cloning factories); I disagree with this because of a number of other very valid sources that have specifically stated about all the cloning that has been done throughout the decades of many politicians, etc. And the other "disagreement" was his statements inferring that Jesus, or the man who is historically known as "Jesus", because of his image always being shown as a very light skinned "Swiss European" type man, as verses the fact that being born in the Middle East, He had to be of a much darker skin color. The guest is a very Spiritual person, not religious, and has obviously a few "issues" with the whole "orthodox religious version" of who we refer to as "Jesus." But, again, this is his position. But as far as most everything that he is sharing, as stated, I Am totally in agreement with, and feel that this IS definitely the best radio interview to summarize and "put in a [large] very accurate nutshell" all that has occurred "behind the scenes," that the cabal controlled media just "conveniently forgot" to tell us, that absolutely Guarantees the Victory of Light for the planet.

And Celeste, my Beloved and Divine Goddess, totally 1000% Confirms this other 95% of what he is sharing. Please share this with as many people as possible, to also help "wake them up a lot faster" and to prepare for so many exciting things yet to occur. Yes, "the Best Is Yet to Come"!

Here is the Link: https://www.youtube.com/watch?v=_jl7N4iM4Yg&feature=youtu.be (GVP#161—Charlie Freak & Colleen: Further Trump & Q Insights)

The Star Trek Golden Age is Coming

Those of us who know this truth, also know that the future holds a great and wonderful promise of what many have termed a "Star Trek Golden Age." Our world is about to drastically change for the better. Once we move into 2021, things are going to begin to powerfully shift so much to the better.

I know that it is Destiny, a Sacred Promise, a Cosmic Done Deal, that this is to occur (unless it already has, and you are presently just Blissed Out with your Beloved—if so, Celeste and I are so happy for you!). All the rest of you will soon be Blissing out as well, so that you can also, as I have with Celeste, be "Blessed and Blissed!"

I could also say (using a famous phrase from the 1960's/70's) that ever since Celeste, my Beloved, came into my life, I have been "Trippin' the Light Fantastic" with her! In case you are not familiar with or do not remember these slang terms from that "psychedelic drug culture" of that time: They used the phrase "Trippin' the Light Fantastic," to mean that they had a "good (drug) trip," as opposed to a "bad trip". Sometimes they would say "Man, you're trippin' me out" or "freaking me out," or "I was trippin' on those psychedelics." When the "trip" was a more incredible, "out-of-this-world" cosmic type of trip, they would say it was "Trippin' the Light Fantastic!"

I never got into drugs because I was into meditating, etc., and because it has been said that "drugs are the 'back door to God', while meditation, Light Decrees, prayer, etc., are the 'front door to God.'" Instead of me ever "getting high" on any drugs, I am "Getting High" from Celeste and her awesome, wonderful Divine Feminine Goddess presence. I am "Trippin' the Light Fantastic" with her!

Celeste and I wanted to share her and my own romantic story in this book, share our reconnecting and how wonderful it is to be with one's Cosmic True Love, so that all of you who have that Pure, True Heart's Desire for this to happen, will indeed experience it yourselves. No matter how many times you have thought you had met the Love of your life, only to discover that, for whatever reason, you had "misinterpreted" who that person actually was, do not ever give up Hope.

Know that the Divine Creator of all the Universes created someone for everyone. There is, indeed, a Divine and Scared Plan which is starting to unfold, a Plan to reunite you and your True Beloved Cosmic True Love at long last. And, you are now much more emotionally balanced and mature, so much more Truly Ready than you were before. Remember, "Timing is Everything"; you just needed to wait a little longer and to develop a little more patience (and wisdom) than you had before.

Celeste wants all of you to know that as the Cosmic Match Maker that she is, and as a member of the Love Ops/ Special Forces of Romantic Love: Do tune into the energy of IntergalacticMatch.com and call on her—she will be very happy to help you find your Cosmic True Love, so that you both can now truly Live Happily Ever After!

NASA STAR PEOPLE CHARACTERISTICS LIST

UFO Researcher Brad Steiger's profile of the Star People contains the following elements. Few Star People have all the characteristics, but all have at least several or up to a third of the elements. (James Beal, a former NASA engineer, and Dr. Norman Cooperman, a psychotherapist from Miami, researched this entire subject back in the 1970's and 80's.) TheStar People Characteristics include:

- Compelling eyes and personal charisma
- Unusual blood type (such as A-, B- or AB-)
  - I have AB-, the rarest blood type upon this planet. Approximately one out of every 10,000 people has this very rare type. It is also the type of blood found on the Shroud of Turin.
- Lower than normal body temperature
- Was an unexpected (or "unplanned") child
- Extra vertebrae, transitional vertebrae, fused vertebrae, and lower back problems
- Extra or "misplaced" ribs
- Thrive on little sleep and do their best work at night

- Hypersensitivity (or feeling sensitive) to electricity and electromagnetic force-fields (may also be termed "environmentally sensitive")
- Unusually sharp (or above "normal") hearing and eyes that are very sensitive (or above "normal" sensitivity) to light (or sunlight)
- Seem to have been "reborn" in cycles—for example, 1934–38, 1944–48, 1954–58, and so on
    - Actually, (some) of the majority of the Volunteers who have come to Earth have been born within a year or two of particularly "intense" and/or "challenging" times. In fact, some of the largest number of Volunteers to take Earth embodiment occurred right after the bombs that were dropped on Hiroshima and Nagasaki in WWII. This happened because of the concern on Higher Worlds (observed from Lightships) that the next generation could possibly destroy the planet. It was decided that the Volunteers would come in greater numbers than ever before into Earth embodiment. Thus the "baby boom generation" appeared, to make sure that never again would this planet be allowed to be destroyed. Now in these more recent decades, an even much greater number of Volunteers—over half the entire world's population—are "from somewhere else," making this literally the largest number of Star People to ever take Earth embodiment at the same time!

- Feel that their (Earth biological) mother and father are not their real parents
- Feel a great urgency (or strange "restlessness," feeling like they have been in a type of "holding pattern" for too long) a short time before completing an important goal or "special mission" of some kind
- Lower than normal blood pressure
- Chronic (or "semi-chronic") sinusitis (also known as "irritation in the nose or nasal passages")
- Feel or sense that their true ancestors came from another (much more beautiful, evolved, peaceful, and sane) world, another (Higher) dimension, or another level of consciousness, and they yearn for their true place of origin, their real home "beyond the stars"
- Had "unseen companions and/or friends" as a child
- Natural (or "above normal" or "unusual") abilities in specialized areas, such as art, music, mathematics, healing, acting, natural sciences, etc.
- Experience a buzzing or a clicking sound or a high-pitched mechanical whine in the ears prior to or during some psychic event, or as warning of danger. This can also be in the form of a "synchronicity" and/or a vision of some kind
- Had a dramatic or unusual experience around the age of 5 or 6 (or at least when they were very young, before the person's early teen years), which took the form of a white light and/or a visitation by human-appearing beings who gave information and comfort

- Have since maintained a continuing contact with beings which they consider to be angels, masters, Elves, spiritual teachers, or openly declared UFO intelligences (that is, beings who are benevolent in nature, as opposed to the "grays" or "reptilians"), and have not been abducted, only contacted to help, guide, inspire, uplift, empower, etc.
- Had a serious accident, illness, or traumatic experience around the age of eleven or twelve (or early teens) which encouraged them to turn inward
- Their artwork, dreams, or fantasies often involve an alien, multi-moon (and /or multi-dimensional, inter-) planetary environment
- Children and animals are attracted to them
- May have mystic crosses, mystic eyes, or mystic stars on their palms
- Have unusual abilities that are considered paranormal by their peers and family (such as being psychic, doing channelings, and/or being involved in psychic/spiritual healings and psychic surgery, telekinesis, etc.)
- Experience a strong attraction to quartz crystal and natural gemstones
- Have flying dreams or "out-of-body"/"astral travel" experiences
- Have the ability to take on the role of an empath (extreme compassion and feelings for what the other person or animal (and even insects and bugs) are going through)

- Have a strong affinity to past eras and places such as of Atlantis, Lemuria, ancient Egypt, King Arthur and Camelot, the Tantra Temples of India, and other ancient, biblical or "mythical" times of history (such as J. R. R. Tolkien's "fictional fantasy" past ages) when contact and interaction with multi-dimensional beings (and the Elvin race) was conducted on a more open basis by the entities themselves
- Have recently received the message or inner feeling, or message from one's Higher Self, that "Now is the Time!"

This was the end of the NASA Star People list from Brad Steiger's research, but I also added a few other characteristics:

- Have experienced at least one or more "close calls" through the years and have felt that they were being watched over and somehow Divinely Protected time and time again. Experienced either life-threatening situations in which one should have been either killed or at least severely injured but instead was protected from it, or experienced sickness or disease that should have killed one, but from which one fully and quickly recovered
- Have often experienced through the years, while glancing at a digital clock or watch, that the time just happened to be 11:11
- Feel that they are one of the "144,000"
- Feel like they are "A Stranger in A Strange Land"

- This was the title of a famous science fiction classic by Robert Heinlein, which accurately describes what Volunteers intensely feel while here in 3D Earth embodiment. Of course, reality is so much stranger than fiction, but truth has often been presented in so-called fictional form

To order more copies of this book, please go to
Michael & Celeste's website, IntergalacticMatch.com. Thank you.

CPSIA information can be obtained
at www.ICGtesting.com
Printed in the USA
BVHW091746150222
629082BV00003B/36

9 781954 095090